Ritual for
PO & KT.

To complete

this work.

Dig a small hole

2 inches larger

than this book

& twice as deep.

Insert 666

marshmallows

& the book into

the hole.

Bury it.

Black Metal Rainbows
©2023 Daniel Lukes, Stanimir Panayotov, & Jaci Raia
This edition © 2023 PM Press

ISBN: 9781629638812 (paperback)
ISBN: 9781629638829 (hardcover)
ISBN: 9781629639017 (ebook)

Library of Congress Control Number: 2020919415

Cover: Jaci Raia www.kvlt.co

Cover Image: ©O.B. De Alessi, *Swan Song*, 2011,
documentation of live performance, photo by
©Michael Salerno, 2011

Cover *Black Metal Rainbows Logo*:
©Christophe Szpajdel, 2018, color rendition
by Jaci Raia, 2020

Interior art direction and design by Jaci Raia

Excerpt from Catherine Fearns, *Sound*
(London: darkstroke books, 2019), 69-70,
published by permission from the publisher

All artworks not originally commissioned for
this book are reproduced by permission from
their authors and/or copyright holders

10 9 8 7 6 5 4 3 2 1

PM Press
PO Box 23912
Oakland, CA 94623

www.pmpress.org

First published in Canada in 2023
by Between the Lines
401 Richmond Street West, Studio 281,
Toronto, Ontario, M5V 3A8, Canada
1-800-718-7201
www.btlbooks.com

Canadian Cataloguing in Publication
information available from Library and
Archives Canada

ISBN: 9781771135764

–
black
metal
rainbows

black metal rainbows

Edited by Daniel Lukes
& Stanimir Panayotov

Designed by Jaci Raia

Jonathan Mayhew
*Blink. 2.0 (For Pelle Ohlin
& Kiriko Takemura)*, 2019
a work for a book, instructions
courtesy of the artist

Christophe Szpajdel
Black Metal Rainbows Logo (Rainbow Version), 2018
ink on paper, 29.8 x 21 cm
courtesy of the artist
color rendition by Jaci Raia, 2020

Contents

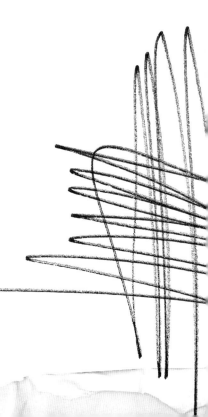

Johanna Mueller
Antelope Dreams, 2015
relief engraving and
marker, 23 x 15 cm
courtesy of the artist

Heather Masciandaro
Love of One's Own Fate, 2012
oil on linen, 122 x 81 cm
courtesy of the artist

Somewhere Over a Black Metal Rainbow

DANIEL LUKES AND
STANIMIR PANAYOTOV

You may think that *The Wizard of Oz* and black
metal are two completely separate things, but
if you watch Immortal's "Call of the Wintermoon"
video, it's clear there's a connection. Immortal
are following their own yellow brick road through
the forest, and who knows where they will
end up.

Of course, someone has already made a death metal cover of Judy
Garland singing "Over the Rainbow" and posted it on YouTube.[1] In a
way, this book is the black metal version of that song. The Wizard of
Oz and Judy Garland as Dorothy are queer icons and gay emblems
because of how the film represents a technicolor utopia where all
are accepted for who they are: from black-and-white 1930s Kansas
to full color Oz.

Black metal is for everyone. Everyone, that is, who wants to listen
to it, play it, think or write or make art about it. Sonically, it can be
harsh (it can also be very soft and tender). Sometimes it sounds like
a bee buzzing around in a paper bag. Plenty of people don't need

or want music that's noisy and evil. But black metal *is* for *anyone* who does. That is essentially the message of *Black Metal Rainbows*, which is a joyful celebration of all the cool stuff you can do with black metal, and how ripe it is for cross-pollination, hybridity, appropriation, obliteration, resurrection, how it stretches and bends into a plurality of glimmering configurations and evolves in constant mutation without ever losing its black metal spirit. Gatekeepers get lost! Go disappear in a pile of rubble and dust. You are history, because everyone is listening to black metal now and having one hell of a time enjoying it, whether you like it or not.

A black metal rainbow is a paradox: an affirmative one that says *yes*. Black metal rainbows—in the plural—are feminist, gay, tomboyish, emo, queer, trans*, fat, disabled, you name it. Yes, we know how fucked up this is for fans who can't stop loving their cis het/cis homo identities. Yes, we are curious as to why you are not curious or, better yet, why your spewing curiosity is presented as rejection. *No*, we don't think black metal rainbows is a jolly-be-good umbrella for everyone. Black metal rainbows include and affirm every difference, because it is in difference that we are created as identities. And since everyone is invited over this black metal rainbow, nobody is invited too. Do you see now what a yes could do? You can hate black metal rainbows all you want. All you get in return is a cosmic picturesque indifference.

Black metal is not black-and-white! There is a multiplicity of colors oozing through it; there always has been. There always have been queerness and diversity and plurality, under the surface and peeping through. Black metal is black because black/ness is a noncolor and, as such, it is a mix of all the colors. Black metal was never just black-and-white but always was a shining rainbow. We are not turning black metal upside down or inside out; we are not inventing anything but are merely showing what was always trve. We're not reimagining black metal but showing what it always was/could be/can be if you can see it prismatically. Black metal is art, including visual art, and this is an art book: a curated space that celebrates and challenges and transgresses black metal's aesthetic parameters, its uniquely recognizable look.

With this motley collection of documents, scribblings, manifestos, confessions, tears, ejaculations, and sighs, we simultaneously historicize and cocreate black metal as a utopian art form, a utopia that can say both yes and no to its histories, that transcends its black-and-white origins and the sacred cow of corpsepaint as its unquestionable face.[2] No, we do not posit that black and white are obsolete; we unearth them from an origin story of the rainbow of black metal that has always been there to see. There is nothing wrong with dualism per se, but, for fuck's sake, fifty or so years on and black metal is still advertised as fascistic, protean, and Nietzschean power fantasy kink. No more black repression: let the rainbows bleed out of blackness!

Things have dramatically changed since the 1990s;[3] art carries a different weight in today's precarious and hyper-unequal world. It interacts with politics in a more direct and impactful way, in large, thanks to the tentacular spread of social media, and so it must be judged by a different standard. Silencing those who want to kill you is a no-brainer. Black metal is a cultural battleground and, as such, is fair game for reterritorialization. Black metal is so much fun! And mucking around with it, playing with and transgressing its conventions, is something practitioners of the genre have been doing since its foundation. Do you think lo-fi symphonic screeching legendary thrash punk just came into being fully formed? Black metal itself is a glorious mess of styles that keeps evolving, and black metal embracing its color spectrum is simply the next step. Pvrity be damned.

The falsely fascistic aura of black metal stems from the feelings of impotence and alienation under late capitalist modernity. As capitalism and postmodernity changed, so did black metal. But alienation is here to stay; it is the condition of progress, and not even capitalism is entirely responsible for the cosmic and creationist injustices black metals feel reverberating through them. In alienation, black metal offers a paradoxical community. One can both cut off from the world and be alone and rejoice in this solitude with others: "Silence, the new aristocracy" (Ulver), if you like your metal with a pinch of snobbery. Whether you want to love your friends in togetherness or separation is not the question; you can do both as you see fit. In either case, you will be on a journey with them, through strange forests and weird fields. You will eventually grow as a person and learn to love yourself and understand who you are. Black metal is a "negative kingdom" (Arcturus), an upside-down topsy-turvy world in which powerlessness is traded for empowerment, and hate is vanquished by love—of all kinds, but starting with self-love. Yes, black metal is some sort of musical comfort food, nursing the super-inflated hypersensitively bruised ego with its soothing sounds of otherworldly monstrosity.

Black metal likes to trade on being a *no* genre: *against* the world, *against* life itself. Do you think black metal wants to mock and offend and desecrate everything, except itself? LOL. If you think that black metal wasn't poking fun at itself, deflating its own pretentiousness and self-seriousness pretty much every step of the way, then you're not seeing the full picture; you're missing out. Have you even read Nietzsche? Black metal, burner of churches, vengeful destroyer of sacred spaces; it would be a bit ironic if black metal itself wanted to be some kind of safe space, but for white male tears only. *No.*

Many metalheads think of other metalheads as "gay," and black metal has, of course, been called "gay." These detractors say this all the time, and they are not wrong. They are wrong about that being a bad thing, though. Bad is being forever trapped in hatred as your identity. Hate and negativity are perhaps part of all of us, but such detractors identify with hatred and bask in the sumptuous irrelevance of murders and rapes they will never commit, glorifying acts they can hardly perceive, with a cooler and trvuer than thou mentality. In violence, black metal is supremely masturbatory. It is indeed extremely gay, so to use gay as a term of derogation is stupid and tautological, not funny or cool. And if Venom's 1982 act does not look gay to you, you should probably visit a gay club to see the differences.

Did black metal evolve out of Scandinavian boyish cruelty and juvenile middle-class boredom? Partly, yes, and the founding acts of terrorizing the surrounding world are not to be vanquished or forgotten. The facts and history are very important, because they create a sentimental community, however performatively alienated. If you kill someone, if you hurt someone, if you want to hurt anyone, what is the point of doing this, or thinking of doing this, all the time? Can Georges Bataille's *Acéphale* be all there is to human transformation? As with Bataille's philosophy of erotic transgression, black metal music is about transforming the self—not killing it.[4] This sentimental and hurting *no* lodged in your bosom transforms you forever. Black metal truly transforms the a/social self. This is why it is not strange or gay to talk about its gayness: not only because black metal is socially atypical in its very core, but because by ridiculing difference one betrays the very core and trvth of black metal—even its murderous trvth.[5] The scandal is not that black metal is gay; the scandal is that this is a fucking scandal. If you really want to reject society and *become* yourself, gayness is as good as it gets.[6]

We are certainly not the first to notice how gay black metal is. In culture and fashion, just look at Kenneth Anger's leather bomber jacket and his rainbow

Lucifer. In academia and journalism, a look at the scholarship (which is predominantly focused on heavy metal) reveals as much with its disproportionate focus on studies of metal masculinities, their theatricality and performativity, and, on the other hand, a more niched scholarship on female exclusion and mis/representation.[7] Gender performativity is now a scholarly cliché, but it is far from truism among black metal journalism or fandoms. If questioning yourself and the world around you is such a black metal obsession, why not include gender and sexuality along the way (or before all else)? It is this disconcerting paradox that animates much of the critically joyous perspectives in this book.

There is a precritical focus on murder and rape in the Scandinavian *father*land of black metal, and the notion that if it is not about hate and rape, it does not hold trve. Yet the truth has evolved.

Black metal is now an archive of truths about a myriad of genders and desires: the murder fetish is a bland and useless narrative, and for years now bowing down to it has been pointless. Black metal has always been queer. All we need to do—in order to ascend to its own trvth—is showcase its queerness spreading out of its multiple histories. There is now a niched but unrelenting and proud queer black metal, including Straight Panic, notably the authors of the only black metal tribute to Magne Andreassen (2016), murdered by Bard "Faust" Eithun of Emperor in Lillehammer, Norway, in 1992, and Homo Erektion's *Gay Black Metal War* (2019).

Black metal is not closed but open. Its boundaries are porous; it is wide open (even gaping like a Goatse). Yes, it's a wintry forest with howling winds and whirring cacodaemons hiding in the buzzing mists—and black metal finds in the winter a place of great comfort, a hibernation from modern life's incessant demands, and the Romantic fantasy of a timeless forest, a simpler place where humans can retreat, at least in spirit; recall T.S. Eliot's "Winter kept us warm." But black metal is also a meadow in a valley with the sun peaking over the mountains (and some unicorns fancily prancing through it). Yes, there are plenty of black metal songs about spring,[8] despite the genre's protestations—born of both the objective fact of the cold Scandinavian climate, with its long winters, and 1980s geopolitical nuclear winter fantasies—that spring will never come and winter will reign forever, like in Narnia.

Black metal is an ecology: an ecology of ideologies, of political and aesthetic ideas. Black metal has been going green for a while now, from Wolves in the Throne Room and Panopticon and Cascadian and post-black metal and blackgaze's musical softening of black metal's hard stance, into softer, more melodic stances, with sounds that are lush and bubbling, to Scott Wilson's *Melancology: Black Metal Theory and Ecology*, which contains such wonderful and perception-altering essays as Niall W.R. Scott's "Blackening the Green" and Ben Woodard's "Irreversible Sludge: Troubled Energetics, Eco-Purification, and Self-Inhumanization." Black metal as an ecological practice is critical of and an alternative to the machinist industrial world, and post–black metal presents plenty of crossover with drone, sludge, and metalgaze, and their dystopian and postcapitalist themes of ecological disaster and climate change (Sunn O))), Locrian, The Body, the art of Terence Hannum). Not far off is also the swelling genre of aquatic-themed post-metal (Isis, Pelican, Giant Squid, The Ocean, Mastodon's *Leviathan*) that imagines the marshy, fecund, and waterlogged paradigm of a heating rather than a cooling planet, governed by the demonic viscous petropolitical presence of black oil—"hydrocarbon corpse juice" as Reza Negarestani calls it in *Cyclonopedia: Complicity with Anonymous Materials*. It's always worth remembering that oil is one of black metal's great repressed elements, being at the basis of Norway's rich economy, and, thus, the high quality of life that Norwegians enjoy. Black oil that releases its rainbow iridescence.

Of course, "hipster black metal" excites us; it is sexy as fuck. Especially pink black metal, such as that offered by Deafheaven, Zweizz, The Soft Pink Truth, Fullmoon Bongzai, often under the mighty influence of that ultimate pink noise album, My Bloody Valentine's *Loveless* (1991). There is a whole blooming field now of pinkgaze black metal, all those bands using pink, purpleish, blue, soft tones and pastel colors in their album art: a flowering palette, a natural world opening up, with pink as its entrance point, shockingly critiquing black metal's grey zones, musically dipping liberally into post-hardcore romanticism and melodicism, pop, and post-punk. Bands and albums such as Underdark's *Mourning Cloak* (2017), Show Me a Dinosaur, Laster, Vaura, An Autumn for Crippled Children, and Fullmoon Bongzai's trippy *Noisense: A Voodoo Beach Party Celebrating the Unholy* (2008). Pink is a wildly anti-social color (unless you're a little girl, in which case it's imposed upon you), churning up so much of what black metal works hard to suppress or deny: girliness and gender, homosexuality, androgyny, glam and punk, childhood and femininity. (What is presumably less black metal than Disney princesses? Yet, of course, princesses can be black metal.) But pink was there from the beginning; just check out the original hot pink vinyl pressing of Mayhem's 1987 EP *Deathcrush*,[9] as well as the pink Carpathian Forest logo on their 1995 EP *Through Chasm, Caves and Titan Woods*.

Black metal is ripe for pinking, for being reterritorialized along lines of pinkness: an active reclamation of humanity in the face of belittlement and accusations of deviance. Of course, as the dangerous and violent and antisocial and affirmative and identity-building form of music that black metal knows itself to be, there is no reason why it shouldn't proudly embrace the color pink. Probably the loudest and proudest pinkening of black metal is The Soft Pink Truth, a side project of Drew Daniel of Matmos, whose 2014 album *Why Do the Heathen Rage?* is a gay disco industrial, house, and techno subversion of black metal, including suitably strutting covers of Venom's "Black Metal," Sarcófago's "Ready to Fuck," and "Grim and Frostbitten Gay Bar," by Anal Cunt side project Impaled Northern Moonforest. What is black metal's soft pink truth? Surely its racism, its antiblackness. As some black metal elements seek to disavow African blackness, The Soft Pink Truth points its finger at the pink skin hiding beneath corpsepaint's powdery dusted skin, bringing out the latent would-be white supremacy at the heart of the black metal project. Queering black metal by turning it into pink disco (a genre that black metal would reject as both "gay" and "black"), The Soft Pink Truth brings out into the open black metal's problematic pink whiteness *and* its undeniable gayness: black metal as both a homosocial and a homoerotic project, which does not diminish male friendship per se: even on stage—think of the countless mouth kisses between Bruce Springsteen and Clarence Clemons.

Pink black metal is like life renewed after black metal's death hole, spring following the winter; prettiness is a virtue, making black metal beautiful and cute. Lush, orchestral, filtered with post-rock swirls; Sunn O)))'s *Life Metal* (2019), with its glorious clouds, a swinging back of life. Pink (mixed with orange etc.) is sunset and sunrise, Homer's "rosy-fingered dawn." The pink triangle was used in Nazi concentration camps to identify gay prisoners and is a symbol of the modern gay rights movement, but neither pink nor gay in black metal necessarily mean anti-fascist, whether we be talking about Gaahl (with his history of racist comments and assault) or the striking image on the cover of NSBM band Kataxu's *Hunger of Elements* (2005): a cosmic shining swastika sword against a universe that glows with a pink tinge crossed by pink lightning.

Pink flows into red, to the bloodied thrones of red and anarchist black metal (RABM). But first let's make a brief stop at the gunslinging/proletarian communist/whore, the castrating rifle woman (*flintenweiber*) or "red nurse" of Klaus Theweleit's *Male Fantasies* (1977): out to shred men to pieces, scourge of the Freikorps, the World War I veteran militias that laid the foundation for the Nazi party, which nurtured a pathological hatred of women and idolized the virginal pure "white" woman who would rear the next generation of the Aryan race. The red woman must be defeated as part of the effort to prevent a "red flood" of communism coming from the East into Western Europe.[10] Red in black metal is not a common color, despite it being the color of blood, and thus suitable for battle slaughter scenarios: the memorable cover of Marduk's 1996 album *Heaven Shall Burn… When We Are Gathered* has a red logo, and takes place under a nice purple sky. Some bands splatter themselves in blood when they play live. Nattefrost on the cover of Peter Beste's *True Norwegian Black Metal* book is an iconic example. Then you have Urgehal, Gorgoroth, Shining, and Watain, who play covered in blood and accompanied by rotting animal body parts. While Amenra's use of blood is closer to performance and the tradition of body radicals. Vampiric blood is present in Cradle of Filth's tribute to Elizabeth Báthory *Cruelty and the Beast* (1998), and it's always worth recalling the album cover of Teen Cthulhu's 2003 *Ride the Blade*, featuring a young person in a bathtub splattered in dark red blood. Yet despite its alleged interest in mass slaughter, black metal is quite a bloodless genre; it's not brutal death metal or slam, obsessed with rotting bodies and gore, but tends toward being a more abstract, philosophical, and evanescent genre, like a bodiless and disembodied death metal that has died twice and now appears in ghostly form.

Injecting the red back into black metal is RABM: not so much a subgenre tied together by any musical affiliation, but more a network of bands that share a commitment to left-wing, socialist, communist, and anarchist politics and organizing. From 2009 to 2019, the RABM blog Red and Anarchist Black Metal (r-a-b-m.blogspot.com) chronicled dozens of bands "charged with radical leftist (anarchist, libertarian socialist, eco-anarchist, etc.) political views," including "blackened crust/hardcore/punk" and also dark ambient, neofolk, post-rock, and hip-hop. Notable names in RABM are Iskra, Sankara, Dawn Ray'd, Ancst, Underdark, Yovel, and there is Cascadian crossover with the anarchist Panopticon. The *Crushing Intolerance* compilations from the Black Metal Alliance (2015–2017), the two Blackened Death Records compilations *Worldwide Organization of Metalheads against Nazis* (2018), as well as projects such as Kim Kelly's compilation *Riffs for Reproductive Justice* and her Black Flags over Brooklyn festival (2019), illustrate the growing global reach of RABM. St. Louis, Missouri, "Midwestern proletarian crust" band Redbait are exemplary of a new breed of explicitly political left-wing metal, led by the dual vocal attack of Rebecca Redbait and Madeline. To "red bait" means to attack or denounce an opponent by calling them a communist, anarchist, or Marxist, a term which is losing meaning in our political moment, because it is becoming socially acceptable to identify as a socialist in the US. What has also changed in the last two decades is the weight of politics in art: aesthetics and reality grew closer.

Says former Redbait guitarist W:

Astral Noize did an interview with Feminazgûl and Maggie Killjoy said something that struck me, something like "Nazism isn't the abstraction it was twenty years ago." Fascism has never been acceptable, but when a lot of us started listening to black metal a decade or more ago, we weren't aware of violent, organized white supremacist groups marching through the streets, but they're here now and they've murdered people who showed up to tell them they weren't welcome. I don't know what to say to somebody who's seen what happened in Charlottesville and still walks around in public with some Nazi eagle shit on their back, except "go fuck yourself."[11]

On the subject of fascism in the black metal mist, the color grey may serve us well; black metal remains a grey area when it comes to the specifics of its actual relationship with Nazi ideology and/or aesthetics. You don't hear too much about grey in black metal; beginning with its classic panda corpsepaint, there is a lot invested in separating the black and white, as if they should stay apart and not mingle. Yet sometimes they smear together, and you get a strange and uncanny effect (Gaahl's corpsepaint, for example). These days, as black metal musicians age, you also get grey hair and grey beards: the black metal greybeards and the adjacent gayish lumberjack hipsterism. Black metal is awash with swirling greys, mists, skies. The cover art of Posthum's self-titled debut (2009) figures a posthuman world devoid of humanity, with the black of the trees blending into the white. Merrimack's *Grey Rigorism* (2009), an album that has a notable industrial influence, especially in the martial drums, posits black metal as a grey world; and Jute Gyte's "Grey King" is almost a parodic pastiche of death and doom metal with its sincere debility. Black metal arguably constructs a black-and-white world, a return to a BW past before color photography, an othering separating the historical world as different from ours (BWBM?). It also generates grey worlds, where black and white mingle in grey misty fogginess, where boundaries are blurred between human and non-human, animate or inanimate, animal, vegetable, or mineral, the rational and the fantastic: Theodor Kittelsen's imagery used on Burzum's albums, and Kittelsen's trolls poised between atavistic menace and old-world whimsy. Black metal is cute, and often cuddly, from cozy pictures of Fenriz as a domestic god to the Black Metal Cats.

Fascism hides within the black metal mist but ever eludes simple identification with the genre. Burzum is often characterized as NSBM, but their early albums and their music in general is not explicitly political, even by "apoliteic" standards. But just like Salman Rushdie's fatwa becomes the story that overshadows his actual writing, so the story of Count Grishnackh killing Euronymous becomes the story of the Nazi heart of black metal triumphing over its communist heart. The misty sublime that black metal rests upon is the mystery of its relation to Nazism. "To what extent is black metal really a Nazi art?" they breathlessly ask. "Black metal cleaves to Nazism as an expression of ultimate evil!" they respond, but then you get reports of members of Marduk handing out neo-Nazi pamphlets, and the sublime is revealed as banal. Not even romanticism is left. But good humour comes to help, as the circle turns to satire with Neckbeard Deathcamp's *White Nationalism Is for Basement Dwelling Losers* (2019).

We need to move beyond, not negate, the founding acts of terror and the flirtation with black metal's ideological riffraff. This is precisely where the grey truth of black metal shines forth. But where is the line between performing a shocking Nazi aesthetic and buying into the ideology as everyday political practice? Liberal commentators like Dick Hebdige bought into the idea of the swastika as an empty signifier,[12] but the history of our current political moment has not borne that perhaps rather naïve belief out: even Johnny Rotten is a Trump fan these days, and Morrissey believes he is a misunderstood liberal. The grey area of black metal comes from the habit of obscuring the issue of black metal's Nazism. All that noise and swirling in the cosmic snowstorms is a kind of white noise that covers up the answers to that question, answers which are lost and inaudible in a swirling snowstorm-cum-shitstorm, howling over a straight answer. If fascist creep is inevitable in black metal and forms part of its mystery and sublime, resisting that pull is healthy practice.

Rainbows in sunlight dissolve the mist and melt black metal snowflakes.

White Tears, Black Metal: Hari Kunzru's 2017 novel *White Tears* tells the story of two white record industry dudes who appropriate an old blues track from a mysterious and forgotten musician, whose ghost begins to haunt them. The novel is an insightful metaphor for rock music in general, which from Elvis onward has been very invested in appropriating black music, and then disavowing the appropriation: Varg Vikernes is merely the latest in a long tradition of black erasure. To what extent has black metal become, or always been, the music of white tears? Adam Lehrer makes the valuable point that second-wave Norwegian black metal was a white middle- and upper-class product: "a counter-cultural movement rooted in white privilege and a kind of rebellion against the musicians' own privileges...in actuality a reaction to the very high quality of life found in Norway."[13] It's hard not to read 1990s second-wave black metal through the lens of (and as anticipatory of) the current wave of white male revanchism supporting totalitarian politics across the globe, feeding into an organized movement of purism claiming black metal as a safe space to promenade and peacock white supremacist ideas, all wrapped up in an allure of curated self-pity and misery, a sadness about "the death of the West," in short—an incontinent white fragility contest and image where all life is dead, because they feel their supremacy threatened. In other words, black metal as a conservative force fighting against what it perceives as an excessively liberal, or liberalized, society.

Was this the guiding sentiment of black metal all along? The facts check out: liberal critics and fans at the time enjoyed black metal's "flirtations" with fascism as a bit of naughty frisson. Even Varg's killing of Euronymous was treated by the tabloid metal media (*Kerrang!* in the lead) as shocking but, nonetheless, a *cultural* event that made rock 'n' roll exciting again. Faust of Emperor's homophobic killing of Magne Andreassen, Hellhammer of Mayhem's comments about black metal being only for white people ("we don't like black people here"), Jon Nodveidt of Dissection's racist killing of Josef ben Meddour, recently unearthed comments by Dimmu Borgir in a *Darkness* zine interview from 1995.[14] Etc., ad nauseam. From this point of view, it is easy to see black metal as the voice of white male racism, generously gathering its revanchist tears and spreading them all around wherever they may flow. A band like Taake, with its anti-Islamic sentiment, belies the notion that black metal is an equal opportunity misanthropist. Under the guise of hating all humans equally, it actually hates some (the black and brown ones) more than others (the white ones). When thinking about race and black metal it's always worth remembering why there are comparatively so many fewer musicians of color in black metal than, for example, in death metal.

The problem with *accepting* this version of events is that it lets them win; it lets the racists and the Nazis have black metal for their own. And why should they? Why should they be allowed to take black metal for themselves just because some of its key players were or are racist shitheads? Exactly, they shouldn't. We metalheads, in all our plurality and diversity, have somehow allowed black metal to become an authenticity race of rejectionism, obliterating whatever cultural value there is in negativity (which is *not* the same as hatred). Black metal as a music is too good to let racists have it; they didn't invent it, they didn't give us corpsepaint, they don't own it, and they never will, because there is more to black metal than its Nazi associations, which we don't need to downplay or ignore.

In fact, we need to recognize them so as to be able to reclaim the genre, not without or in spite of them, but against and beyond them. A black metal rainbow shines over Nazism's graveyard!

We must move beyond black metal's founding mythology (the *Lords of Chaos* type); it no longer determines the ethical ramifications of musicians and fans, including a continual move away from a dishonestly rehearsed Satanism toward spontaneous or reflected forms of Gnosticism and mysticism writ large. Whether it is Fushitsusha, Ulver, Liturgy, or Myrkur, there is a clear move *toward* an anti-cosmic interpretation of the social worlds we inhabit. Since the early 2000s and the rise of nu metal, the limits of Satanism have been commercially exhausted, and the proclaimed ethical coordinates of individualism have evolved to articulate black metal as something more than a love-hate relationship with the media and the market. Renihilation now coexists with annihilation. Because there is both a picturesque history and evolution in focus, one of the main points of this book is that Nazis don't own black metal, and they never will! Just like rock music does not belong to Rock Against Communism or Oi punk to the likes of Nicky Crane.[15] No matter how many times they try to own it, wank on Varg Vikernes, or try to argue that black metal's true core is hate and intolerance. Of course, this rejection is exclusionary and risks making Nazis the losers they secretly want to be, but the historical justice here is that *they* will have to hide in and then crawl out of their closet. Nazis' perpetual romance with rejection paradoxically obliterates their pretension for self-transformative triumph of the will. Black metal is a utopian art, and that is why it will never fit into their narrative. Art will always elude ideology, and this is partly because of reception theory: you can enjoy Burzum even if you've never heard of Adolf Hitler. Black metal and its rainbows are spontaneous inversions.

Black Metal Rainbows is not a "critique" of black metal's Nazi tendencies or a list of problematic bands you should avoid. *Black Metal Rainbows* celebrates black metal being a place for everyone, not the domain of Nazis; they have no right to it, whatever their place in its history. NSBM does not represent black metal however hard it may try.[16] And the reason for that is that Nazis falsely ascend to the gnosis of black metal, which they always fail to comprehend: transformation and change. Black metal is pluralistic, because it is transformative, and now is its Golden Age of Rainbows.

This book advances the point of view that black metal is a type of carnivalesque, in the Bakhtinian sense: an art form that presents a carnival world, in which the cross is reversed and hangs upside down, Satan is queen, and the old order of the world sloughs away while every god or master is torn down. Bakhtin's carnival is ever a double-edged sword; just as it creates the conditions for the possibility of progressive thought, it is also an allowed feast, a sanctioned holiday that tilts right back into Monday at work, everyone in line again. Black metal as carnival also cuts two ways; it is not just Dødheimsgard in their flamboyant multicolored corpsepaint in the 1990s but is also Peste Noire and their accordion-wielding nationalist troubadour black metal, Richard Moult's classicist influence on Satanism, and the reputation of Les Légions Noires. One of the desolations of the cultural left right now is the realization that the right-wing is in full carnival mode; their politics are literal spectacles of cruelty, with open mockery of the disabled, immigrant children in cages, police officers brutalizing, wounding, and killing black people and protesters on video broadcast for the world to see. Their culture is now counterculture, a bad-taste whirlwind of Pepe, Groyper, Honk Honkler, and clown world memes, Wojacks and grey NPC faces, revelling in the self-exiled forest of the margins, deplatformed yet ubiquitous online, self-professedly "adorably deplorable," chasing conspiracy theories from Alex Jones to QAnon, redpilled and blackpilled, alt-right and 4chan. There is energy piled behind the right-wing revolutionary impulse, which in an era of wokescold, liberal guilt and white self-shaming, sees the temptations of the far-right forbidden taboo topics, from racism and sexism to Nazism, pedophilia, and lolicon, as indicators of freedom, as culturally invigorating.

Black metal drips down into popular culture, from Brian Manowitz's *Vegan Black Metal Chef* to Rarecho's *Aggretsuko*, and is, in turn, reinvented through it. Anything can be "blackened" and, thereby, become part of black metal's larger cultural quagmire: Harmony Korine's *Gummo* and the high-end conceptual art of Banks Violette, the metal-cum-expressionism of Bjarne Melgaard or the photo doom naturalism of Torbjørn Rødland, Kanye West wearing a Vetements $800 designer black metal hoodie,[17] Taylor Swift's 2020 album *Folklore*, which was seen by some as partaking in black metal forest aesthetics, cultural mash-ups like Curezum and Marxthrone. Despite its protestations that it stands alone, black metal fucks with the internet and online meme culture; there are blackened *Teletubbies* memes, and there is the Modern Black Metal Classics Facebook page—a series of black metal album cover parodies—Varg is almost a living alt-right meme at this point, and Pepe black metal (Fatelancer) is actually a thing. Reputations are ruined online by journalistic and social media exposés of everything from Nazi affiliation and antisemitism to child pornography and pedophilic subject matter (Dagon of Inquisition, Mikko Aspa of Deathspell Omega/Clandestine Blaze/Nicole 12, Mikołaj Żentara of Mgła/Leichenhalle), cancellation campaigns are fought online (recent cases include Deströyer 666, Horna, and Taake, the latter involving rapper Talib Kweli), and abusers in bands are routinely outed on Left Metal Twitter—a scene which is a big inspiration for this book.

The crossover from a Satanic fairy tale to doomsday reality is clear in what Peste Noire front man Famine, now living in Ukraine, says of the cultural right: "In Ukraine being NS, natio, pagan is a winner's trick, it's stylish, young people want to be part of it, they attract girls, when the extreme French right only likes forest trolls or old girls with problems."[18] Peste Noire—and we don't need to think too deeply as to which black plague they are referring to, with all Famine's talk of ethnically white people living happily together and multiculturalism being a cancer. Black metal cultivates a reputation that it is above and beyond ideology, but why should only its leftward leanings be critiqued, and its right-wing faction be elevated as its trve essence? If metal orthodoxists insist so much on the dualism traversing all Satanism, Gnosticism, and mysticism that make the genre of black metal, then their opposition to the political opposite is at the very least hypocritical.[19] And when it is not, it is just murderous.

Black metal is infinite potentiality—to do better.

Black metal is a cultural battleground, and its rainbow contains black and brown like the Philadelphia 2017 Pride flag, which included them in recognition of LGBTIQ+ people of color. The left already owns the carnival and the parade; what remains is to reclaim ownership of it through the shimmering loops of intersectionality, punching upwards, and dragging down the aristocracy and its minions. The right-wing carnival is over!

The story of *Black Metal Rainbows* stems from Coloring the Black: A Black Metal Theory Symposium, organized by Daniel Lukes and Michael O'Rourke, at Gallery X in Dublin, on Friday, March 20, 2015.[20] This event was part of—and also an act of theoretical renegadeship against—so-called black metal theory (BMT), a field of theoretical writings on black metal spearheaded by Nicola Masciandaro and the Hideous Gnosis symposium in Brooklyn in 2009 and continuing over the subsequent years with various events and publications.[21] The idea of not just academically studying black metal but doing critical theory with and through it was and remains fascinating and invigorating, stenching up the often obscure world of theory with pestilential delights. But the various blackenings and pesterings that had come out of BMT thus far did not seem sufficient, in that the politics remained largely unquestioned.[22] There is no question of handing over black metal or BMT to the Nietzschean fanboys, the incel edgelords and alt-right keyboard warriors, and the neo-Nazis who hurt and kill people in the streets. And BMT had, unwittingly or not, been going in the direction of reproducing that vision of black metal: overly kvlt, narrow, elitist, and precious.

Coloring the Black sought to throw a bucket of rainbow splatterings into BMT's chin-stroking milieu, to "open up black metal theory to a broader spectrum beyond the black...more prismatic and multicolored,"[23] extending and seeking to fulfil BMT's promise of blackening the wider canvas of critical theory (including queer theory), as well as departing from and looking beyond BMT. The call for papers announced three primary aims: "to challenge the potentially ponderous and serious nature of black metal theory; to question the black/white binary which dominates theorizing about black metal music and aesthetics; to foreground diverse, marginal, and intersectional black metal voices, readings, and practices." In addition, there was the desire to "open up the more comedic, playful, camp, ludic, carnivalesque dimension of black metal and black metal theory...questioning its more nihilistic impulses ('blackening' and more 'blackening') in favour of more affirmative approaches and utilizations." The aim was to "pink" BMT, by thinking about The Soft Pink Truth, Pinkish Black, Zweizz, Deafheaven, My Bloody Valentine, Nicki Minaj, and Pink, furthering BMT from a range of feminist, LGBTIQ+, and intersectional perspectives, including disability studies, animal studies, and cute studies, to consider and destabilize the racial normativities of black metal musical and theoretical traditions.

And then shit hit the fan. Once the call for papers was posted publicly, there was immediate interest and responses: positive, negative, outraged, apoplectic; the goons of deathmetal.org led the charge, attempting a #MetalGate campaign, which fizzled out poorly.[24] There were death threats. Nicola Masciandaro felt (correctly) called to account and penned a lengthy article (since taken down) densely arguing that black metal theory already took into account the colors within the black.[25] In spite of these detractors, the symposium was a glorious success. "Lord of the Logos" Christophe Szpajdel, fresh from working with Rihanna on a wonderfully multicolored black metal logo of her name, designed the symposium's Coloring the Black logo and opened up a contest for collaborators to color it, for which he received his fair share of angry naysayers. The symposium saw contributions from Drew Daniel of Matmos/The Soft Pink Truth, Andy Curtis-Brignell of Caïna, Laina Dawes, Christophe Szpajdel, Stanimir Panayotov (whose paper "Sad Rainbows" would inspire the title of this volume), and many others. You can still stream it on YouTube.[26] In 2016, Daniel invited Stanimir to be his coeditor, and work on this project began, with the blessing of Michael O'Rourke, to whom we are thankful. We invited Jaci Raia to design the book:[27] Jaci is fully our coauthor; her work is not an illustration but an actual coloring of the rainbows we imagined together. We three are equally responsible cocreators of this project. *Black Metal Rainbows* is thus not merely a conference proceedings but the next step. It is not a lone instance but one of many steps occurring globally illustrating the broad and inclusive appeal of black metal and of metal in general: it is part of a wave, in music journalism in particular, giving a strong boost to critical debates in metal and extreme music more broadly construed.[28] It is a middle finger firmly raised to cultural gatekeepers who take it upon themselves to try to carve out spaces of exclusivity and exclusion.

Our approach is not musicological; it is open and eclectic. It originates within fandoms of blackening, as did the original black metal theorists. We acknowledge the work done by various authors, organizers, and editors, such as Nicola Masciandaro, Edia Connole, Keith Kahn-Harris,[29] Scott Wilson, and Amelia Ishmael. We are informed by various approaches in both the humanities (in particular cultural studies) and the social sciences. We share in this volume many of the worries and research agendas of social scientists and researchers who speak to an audience of fans and theorists alike about ethical and sociopolitical concerns in metal via disciplinary frameworks. There is now a plethora of work to be consulted in both "high theory" and the social sciences.[30] This is also an artistic project; it is not meant to be merely descriptive or analytical. What distinguishes our approach to thinking about "black metal rainbows" from musicology, or even so-called metal music studies, and, to some extent, BMT itself, is that we do not imaginatively prohibit an *affirmation*. Black metal rainbows, if they are to proliferate in the way the genre has, include affirmative cosmologies: a reversed Gnosticism of the will to create worlds and spaces of resistance. Do we know the addressee of such a cosmology? Not really. This is a messy project. Nothing wrong with the blood fetish per se, but there are other bodily fluids and solids to be played with (like spit, cum, piss and shit), and black metal's troubled relationship with the body is often on our minds here. Black metal can be incredibly sexy, as you will see once you delve into this NSFW volume—there is now black metal porn, and it whips.

This introduction began with a film (*The Wizard of Oz*) and can end with another: Clive Barker's *Nightbreed* (1990), based on his own novel *Cabal*, about the mythical city of Midian, a utopian place for the monstrous, the outsiders, the queer, destroyed yet ever renewed, which Cradle of Filth carried into their sumptuous album *Midian* (2000).

Black metal is for everybody and nobody, and may this black metal rainbow be a glittering path leading to that nowhere!

In our interview with Svein Egil Hatlevik (Fleurety, Dødheimsgard, Zweizz et al.), one of the inspirations behind this book, he ponders the value of this particular moment in black metal history. "It seems very much more pluralistic now," he says. "I guess that's because there's more space. So you can have your very conservative or formulaic record labels for the people who like that, and then you can have record labels with people who make something more like you who aren't interested in that at all. And then you can have festivals and social get-togethers and everything. I guess that thing is peaking now."

The golden age of pluralistic black metal is happening not in the nineties but now. Black metal is a party, and you are invited!

Welcome to Black Metal Rainbows.

Notes

[1] In this case, Andy Rehfeldt and Chavdar Zhechev's "Judy Garland Sings Death Metal," YouTube, July 30, 2014, accessed February 23, 2021, https://www.youtube.com/watch?v=QcBYpmD29ik&ab_channel=AndyRehfeldt.

[2] Corpsepaint deserves its own special mention: there's lots of writing and speculation on its origins, and the upshot seems to be that it has multiple roots; Drew Daniel, "Corpsepaint as Necro-Minstrelsy, or Toward the Re-Occultation of Black Blood," in *Melancology: Black Metal Theory and Ecology*, ed. Scott Wilson (Winchester, UK: ZerO Books, 2014), 26–49, identifies Brazilian band Sarcófago as potential originators of black metal corpsepaint; drawing upon the Latin American *calavera* tradition and discusses its ambivalent relationship with minstrel show blackface, which is reflected in certain modern uses of fully black corpsepaint, such as Cradle of Filth in their "Heartbreak and Séance" video and the *Cryptoriana: The Seduction of Decay* photoshoot (2017), Samael in their "Black Supremacy" video (2017), and actual blackface, in the case of the artwork of Peste Noire's 2018 self-titled album, on its "Degenerate" side. Also see Jeremy Ulrey, "A Visual History of Corpsepaint," Metal Injection, February 19, 2016, accessed February 23, 2021, https://metalinjection.net/black-metal-chronicles/black-metal-history-month/an-illustrated-history-of-corpse-paint.

[3] Brad Sanders, "Untrue and International: Living in a Post Black Metal World," Quietus, April 9, 2012, https://thequietus.com/articles/08463-post-black-metal-liturgy-leviathan-alcest; Sasha Frere-Jones, "The Dark Arts: How to Approach Black Metal," *New Yorker*, October 3, 2011, accessed February 23, 2021, https://www.newyorker.com/magazine/2011/10/10/the-dark-arts.

[4] Cf. Deathspell Omega's *Fas—Ite, Maledicti,*

in *Ignem Aeternum* (2007). On Bataille, black metal theory and transformation, see Edia Connole, "Black Metal Theory: Speculating with Bataille's *Unfinished System*—'Mystical Vomit' from Neoplatonism to Neroplatonism," in *Georges Bataille and Contemporary Thought*, ed. Will Stonge (London: Bloomsbury Academic, 2017), 173–216.

[5]Kevin Coogan's argument best captures the betrayal of black metal by the likes of Burzum; see Kevin Coogan, "How 'Black' is Black Metal? Michael Moynihan, *Lords of Chaos*, and the 'Countercultural Fascist' Underground," *Hit List Magazine* 1, no. 1 (February–March 1999), 32–49.

[6]See the useful summary of gay metal icons for the perplexed by Amanda Hess, "Top Five Gay Metal Icons," *Washington City Paper* (August 26, 2009), accessed February 23, 2021, https://www.washingtoncitypaper.com/columns/the-sexist/blog/13118298/top-5-gay-metal-icons.

[7]While not an exhaustive list, the major books to be credited here are: Florian Heesch and Niall W.R. Scott, eds., *Heavy Metal, Gender, and Sexuality: Interdisciplinary Approaches* (London: Routledge, 2016); Sonia Vasan, *Women's Participation in the Death Metal Subculture* (PhD diss., University of Houston, 2010); Rosemary Lucy Hill, *Gender, Metal, and the Media: Women Fans and the Gendered Experience of Music* (London: Palgrave Macmillan, 2016); Amber R. Clifford-Napoleone, *Queerness in Heavy Metal Music: Metal Bent* (London: Routledge, 2015); Laina Dawes, *What Are You Doing Here? A Black Woman's Life and Liberation in Heavy Metal* (New York: Bazillion Points, 2013); Robert Walser, *Running with the Devil: Power, Gender, and Madness in Heavy Metal Music* (Hanover, NH: University Press of New England, 1993).

[8]Including: Wolves in the Throne Room, "The Old Ones Are with Us"; Elderwind, "Приближение Весны" (The Coming of Spring); Winter Dynasty, "句芒" (God of Spring); Black Lotus, "Terra Hiberna" and "Wreath of the Triumphant Sun"; Lustre, "They Awoke to the Scent of Spring"; Nocte Obducta, "Frühling: Des schwarzen Flieders Wiegenlied"; UADA, "Black Autumn, White Spring"; Wintersun, "Awaken from the Dark Slumber (Spring)."

[9]J. Bennett, "White Whale Vinyl: Mayhem's *Deathcrush* Comes Pretty in Pink," *Revolver*, September 30, 2020, accessed February 23, 2021, https://www.revolvermag.com/culture/white-whale-vinyl-mayhems-deathcrush-comes-pretty-pink.

[10]Metal has often articulated a kind of appropriated femininity and acted as a kind of becoming-woman, from Iron Maiden to Cinderella, Alice in Chains, and Black Veil Brides: and along with this becoming-woman, the fear of letting actual women into its spaces. If glam metal is black metal's mirror image, its party girl persona is substituted in black metal by a monstrous sorrowful woman, a crone shrieking in the marshes and woodlands. As has been the case with Myrkur's entry into the scene, women in black metal are still all too often perceived as intruders.

[11]George Parr, "Redbait's Proletariat Crust Is Precisely What the World Needs in 2018," Astral Noize, August 1, 2018, accessed February 23, 2021, https://astralnoizeuk.com/2018/08/01/redbaits-proletariat-crust-is-precisely-what-the-world-needs-in-2018.

[12]Dick Hebdige, *Subculture: The Meaning of Style* (London: Routledge, 2006), 116–17.

[13]Adam Lehrer, "Norwegian Black Metal as a Conceptual Lens in Contemporary Art," *Forbes*, June 11, 2018, accessed February, 23, 2021, tinyurl.com/25nzenz7.

[14]"Do you agree with me, that black metal should be for white people?/Yes, I do and I would gladly cut the throat of every black person in the world," *Darkness Zine* no. 1, August 1995, 19, accessed February 23, 2021, https://hatpastorn.files.wordpress.com/2010/12/dimmu-borgir-darkness-zine-1995.jpg.

[15]See the important documentary work done by the website Who Makes the Nazis?, accessed February 23, 2021, unavailable September 15, 2021, http://www.whomakesthenazis.com.

[16]See the painfully simplistic and illuminating *How to Oppose Fascism in the Extreme Metal Scene: A Beginner's Guide for Comrades and Fellow Antifascists*, Barbarie, 2017, accessed February 23, 2021, https://barbarie.noblogs.org/files/2017/08/How-to-oppose-fascism-A5-EN-1.0.pdf; also see the important historical work done at the Red and Anarchist Black Metal blog, accessed February 23, 2021, r-a-b-m.blogspot.com; Dylan Miller, "Why We're Investigating Extreme Politics in Underground Music," Quietus, November 26, 2018, accessed February 23, 2021, https://thequietus.com/articles/25682-fascism-underground-music-racism-industrial-black-metal-noise; Stephen O'Malley, *Fuck Fundamentalist Pigs* (iDEAL Recordings, 2015), a reaction to the Charlie Hebdo killings.

[17]Jake Woolf, "There's an $800 Hoodie That's Selling Out Everywhere," GQ, February 22, 2016, accessed February 23, 2021, https://www.gq.com/story/vetements-hoodie-buy-sold-out-price.

[18]"Interview with Famine (KPN) from Kiev," Le Scriebe du Rock, September 2, 2019, accessed February 23, 2021,

https://www.webzinelescribedurock.
com/2019/09/english-version-interview-
with-famine.html.

[19] A great deal of black metal "wokeness"
in the world of journalism is indebted to
the writing of Kim Kelly; see, among many
texts, Kim Kelly, "Riding the New Wave of
Anti-Fascist Black Metal," *Vice*, August 23,
2018, accessed February 23, 2021, https://
www.vice.com/en_us/article/ywkj8y/riding-
the-new-wave-of-anti-fascist-black-metal?;
Kim Kelly, "Fuck Nazi Metal Sympathy,"
Vice, October 25, 2018, accessed February
23, 2021, https://www.vice.com/en_us/
article/598xdb/fuck-nazi-metal-sympathy;
also see Colin Moynihan, "Heavy Metal
Confronts Its Nazi Problem," *New Yorker*,
February 19, 2019, accessed February 23,
2021, https://www.newyorker.com/culture/
culture-desk/heavy-metal-confronts-its-
nazi-problem.

[20] See Coloring the Black: A Black Metal
Theory Symposium, accessed February
23, 2021, https://www.facebook.com/
events/1543138352628663; http://
coloringtheblackmetal.tumblr.com.

[21] Nicola Masciandaro, ed., *Hideous Gnosis:
Black Metal Theory Symposium I* (Charleston,
SC: CreateSpace, 2010), accessed May
21, 2021, http://hugoribeiro.com.br/
biblioteca-digital/Masciandaro-Black_
Metal_Theory_Symposium.pdf; Scott Wilson,
ed., *Melancology: Black Metal Theory
and Ecology* (Winchester, UK: ZerO Books,
2014); Edia Connole and Nicola Masciandaro,
eds., *Mors Mystica: Black Metal Theory
Symposium* (London: Schism Press, 2015);
Nicola Masciandaro and Edia Connole,
Floating Tomb: Black Metal Theory (Milan:
Mimesis International, 2015); *Glossator:
Practice and Theory of the Commentary* 6
(2012), special issue on Black Metal, eds.
Nicola Masciandaro and Reza Negarestani;
Helvete: A Journal of Black Metal Theory
1 (2013), eds. Amelia Ishmael, Zareen
Price, Aspasia Stephanou and Ben Woodard,
Helvete: A Journal of Black Metal Theory
2 (2015), eds. Niall W.R. Scott and Steve
Shakespeare, *Helvete: A Journal of Black
Metal Theory* 3 (2016), ed. Amelia Ishmael;
P.E.S.T.: Philial|Epidemic|Strategy|Tryst,
Radical Matters, November 20, 2011,
accessed February 23, 2021, http://
www.radicalmatters.com/metasound/pest_
metasound_20_nov_2011.pdf; also see Eugene
Thacker, "Black Metal," Mute, August 24,
2010, accessed February 23, 2021, https://
www.metamute.org/editorial/occultural-
studies-column/occultural-studies-1.0-
black-metal; Eugene Thacker, "Three
Quæstio on Demonology," in *In the Dust of
This Planet: Horror of Philosophy*, vol. 1
(Winchester, UK: ZerO Books, 2011), 10–48;
Lieut. Nab Saheb of Kashmir, *Bergmetal:
Oro-Emblems of the Musical Beyond* (Austin,

NY: gnOme books, 2014). Black metal
theory as a movement was itself partially
influenced by preceding events, such as the
first global conference on heavy metal music
held in Salzburg, Austria, in November
2008, the founding of the International
Society for Metal Music Studies, and the
landmark volumes: Rosemary Hill and Karl
Spracklen, eds., *Heavy Fundametalisms:
Music, Metal, and Politics* (Oxford: Inter-
Disciplinary Press, 2010); Niall W.R.
Scott and Imke Von Helden, eds., *The Metal
Void: First Gatherings* (Oxford: Inter-
Disciplinary Press, 2010). This line of
work led to founding the journal *Metal
Music Studies*, published by Intellect Books
(Bristol, UK).

[22] Ben Ratliff, "Thank You, Professor, That
Was Putrid," *New York Times*, December
15, 2009, accessed February 23, 2021,
https://www.nytimes.com/2009/12/15/
arts/music/15metal.html; also see the
cogent summary of Peter Pichler, "The
Cultural History of Black Metal Theory
and Philosophy—Extreme Metal Music as a
'Schrödinger's Cat of Culture'?" Peter
Pichler's Website, August 1, 2016,
unavailable February 23,2021, http://www.
peter-pichler-stahl.at/artikel/black-
metal-and-philosophy-extreme-metal-as-a-
schroedingers-cat-of-culture.

[23] The approach to an opening for "coloring"
was inspired by the essays in Jeffrey
Jerome Cohen, *Prismatic Ecology: Ecotheory
beyond Green* (Minneapolis: University of
Minnesota Press, 2013).

[24] Cory Van der Pol, "#MetalGate," Death
Metal Underground, December 12, 2014,
accessed February 23, 2021, http://www.
deathmetal.org/article/metalgate; Cory Van
Der Pol, "#MetalGate Hipsters Continue
Faking the News," Death Metal Underground,
January 31, 2015, accessed February 23,
2021, http://www.deathmetal.org/article/
metalgate-hipsters-continue-faking-the-
news; Brett Stevens, "The Historical
Background of #MetalGate," Death Metal
Underground, April 20, 2015, accessed
February 23, 2021, http://www.deathmetal.
org/news/the-historical-background-of-
metalgate.

[25] A close argument, via research on the
thought of Meher Baba, is contained in
Nicola Maciandaro, "The Inverted Rainbow:
On the Color of Love," in *On the Darkness
of the Will* (Milan: Mimesis International,
2018), 139–54.

[26] Coloring the Black: A Black Metal
Symposium, YouTube, March 20, 2015,
accessed February 23, 2021, https://www.
youtube.com/watch?v=3Ro7LKac4mO.

[27] See Jaci Raia's work at KVLT, accessed
February 23, 2021, http://kvlt.co; also see
her work on American Nihilist Underground

Society, *The History of Metal* (San Francisco: Blurb, 2011).

[28]Among a plethora of current writing on homophobia and misogyny in metal, see Tom Dare, "Heavy Metal Is Gay: Why We Need to Tackle Our Homophobia," *Terrorizer*, July 23, 2014, accessed February 23, 2021 http://www.terrorizer.com/news/features-2/heavy-metal-is-gay-need-tackle-homophobia; Kristy Loye, "Metal's Problem with Women Is Not Going Away Anytime Soon," *Houston Press*, November 11, 2015, accessed February 23, 2021, https://www.houstonpress.com/music/metals-problem-with-women-is-not-going-away-anytime-soon-7858411; Jill Mikkelson, "It's Time to Stop Making Excuses for Extreme Metal's Violent Misogynist Fantasies," *Vice*, January 20, 2016, accessed February 23, 2021, https://www.vice.com/en_ca/article/rb8bnd/death-metal-misogyny; Beth Winegarner, "Smashing through the Boundaries: Heavy Metal's Racism and Sexism Problem—and How It Can Change," *Bitch Media*, May 17, 2016, https://tinyurl.com/27sj3djd; Stephen Hill, "Metal's Most Interesting Voices Are All Female—And It's About Time," *Metal Hammer*, February 12, 2019, accessed February 24, 2021, https://www.loudersound.com/news/metals-most-interesting-voices-are-all-female-and-its-about-time; Bradley Zorgdrager, "How Brutal Death Metal Is Confronting Its Misogyny Problem," *Kerrang!*, August 29, 2019, accessed February 24, 2021, https://www.kerrang.com/features/how-brutal-death-metal-is-confronting-its-misogyny-problem. Although not focused on (black) metal, the approaches to ethics and female fandom in Rhian Jones and Eli Davies, eds., *Under My Thumb: Songs that Hate Women and the Women Who Love Them* (London: Repeater Books, 2017) should be greeted too. On female voices in metal specifically, see Kim Kelly, "With #KillTheKing, Heavy Metal Is Having Its #MeToo Moment," *Vice*, March 19, 2018, accessed February 24, 2021, https://www.vice.com/en_asia/article/9kg9ez/with-killtheking-heavy-metal-is-having-its-metoo-moment. There is a long list of female metal vocalists and musicians now, including such notables as Lingua Ignota, A.A. Williams, Larissa of Venom Prison, Chelsea Wolfe, Emma Ruth Rundle, Kayla Phillips, to name but a few.

[29]See especially Keith Kahn-Harris, *Extreme Metal: Music and Culture on the Edge* (Oxford: Berg, 2006).

[30]Along with *Helvete* and *Metal Music Studies*, see the following special issues on metal: *Journal of Cultural Research* 15, no. 3 (2011): Metal Studies? Cultural Research in the Heavy Metal Scene, eds. Karl Spracklen, Andy R. Brown, and Keith Kahn-Harris, https://www.tandfonline.com/toc/rcuv20/15/3; and *Volume!: The French Journal of Popular Music Studies* 9, no. 2 (2012): Dossier Metal Studies, eds. Gérôme Guibert and Jedediah Sklowe, accessed February 24, 2021, https://journals.openedition.org/volume/2946. Apart from those already referred to above in note 7, some of the more prominent (but not all) names that have done the important work of unearthing the picturesque and ludic qualities of metal broadly construed are Deena Weinstein, *Heavy Metal: A Cultural Sociology* (Lanham, MD: Lexington Books, 1991); Deena Weinstein, *Heavy Metal: The Music and Its Culture*, rev. ed. (Boston, MA: Da Capo Press, 2000); Jeffrey Jensen Arnett, *Metal Heads: Heavy Metal Music and Adolescent Alienation* (Boulder, CO: Westview Press, 1996); Mark LeVine, *Heavy Metal Islam: Rock, Resistance, and the Struggle for the Soul of Islam* (New York: Three Rivers Press, 2008); Mark LeVine, *Headbanging against Repressive Regimes: Censorship of Heavy Metal in the Middle East, North Africa, Southeast Asia and China* (Copenhagen: Freemuse, 2009); Pierre Hecker, *Turkish Metal: Music, Meaning, and Morality in a Muslim Society* (Falmouth: Ashgate, 2012); Andy R. Brown, Karl Spracklen, Keith Kahn-Harris, and Niall W.R. Scott, eds., *Global Metal Music and Culture: Current Directions in Metal Studies* (London: Routledge, 2016); Gabby Riches, Bryan Bardine, Brenda Gardenour Walter, and Dave Snell, eds., *Heavy Metal Studies and Popular Culture* (London: Palgrave Macmillan, 2016); Jeremy Wallach, Harris M. Berger, and Paul D. Greene, eds., *Metal Rules the Globe: Heavy Metal Music around the World* (Durham, NC: Duke University Press, 2011).

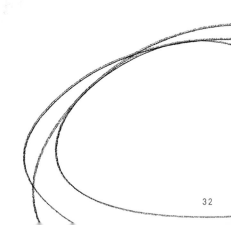

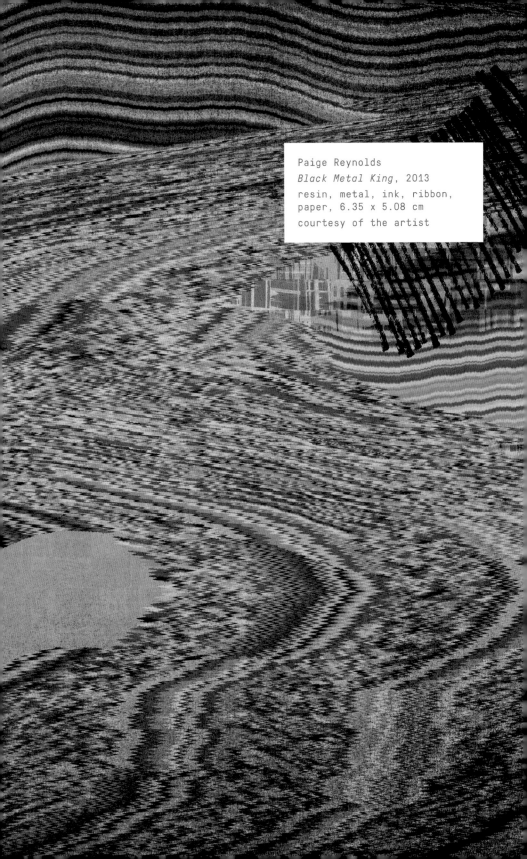

Paige Reynolds
Black Metal King, 2013
resin, metal, ink, ribbon,
paper, 6.35 x 5.08 cm
courtesy of the artist

PUTTING THE FAG BACK IN

SARCÓFAGO

DREW DANIEL

Years ago, in a bar called The Fighting Cocks, I stood in front of a microphone and read the following:

To state the obvious, though the jury is out on the question of whether such encounters are long overdue or preemptively rigged, black metal theory awaits its rendezvous with both queer theory and critical race theory. Given the presence of nationalist and racist rhetoric, images, lyrics, and opinions within some but by no means all of its practitioners, black metal's partial overlap with neo-Nazi politics and crypto-supremacist or openly white supremacist positions at once calls out for theorization precisely as a counterpart to, and component of, any ethical judgment and at the same time raises basic questions about the fundamental disjunction of aesthetics and ethics. Mention of such facts and indications of such problems typically cues the presentation of well-meaning apologias, numerous counterexamples of nonracist black metal, and awkward changes of the subject from fans and, by extension, fans who theorize (myself occasionally included).

I am pleased to say that the waiting is over and a day of judgment with these perspectives has come: as with all days of judgment, the task of separating sheep from goats is precarious, and the question of whom shall be master looms. I want to offer satanic hails to the organizers of the Coloring the Black event (and editors of the subsequent volume), and to the participants, both virtual and present in meatspace, for rendering my remarks of five years ago obsolete. It's high time that we colored in the black, or, conversely, pressed ever deeper into the darkness to see what colors and forms it already contains and already affords. To that end, what follows is an articulation of self-critique, both of my contributions to black metal theory in its past iterations and of my last album as The Soft Pink Truth, *Why Do the Heathen Rage?*, which positioned itself as both a gesture of homage to black metal's energy and power and a blasphemous queer critique of black metal's outmoded pieties, its enabling rhetoric, and its ongoing status as political disaster area and racist dumping ground.[1]

Like my cover of Impaled Northern Moonforest's "Grim and Frostbitten Gay Bar," my title phrase, "Putting the Fag Back in Sarcófago" is a parody of a parody. In this case I am parodying a song title by Bay Area math-rock pioneers A Minor Forest, "Putting the Gay Back in Reggae." It is an apt starting point because A Minor Forest are already flagging the ludicrously gratuitous yet also necessary and utopian reparative work of talking about queer space and musical subculture. I call this gratuitous because there's something possibly unnecessary, not to mention self-serving, about a formulation that posits a genre as in need of being territorialized on behalf of minoritized subjects who are set up through that very formulation as necessarily already excluded in advance, shut out, oppressed, marginalized. What if they are already inside? What if the call is already coming from inside the house? No doubt gay people made and make and enjoy reggae, just like there are and will be and have been gay and lesbian and bi and trans and unclassifiably other subjects within and inside every other subculture on the musical map.

To go from A Minor Forest to my own test case, no doubt queer people made and make and enjoy black metal, just like there are and will be and have been gay and lesbian and bi and trans and unclassifiably other subjects within and inside every other subculture on the musical map. Hello, Gorgoroth! So the gratuitous nature of "Putting the Gay Back in Reggae" is also true of "Putting the Fag Back in Sarcófago," at the level of the phoneme, because "Fag" is already in "Sarcófago" just as "Fun" is in "Funeral," but also, because, while I have no inside information about whether any actual member of Sarcófago was or would have considered themselves fags, there is already something deeply "Faggy" about the premise of "Sarcófago," with their bullet belts and white face makeup and black lipstick and outrageous eyeliner and Kisser-than-Kiss representation that is screamingly, massively, utterly faggy, even as there is also something screamingly, massively, powerfully metal about their presentation, their power fantasies, their hymns to the devil, their red light district jams about sucking and fucking.

To borrow an old riff from the 1980s (not in this case an old guitar riff but an old theory riff), if deconstruction loved to announce that one did not need to deconstruct canonical texts of philosophy because they were, all unto themselves, already "in deconstruction" insofar as their organizing and structuring systems of binary opposition were self-evidently unstable, mutually derivative, and hence tenuous, then one might say the same about the project of queering black metal: black metal does not need the work of theoretical queering because black metal is already "in queerness" all unto itself. Think about it: a pack of wimpy guys with long hair wearing makeup and tight jeans singing about crying in forests. This is hardly the meat-and-potatoes masculinity of Manowar.

And yet: just as A Minor Forest were flagging a received narrative of tension about discrimination in Jamaican dancehall culture epitomized in Buju Banton's anthems about "batty boys," so too with my own work, I was guilty of playing the gay card, flagging the extent to which the allure of criminal violence in which black metal as received media narrative was a baptism in queer blood, specifically Magne Andreassen's murder at the hands of a member of Emperor, and its grim sequel, Josef ben Meddour's murder at the hands of a member of Dissection. By invoking this worst case scenario for a subculture which inspires homophobic murders in cruising grounds, I set up black metal as a scene in need of a radical queer response, a scene in need of correction and retaliation, a place of danger and oppression for queer people, a target in need of calling out. Which, sometimes, in some contexts, it has been, and remains. But: let's not ignore the extent to which that very oppositional framing plays into a mainstream musical journalism landscape of placid liberal middle-ground, eager to fetishize and yet denounce the intolerant fringes on its periphery in order to preserve and maintain their own *bien pensant* credentials as a tolerant zone of inclusion.

It would be far too easy to bask in the afterglow of having achieved my direct political goals if I simply listed all the hateful homophobic and racist bullshit that was directed at me on various black metal discussion boards online because of this album; it is not enough to say that my enemies have online avatar names like "n*****slayer," as if that verified that I must therefore be on the side of the angels. We ought to beware of white men bearing good intentions, me included. I am most ashamed when I look back on the press rollout for this album and see my hapless gestures towards an innocence that I treat as my birthright; that is standard white behavior and it is all too typical: it is me saying "Please oh please don't think that I, me, Drew Daniel, the person, am a racist. Think that I am a good gay man. Trust me on this one, etc." The gestures of disavowal that I performed with respect to black metal are understandable but worryingly smell like marketing and white fragility, the performative wokeness of the ally who comes bearing products for sale.

I am happiest when I reflect upon the thoughtful critiques that this album received from those who clearly get what I am trying to do but proceed to point out the flaws, limits and edges of the work in its queer theorization. In his article in *Texte Zur Kunst* "Profaning the Unprofanable," Tavia Nyong'o puts his finger on this latent limit: "the last thing we need is for another subcultural space to be pervaded by homonationalism (and if that seems like an overstatement, consider the unsettling recurrence of openly gay politicians on the far right of Europe's political spectrum)."[2] As the history of industrial subculture in general and Death In June fandom in particular, not to mention Milo Yiannopolous and Peter Thiel, have amply demonstrated by now, the presentation of legibly gay subjectivities is often cheek by jowl with shitty reactionary racist politics, thus calling the bluff on any naïve assumption that the politics of gay visibility are always necessarily and inherently liberating.

Pinkwashing by the state of Israel is another flagrant case in point; civil rights for gays can and do sit side-by-side with an apartheid state that oppresses Palestinians who are thereby constructed as "homophobic" and "medieval." This sense of needing to make black metal somehow "good for the gays" is, Nyong'o points out, the least interesting possible direction. I do not want black metal to become a rainbow flag safe space because I am attracted to the spirit of delirious negation which drives black metal to affirm the nihilist flag of *no colors*, but I do want a radically queer eruption of virulent/shameless faggotry from within to pose a withering challenge to black metal's safety with itself, and thus to un-settle black metal in order to force a doubling down upon the spirit of lawless chaos that it invokes: a lawless chaos would not be legibly heterosexual or legibly homosexual, but would be queer with respect to itself, that would experience the incoherence of race on a molecular level and abandon its campy Viking monocultural fantasies in favor of an endlessly recombinant space of becoming as permanent revolution.

Going beyond a referendum on the success or failure of my album, Nyong'o speaks to something more broad and open-ended: how race and genre contour the hierarchical logic of the dominant styles of discourse and its accursed-yet-irresistible supplement via the relationship between black metal and dance music. As he notes, it is an essentially Derridean claim: "At a meta-level, the musical hybridization of the album is constantly asking 'What's black about black metal?' and daring to suggest that the answer might be, well, black."[3] Who claims blackness? Who speaks for/to/from the space that is defined as black? How could black metal's endless articulation of blackness as zone of evil, lack, cruelty and atavistic tendencies not be necessarily and constitutively in dialogue with the blackness of black people, as both fact of embodiment and cultural zone of fantasy?

The entire conceptual architecture by which blackness and evil are aligned has, in the experience and lived reality of America, forced a short-circuit of ethics with lived histories of enslavement in which racism and white supremacy cathected negativity onto the space of the black. But we cannot claim that that history is simply an American obsession; we are talking about a subgenre of rock music, and rock music has a history, and that history is racialized. No articulation of "the black" within the context of rock music, however abstracted and deracinated that context might be in its coldest and whitest Norwegian forest enclave, can complete the work of purification by which this blackness over here and that blackness over there can be finally and utterly and categorically disjoined. Because cultures touch, repel and contour each other.

Given Varg Vikernes's prison interviews in which the guitar was excoriated as a black slave instrument best abandoned in favor of the funkless white purity of the synthesizer, the crude isometric mapping of races onto genres is obviously rendered deeply suspect, and nobody wants to reify such one-to-one correlations, even if we cannot proceed without acknowledging the painful histories which bequeathed racialized genres (remember "race records"?). Yet if the unfinished business that black metal has with electronic music has been the case since Mayhem conscripted Conrad Schnitzler to contribute an ominous intro drone, the precise status of black metal's indebtedness to house and techno specifically seems like a touchier subject. The working title of my own album was *Fenriz Has a Guidance Tattoo*, a factoid relayed by a photoshoot of Fenriz in a bathing suit that opened him up to the erotic gaze of the viewer and, in so doing, also relayed the existence of lines of influence, admiration and connection between black metal and functional dancefloor-oriented genres. Given the fact of these linkages, my own contributions to the reinforcement of that pre-existing bridge are, in some senses, gratuitous, unnecessary, a matter of "gilding the lily": over and above my efforts and the efforts of people who share my mixed emotions, black metal is already queer, and already imbricated in a web of relationships to the genres and populations that its practitioners nonetheless all too often continue to excoriate and reject (looking at you, Inquisition). Black metal is already "in queerness" over and above and in advance of the work of queering which we must nonetheless insist upon.

As far as my own attempts to go forward with the task of thinking in conjunction with black metal theory, I took part in the Mors Mystica conference on the sensorial experience of rot and putrefaction at Watain concerts that I have attended, and which has since been published in the volume by that name.[4] I am interested in this as a material experience of death and decay which ruins aesthetic values (sublimity/beauty/melancholy) in favor of the collectively experienced, communal fact of a visceral disgust that enacts black metal poetics in an immanent way. To me, the production of a "black metal theory" needs to start from within the context and concerns and images and sounds and performances of black metal, but that does not need to pre-empt or script in advance a credulous, mimetic or derivative form of thinking. We need not practice what Dave Hickey with reference to art criticism dubbed "Air Guitar," but can instead work towards the blackening and harrowing of concepts, deliberate acts of critical satanism in which the theorist stages a satanic betrayal of pleasure and belonging and turns upon and distorts or profanes the objects venerated by a subculture.[5] Going beyond this Father-slaying, black metal theory might encourage the cultivation of a sensibility that is "necro" with respect to the neoliberal values (productivity, growth, adaptability, endlessly scalable and portable forms) of the contemporary capitalist marketplace. To insist upon a world where "flowers smell of black" is to fast-forward ongoing scenarios of slow violence, to speed them up to a blast-beat blur in order to see them through to their endpoints and beyond. To draw a final link to the prismatic as a mode of theoretical engagement in dialogue with the theorization of colors as aesthetic-material manifolds in the *Prismatic Ecology: Ecotheory Beyond Green* anthology edited by Jeffrey Jerome Cohen, black metal's insistence upon scenarios of death and extinction might yet offer us aesthetic purchase upon, if not immanent experience of, the futures towards which we are already hurtling, cracking open a present by drawing into it a futurity we tend to disavow: annihilation.[6] Far from an escapist fad that peaked in the 1990s and is now in terminal self-citation and decadence, black metal's *longue durée* offers a lesson in the virtue of fanatical recalcitrance.

Notes

[1]The Soft Pink Truth, *Why Do the Heathen Rage?* (Thrill Jockey, 2014).

[2]Tavia Nyong'o, "Profaning the Unprofanable," *Texte Zur Kunst* 95 (September 2014): 192-96.

[3]Ibid.

[4]Drew Daniel, "Following the Stench: Watain and Putrefaction Mysticism," in *Mors Mystica: Black Metal Theory Symposium*, eds. Edia Connole and Nicola Masciandaro (London: Schism Press, 2015), 53-69.

[5]Dave Hickey, *Air Guitar: Essays on Art and Democracy* (New York: Art Issues Press, 1997).

[6]Levi Bryant, "Black," in *Prismatic Ecology: Ecotheory Beyond Green,* ed. Jeffrey Jerome Cohen (Minneapolis: University of Minnesota Press, 2013), 290-311.

Acid Lich
Forest Friends, 2019
copics on mixed media paper,
22.86 x 30.48 cm
courtesy of the artist

Sad Rainbows

STANIMIR PANAYOTOV

Is black hopeless? Doesn't every dark thundercloud have a silver lining? In black lies the possibility of hope. The universal sleep is hugged by black. A comfortable, warm black. This is no cold black, it is against this black that the rainbow shines like the stars.

— DEREK JARMAN, "BLACK ARTS"[1]

Coloring black metal is not possible through a "reformist" rejection of black or its "revolutionary" and carnivalesque diluting. Excising blackness from black metal is not the aim in offering a reading of black metal's vivacious diversity. From the very beginning, a discourse on "queering" black metal is perceived as the manifest sensitivity of paradoxical antisocialites who "just can't fucking handle it"—"it" being rage, rebellion, solitude, suicide, morbidity. Queering the musical scenes of metal, weeping with blackness as they do, demands a reading that is invariably *seen* as a "reformist," left-wing, nagging banter of will-less SJW pseudo-connoisseurs. Why? Because the founding acts of trve black metal are somehow always represented and perceived as those total excesses of will that have no repressed (in the Freudian sense), and hence its queering is always already obsolete. Because "it"—the human sacrifice—has already happened in murder and suicide. "Only a trve man can do it": one can hear the stench of greasy-haired, self-deprecative masculinity from the mommy-owned basements of the world.

If there is one thing we have learned after the iconoclastic phase of such trveness—that epistemological blunder of fan-made self-perception—it is that repression there was. Gaahl's homosexuality is not just a mindless cliché. As if this was not enough, there is the argument that virulent masculinity is itself the result of some form of preceding repression. Queering black metal as the natural phenomenon of rainbow or as the very exegesis of nature, which I attempt in this chapter, appears as a game of causal relations between repressor and repressed only because a contingent correlation between masculinity and violence has ingratiated us with its *mythos* of superhuman exceptionalism. Thus, if "coloring the black" of black metal vexes the imagination, it is only because we have agreed in advance to present our archeology of the genre as some sentimental democracy. Which it is not. Queer murderers there are.

Let us discuss two natural phenomena: the forest and the rainbow. The first, the forest, is naturalized and implied in the representational politics of black metal; I propose to read it through the reactionary metal archives of the forest and the latter's intellectualization in postwar (meta)politics and the notion of *apoliteia* integrated in black metal scenes. The second, the rainbow, is implied within the forest itself but is missing from the representation altogether (or so it is in the sectarian lodges of black metal trveness); and I propose my own reading that partly relies on Aristotle and Laruelle, trying to interpret the forest, occupied as it is by reactionary metapolitical sentiments, via what I call "sad rainbows," a form of immanent and naturalistic (meta)politics of black metal music. Both phenomena are metapolitical.[2]

BLACK METAL IN THE FOREST

This is a very concise political history of the appropriation of nature and the forest in metal. In apocalyptic and symphonic black metal's imagery and lyrics, as in martial and neofolk music, often it is the figure of the forest that offers a radical individualist retreat from the world, based on a sacral sentiment of self-awareness and self-reliance in resisting the secular world. This is manifested across the entire spectrum of production. Consider various albums from Burzum (*Hliðskjálf, Belus, Forgotten Realms*), Darkthrone (*Under a Funeral Moon, Panzerfaust, Ravishing Grimness*), Toroidh's *Alliance Proditorum*, Dimmu Borgir's *Inn I Evighetens Mørke* to Myrkur's *M* and *Juniper*, Ulver's *Bergtatt—Et Eeventyr I 5 Capitler* and *Kveldssanger*, Black Lord's *Black Ritual Forest*, Hanzel und Gretyl's *Black Forest Metal*, and Astral Winter's *Forest of Silence*; bands' names such as Carpathian Forest, Hate Forest, Forest of Shadows, Dark Forest, Old Forest; and some of the lyrics like Emperor's "Beyond the Great Vast Forest" ("Beyond the great vast forest/Surrounded by majestic mountains/Dark rivers float like tears of sorrow/Frost submerge the holy ring of fire"), Striborg's "Black Metal Is the Forest Calling" ("Endless journeys through the bush/Endless journeys through the forest/Across paddocks to the enlightened land/This is far away from any man"), or Behemoth's "The Dark Forest" ("As night raises over dreaming forests/She [darkness] awakes Gods and Goddesses, unsilently...Dies in me with barbarous voice/The dark forest enchant me!"). The entire genre of Cascadian/atmospheric black metal is in itself a musical eco-spiritual and mystical movement.

Generally, in metal the forest functions as the ultimate church of anti-secular separation, a synecdoche for and against a failed modern society. It is especially persistent in the imagery of black metal meeting neofolk and sometimes martial/industrial/neofolk. One banal reason is that the forest is a dark place and, thus, difficult to navigate, just like the distorted black metal logos and vocals are. The forest is an escape, expressive of so-called ethnic paganism against Christianity or Christian quasi-secularism, and ethnic paganism in turn is often a converted form of naturalistic fascism. Indeed, the forest provides a suitable and literal shortcut to the *fascio*—a bundle of individuals who seek a radical retreat into the nethers of nature to politically reorganize themselves and society. The final conquest of society is hosted by a rebellion choreographed in the forest. When blending with paganism, black metal offers a critique of modernity and, hence, a glorification of nature. The synecdoche of the forest implies a purity untouched by modernity.

How did the forest come to be such a synecdoche of traditionalist and quasi-fascist political sentimentality? What provoked the identification of black metal with fascist naturalism? With the notion of "metapolitical fascism," Anton Shekhovtsov explains the intellectual appropriation of the forest.[3] According to him, two sources of postwar inspiration generate this naturalist infatuation: the concept of *der Waldgang* (variously translated as "retreat into the forest" and the "forest passage") from Ernst Jünger's "Retreat into the Forrest" (1951) and the concept of *apoliteia* in Julius Evola's *Ride the Tiger* (1961).[4] Shekhovtsov prefaces these two concepts with Armin Mohler's *Die konservative Revolution in Deutschland 1918–1932*, published a year before Jünger's essay. Mohler "argued that, since fascist revolution was indefinitely postponed due to the political domination of liberal democracy, true 'conservative revolutionaries' found themselves in an 'interregnum' that would, however, spontaneously give way to the spiritual grandeur of national reawakening."[5] This interregnum is a corrupted but necessary phase for a conservative transformation. Both Jünger and Evola follow the precept that a reawakening can only happen with an anti-systemic approach to organized political systems, be they fascist or liberal democratic. This anti-systemic and aristocratic posture was translated into both of these concepts (*der Waldgang* and *apoliteia*) to offer a path for an "inner emigration" into nature, where the aristocratic soul could develop its militaristic proclivities and arm itself intellectually and physically for a final battle with the modern world, such that it ultimately wins "hearts and minds."

Jünger stretches his forest metaphor as far as Socrates, who has "called the sphere where he was counseled by a voice not to be expressed in words, his *daimonion*. It might also be called the forest."[6] While for Jünger the forest is a means, a topos to resist the age, some ten years later Evola provided the inner ethos for this retreat of *l'uomo differenziato*, a man who should practice "disinterest, detachment from everything that today constitutes 'politics.'"[7] We are speaking here of postwar fascism and the New Right, which, to gain significance and dominance, for Jünger, should be treated as a temporary interregnum.[8] Nature and the forest is, thus, not a final destination of retreat nor an object of aimless adoration.

Numerous black metal acts have retained and perpetuated the imagery of this interregnum, at times more so as a visual habit than a credible ideological credo. As a result, the splicing of nature and fascism have translated into black metal's aesthetic ideology from the get-go. The retreat into the forest, "the forest passage," is similar to some of black metal's critiques of both Christianity and modernity, audible in Jünger's statement that "increasing automatism and anxiety are closely related."[9] To reclaim society, the individual should be as "a tree in the forest."[10] In his solitary stay in the forest, the individual needs to again see "the prime depths of Being." Because the forest is "a symbol of supratemporal Being," "[w]e shall call this reorientation toward Being the retreat into the forest (*Waldgang*), and the man who carries it out the wanderer in the forest (*Waldgänger*)."[11] The radical retreat into the forest is a kind of super-social individualism in the name of a Being forlorn, for "[l]ife has become grey, but it may well seem bearable to the man who, next to himself, sees the absolute black of utter darkness."[12]

With or without the intellectual luggage of Jünger's *Waldgang*, this willingness and ability to both *see* and *experience* darkness is easily rehearsed in black metal: "It's a victory over fear! In order to encounter community, one should encounter identity."[13] To retreat into the forest is to encounter your own Ego, in order to develop a temporal endurance as to reenter the stage of history: "Wanderers in the forest (*Waldganger*) are all those who, isolated by great upheavals, are confronted with ultimate annihilation."[14] The forest, then, is the *gymnasion* of the historical loser: after the experience of utter darkness and ultimate annihilation, the retreated one can finally practice resistance. This is not an anti-modernist project, for the question is not to choose the forest over the Titanic but to choose both: a dualism typical of postwar intellectual fascism. As Shekhovtsov says, the task of the retreated is a "re-enchanted alternative modernity of the reborn nation."[15]

Evola's apoliteia is also not an anti-modernist project but a nationalist correction to coercive forms of liberal democracy. As Shekhovtsov sums this up, "While *apoliteia* does not necessarily imply abstention from socio-political activities, an apoliteic individual, an 'aristocrat of the soul'...should always embody an 'irrevocable internal distance from this [modern] society and its 'values.'"[16] In *Ride the Tiger*, Evola openly exclaims that the aristocrat of the soul should learn to live between the modern and the primitive:

As for the "sentiment of nature," in general, the human type that concerns us must consider nature as part of a larger and more objective whole: nature for him includes countrysides, mountains, forests, and seacoasts, but also dams, turbines, and foundries, the tentacular system of ladders and cranes of a great modern port or a complex of functional skyscrapers. This is the space for a higher freedom. He remains free and self-aware before both types of nature—being no less secure in the middle of a steppe or on an alpine peak than amid Western city nightlife.[17]

It is this duality between the "traditionalism" of the forest and the "modernity" of the industry that opens the secular vistas of a nature-clad nationalistic black metal, with its sinister imagery of beautiful forestscapes. For this is the quality of the differentiated man—and by extension the black metal (aristocratic) musician—that for him "the stone and steel panoramas of the metropolis, the endless avenues, the functional complexes of industrial areas are on the same level."[18] With black metal, one can practice the retreat into the forest inside the very industrial world and the audio bedroom: the aristocratism is predominantly representational. For the differentiated man, the position of utter darkness is one where, in discovering the hopelessness of his fight against the modern world, he will continue to wrestle with society inside nature as the passage way to supranatural Being—even in the world he resists by encountering his Ego in the forest. But before this fruitless fight, one becomes himself through the principle of *apoliteia*—the detachment from politics—by achieving an "inner attitude."[19] This is so radical a detachment that *apoliteia* has no specific consequences to anything outside the forest in terms of one's practical abstention from the world. Being apoliteic entails a temporary aristocratic subterfuge that at its essentialist core *is* political, but this is willfully suspended as metapolitical act. Once one knows that nothing constrains his being, the aristocrat can truly become a soldier. The black metal aristocrat (musician or fan) does easily reproduce something of this postwar metapolitical sentimentality in a radical isolation to index his own individualism of the soul and the rebellion of his mind as a double gesture against "politics" altogether; the radicalism of seclusion into nature/the forest figures him as an aristocrat, for only the elevated spirit of a "tree in the forest" can transcend worldly platitudes and incorrigible injustices against one's desecrated individualism. *Apoliteia* is thus just "the inner distance unassailable by this society."[20]

Black metal is often caught between radical individualism and group identity. Both the *Waldgänger* and the apoliteic man, especially when interpreted as a unity, suffer this bipolar fate of surviving their historical catastrophism. According to Benjamin Olson, this bipolarity often happens through a dual use of anti-Christianity and nature; in this process, both are "uniting each individual under the banner of the spirit of Satan and/or Odin and/or Nature."[21] The transcendental reign of black metal is one that is closer to Jünger and Evola's strategies of social avoidance as divine transcendence in the name of (a new) society. None of this transcendental spirit would be of any significance if there was no radical detachment from history. In black metal, it is the forest that serves this synecdochic role. After all, the detachment *from* requires also an attachment *to*. As Jünger says, "Therein resides the real substance of history; in the encounter of man with himself, that is to say, with his own divine power."[22] By becoming a truly social rebel who, desiring as he does to learn how to resist a disintegrating pluralist society of egalitarianism, and by learning to divinate his own powers, one transforms the very topos of the forest into a metapolitical fascism—and it becomes the *fascio* of the apoliteic aristocratic rebels. As Shekhovtsov says, "the adherents of the ENR [European New Right] believe that one day the allegedly decadent era of egalitarianism and cosmopolitanism will give way to 'an entirely new culture based on organic, hierarchical, supra-individual, heroic values.'"[23]

Yet to the extent that subgenres of black metal and neofolk have incorporated the ideology of the European New Right and the retreat into the forest, they have also embraced the ideology's cultural implications. In the aftermath of World War II, neither Jünger nor Evola tried to base their strategy—let us call it a socialized transcendentalism—on race. Rather, they retreated into both the forest as an individualist strategy and the culture as a collective tactic for the individual to reclaim a society akin to supranatural Being, which in turn is expressive of a spiritual aristocratism regained.

This intimate interface between the human and the forest is particularly fitting for the sonic ideology of black metal, because the forest provides itself as darkness par excellence; its authentic darkness does not imitate anything. What the metalhead can do is thus learn from the forest how to resist society as its other, how to confront annihilation and the absolute black in their very wellspring. But when black metal acts use the imagery of the forest, they promote a kind of spontaneous right-wing Gramscianism. The forestscapes in black metal and related subgenres express exactly how a right-wing Gramscianism has migrated into urban black metal subcultures and how it serves as a kind of aural metapolitical fascism. Yet, in the end, this recourse to the forest is not a struggle for cultural hegemony; it is a struggle for aristocratic dominance, a struggle of who is going to preside over Nature and the Supernatural Being of the Ego in the name of society, for only by miming the alienating quality of nature can the aristocrat of the soul bring history to a standstill. This is why culture is only a tactical vehicle, and the more black metal invests in the ideological trepidation of the forest, the more it reduces itself to a non-transcendent and self-centered form of right-wing Gramscianism.

BLACK RAINBOW IN THE METAL FOREST

Illuminating the history and the appropriation of the forest in black metal was not to claim this ideology should be simply resisted by abandoning the aesthetics and the ideological underpinnings seen in Nature, on which a great deal of black metal is so reliant. Nor is it my aim to propose a narrative against naturalistic transcendentalism, which can be entirely anodyne, unpolitical, and fetishistic (especially in blackened doom, shoegaze, drone, etc.). After all, what is the point of offering the aristocrat of the soul to leave the forest? Rather, what is more important is: How can the egalitarian mind enter the forest?

This is possible through a vision of the rainbow in the forest.

Both *der Waldgang* and *apoliteia* can be read from an egalitarian perspective: metapolitics is not immanently fascist. Against a naturalistic transcendentalism of blackness and inegalitarianism stands the immanent naturalism of colorfulness and the rainbow of egalitarianism. In neither case need we reject the naturalistic experience of the self. The solitude of the rainbow suffices in itself. The forest rainbow is an extremely solitary egalitarianism.

What is a rainbow? It is this morsel of prismatic darkness within the grim and solitary nature that is neither darkness nor color. It is not the totality of darkness, and it is not the totality of color. What is a black metal rainbow? It is the piece of metal forest that is *not* black. The rainbow in the forest, a nature within a nature. The black metal rainbow is Nature's apophasis. It is through the *vision* of the rainbow *in* the forest that we explain the naturalistic and crypto-fascist audiovisual assemblages of black metal, and, more specifically, the visual representation of nature as defining black metal's "nature." It is through a vision that we again can see it as the depressive liberation of the self.

What is a rainbow in the forest? Just as the rainbow is imminent and possible in the forest, so is color immanent within the black. If the rainbow's picturesqueness is naturally part and parcel of the forest, of nature itself, then there is nothing inherently joyful, and, thus, radically gay, in the rainbow. A black rainbow that stands for nothing. A sad rainbow that appears for nobody. A nemofocal forest rainbow seen by no one but stands there despite humanity as a (meta)political potentiality.

If the rainbow as the symbol of queer solidarity and struggle is a social symbol of resistance, what of it is there in the solitary forest rainbow that no one ever sees? As a thing for itself, as a symbol without a fan base, the rainbow in the forest is as suicidal and dire as the black tunnel of forest's nature.

Just as, per Aristotle, black is the transmutation of the color, so black metal manifests itself as the avoidance of color's consequence, its picturesqueness.

The natural/ist environs of black metal—the forest—is the avoidance of the colorful. But the rainbow is there. It is a sad rainbow only from the perspective of the egalitarian self who does not know how to enter the forest, because she has given it up to the aristocrat of the soul. In the shrine of blackness, we pray for the perpetual retention of black, we lament black's potential transformation in other colors.

In the forest, you can hardly ever see a rainbow as-is. You have to go up the mountain, up the hills, or down the valleys, to see the rainbow in its realness or else rely on the chance event of a rainbow in the urban surrounding. Seeing the rainbow is to have your vision endowed with the ability to see primordial blackness transformed. The rainbow and the black constitute a paradoxical separation of the vision of color itself.

Even if and when in the forest, the egalitarian mind can never see the rainbow in its curving beauty and, thus, cannot see the full spectrum of colors it offers, just as the aristocratic soul cannot see the entire forest, because it sees it only as/through society's dysfunctionality, as the disfigurement of pure blackness, and not through the immanence of nature—what one experiences is the rainbow's chromatic interruptedness from within—and because of—the forest. The rainbow contains a spectrum that does not include black, but implies it on one of its ends, and so it is open-ended to blackness and its opposite. One can imagine that in the sad rainbow "[t]he blackness and the luminosity, the absence of color in the singularity of pain and the radiant colorfulness of craving memories, begin to merge, to create a fusion that will be the gloomy point of genesis of new light and color."[24] The absence of color—the blackness of the forest, the radiant colorfulness, the picturesqueness of the rainbow—when converging in a forest rainbow—produces an elemental and insatiable sadness that no Church of Satan can ever quench. On one of its sides it is "radiantly colorful," and on the other side it is "gloomy." In this sense, the rainbow itself is expressive of a duality that is inherent in the forest too; while the forest is conquered as the temporary training camp for the aristocrat who has to become a soldier, the rainbow in the forest, which is never black but only implies a blackness transformed, is already part of the Church of Evil. It is the assemblage of Evil and, as such, it is already immanently social. For Evil is always for the Other. We need do no more than admit that to color black metal, we have to see the rainbow as the obscure background of the Church of Evil, as the arcade of its obscure progeny. And then even the forest rainbow, which you never get to see, is seen as the already distorted society, just as fascists would see it as a distorted blackness.

THE METAPOLITICS OF SAD RAINBOWS

The rainbow in the forest is sad, because it is blackness transformed and unseen. Thus, it does not do away with black metal's sensitivity for pessimistic realism or grim transcendentalism. What is more, considering that so many black metal connoisseurs are both enchanted by its grim and hopeless aesthetics, which are largely reactionary in origin, and, at the same time, share egalitarian sentiments, what do we do with archives of beauty such as Burzum's *Filosofem, Hliðskjálf or Belus?* (After all, there is no other musician that has been so cherished against the grain of his own beliefs.) Indeed, if the egalitarian minds of queer radicals and the inegalitarian souls of the cis het aristocrats are united by something, it is depression and detachment from the social.[25] But there is a difference. The first see nature as constructive, as the church of universal Evil that has an inherent continuity with society as its outside, as its double. The latter see it as reparative, as the merely temporary temple of individual virtue, an in-between space that will enable individual continuity with social views that one deems broken and interrupted by history.

We should be able to think and enjoy the sad rainbow within the forest, to the extent to which we do not see nature as passive shelter of an idealism so morally persistent that it becomes a vulgar materialism. In this sense Evola's *apoliteia* and its moral detachment from society holds true also on the ground of egalitarian sad and black metal rainbows.

The colorfulness of the rainbow *in* the forest is rich in both hyperborean and hypoborean intensity.[26] If depression and darkness, blackness and luminosity, are what unite both homophobes and queers in black metal, then this unholy union is lodged within those sad rainbows that we have yet to see—in the forest. Sad rainbows that express both an explicit divisibility of the colorful and an implicit unity of the black. It is this double quality that can be called and experienced as a "sad rainbow." It is sad and suicidally isolated, so much so that it can hardly become a metapolitics. But the sad rainbows of black metal are exactly metapolitical.

How to do the *meta-poli-tiká* of black metal's sad rainbows, black metal's after-the-fact common things? Can they become *meta-a-poli-tiká*, that is, can such rainbows represent an after-the-fact abstention from the common things of the black metal "cities," and should they? If it is safe to assume that progressive metalheads are not ready to denounce either their egalitarianism or depressive proclivity, then the bipolarity of utter darkness in ulterior hopelessness and the cheerful naïveté of a finalist hyperteleology are not enough. We also need a passageway from the fascist forest to the egalitarian rainbow in the forest, a place where it can be *seen*. The sad rainbow can be seen from both the robust vista of the mountain peak and the modern rooftop of the skyscraper. But, to the extent to which it implies the transformed darkness of black *and* the darkness of social disillusionment, the sad rainbow in the forest is already its own passageway.

The metapolitical drama of the sad rainbows: they can neither be hidden nor seen in their entirety. An a-theological rainbow that bestows upon us so radiant a blackness that it culminates in an unbearable joy we cannot hold in ourselves.

MELANCODA

We need not "subvert" or "reclaim" Jünger and Burzum in our pursuit of "the absolute black of utter darkness" or in confronting "ultimate annihilation." There is another shortcut to the sad black metal rainbow: asking ourselves, "What is black, and how we see and experience it?" "Black" is a kind of chromatic escape, a colorless avoidance, an iconoclastic and vanishing docetism. It is a color of no(n)color. Black is both the generation and the avoidance of color. Before all discourse on the ludic grimoire that the rainbow is, black should be understood and refounded.

Aristotle taught that the list of primary colors is very short: black and white. More generically, he defined color itself as "the limit [*peras*] of the transparent in a determinately bounded body,"[27] while elsewhere he described it as what "is capable of setting in motion that which is actually transparent [*diaphanes*]."[28] Black and darkness are subject to their relation to form and shape, and, for Aristotle, this relation was indefinite and lacked shape: "darkness, unlike all other objects of vision, is never perceived as having any definite magnitude or any definite shape."[29] All other colors and their "chromatic effects" are derived by blending black and white.[30] He also defined black more specifically as "the proper color of elements in process of transmutation."[31] Just as with the Platonic-Plotinian teaching on evil, by way of associating black with darkness, he defines dark as the privation of light.[32]

Now, if black is the transmutating color, it has a spurious relation to limit/edness, and if it has no definite magnitude, it cannot be a proper color. There is no vision without colors,[33] but black offers a vision on all colors. Ultimately all color is a mixture of black plus some light and is revealed to us through seven basic colors, lodged as they are in the rainbow.

There need not be an opposition between color and black if black is a *noncolor*. It is a question of vision, or of vision in black. The cascading richness of blackness is immanent to its opacity, not its transparency (*diaphaneia*), as Aristotle had it.[34] Against the philosopher's world, the non-philosopher Laruelle teaches that "[t]he Universe is an opaque and solitary thought."[35] It is due to man and man as philosopher that all things become both the Universe and (its) opacity. He contends that "Black is anterior to the absence of light...The black universe is not a negative light,"[36] for in the Aristotelian version the origin of blackness's diversity is reduced to light's suppression. That Black is a noncolor is not enough to dissipate it into the world of man, because blackness was smuggled in man's world before its creation and never leaves it.

If, for Aristotle, "black is the original color of the substance,"[37] François Laruelle exhorts that "[b]lack prior to light is the substance of the Universe."[38] It is a difference of Universe creation and not color scales upon which a vision depends. In the science of color, black is the already manifested and is, hence, the "vision-in-Black:"[39] the singular color that cannot be excised from the universe (not the world or the earth). The Aristotelian black noncolor is the spectrum of vision for all colors, while the Laruellian black color is the vision-in-Black for all Universes. A blackness that sees itself unto itself before all creation, a paleo-metaphysical joke on all subsequent worlds and their spectral colors.

Notes

[1] Derek Jarman, "Black Arts," in *Chroma: A Book of Colors* (Woodstock, NY: Overlook Press, 1994), 138.

[2] There is a plethora of theories about the metapolitical, and here I do not engage with any of them. Suffice it to say that I treat the "metapolitical" as that attitude toward politics that prepares the individual for political dealings beyond so-called formal or representative politics.

[3] Anton Shekhovtsov, "Apoliteic Music: Neo-Folk, Martial Industrial and 'Metapolitical Fascism,'" *Patterns of Prejudice* 43, no. 5 (December 2009): 431-57, accessed February 24, 2021, http://www.shekhovtsov.org/articles/Anton_Shekhovtsov-Apoliteic_Music.html.

[4] Ernst Jünger, "The Retreat into the Forest," trans. anonymous, *Confluence: An International Forum* 3, no. 2 (1954): 127-42, accessed February 24, 2021, https://counter-currents.com/2013/04/the-retreat-into-the-forest; Julius Evola, *Ride the Tiger: A Survival Manual for the Aristocrats of the Soul*, trans. Joscelyn Godwin and Constance Fontana (Rochester, VT: Inner Traditions International, 2003).

[5] Shekhovtsov, "Apoliteic Music," 437.

[6] Jünger, "The Retreat into the Forest," 136.

[7]It is significant to mention that Jünger's (politics of the) forest is purposefully connected to Nietzsche's Zarathustra (cf. "The desert is growing; woe to him who contains deserts within himself"). To escape one's desert, one should escape into the forest. Similarly, Evola refers to the Zarathustran desert: "to defend the world of being and dignity of him who feels himself belonging to a different humanity and recognizes the desert around himself"; Evola, *Ride the Tiger*, 176.

[8]Jünger, "The Retreat into the Forest," 141.

[9]Ibid., 127.

[10]Ibid., 128; note that there is no explicit discussion on being alone or being with others.

[11]Ibid., 131-32.

[12]Ibid., 130.

[13]Ibid., 141.

[14]Ibid., 132.

[15]Shekhovtsov, "Apoliteic Music," 441.

[16]Ibid., 437-38.

[17]Evola, *Ride the Tiger*, 123-24.

[18]Ibid., 126. It is noteworthy that this modern quality cannot explain why the apocalyptic post-industrial imaginary that has so permeated subgenres, such as drone metal, is politically very different; in short, representations of the nature of industrial decay are not fascist metapolitics, which is prone to lament the decay of the industrial world.

[19]Ibid., 174.

[20]Ibid., 175.

[21]Benjamin Hedge Olson, *I Am the Black Wizards: Multiplicity, Mysticism and Identity in Black Metal Music and Culture* (master's thesis, Graduate College of Bowling Green State University, 2008), 68.

[22]Jünger, "The Retreat into the Forest," 136.

[23]Shekhovtsov, "Apoliteic Music," 438.

[24]Katerina Kolozova, *Cut of the Real: Subjectivity in Poststructuralist Philosophy* (New York: Columbia University Press, 2014), 129.

[25]This is partly the message of Drew Daniel's inversions of black metal in his solo project The Soft Pink Truth's *Why Do the Heathen Rage?*

[26]I use the term *hyperborean* in Hunter Hunt-Hendrix's sense: "lunar, atrophic, depraved, infinite and pure." See Hunt-Hendrix, "Transcendental Black Metal," in *Hideous Gnosis: Black Metal*

Theory Symposium I, ed. Nicola Masciandaro (Charleston, SC: Create Space, 2010), 54, accessed May 21, 2021. By *hypoborean* I do not mean *transcendental* as an opposite proposed by Hunt-Hendrix, which is affirmative and solar, but an inactive and sleeping hyperborean intensity.

[27]Aristotle, *De Sensu*, 439b11-12.

[28]Aristotle, *De Anima*, 418a31-b1.

[29]Aristotle, *De Coloribus*, 791b7.

[30]Ibid., 792a5-792a28.

[31]Ibid., 791a10; also see Jarman, *Chroma*, 26.

[32]Aristotle, *De Coloribus*, 791a13.

[33]On the problem of transparency, see Katerina Ierodiakonu, "Aristotle and Alexander of Aphrodisias on Color," in *The Parva naturalia in Greek, Arabic and Latin Aristotelianism*, eds. Börje Bydén and Filip Radovic (New York: Springer, 2018), 78-84.

[34]The following statement could easily trigger an Aristotelian black metal followship: "In the case of objects burning, dissolving, or melting in the fire, we find that those have the greatest variety which are dark in color"; Aristotle, *De Coloribus*, 793b3-793b8.

[35]François Laruelle, "On the Black Universe in the Human Foundations of Color," trans. Miguel Abreu, *Recess Art* (2012), 2, accessed February 24, 2021, https://www.recessart.org/upcoming-dark-nights-of-the-universe.

[36]Ibid., 4.

[37]Aristotle, *De Coloribus*, 793a18.

[38]Laruelle, "On the Black Universe in the Human Foundations of Color," 3.

[39]Ibid., 4.

Mimi Chrzanowski
Mother Knows Best, 2019
ink on paper
courtesy of the artist

You Don't Win a Culture War by Giving Up Ground

MARGARET KILLJOY

Sometime around fifteen years ago, I got on a bus in Amsterdam to go to Rotterdam to try to fight Nazis. I'm not much of a street fighter, let's be honest. These days especially, I'm more of an anti-fascist cheerleader than anything else, so I milk this story for all the street cred it's worth. But it happened, and it's relevant, so I'm going to tell it.

Some Nazis in Rotterdam had burned down a mosque. When the community tried to rebuild, Nazis threatened to stop them. So anti-fascists from all over the country got on buses to head over there and defend the mosque.

My bus didn't make it. The Dutch police arrested every anti-fascist they could find before we even reached the city, and when we got there, they made our bus driver drive the lot of us to jail. Everyone on the bus, none of whom I knew, wanted to protect me, because I was a foreigner. All of them pretended they weren't Dutch, that they only spoke English. Four of them went to foreign detention with me and only admitted their own nationality when I was being released.

Those anti-fascists were and are some of the bravest people I've ever met. They weren't particularly kind, or caring, or empathic...no more or less so than anyone else. They defended me from the state for the same reason they defended Muslims from Nazis, because they were anti-fascists, committed to fighting against systems of oppression.

Oh, and those anti-fascists, an awful lot of them were skinheads.

Skinhead culture started as a multiracial working-class subculture, and a lot of skinheads, maybe most of them, refuse to let Nazis take that away from them.

A friend of mine, she's this tiny woman who spends her days hating everyone, scowling, listening to black metal, worshipping the old gods, and getting Norse pagan symbols tattooed on her body. She also writes poetry. She also tracks fascist activity. When the Nazis came to her town to parade around in their swastikas, she got in her truck and drove all over the city. Not to fight Nazis, not necessarily. To look for anyone who needed rides away from danger.

She won't let Nazis have her subculture, her heritage, or her religion.

She's one of my heroes.

Black metal is a politically contested space. There's a wide swath of leftist and anarchist bands and fans. There are, quite famously, more than a few Nazis. Of course, most of the fans and bands aren't particularly politically engaged in one way or the other and are just into grim, extreme, beautiful music.

I'm an anarchist and an anti-fascist, and my problem isn't with Nazis playing shows, it's with Nazis breathing air into their lungs. But I understand why they're attracted to the genre.

Even though fascism, perhaps the clearest example of an authoritarian ideology ever created, is the polar opposite of anarchism, I understand why we're both drawn to drink from the same dark pool. A musical subculture is also an aesthetic culture. We make music—and visual art and fashion—to aesthetically express certain ideas. There are plenty ideas to choose from in black metal. The wild, chaotic, dark beauty of nature. The wars we fight against society. Isolation and grief and loss. The acceptance of, and reveling in, our mortality. The old gods, or Satan, or whatever spirits we draw power from.

Anarchists have reasons to romanticize those ideas. So do fascists. It's dangerous shit to romanticize ideas that Nazis might romanticize as well. We have to be careful, be alert. But what we can't do is abandon these ideas, this cultural and aesthetic terrain, to fascists. We have to fight. Both sides of an ancient battle might worship a god of war. They might even worship the same god of war. But that doesn't mean either side is wrong to do so. We venerate gods, or concepts, to draw courage from them—to draw power.

Holding on to aesthetic and cultural terrain gives us power.

There is a cultural war raging around us. There are literal wars, and there are also political wars, but the cultural war matters too. Fascists have consciously engaged in this war for some time now. As I've heard from harder-working anti-fascists than I, a while back some Nazis realized they weren't getting anywhere with swastikas and shouting, so they started to work "apolitically." Specifically, they decided they wanted to promote cultural values that lend themselves to the Nazi agenda. Some of those values are reasonably obvious red flags: nationalism, blood-and-soil, antimulticulturalism. Some of those values are far more complex: glory, honor, loyalty, the reverence of family.

As an anarchist, I prefer to wear my heart and my politics on my sleeve. I have no desire to trick anyone into being an anarchist. I don't believe my values should be the values shared by everyone in the world. I don't believe in my own ideological supremacy. I only believe in my own personal autonomy. When I work to share cultural values, I want people to know where I'm coming from, so they can make up their own mind about whether or not I'm to be trusted. To me, this is one of the cornerstones of antiauthoritarian cultural work.

Yet I sometimes find myself promoting somewhat similar cultural values as fascists. I need to be careful when I do that. Take the idea of loyalty. I don't believe in loyalty, not as such. I believe in solidarity, instead. These are comparable social values, but the difference matters. Loyalty, as I understand it, is about allegiance. Allegiance is about the subordination of one to another. Loyalty happens, by and large, in a hierarchical fashion. Solidarity is performed between equals.

I also hate quibbling over semantics, and there are plenty of people who use the word loyalty without regards to hierarchy. Or people who see their loyalty as themselves acting subordinately to a certain value. Loyalty to one's family or friends, for example, might be the loyalty an individual shows the larger social body. That's not how I'd prefer to describe things, but I don't have a problem with people who do.

The idea of the individual showing loyalty to the larger social body isn't very black metal, of course. Black metal seems to me to be far more often concerned with the war of the individual against society than one's subservience to it. Frankly, black metal always feels like an odd thing for Nazis to be obsessed with, beyond a youthful rebellion and a general bloodlust. Fifteen years ago, at least Scandinavian black metal Nazis were the laughingstock of the Nazi world, and that makes sense to me.

Black metal has long concerned itself with trying to be evil, whatever the fuck *evil* means. There might not be any other concepts in the world as subjective as the concepts of good and evil. Most of the time, the idea of *good* roughly means aligned with the individual's or community's moral values, and evil means everything that isn't.

I don't know if I'm evil. Depends on who's labeling me. Anarchists have always been painted as evil by governments and capitalists, but our genocide count is a hell of a lot lower than that of pretty much every other political ideology anyone has tried out in the past five hundred years. I don't actually think anarchists are very evil. I think authority has a better claim to that word.

Personally, I'm drawn to revel in a separate but comparable concept: *monstrosity*. I can't find the quote anymore, buried in the endless expanse of the internet, but I once read another trans woman's post about metal. If I recall correctly, she'd basically been called a poser after talking shit about some white cis dude for wearing a Nazi black metal shirt. She said, and I paraphrase, "I am a trans woman. I inject the concentrated urine of mares to become something monstrous to society. I am more metal than you will ever be."

I don't know whether or not I'm a monster. That decision is up to society.

I do know that being a monster is very, very metal.

Fascism isn't the only thing I'm trying to destroy, of course, and anti-fascism isn't the only thing I'm trying to hold space for in the black metal scene.

I want to destroy patriarchy too. I'm not trying to destroy men—well, not most of them—but I have every desire to drive the forces of male domination back into the abyss from which they crawled.

I never want to go to a show only to find out that the singer advocates the holocaust of ethnic minorities. I also never want to go to a show to find out that the singer is unrepentantly a rapist. I never want to overhear racial epithets aimed at minorities. I also don't want to overhear some group of men complaining about sluts or the friend zone. I don't want some cis dude to fucking put his hand on the small of my back as he passes in the crowd. I don't want to play shows for all-male audiences, to keep sharing the stage with only men.

I'm fighting for cultural space as an anti-fascist, but I'm also fighting for cultural space as a woman. I started my band Feminazgûl partly to do that.

I named the first EP *The Age of Men Is Over* quite explicitly to do that. I'd been listening to black metal for ten or fifteen years. One depressed winter while getting over my sweetheart deciding she was too straight to date a girl after all, I threw together twenty minutes of bedroom-produced black metal. I just needed a way to get out some feminist angst.

I never expected anything like the response I got.

As a trans girl, I'm always afraid of taking up space in feminist circles. Afraid that I'll be rejected by other women. That didn't happen. Quite the opposite. One woman reposted the album saying she was going to listen to it when she went into labor.

What caught me off guard but shouldn't have is the overwhelming support we (Feminazgûl is now a two-piece) have gotten from cis men. A lot of men are nearly as sick of black metal being a boy's club as women are. Men are realizing that patriarchy forces them into shitty, painful boxes and isolates them from half the world. We're winning the cultural war.

There's a downside to all our advances on the cultural front, unfortunately. We've made enormous strides in the past decade in LGBTIQ+ acceptance. As far as I can tell from my position as a white person, it appears that larger chunks of society are making some progress against racism, as more people look at power systemically and understand that white supremacy and colonialism are problems we can't just fix by "treating everyone equal" like my parents' generation tried to tell us. We have gay marriage and an awareness that "reverse racism" is no more real than the tooth fairy. There's a whole generation of Americans that are no longer afraid to criticize capitalism and to call themselves socialists or anarchists. We care about the freedom and autonomy of sex workers. Trans people are coming out of the closet left and right, and some of us even dare to piss in public restrooms or read books to children.

All of this freaked the right-wing the fuck out, and they're in the process of making one last, desperate grab at power. The far right has always been terrible at creating and shaping culture, but, unfortunately, they're pretty good at political power, so they're taking it, as fast as they can, and a lot of our hard work is slipping away from us—fast. It's a last-ditch effort, but it's not necessarily a death knell. We have to keep fighting.

The cultural war isn't the only war. Aesthetic ideas and subcultures aren't the only thing we can't cede to fascists.

Some of the fights are a lot more physical.

Myself, I just want to make music, write books, and live my queer life here in Appalachia. But I can't. Fascism is ascendant politically, even while liberation is on the rise culturally. So I have to fight. I also can't sit back and just live my life, because the local Nazis are stalking me. They send me e-mails, telling me what car I drive, telling me where I hang out.

The local Nazis do a lot of things but playing black metal worth a damn ain't one of those things.

Scare me ain't one of those things either.

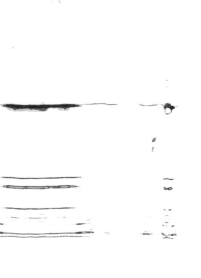

Ezra Rose
Minerva Metalhead, 2019
pen and ink with collaged
vintage doll ad, 23 x 30.5 cm
courtesy of the artist

Why Us? Why Now?

DISCUSSING THE RISE OF
ANTI-FASCIST BLACK METAL

STUART WAIN

When you think of politics and black metal, there is every chance that your thoughts instantly jump toward bands on the right. Ever since the second wave, black metal has been haunted by the specter of far-right politics and bigotry, most notably with the explicit racism and ethnonationalism of Varg Vikernes of Burzum.

The homophobic murders committed by Jon Nödtveidt (Dissection) and Faust (Emperor), the antisemitic language used by Darkthrone around the release of *Transilvanian Hunger*, and the use of fascist-inspired artwork on merchandise and artwork by bands like Mayhem and Marduk have also all attracted considerable attention. Granted, use of such iconography has long been a part of rock and metal, perhaps most famously with Motörhead and Slayer, but a line was crossed here between mere shock value and something more dangerous. I imagine most of us have had some variant of *that* conversation, where well-meaning friends who know a little about black metal's controversies take us aside and ask why we are suddenly so into music that is seemingly so comfortable with hate, murder, and Nazism. Sure, Lemmy may have worn an Iron Cross as part of his on-stage garb and was an avid collector of Nazi memorabilia, but it was obvious from interviews that he was just into the imagery, while being deeply opposed to the politics of hate and division. Can you really say the same about the members of Marduk?

In recent years though, there has been a rise in black metal bands making explicitly anti-fascist music, standing in opposition to those old ideas of hate and fascist supremacy. Such sentiments are nothing new, having been present in certain sections of black metal for years now, with bands such as Neverchrist making explicitly anti-fascist black metal for over ten years, while other notable bands—including proto–black metal figureheads Sodom and Tom Warrior (Hellhammer, Celtic Frost), as well as members of more recent high-profile bands such as Wolves in the Throne Room and Summoning, hold anti-fascist views, even if it is not always explicit in their music. But, now, bands in the underground such as Ancst, Dawn Ray'd, and Neckbeard Deathcamp, among many others, are making anti-fascism a central part of the identity of their band's and music. Some older bands are also responding to the growing fascist threat with a shift in lyrical stance, making their private views more visible.

Central to understanding this shift is asking, "Why now?" It is a simple enough question, but one with a myriad of possible answers, which I explored with several bands via e-mail interviews from September 2018 to May 2019. Simon of UK folk/black metal trio Dawn Ray'd explained:

I feel more and more obliged to write political lyrics, as it seems so much more urgent and important all the time, and our band is primarily anarchist and being anti-fascist comes along with that. These are the urgent issues I can see outside my door, they are the maelstroms brewing on the horizon, I believe that we all have to resist, agitate, and organize in every way we can think of to try to stop all these issues getting any worse.

Likewise, Tom from prolific blackened crust band Ancst says:

I deal with lots of different topics. [Anti-fascism] is just one of
them. The reason I chose to write about that stuff is that it's a
reflection of what I see on a daily basis. It reflects our society. I'm
sure the turn to the right all over the world has a strong influence
on that but, on the other hand, I feel like I have been writing about
that topic, like, forever.

That Tom considers anti-fascism to be only one of the themes his band deals with
also indicates the intersectional nature of anti-fascism and how concepts as
diverse as environmentalism, feminism, and anticapitalism can coalesce under
the umbrella of anti-fascism.

Further to this, the ongoing persistence and growth of fascism and hate in
modern times is undeniable. While the rise of so-called "populists"—in the
form of Trump in the US, Bolsonaro in Brazil, and the Brexit movement in the UK,
among many others around the globe—has brought such forces to the fore, they
represent something that has been simmering for many years. That there are so
many people who support fascism or are willing to tolerate fascism and bigotry in
whatever form it takes initially came as a shock for some of those who now make
anti-fascist music, such as Dan, drummer in UK post-black metal band Underdark:

When we first started the band, I had no idea that the ideals and
morals I upheld personally were called anti-fascism. Personally,
I thought they were just general beliefs on how not to be a shitty
human being, but then other members informed me and showed me where
to look further. That being said, we all shared the same views on
politics, racism, and the like. That and discovering that there's
such an abhorrent thing as NSBM, or other far-right beliefs rife
within a small area of black metal, its history, and its fan base.
So it was a pretty easy decision to make for the five of us.

Experiences such as this can be seen as a reflection of those parts of society and
the media who never expected Trump or the forces behind Brexit to be victorious—
that it can be easy to delude ourselves into thinking that the tolerant people we
try to surround ourselves with are the norm, and that racism and authoritarianism
has been banished to history.

This rising tide of hate did not just influence new bands either. Chris Grigg of USBM stalwarts Woe states:

I was raised to be an outspoken anti-fascist. For most of Woe's history, I was too preoccupied with my own issues and growth to commit it to original songs, but a few things—the clearing of the fog of depression, the rise of Trump and authoritarian movements, the continued failure of America's government to address the failures of capitalism, and good old-fashioned perspective and experience—really made me feel like I should do more for a cause bigger than myself.

This shift in perspective, widening from the personal to encompass the explicitly political, is superbly expressed in the song "No Blood Has Honor," from 2017's *Hope Attrition*, a blistering critique of the forces that drive authoritarian governments and prejudice.

Even if one accepts the mindset of negativity that so many people take as being a key part of black metal, there is potential here for anti-fascist thought too. Libtrigger are a relatively new band, inspired by Neckbeard Deathcamp's comic parodies of fascist black metal, which combine anti-fascism with black metal negativity—even if they did not initially set out to write anti-fascist music. They explain:

We didn't set out to write anti-fascist songs initially. We set out to write good black metal. Thematically, we believe in writing about anything you want to write about, and dark and unsettling topics are part of what has made black metal the challenging genre it is today. We were watching the fallout of another effort to cancel a Marduk show, and we saw the reaction online, and it was enormously disappointing to us. Not because some people were trying to cancel a band's show because of something they have said or written, but because people were disowning black metal because of it. People were disowning black metal as "Nazi shit" and "bedroom music for the alt-right." Fuck that! Black metal is anti-everything depending on where you look. It made us sick because it looked like the people whose personal politics we don't agree with had somehow managed to own black metal and to speak for it, and that is fucking bullshit. Black metal is chaos and war, it is not a recruitment campaign for right-wing grifters and the president of the fucking USA. Fuck them.

To hear a band embrace the negative side of black metal while also rejecting fascism is refreshing. Nihilism has long been a part of black metal's character, and such nihilism seems incompatible with the desire for a fascist state or for the misguided "protection" of the "white race" that many neofascists espouse.

This argument that black metal is somehow inherently evil is one that comes up repeatedly in discussions among fans and musicians, as if the ability to tremolo-pick leads is somehow only possible by rejecting notions of goodwill toward other humans. Like many black metal tropes, this idea of black metal being evil seems to originate from the Norwegian scene, expressing an idea regularly voiced by Euronymous, who argued that black metal must be Satanic,[1] and whose interpretation of Satanism was "against goodness."[2] Given the links between certain notorious members of that scene and the politics of prejudice and the high regard that scene is still held in by many, it is no surprise that the concept that "black metal is evil" is a serious idea—rather than the more theatrical concept demonstrated by Venom—that has taken root. It seems to pose the Satanic (whether serious or not) basis of black metal as being rooted in evil, taking Lucifer as the traditional symbol of evil in Christian doctrine and emphasizing this aspect at the expense of the interpretation of Lucifer as a symbol of freedom. This later interpretation, if followed through to its logical end, makes anti-fascism an integral part of black metal; after all, anti-fascism is, in effect, a struggle for freedom. The mutable, shifting concept of Lucifer, including as a symbol of freedom, has been explored by Elaine Pagels in her book *The Origin of Satan*.[3] Pagels shows that the concept of Lucifer, an angel of God and the "light bearer," was later transformed into the protagonist of Milton's *Paradise Lost*, who famously stated following his failed rebellion against God that it is "better to reign in Hell than serve in Heaven." Pagels's book also illustrates how the mutable concepts of Satan and Lucifer have effectively been used to "other" those who have stood against Christians, claiming that they were possessed by or were agents of Satan: initially those who persecuted Christians but later those who opposed Christian doctrine and control. It is this later aspect that links Satan and Lucifer with the struggle for freedom, and, hence, anti-fascism.

This can also be linked to Aleister Crowley's writings, which have been a huge influence on Satanism, where the concept "do what thou wilt shall be the whole of the law" stands strong. This concept is incompatible with authoritarianism, given that Crowley considered this central aspect of Thelema to mean that one should not interfere with the rights of others. Such concepts also stand in stark contrast to what Massimo Introvigne would likely term the "adolescent Satanism" displayed by many black metal bands,[4] which revels in "evil" for the sake of shock and intimidation. While there are certainly bands who take their Satanism seriously in a theistic sense, these are almost certainly a minority among bands who use Satanic iconography and themes. This is not without irony when it comes to those bands who combine far-right sympathies with Satanic belief, considering the long history of fascist movements opportunistically attempting to appeal to religious groups, including in Nazi Germany and fascist Italy, or the Ku Klux Klan's claim to be a Christian organization.

Another idea often raised in black metal circles is that the music should somehow be "dangerous." This is normally meant to imply something sinister—that extreme metal goes hand-in-hand with extreme politics, which supposedly finds its natural expression in the far-right—after all, many will surely think that nothing is more dangerous and extreme than Nazism and fascism. The idea that black metal should be dangerous is one many of the bands I interviewed agreed with—but their thoughts about who should feel threatened are at odds with those who would use black metal to promote bigotry. Chris Grigg stated:

Metal should be dangerous! The idea that we should make black metal safer or friendlier helps fuel the narrative that we don't understand it, that we are an existential threat to it, that they need to rally around the ideas of old white men to protect the thing they love. Fuck all that. Keep black metal dangerous: dangerous to gods, to rules, to order, to the establishment.

It is a view Libtrigger agree with.

We believe that extreme metal should be dangerous—not to its fucking fans but to their enemies. We just don't think there's anything particularly edgy or dangerous about sharing the political views of the president of the USA or the president of Russia. How is that edgy? How is that counterculture? To us, anarchism represents a far more extreme kind of politics, talk of revolution, and deconstruction of power structures.

I completely agree with this statement and want to emphasize the way that central tenants of far-right belief are integral to modern Western society—for example, the relationship between racism and capitalism.[5] In comparison, concepts such as communism and anarchism are treated by large sections of the mainstream media as inherently extreme, outlandish, and incredibly dangerous.

Simon of Dawn Ray'd takes a similar view:

I think the bands that use fascist iconography and ideas to seem extreme are the lesser bands; it is a very cheap and unimaginative shock tactic. The bands with any sense know full well where the line is and what is not acceptable. Also, if you think there is any merit in being dangerous or edgy by being a paedophile (Inquisition) or targeting Muslims and gay people (Taake) then you are a spineless coward. Fascism doesn't have a monopoly on violence or the extreme, quite the opposite, it is actually a very conservative and old-fashioned set of beliefs.

Dan of Underdark is in broad agreement:

The whole "black metal should be dangerous" mindset is quite possibly one of the biggest loads of shit I've ever come across. The general case I've found with this is people use this phrase to justify their own shitty behavior and/or choice of music and ideals. The use of fascist symbols and imagery nowadays is nothing more than a redundant edgelord take. While genres like death metal have been talking about hatred, death, and the like for a long time, you very rarely see this sort of problem within the genre, so what makes black metal so different?

Death metal also has problems with fascism, as demonstrated by individuals such as Craig Pillard (former vocalist of Disma and Incantation, who has proclaimed an admiration for Nazi Germany in interviews and through his Sturmführer project) and Patrick Mameli of Pestilence being accused of making racist and antisemitic statements on Facebook in 2017, but it is not as central an issue and is not viewed in the same way as black metal's problems with fascist bands and individuals. This raises the question: Do those playing anti-fascist black metal see it as an effective way to encourage listeners to do more than just listen to music and to become more politically active?

"I hope so," says Simon when asked if anti-fascist music helps fuel anti-fascist politics and activism. "I think the purpose of political music is to signal boost different struggles, to be part of education and development, and to help build communities that can resist." In the view of Chris Grigg:

It depends on the individual, who and where they are when they discover the music and how developed their ideas are when they encounter it. I believe in the power of art to shape ideas and change lives, so I obviously think that political music has a role in that. At the same time, I also think someone's about as likely [to] stitch a sunwheel onto a jacket upon first hearing Graveland as they are to immediately go out and burn a cop car upon first hearing Propagandhi.

It's certainly true that while some listeners will take political messages from bands to heart, other fans will not—as evidenced by Republican politician Paul Ryan claiming, in 2012, that Rage Against the Machine was one of his favorite bands.

Of course, this works for both those opposing fascism and those bands that wish to promote it. Tom of Ancst states that "[NSBM] clearly feeds more into [political activities] than leftist black metal does. I mean, if you look at the NSBM scene more closely you find out that there is a politically active network behind it. Nazis have always used music for propaganda. NSBM is no exception."

"I think it emboldens other Nazis, and it also threatens to normalize really awful ideas" is the view of Simon from Dawn Ray'd. "Most people who hear those bands won't be won over to Nazism in any way, but it does create a tolerance for it, which is dangerous." Likewise, Dan of Underdark states: "I don't believe it normalizes NSBM as a whole, but I do believe it gives justification for their own shitty beliefs such as the white genocide myth they all seem to be peddling at the moment."

The danger of the link created between music and the politics of bigotry by Nazi black metal is well summarized by Libtrigger:

We think it helps create a culture associated with "whiteness" or "nationhood," which, in turn, then makes it much harder to change your worldview, because in order to leave your awful toxic views on what "whiteness" is and why you believe it's so powerful, you need to leave things you enjoy behind (music, food, clothing), as you've attached your identity to entertainment.

That's insightful—while "but the riffs!" may be something of a comic meme as a justification for listening to fascist black metal, the Libtrigger statement carries with it a wealth of meaning. If those riffs and that music have somehow become a key part of your identity, even if you disagree with the politics espoused in the songs, then leaving them behind or challenging their creators is no small task, especially if the band in question does not write political lyrics but, instead, promotes bigotry through their artwork, merch, or interviews.

The dual nature of political music is perhaps best summed up by Chris Grigg, who also notes that music as lifestyle is very powerful:

Someone with a strong sense of identity is unlikely to be swayed by art from the other side that challenges them. If one chooses, a confident adult should be able to listen to some Burzum without going full Varg. Sadly, [no] protest song is going to get Varg to have a change of heart either. So where does this leave us? I'd say that the power of sociopolitical music is simultaneously overestimated and underestimated, strange as that sounds. It means that the war against fascism, the introduction of people to our message, needs to be subtle at times, overt at others, but abundantly represented.

It is this need for a mixed approach that makes the comedic stylings of Neckbeard Deathcamp every bit as important as the more straight-forward lyrics of Dawn Ray'd.

Of course, while the struggle against fascist black metal and fascism more generally has the obvious benefit of us all helping to stand against the rising tide of hate, bigotry, and intolerance, anti-fascism at its most effective has always been an intersectional movement, both in terms of the people involved and the approaches taken. The struggle against fascism is also inherently linked with those against racism, homophobia, sexism, and other forms of bigotry, and there is also considerable crossover between anti-fascist, anarchist, and anticapitalist movements.

Chris from Woe argues that the fight against such prejudices is inherent to black metal—a view I would strongly agree with. If one sees black metal as rooted in Satanism and Satanism as a struggle against control and authority, it is clear that this must be accompanied by the fight against prejudice and authoritarianism—or, put another way, the Satanic origins of black metal link with anti-fascism and the associated movements of antiracism, anticapitalism, and feminism.

If we are to agree that black metal is a "thing" with inherent meaning or value, I would say that a crucial element of it is the rejection of authority, the destruction of the rules and rulers forced on us. It is about the cultivation of the individual, the empowerment of every person to be powerful and free to build their own worlds and lives. The fight against all forms of bigotry is inseparable from this, just as the fight to protect the status quo or build happy white families is utterly incompatible with it.

As Simon of Dawn Ray'd puts it, "If you aren't intersectional then you aren't anti-fascist in my opinion. Those struggles are inextricably linked, and from personal experience there are very few people that would care about one at the exclusion of the others." Or, more directly, when I asked Libtrigger about fascism, racism, and other forms of bigotry: "Fuck all of those things." I strongly agree with that. Anti-fascism should not simply be viewed as a struggle against overt authoritarianism but also as a struggle against the different aspects of modern fascism—sexism, racism, unchecked capitalism, imperialism, anti-environmentalism, homophobia, and so on. These are not isolated challenges, and they can all come together under the broad umbrella of anti-fascism.

Associated with this intersectional struggle, the growth of anti-fascist black metal means there is more potential for people who might otherwise not have been able to be a part of black metal to become involved. As Simon points out:

Metal as a whole is actually a very diverse scene anyway, more so than it is given credit for, in my experience. It is a scene that requires only that you be into metal, despite the best efforts of a few fringe bigots. It obviously has its share of problems like any music scene, but that is what makes the whole white supremacist metal thing such a fucking joke. Metal has never been this pure white, straight, cishet scene that a few dickheads want it to be. A quick glance at the musicians that pioneered this genre is testament to that fact. Obviously, there is a lack of representation for a lot of people, and that needs to change. I hope this new influx of left-wing bands will contribute to that.

Dan of Underdark agrees, saying, "There is nothing I want more to see than more people of different races, genders, and sexualities in the scene."

Not everyone is equally convinced about a growth in diversity taking place within metal, though. Chris from Woe argues:

Increasing the diversity within metal is going to require a lot more than pushing back on the Nazis hanging around. Instead, my hope is that it acts as a counterbalance to the right's attempt to normalize Nazi music in black metal. I want it to get smarter, nastier, and do a better job of fighting this notion that "black metal is evil, racism is evil; therefore, racism in black metal makes sense!" Instead, the message should be, "black metal is against control and authority, and bigotry is the ultimate expression of control and authority, therefore, bigotry has no place in black metal!"

Which leads us to the elephant in the room. For all this talk of the dangers of fascism within black metal, just how big a scene is National Socialist black metal perceived to be? One Nazi band is one Nazi band too many, but is it a case of a small number of bands making a lot of noise and making themselves seem like a bigger movement than they actually are? Is there an apathy toward such bands within the wider black metal scene? We find little consensus among the bands interviewed—while all agreed that Nazi black metal is to be opposed, there was little agreement on how many of the so-called Nazi bands are serious rather than just using the symbols and language for shock value and attention and to make themselves seem larger than they actually are.

Chris Grigg says, "I do think that the attitude described earlier (black metal and racism are evil and belong together) is pervasive within the black metal scene, but this has more to do with there being too few good bands going to bat with a better message that really feels natural in the context of black metal. Get more bands taking a stand, and you'll see some improvement." It's certainly true that relatively few anti-fascist black metal bands are playing what can be termed "trve" black metal, as defined by the second wave in the early 1990s—all of the more high-profile anti-fascist black metal bands have considerable "external" influences on their sound. Only a handful of bands, such as Libtrigger, Trespasser, and Operation Volkstod, all of whom have a much lower profile than the likes of Dawn Ray'd and Woe, are writing second-wave black metal with explicitly anti-fascist lyrics.

Simon from Dawn Ray'd takes the view that the danger of Nazi black metal is underestimated by the wider metal scene and metal press.

For a while people have just rolled their eyes at the right-wing bands and treated them as fringe weirdos, but with the huge surge in fascism globally, I think people are much keener to stamp it out now. We can see evidence of this in Graveland and Taake getting shows cancelled for their far-right views, and bands like Marduk, Shining, and Watain coming under heavy criticism for similar things. Very few of the right-wing bands actually have politically active members, so I think for a while they weren't much of a priority, but there seems to be much less tolerance for those ideas everywhere now and a fresh understanding of how dangerous they can be if allowed to grow.

Such bands having shows cancelled is far from consistent, however, and there are instances of them playing shows where their views seemingly conflicted with those of the organizers. It was bleakly ironic to see that Taake, a band with explicitly Islamophobic lyrics, headlined the Sophie Lancaster stage on Saturday at Bloodstock 2019, given that stage's links with the Sophie Lancaster Foundation, which aims to combat hate crimes.

Dan from Underdark agrees that the danger of Nazi black metal is underestimated, while also noting the irony that the very nature of anti-fascism will inevitably draw attention to Nazi black metal.

I believe that NSBM is a small minority part of the wider black metal scene. Sadly, it seems to be getting more press in recent times, and more bands being outspoken toward it sort of brings some attention to it. Alongside this, it seems it's that every other week another band within black metal gets outed for being complete shitheels. However, I do believe the links to wider fascist movements are there. Using the example of the recent Horna shows in the US, where I saw known members of a far-right group standing outside the venue they were due to play *Sieg Heil*-ing. To me, that shows there is links within NSBM that can go further.

Not that everyone agrees that Nazi black metal is as big a scene as it is sometimes portrayed to be. As Libtrigger put it, "We don't think it really is as big or as popular as it'd like people to think. Isn't it just a handful of turds floating around in the bowl desperate for press attention and trying to look dangerous?"

And Tom from Ancst says:

Symbols and speech connected to fascism and the Third Reich are still being used for shock value and marketing. But if you dig deeper you can clearly find bands and labels that are connected to organizations such as the Greek Golden Dawn movement, the Blood and Honor network, and other political organizations. Some individuals clearly pose a threat to an open and peaceful society; others are just kids who want attention.

Nor is there agreement about how Nazi black metal is perceived or should be termed. Chris Grigg of Woe argues that even the label commonly given to it—NSBM—sanitizes and normalizes fascism and prejudice within black metal. "It is Nazi music. Its listeners should tell others they enjoy Nazi music. It should not slide under the radar. It should not be normal. It should stick the fuck out wherever it goes. NSBM as a label infuriates me." Dan from Underdark believes that this labelling of Nazi black metal as NSBM is part of a wider trend within fascism of adopting names to disguise true intentions, stating "I think a lot more people would oppose it if they called it what it is: white supremacy music or something along those lines. Like most right-wing groups, such as the Proud Boys, for example, it's just another dressed-up phrase for Nazi." On the other hand, Simon of Dawn Ray'd says, "I think everyone knows what [NSBM] is, and it is a term that carries a lot of weight, so I don't personally think that any of the gravity is lost. No one is under any illusion as to what it stands for." However, having spoken to fans who saw the term NSBM used in magazines for years without ever having it explained that it denoted fascist bands, I think the term NSBM serves to sanitize fascist black metal and is part of the long history of fascist movements trying to disguise themselves to infiltrate scenes viewed as potentially sympathetic.

There is, however, a sense of optimism about the direction of change. Above, Simon points out that it is increasingly common for bands to be dropped from tours or record labels for things they have said or done—something that was unthinkable ten years ago. Likewise, Chris Grigg of Woe comments:

I think things are much better than they were ten years ago. What we might be seeing is an increase in connectivity to remote scenes due to the internet, greater accessibility and visibility, more opportunities to stumble upon it without looking for it. I remember when this shit was so much more normal, when the idea of discussions like the one we're having were unheard of.

Dan from Underdark also points out that political music can help turn people on to political action and education. "It may come across as preaching to the choir at times, or even screaming at a wall, to those who couldn't care less, but if you can get one person even remotely interested, then it's worth it."

Libtrigger takes a dissenting view, arguing that fascism in black metal is increasing, reflecting wider trends in the world.

I think the election of Trump, and then the rise in individual far-right politicians globally, has emboldened the right, including right-wing musicians, who believe that their time is now. I also believe that it is considered by people who wish to empower the far right as a method of accessing and converting young people into voters and followers. In the same way young people were being recruited from online movements like #GamerGate and the mainstreaming of conspiracy theories, the far right believes that it may be able to recruit using extreme music.

Yet Tom from Ancst argues that "there is a stronger anti-fascist mindset becoming popular due to the increase of right-wing politics all over the world"— that the growing visibility of fascism is, in turn, fueling a stronger pushback against the politics of hate.

On one point, though, there is almost total agreement—unlike with Nazi black metal, there is no wider united anti-fascist black metal movement or scene. Simon of Dawn Ray'd believes that this is due to the relative youth of anti-fascist black metal and RABM (red and anarchist black metal), arguing that "it will take time to build all those networks for sure, but a few years ago an anti-fascist black metal scene was unthinkable, so times are rapidly changing!" Likewise, Dan from Underdark feels that there is a growing scene that may even transcend genre, stating:

Meeting other like-minded bands both in person and speaking to them online, there's a really strong support for each other. Even with other artists that wouldn't be considered black metal, or even labels. If the ideals are there, we've got each other's backs.

While Tom of Ancst says:

The scene for that is too small and isolated and isn't sure what it wants to be...There have been some attempts and I'm sure there are a few loosely organized people out there, but it doesn't feel like a scene to me. Still, I would love to see a political and socially aware subculture rising from the small pool of bands that really mean what they say.

Some bands, though, are resistant to the idea of any unified scene or movement— as might be expected from a movement so heavily steeped in individuality and resistance to hierarchy and structure.

Chris Grigg says:

I'm not interested in being involved in what I'm sure would become an in-fighting mob, constantly seeking traitors who don't live up to their standards. We need bands with backbone and superior alternatives to the music and narratives pushed by the right. We need genuine artists with true black metal spirit who also happen to be on the left, even if they don't want to make it their band's focus.

While recent developments such as the Black Flags over Brooklyn festival show that there is an appetite for and growth of anti-fascism within extreme metal,

Ivan Belcic
We Share This Spirit, 2019
pen and digital
courtesy of the artist

these events do not have the same profile or political links as their fascist equivalents, which, in some cases, double up as militia-style training camps, taking the culture war within black metal onto more dangerous terrain. Ironically, it is this that convinces me of the importance of anti-fascist black metal bands and fans networking to create a unified movement that can push back against the more well-organized fascist bands and labels. This matters not only in terms of the "culture war" and ideological conflicts around black metal but also for self-defense against actual violence. While there would inevitably be issues like those identified by Chris Grigg, the benefits of an explicitly anti-fascist black metal scene outweigh the negatives.

All of this shows that the recent growth of anti-fascist black metal is organic, with a multitude of origin stories and viewpoints. There is no single scene or nexus to the movement—if it can even be called a movement—and, instead, in true underground style, it is a case of artists creating the art they want to see in the world on their own terms. The music itself is diverse, with bands united by thought more than sound, as demonstrated by Woe's punk-infused USBM, the atmospheric black metal of Feminazgûl, the English folk/black metal mix of Dawn Ray'd, the blackened crust of Ancst, the second wave–influenced fury of Trespasser, the combination of harsh noise and war metal made by Archgooch, and the blackgaze of Underdark—and there is no single label or nexus driving the scene forward. That is, perhaps, both the greatest strength and the greatest weakness of anti-fascist black metal. Its variety helps ensure there is something for (almost) everyone, while Nazi black metal has a well-defined sound and scene in terms of labels and festivals, with terms such as NSBM and RAC (Rock Against Communism) describing both a musical style and a far-right mindset, making it easy for fans and bands to present themselves as part of a wider movement. Recent festivals, such as Black Flags over Brooklyn, and the accompanying *Riffs for Reproductive Justice* compilation—both organized by writer and activist Kim Kelly—represent the most notable recent developments in an explicit anti-fascist underground metal movement, but neither the festival nor compilation is solely focused on black metal.

Instead, anti-fascist black metal has the anarchic feel of the proto–black metal of the 1980s, when bands, including Venom, Bathory, and Sarcófago, independently struck forward with singular visions of what extreme metal could be, and it was only in hindsight that common threads could be identified. It may well be that we are witnessing something similar now, with artists reaching similar end points independently—that, no matter the exact style they play, anti-fascism fits perfectly within a black metal mindset, one that defies authority, promotes individuality, and pursues freedom, and that such an approach has rarely been needed more than it is now.

Notes

[1] Dayal Patterson, *Black Metal: Evolution of the Cult* (Port Townsend, WA: Feral House, 2013), 151.

[2] Benjamin Hedge Olson, *I Am the Black Wizards: Multiplicity, Mysticism, and Identity in Black Metal Music and Culture* (master's thesis, Bowling Green State University, 2008), cited in Massimo Introvigne, *Satanism: A Social History* (Leiden, NL: Brill, 2016), 480.

[3] Elaine Pagels, *The Origin of Satan: How Christians Demonized Jews, Pagans and Heretics* (New York: Vintage Books, 1996).

[4] Introvigne, *Satanism*, 9.

[5] For an in-depth discussion of this, see Carter A. Wilson, *Racism: From Slavery to Advanced Capitalism* (New York: SAGE Publications, 1996).

Ry Cunningham
Black Kaleidescope, 2019
digital illustration
courtesy of the artist

Black Metal under the Black Flag

KIM KELLY

We are only alive in these songs
And the songs belong to the land
We must bury all those that divide us
Under the ash of every national flag!

—DAWN RAY'D, "FIRE SERMON"

I believe there is no peace now, and there
will never be peace, so long as one rules over
another; I believe in the total disintegration
and dissolution of the principle and practice of
authority; I am an Anarchist, and if for this you
condemn me, I stand ready to receive
your condemnation.

—VOLTAIRINE DE CLEYRE

Black metal has always been a study in contradictions. The genre—
itself a bastardized offshoot that whips together basic elements of

thrash metal, the new wave of British heavy metal, classical music and punk, and filters them all through a veil of distortion and a theatrically evil atmosphere—has been knocking around since the late 1980s by virtue of early pioneers like Hellhammer, Sodom, Venom, Tormentor, and Mercyful Fate. Despite its scrappy, punk-inflected roots (especially in the case of Venom, a schlocky, gritty NWOBHM band who coined the term), black metal quickly became a symbol of something darker.

These early European adapters were surrounded by their peers in the 1980s punk scene, who stayed busy grinding out short, sharp musical shocks and making their anti-establishment, overwhelmingly leftist political sympathies known. But Venom's tarnished version of British steel was unconcerned with capitalism or the Queen; rather, their lyrics and image were pegged to black leather and black magic. Satan, laughing, had spread his wings, and those primordial stabbings at evil and darkness spawned a genre with a theatrical commitment to nihilism—and a mean streak.

1982 was a year of change, particularly in the countries that gave rise to black metal's early stirrings, now canonically known as its "first wave." Anarcho-punks Crass released *Christ—The Album* in 1982, the same year Venom's *Black Metal* LP came out. While the Falklands War raged and British punks railed against the cruel austerity policies of hated prime minister Margaret Thatcher, their counterparts across the pond protested US president Ronald Reagan's brutal arch capitalist agenda. In Germany, where Sodom's "witching metal" was birthed in 1982, protesters flooded the streets to advocate for nuclear disarmament, while in Sweden, the left-leaning Social Democratic Party swept the 1982 election (while, in 1983, Bathory's Quorthon began work on his demo). Nothing, even the most willfully antisocial, cerebral art, is created in a political void—and whether or not they realized it at the time, early black metal was barely removed from punk in its execution, if not its message.

Despite the historical context, when black metal's fitful, bloodstained march toward global popularity first truly hit its stride in the 1990s, those involved in the genre's second wave rejected any notion that their creation was based in anything but pure hatred. Norway and Sweden dominated black metal discourse throughout the 1990s, while South American bands forged their own concurrent path in relative obscurity. Norwegian bands, in particular Burzum, Mayhem, Darkthrone, Emperor, and Thorns, became the face of the genre and reveled in their social and musical transgressions as they raked in attention from horrified journalists and befuddled music critics alike.

Even then, as the genre was finding its first set of sea legs, there was something rotten in the state of black metal. Racism, antisemitism, and misogyny were rampant within the second wave, and escalating violence became its hallmark, with several of its biggest names engaging in racist attacks, homophobic hate crimes, arson, and murder. Jan Axel Blomberg, better known as Mayhem drummer Hellhammer, made the black metal scene's deeply rooted white supremacy problem clear when he told one of the authors of the influential book *Lords of Chaos: The Bloody Rise of the Satanic Metal Underground* (which was cowritten by the openly fascist musician Michael Moynihan), "Black metal is for white people."

Those events and the influential recordings that were released around them would set the stage for the decades to come, scrawling a blueprint for black metal bands to couch or openly peddle far-right views under the guise of extremity for extremity's sake, shock value, and, later, "free speech."

The philosophy of black metal cannot be nailed down into one specific school or line of thought; as with any complex art form, the genre contains multitudes. Given how much black metal has evolved since the early 1990s, it can be difficult to generalize anything about it at this point, but one of the major tenets of black metal has always been a total rejection of oppressive societal structures like organized religion and the idea of "polite" mainstream society. It is about power, extreme emotion, and individualism as much as it is about evil or esoteric philosophies. Darkness as a concept, an aesthetic, and an experience is an integral component, along, of course, with hatred in its myriad forms.

Andy Curtis-Brignell, better known as the force behind British experimental black metal/noise project Caïna, has been involved in the black metal scene for decades and has been an anarchist for nearly as long. In his estimation, the combination makes perfect sense once one is able to peel back a few spiky layers and recognize the ideological fallacies that black metal often seeks to perpetuate.

As Curtis-Brignell explained in a 2020 interview for this piece:

Black metal is a philosophically dualistic creature, in that, on the one hand, there's a perception—at least certainly an internal perception—of itself as uncompromising, thematically, sonically, and politically conservative and rigid, and so on. But if you actually look at the genre, there's a tremendous plurality of opinion, approach, and attitude that I think is broadly anarchistic in nature. It's iconoclastic, says "Fuck you!" to the top-down hierarchies of both music theory and the Byzantine hellscape of the music industry in general and has stuck more rigidly to its founding inherently proletarian DIY community principles than any other subset of heavy music.

The contradictory character that Curtis-Brignell describes is indeed made plain as one digs a bit deeper into black metal ideology, if that label remains appropriate. The "anti-human, anti-life" rhetoric common to its second wave and prevalent throughout the genre's history is countered by equal exhortations to support a chosen community of like-minded people by rooting out "posers" (and, later, "hipsters" and "social justice warriors"). Its pagan roots and connection to heathenry opens up a dangerous avenue for white supremacist poison to filter in, but it also opens up space for ideas around mutual aid and collective living. The genre's well-known connection to Satanism offers another line of contradiction, one that connects ideas about free love and self-determination to more problematic and harmful viewpoints. There are as many ways to be a Satanist as there are to be a black metal band, and, at this point, many artists have eschewed the association altogether, particularly those who have chosen to pursue a more political bent.

Black metal's political and ideological ambiguity remained elastic during the first wave's punk-influenced early stirrings, but then hardened as the second wave crested. This is what still allows it to be interpreted so broadly and to be claimed by so many conflicting perspectives. It is why anarchist black metal coexists (albeit extremely uncomfortably) with neo-Nazi black metal and why both camps are able to lay some legitimate claim to the genre. The far right has been more successful in claiming black metal as its own for a variety of reasons, but those on the left have never ceded that ground without a fight. That tension between the two camps has reached a boiling point in recent years, and one must ask: If black metal is truly about freedom, then how could it be anything *but* anarchist?

Before we can get into the justification for black metal being sorted firmly into the anarchist tradition, we must first break down why exactly fascists have had such a strong track record in claiming it for their own. Black metal's fiercely guarded relationship with hate itself is a core tenet, though the community has struggled to reach consensus over exactly what—or *who*—that hatred is being beamed toward. For some, it is conformity and the grating demands of mainstream polite society; for others, it is authority and oppression; while for others still, it unfortunately boils down to hating those who do not look or sound or believe exactly the same as they do, and manifests as racism, misogyny, antisemitism, Islamophobia, homophobia, transphobia, xenophobia, nationalism, fascism, and white supremacy.

In a 2019 interview for *Metal Hammer*, Dawn Ray'd vocalist and violinist Simon Barr said:

Fascists have always sought to infiltrate radical youth movements and cultural scenes, they tried it with Oi and punk, they have tried it in some sections of electronic music, but they always get disrupted and kicked out. The same will happen in black metal. The far right are a vocal minority in this scene, so a big part of the struggle is being vocal and visible in opposition to those ideas, so as to lessen their influence, whilst actively working to disrupt their shows and networks. Let's be clear: fascism is the most violent and horrific ideology we have seen so far, and we cannot compromise or hesitate in our attempts to stop it.[1]

So how can something so fraught, with so much baggage, be anything but what the fascists have deemed it? How can it be worth saving? The answer is simple. Black metal and anarchism are both based upon the same inherent principle: the concept of freedom. As Lucy Parsons, a black and indigenous woman who was born into slavery and became a legendary labor organizer and one of anarchism's most revered orators, once said, "[Anarchism] has but one infallible, unchangeable motto, 'Freedom': Freedom to discover any truth, freedom to develop, to live naturally and fully."[2]

That sentiment has echoed throughout history, and inspired multiple generations of more recent converts to the cause. Among them are Dawn Ray'd, a trio of working-class Brits who started a band to reflect their politics and inadvertently became one of modern metal's most controversial lightning rods. Their sworn commitment to both anarchism and militant anti-fascism—and refusal to apologize for either stance—won them fans as well as enemies across the metal spectrum after they released their watershed 2017 debut LP *The Unlawful Assembly*. The album remains a tour de force of masterful, potent black metal, with a melodic tinge and Barr's violin adding texture and pathos to the proceedings, and ensuing releases only raised their profile. As one of the most vocal anti-fascist bands in metal, let alone black metal, they endured torrents of abuse, death threats, and mockery but have held firm. To them, this is more than music; it is a battle for a better world.

"Anarchism is the freedom to live your life any way you choose, as long as in doing so you don't affect anyone else's ability to do the same," Barr explains, echoing Parsons a century earlier. "Anarchism means taking responsibility for your actions, it is having direct control over your life, and it is anti-oppressive by its very nature."[3]

As an ideology, anarchism is nearly as fluid as black metal, but while black metal's linchpin is hatred, that of anarchism is, arguably, love. That sounds painfully utopian (and insurrectionary anarchists would surely recoil at such a kumbaya description), but it is true. To fight for collective liberation, for a world defined by voluntary association, solidarity, self-determination, and autonomy, a life without the hierarchy of oppressive power structures, built on consensus and restorative justice, and in which every creature and the natural world itself is valued, requires a deep well of affinity for one's fellow living beings. Whether one is drawn to one of the many different schools of thought loosely grouped under anarchism's black umbrella—mutualism, Black anarchism, anarcha-feminism, green anarchism, queer anarchism—or, in the style of renowned anarchist thinker Voltairine de Cleyre, an "anarchist without adjectives," the core beliefs remain intact.

Satanic anarchism is another option, and while it is certainly a less traditional path, it is one that may at first appear to be a natural fit for black metal's leftist contingent. There is an iconic video clip of Gorgoroth vocalist Gaahl languidly sipping red wine as an interviewer asks him about the biggest inspiration behind his music. The answer: "Satan." And when asked what Satan means to him, Gaahl pauses, levels his gaze at the interviewer, and answers again. "Freedom." (Gaahl is a controversial and problematic figure in his own right—he is one of the most famous queer people in metal and is an undoubtedly influential artist, but he has also committed multiple acts of violent assault and torture, which, black metal being black metal, has only added to his standing in the scene).

Satanism's rejection of moral dogma and religious authority does share some basic commonalities with anarchism, but, after that, the waters become clouded. There are as many ways to follow Satan as there are to be an anarchist, and not every sect is benign. The occult and esoteric arts have long proven to be fertile ground for white supremacy, Nazism, and other hateful ideologies, and Satanism is no exception. The Order of the Nine Angles (O9A, a Satanic fascist Left Hand Path collective with an extremist theology centering Nazism and violence) has a following in the black metal world,[4] with bands like Brazil's Black Devotion, Italy's Altar of Perversion, and California's Hvile I Kaos, as well as popular labels like the AJNA Offensive drawing inspiration from the sect (though, interestingly, Hvile I Kaos's sole member, Chris "Kakophonix" Brown, publicly withdrew his affiliation with O9A once it was exposed by the Quietus in 2018). O9A has been linked to numerous violent events across the globe, and, in 2020, a US Army private was arrested on charges of leaking information to O9A and conspiring to plan a violent attack on his own unit in hopes that it would lead to "a new war."

One could write an entire book on black metal's relationship with Satanism (and a few people already have!) but, politically speaking, in actuality, the Dark Lord has little to do with black flags. For their part, Barr and his comrades are no Satanists; to them, the Devil's work pales in comparison to the grim realities of life under capitalism, and they are certainly not alone in their estimation. As well as being part of a broad leftist metal tradition that has existed for decades, Dawn Ray'd are also a perfect example of what is known as red and anarchist black metal, or RABM for short. Explicitly anti-fascist metal bands began popping up in droves after the 2016 election, but, for many years before, there was just a blog called r-a-b-m. blogspot.com.

R-a-b-m.blogspot.com began as a Last.FM group in the early 2000s and has now migrated to reddit/RABM, but its central purpose remains unchanged: to share and amplify the music of anti-fascist, anarchist, and otherwise leftist bands from around the world and across the metal spectrum, with a special focus on black metal and its grimy cousin blackened crust. As their own FAQ explains, RABM is loosely defined, but you will know it when you see it. Acronyms aside, RABM is not a response to NSBM, it is an entirely separate and self-sufficient community that encompasses "all kinds of black metal–related music charged with radical leftist (anarchist, libertarian socialist, eco-anarchist, etc.) political views," as well as bands that are sympathetic without being overly public with their views. The same FAQ offers some practical advice as well, encouraging readers to do their own research to ferret out bands' dodgy connections (and it also amusingly skewers LaVeyan Satanism as "Ayn Rand with some occult tinge").

Many of today's best-known anarchist black metal bands posted their music on r-a-b-m earlier on, and it remains an excellent resource even now that Bandcamp and social media have reconfigured the ways in which metal fans discover and consume new music. The fact that the site made such an effort to include metal-adjacent punk bands, and specifically blackened crust, was significant as well, because it provided readers with the perfect context in which to discover one of the most important and influential anarchist black metal bands of all time: Iskra.

Formed in Victoria, British Columbia, in 2002, Iskra is a self-described "violent cultural attack on the status quo, its philosophic inquiries, and political structures" that also happens to churn out an incredibly compelling blend of black metal, crust punk, and thrash. Albums like their 2004 self-titled debut and 2008's watershed *Bureval* are rife with lyrics that reference anarchist theory and revolutionary history, as well as the ravages of capital and the state's inhumane war on the people themselves, and are light years ahead of what passed for rebellion in punk and metal during the Iraq War years. For years, Iskra preferred to play in squats and release their albums with crust punk godfathers Profane Existence, and even when they did consent to work with Southern Lord in 2015, they did it on their own DIY terms.

In a 2010 interview, they laid out their philosophy in no uncertain terms, and also pulled no punches in criticizing the black metal scene's lack of political resolve.

Just because someone decides to wear corpse-paint, and propose some kind of holocaust, doesn't mean they're a rebel. Quite often they are nothing more than George Bush in disguise, or any other politician for that matter. When such people suggest a "non-political" stance (often to simply hide a confused agenda) we know it's bullshit. Anyone who takes a position is being "political," after that it's action and intent. Nationalism is not an act of resistance to systems of subservience. It is subservience.

Iskra may have felt like an anomaly in the metal scene, but they did not remain outliers for long. On May 1, 2008, Panopticon released their debut album, and the world of anarchist black metal suddenly expanded in a big way. Helmed by Tennessee-born Austin Lunn, the band was an explicitly anarchist project from the onset. They made that stance clear on the song "Flag Burner, Torch Bearer," where we hear Lunn bellow "There are just a few things that I believe: that people are born free and slavery is murder, that their property is theft, and government is tyranny. Anarchy is liberty!"

Lunn worked at a furious pace for much of the 2010s, writing and releasing slab after slab of righteous, folk-inflected black metal fury. 2011 saw the release of the well-received *Social Disservices* album, which centered on Lunn's horrific experiences working in the grim hell of this country's mental health institutions, where the most vulnerable are warehoused and neglected. It was a searing indictment, a heartbreaking lament, and a purposefully challenging listen. Then, in 2012, Lunn threw listeners for a loop once again with *Kentucky*, the record that really put Panopticon on the map, with its masterful blend of atmospheric black metal, bluegrass, Appalachian folk, and heart-rending coal mining songs puzzling and entrancing critics and listeners alike.

Kentucky conjured a uniquely American, nature-focused, working-class black metal aesthetic that has still not been replicated (though like-minded bands like Merkaba, Skagos, and Twilight Fauna have come close). As writer Craig Hayes explained in a 2012 PopMatters essay about Panopticon's anarchism, "Lunn's rearrangement of black metal's parameters is resoundingly intransigent; hierarchies and doctrines are swept aside. His work challenges orthodox black metal philosophies, but it also challenges his own artistry—it's revolutionary in spirit and substance."[6]

Across the country from Lunn (and only a few hours drive down the West Coast from Iskra), another impactful anarchist metal project was finding its footing in Olympia, Washington. In 2012, anarcha-feminist duo Ragana released *All's Lost*, a muted amalgam of grungy metal, screamo, and doom; a scant twelve months later, they would hit upon the last element of their sound, and cold, gripping black metal melded into their dark oeuvre. By 2016, they had written "You Take Nothing," a gut-wrenching anthem that was released the day of Donald Trump's improbable election sweep and would become the centerpiece of their game-changing 2017 album of the same name. "This constant power struggle is so frustrating—especially for women, especially for queer people—where people are taking so much from you all the time," Maria told me in a 2017 interview. "I wanted to keep the lyrics really simple—just 'you take nothing' over and over again—because I wanted everybody to feel connected to it."[7]

There are great storms of intensity, throat-curdling howls, and swells of brutality galore, but Ragana's music—and their anarchism—leaves space for emotional growth, for trauma, for catharsis, and for care. "Every song we write will come from a feminist, anarchist perspective, and we feel it's important to be political and to make statements and feel like there's meaning to our songs," Maria said. "I'm not against apolitical music but I don't really get it."[8]

"You Take Nothing" would prove to be a harbinger of sorts. Late 2015, and especially 2016, saw the floodgates for anarchist and more broadly anti-fascist metal burst open. Scores of metal fans and musicians alike were driven to a rude political awakening by the racist, xenophobic car crash of Donald Trump's presidential campaign, the brutal shock of his victory, and the ensuing sharp rise in hate crimes and far-right extremism across the US. Bands that had previously avoided political messaging hit the streets and made their allegiances clear, and new bands like Neckbeard Deathcamp, Feminazgûl, Trespasser, Sankara, and Putrescine formed with the unequivocal intent of showing where they stood in the battle against fascism. Big independent labels like Prosthetic Records and Relapse Records began signing politically outspoken bands like Dawn Ray'd, Vile Creature, Ilsa, Amygdala, and Primitive Man. Not every entry in the new wave of anti-fascist metal was a clear-cut anarchist project, but as an elastic ideology that can be molded and shaped to suit nearly any liberation-minded perspective and identity, anarchism proved to be a perfect match for many in the new generation of politically conscious metalheads.

This newly energized microscene grew and spread; new bands formed, new labels got involved, and the community threw itself into organizing benefit compilations and fundraisers. Problematic labels were put on blast, racist and fascist bands were targeted for deplatforming campaigns, and the idea of being "apolitical" eroded even further. (In 2019, I put together a two-day anti-fascist metal festival dubbed Black Flags over Brooklyn that highlighted some of these bands, and facilitated new connections between leftist metalheads and anarchist organizers). As tours were cancelled and gigs were shut down, there was of course pushback from the reactionary forces in the scene, as well as from metal fans who wanted to "keep politics out of metal." In the metal world, anti-fascism—in the guise of fearmongering and anger over "antifa"—became as controversial as the "social justice warriors" and "hipsters" of an earlier generation.

It was not only a metal problem, though; the antipathy toward antifa was amplified a thousandfold by the Trump regime and its allies. In 2020, as the furor around the presidential election reached a fever pitch and, as Trump scrambled to cement his strongman status and punish his enemies, a new Red Scare was born—one that took its cues straight from the Satanic Panic playbook. That summer saw a nationwide uprising over the police murders of George Floyd, Breonna Taylor, Ahmaud Arbery, and countless other Black people, and, instead of responding to the peoples' calls to address the virulent systemic racism and white supremacy fueling these senseless state-sanctioned attacks, right-wing media and government officials instead began blaming the unrest on "anarchists."

Black metal has never been much of a media darling for fairly obvious reasons, and when it does get some attention from the mainstream, it is seldom positive. The flattened caricature of funny-looking nerds sweeping about in capes and weird face paint and screeching about Satan does the genre no favors (even when the portrayal does hit a bit close to home), and its very real history of violence and bigotry adds a further layer of complexity. Anarchists suffer from a similar image problem, though they are far less partial to spiked gauntlets or smoky eyes. While the majority of anarchists can typically be found working in community gardens or creating mutual aid projects for their communities, the fact is that anarchists genuinely do want to see capitalism, the prison-industrial complex, and the state itself destroyed by any means necessary.

This tends to place them at odds with liberal reformists, the media elite, *and* the entirety of the right-wing (as well as various other leftist tendencies), so it becomes easy to fingerpoint and to scapegoat anarchists as bomb-throwing vigilantes with no concern for anything but chaos. That is not the case, but facts are of no interest to fascists. It was far more politically convenient for Trump to demonize any and all protesters as "anarchists" as a means to further criminalize dissent than to take five minutes to Google "what is anarchism," let alone to attempt to understand the nature of the peoples' complaints against him.

Metalheads got a small taste of this brand of state repression in 1994, when the West Memphis Three were imprisoned for decades on false murder charges simply because of their long hair and "Satanic" metal T-shirts. But the US government has been waging a slow-burning war on anarchists and other leftist political dissidents for centuries. It may have turned its attention to anarchists in 2020, but, before that, it was "Black Identity Extremists" and "Radical Muslims"; only a few short years before, there was COINTELPRO and the Red Scares of the World War II era and the 1950s. In 1918, under the Sedition Act, Emma Goldman and Alexander Berkman were deported to Russia because of their anarchist beliefs. It has never been a safe time to be an anarchist in this country, particularly if you are also Black, indigenous, or a person of color, and the same can unfortunately be said about the metal scene, where marginalized people are not always welcomed with open arms.

That is why anarchism's foothold in the black metal scene matters. It is a sorely needed and extremely positive development to see that it has become an established presence, one that will only grow bigger and more influential as more metal fans turn away from apolitical malaise or juvenile attachments to shock value and awaken to the possibilities of metal that actually stands for something. To stymie the fascist creep within black metal, anarchist black metal (and metal anarchists of every persuasion) will need to take cues from less musically inclined anarchists and revolutionaries. "I want the metal scene to grow and become more diverse and to feel safer and to not support fascist bands anymore, but I don't know how to do it, you know?" Maria from Ragana said in 2017. In her estimation, it starts small, with each musician and every band doing their part. "We're in this band, we play shows, people like us sometimes, and we'll be there to support anybody else who wants to play metal."[9]

Those blueprints are already there, and the principles of autonomy and mutual aid translate easily into a metal setting. "We all have different but equally valuable skills, and we just have to look to see where they can be useful," Simon Barr explained. He was speaking of mutual aid and community defense, but could just as well have been speaking to those who want to clean up the rotten corners of black metal's backyard. As Austin Lunn sings on *Kentucky*'s "Black Soot and Red Blood": "Meet them in the streets, meet them in the hollers, meet them in the hills and don't back down, don't back down."

"We need to cultivate a strong leftist presence in the scene, build our own networks of resources and support, and create more left-oriented black metal to crush their influence," Draugr, a leftist black metal artist who had a political awakening of his own and renounced his own past involvement in right-wing underground metal circles, said in an interview for this piece. He has since dedicated his life and music to the anti-fascist cause, proving that it is absolutely possible for even "apolitical" or right-wing metal fans to see the light and change for the better. "In the future, nobody's favorite bands will be NSBM, and those old bands will become ever less relevant as leftist black metal burgeons, moves the genre forward, and chooses instead to take on actual real-world topics like the struggle against capitalism. It's just a matter of time and effort!"

By caring for their communities, and standing up to defend the vulnerable and marginalized, as well as exacting a zero-tolerance policy for far-right infiltrators and sympathizers, black metal's anarchists have the ability to force real change within the metal world and to clear a path for the next generation of revolutionaries to take the stage. As Barr said back in 2019, "There is so much to be done, and there is no one better to do it then you."

Let the fires burn as a signal!

Notes

[1] Kim Kelly, "Black Metal Punks? Meet the Fascism-Fighting Dawn Ray'd," *Metal Hammer*, February 17, 2020, accessed March 28, 2021, https://www.loudersound.com/features/black-metal-punks-meet-the-fascism-fighting-dawn-rayd.

[2] Lucy Parsons, "The Principles of Anarchism," in *Freedom, Equality, and Solidarity: Writings and Speeches, 1878–1937*, ed. Gale Ahrens (Chicago: Charles H. Kerr, 2004), 30.

[3] Kelly, "Black Metal Punks?"

[4] Dylan Miller, "Beyond the Iron Gates: How Nazi-Satanists Infiltrated the UK Underground," Quietus, November 27, 2018, accessed March 28, 2021, https://thequietus.com/articles/25716-ona-fascism-nazis-folk-horror-underground-occult.

[5] "Interview: Iskra (Canada)," Obliteracion Webzine, August 18, 2010, accessed March 28, 2021, http://obliteracionzine.blogspot.com/2010/08/interview-iskra-canada.html.

[6] Craig Hayes, "If It Ain't Got No Blastbeat, It's Not My Revolution: Panopticon," PopMatters, July 19, 2012, accessed March 28, 2021,

[7] Kim Kelly, "Ragana Defies Genre and Gender on 'You Take Nothing,'" *Vice*, April 14, 2017, https://www.vice.com/en/article/3d9qp9/ragana-defies-genre-and-gender-on-you-take-nothing.

[8] Ibid.

[9] Idem.

Queer Kvlt Porn

ESPI KVLT

Being a queer, anarcho-communist sex worker in the black metal community has truly been both one of the most isolating and one of the most rewarding experiences of my life.

I was raised on metal, but as a teenager I grew up in the punk scene. Through the punk crowd, I quickly learned the only way I was going to survive in this world was by unapologetically being myself and never being silent about the things I believed in. Unfortunately, as I ventured into the black metal scene in college, I soon learned that being unapologetically yourself was not welcome (unless that version of yourself was the trve kvlt ideal, of course). I also quickly learned that if you were not silent, you could have half of your community with their backs turned to you in an instant. Still, I have refused to let any of that faze me, and as time has gone by between my introduction to black metal in 2012 and now, I have only gotten louder and learned to be even more unapologetic about who I am. Between marketing myself as a sex worker who loves black metal to coming out as queer to being a loud voice in the leftist metal community, I have not only managed to successfully irritate and deviate from a large portion of the black metal scene, but also been embraced by those I truly love and admire: The Trve Kvlt of Leftist Black Metal.

My journey into the black metal scene happened to begin at the exact same time as my journey into sex work. I had just left home for college and had, therefore, begun the process of blossoming into my own person. I chose the name "Espi Kvlt" as a joke (at least, the "Kvlt" part was a joke—Espi is just short for Espeon, my favorite Pokémon). I was definitely not kvlt, and therefore found naming myself that hilarious. I still listen to country music, pop, rap, you name it. I simply love music. But I also hoped that by choosing that as my model name, I would attract a very distinct crowd. My name is made up of one nerdy thing and one metal thing, and that is exactly the kind of porn I create (and let's be real, black metal is the nerdiest music genre). I will make a video dressed up as a superhero, then in the next video I will be covered in blood. I will make a video cosplaying as a video game character, and in the following video I will be wearing corpsepaint. I have created a niche porn persona of the nerdy metalhead I am in real life and managed to keep my porn persona as close to the real me as possible, with some exceptions (for example: I do not have a thing for incest, and I am not a woman, but if you saw a list of my porn, I have definitely made quite a bit of incest content, and I do play cis for the camera).

I have been accused of "profiting off black metal" and only pretending to like metal "for the money" by many a metalhead. The great irony in this, of course, is that my metal-themed content is generally my worst-selling

Espi Kvlt
2020
courtesy of
the artist

content. My average customer is not going to know the difference between me wearing a Mystifier shirt versus a Slayer shirt versus a Death shirt. My average customer is not in the alternative scene at all, and that alone is what tends to draw them toward me. When I spend hours working on a deeply personal black metal-themed porn, I do it mostly for myself. I do it for the art and my passion for this music genre. I go into those videos knowing they are not going to be top sellers, and instead I focus on creating something that shows my passion for the music. I am so grateful I am able to showcase all these amazing bands I love simply by taking nudes, and it is my hope that someone will stumble upon my porn and find love for a music genre they would have never even known about had they not seen my bare ass.

Espi Kvlt
2020
courtesy of the artist

As I began to venture further into my college career and further into the scene, black metal held my hand and lifted me up through some of the most traumatic, tumultuous, and horrifying experiences of my life. As my ex-boyfriend sexually assaulted me multiple times, *Sunbather* embraced me. It wrapped its cool pink riffs along my body, and as I listened to it, I felt sunlight pouring onto my face. As George Clarke sang about the bliss of death, I somehow felt hope. I took those lyrics as a reason to survive and to conquer the ease of simply escaping my torment by dreaming forever (and I now have those lyrics tattooed on my body as a reminder that if I could survive that, I can survive anything). When you are trapped in a personal hell, you become immediately self-reflective. You consider every version of your life where the pain you are dealing with could have been avoided. It was through this self-reflection that I conjured up a version of my life where the girl I had been in love with in high school loved me back. For the first time, I accepted that the feelings I had had for her were valid, not the consequences of confused teenage hormones. Soon, I came out as bisexual, and soon after that, the community and the music that had once held me up began to make me feel extremely isolated. After coming out as gay, I noticed the people in my black metal friend groups quietly drifting away. I began to feel like I no longer had a place, and I started to listen to more pop and punk (and pop punk) music. I threw myself full force into the sex work community, and, before long, I began to purposefully isolate myself from the black metal scene.

I only became more detached from the subculture after coming out as nonbinary. By that point, I had fallen headfirst back into the punk fanbase. I had become totally jaded by the metal landscape and avoided it like the plague. The few interactions I had with it through Tumblr discourse made me feel justified in my decision, as I was constantly misgendered and told I was not "trve kvlt." The "kvlt" in my name took on an entirely new ironic flair, as I rarely listened to black metal at all during that time, with one of the few exceptions being Deafheaven. I began to wonder if I would ever find a place in the subculture again. I even briefly considered rebranding entirely, changing my last name, and focusing solely on creating video game–related porn. I considered removing the "metalhead" part of my porn persona completely and catering wholly to the nerd niche. For a brief period in my life, I began to feel like an imposter. I began to feel that coming out as queer had accidentally resulted in a total rejection of the black metal community.

Then, something happened.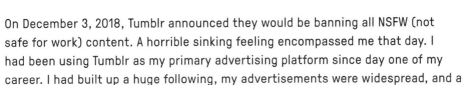

On December 3, 2018, Tumblr announced they would be banning all NSFW (not safe for work) content. A horrible sinking feeling encompassed me that day. I had been using Tumblr as my primary advertising platform since day one of my career. I had built up a huge following, my advertisements were widespread, and a majority of them had over one thousand notes (a number of the cumulative likes and reblogs on a post). I felt as though all I had built and all the work I had put in was going to be taken from me in the blink of an eye. Over six years cultivating a paying audience on Tumblr, and for what? I tried to make other platforms, such as Pillowfort and Sharesome, work for me in the same way as Tumblr had but felt I was getting nowhere. Begrudgingly, I felt my last resort was converting Twitter into my primary social media presence. I had used it as a business platform for as long as I had used Tumblr, but it always felt too impersonal. I would occasionally share personal thoughts and things going on in my life, but it was mostly with an intent to market. The only outreach I did was to fellow sex workers, and all the posts I created were carefully thought out. "Is this marketable?" is a question I would always ask before posting, unlike Tumblr, where I would vomit my thoughts carelessly into the void. Still, I was out of options, and so Twitter became my new home. To my surprise, my sales did not plummet as I had anticipated. In fact, January of 2019 was the best month of my entire career. Then I began getting personal on Twitter. Gradually. Unlike Tumblr, which had a massive anarchist community (cutely nicknamed anarchblr) that I had been fully entrenched in, my Twitter was completely cultivated around sex work. Therefore, I felt odd espousing every thought that crossed my mind, particularly extreme leftist rhetoric. Even though my following on Tumblr had been much larger, it always seemed that the platform had reveled in its unapologetic weirdness. Twitter did not feel quite the same.

Still, I slowly began to say more and more. While, at first, I had deleted most of my anarcho-communist posts, feeling as though they were simply "too much for Twitter," I started to let it go. The more I let it go, the further into leftist Twitter I swam. Until, finally, I went so deep I accidentally dove into the leftist black metal community. It felt like a rebirth. Everything I had become convinced could not be possible as a leftist who loves black metal was proven wrong right before my eyes. Then, just like that, my love for black metal returned full force. My desire to rebrand completely vanished, and I soon found myself making more black metal content than ever before. I found myself surrounded by others who think like I do and who truly want to make the black metal landscape into something bigger than ourselves. I, a queer anarchist sex worker, feel like I actually belong in this community for the first time in my life, and that is something no metalhead Nazi can ever take from me.

On top of the community I have found for myself, I also recently took it a step further when I decided I need to take a stand and make art that represents my values. While there are now plenty of black metal bands out there that refer to themselves as overtly leftist anti-fascists, I still believed I could contribute more to the discussion, so I decided to start a band called Phryne, named after a Greek sex worker. We play blackened grindcore and all of the lyrics are about my experiences as a sex worker, as a victim of abuse, and as an AFAB (assigned female at birth) person navigating the world and dealing both with experiences unique to those perceived as women and experiences unique to trans people. The other band I am now part of, Seas of Winter, is a full-on black metal band in which I take a more abstract approach to my lyrics, writing mostly about nature. However, we are also explicitly anti-fascist, and while writing about nature, I have found that most of my lyrics have been illustrating my anxieties over our uncertain future as a species as climate change becomes a present threat, as opposed to some unforeseen force of the future. I am now more part of the metal scene than I ever have been before, and through my art I am able to speak out as an active leftist, sex worker, and trans person in the metal community.

I am no longer afraid to speak my mind, make enemies, and fight for what I believe in. Feeling ostracized from the black metal scene taught me one of the most important lessons of my life: by letting those who seek to oppress others take control of something I love, I am letting them win. I am giving them exactly what they want. I will never make that mistake again. Black metal has entered a new age, and this age is one of violent rebellion. Being a leftist in the black metal collective is truly one of the most punk things I have ever done.

Espi Kvlt
2020
courtesy of
the artist

Those who oppose the notion that someone can be a leftist metalhead who makes porn can pry black metal from my cold, dead hands.

WHY PELLE OHLIN IS SO SIGNIFICANT TO ME

One of the first things people learn about me is how significant and influential Pelle Ohlin (known as Dead to most, though at this point I honestly feel a bit weird referring to him as such) is in my life. People not only hear me talking about him constantly and wearing shirts and patches featuring his likeness, but they also notice that I have tattoos of his corpsepaint, of his portrait, and of one of his pieces of artwork (which I do not technically have yet but will have when this is published). There are many contributing factors to his influence in my life: I feel a kinship with him due to my suicidal depression, which is something I have been dealing with since I was twelve years old. I have constant dissociation, which causes me to feel at all times like I am either dreaming or watching myself from some other world. Pelle mentioned something similar in his suicide note: "I'm not a human, this is just a dream and soon I will awake."

I am also drawn to him because of his obsessions with horror and death, which are things I have also been obsessed with my entire life and are the reason I am now a published horror writer, as well as a collector of animal remains. I have recently joined two black metal bands, and when I sing, I feel as though he is watching me and manipulating my voice. I feel him with me always, and I live each day of my life trying to honor him and his legacy. Though it may sound ridiculous to some, despite the fact that he died three years before I was born, I feel like I must have known him in some other life, as I feel closer to him than most real people I know, and I do not go more than five minutes without thinking about him. Part of the problem with all of this is that there is no way for me to bring him back, and I spend many waking hours attempting to fight off the pain and difficulty of knowing I will never actually meet this man who means so much to me.

One of the ways I cope with this reality is by using his influence to add new dimensions to my sex work. And one way in which I went about doing this was by making a porn about an exaggerated version of myself who will not sleep with anyone because they are not Pelle and who, therefore, makes men watch as I masturbate to a photo of him. This video, "Cucked by a Dead Dude," was widely circulated on Twitter, more than likely due to how outlandish it is, but it actually meant a lot to me, because I was able to put this pain of knowing I will never be able to bring him back into my art. While some people were put off by it and found it offensive, I did not see it that way. To me, it was purely a love letter to a man taken from this world too soon. Another thing I have done is write erotic fiction and publish it on one of my porn sites. Members can pay to access it and read my fantasies of intimate relations with Pelle. While I do understand why this puts people off, to me it is purely a way of coping with this awful situation and finding healthy ways of dealing with my reality. Because I know Pelle had an amazing and morbid sense of humor, I do think he would laugh if I told him about all of this. While my heart may yearn and ache for him every day, I am attempting to keep the memory of one of the most important figures in metal history alive and burning. All I want to do is make him proud.

Espi Kvlt
2020
courtesy of the artist

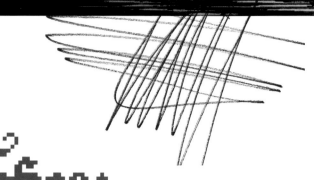

Malefica:

THE WITCH AS RESTORATIVE FEMINISM IN FEMALE BLACK METAL AUTOETHNOGRAPHY

JASMINE HAZEL SHADRACK

Who is she that looketh forth as the morning, fair as the moon, clear as the sun, and terrible as an army with banners.

— PETER GREY, *APOCALYPTIC WITCHCRAFT*[1]

Through my performance as Denigrata Herself in the black metal band Denigrata, something "other" has been advancing in parallel with my onstage persona. She has made herself known in our perichoresis or total artwork,[2] through our promotional pictures, artwork, and videos. While I had no a priori desire or conceptualisation to create Denigrata Herself in these terms, she has evolved this way nonetheless, birthing herself through me in defiant and emancipating glory. Denigrata Herself is a witch, a patriarchally loathed female archetype who embodies freedom of will, sexual desire and power. Witchcraft as a matrifocal ritual practice has developed,[3] particularly for Denigrata Herself and Manea (keys and vocals), into a feminist strategy of resistance that places the women in Denigrata as role makers who "evolve [performance] strategies which 'consume' their own biases as they expose and erode those of the dominant discourse."[4]

Denigrata Herself and Manea's embodiment of the witch archetype on stage and in our perichoresis uses witchcraft as restorative feminism within black metal, subverting its juridical conservatism and masculinity from inside its dominant discourse by positioning women at the front. Whenever women are at the front, that troublesome descriptor *female-fronted* looms out of the abyss like a specter of gender essentialism, waiting to herald the weight of miserable expectation and disappointment. I loathe this term, because women are considered an anomaly in popular music, either addressed and engaged with as exceptions to the category of "woman" or as sexualized objects with no agency;[5] either we are selling points or it is generally accepted that the band will be an aberration against the excellence of male musical practice and heritage.[6] In all honesty, being a woman in black metal is sometimes exhausting; however much metal and its variants claim to be a separatist sociomusical endeavor, none of us can separate ourselves from the dominant discourse of patriarchy. I argue we need feminist witchcraft in black metal as a strategy of resistance, because it arms us in the fight with the hegemony.

WITCHCRAFTING

Witchcraft, as a proto-feminist movement, is not a new concept, but where it does take on a new demeanor is in its setting; witchcraft is our locus for matrifocal black metal performance. When we started the band, our onstage aesthetics were only loosely formed, and they developed as the music did. When we had our first photo shoot with the world-renowned extreme metal photographer Ester Segarra, her perspective created (and cemented) how we were to be perceived. We looked like witches, the absolute of a female legacy, the ruptured power and trauma, that suddenly rushed up to meet us. It shouted, "Look! This is what you are!" and there was no denying it. This realization developed further with our first video for "Kyrie Eleison,"[7] which demonstrated a matrifocal engagement alongside occult imagery and practice, such as scrying, grounding, water work, and connection with our natural surroundings.

Figure 1. "Kyrie Eleison," dir. ©Cavan McLaughlin, 2015.

These concepts merged into an overall, encompassing narrative that positioned women at the forefront surrounded by the tenets and accoutrements of the craft. In black metal, occult renderings and aesthetics have been historically attributed to the masculine, because men were the ones creating the art.[8]

Denigrata is a feminist statement. To appear as witches, and not the stereotypical Disney villainess with a crooked nose and the warts of a crone, which is nothing more than an outward visual manifestation of patriarchy's fear of wise and cunning women. Our representation is wild, free, and obviously black metal, a musical form constructed through and by patriarchal hegemonic discourse that has no place for women in its creative capabilities.[9] Corpsepaint adorned each band member differently and was the chiaroscuro armour of black metal, the makeup that Drew Daniel calls "the cross-identification of the living with the dead, permitting the fantasy of their liminal border as a life-in-death. To wear corpsepaint while alive is to put on a kind of travesty of being dead, which is epistemologically reliant upon the audience's recognition of a fundamental artificiality."[10] Wearing it not only signifies the aesthetic connection to black metal and its heritage but also offers us a mask, a dramatalurgical methodology through which to perform and sometimes hide.[11] Initially, corpsepaint was worn as a black metal aesthetic signifier, now I wear my corpsepaint as armour, something Daniel accurately calls "melancholy self-preservation."[12] In the early stages of gigging with Denigrata, my corpsepaint was a personalized visual dramatic display, a face mask, not to hide anything but to exceed the boundaries of my subjective embodiment as a woman playing black metal. Having these painted marks on my face felt empowering and provocative; it located me as the true "other" who, in my everyday life, I experience as "woman," but, as Denigrata Herself, I am in more control of the construction and presentation of how, why, and when this "other" shall be confronted. Perhaps this can be perceived as "drama as artifice," but I cannot perform as my ordinary everyday self whose interiorities are thinking about my shopping list or taking my dog to the vets and my exteriorities are being addressed as "belonging to the hegemonically constructed category of woman"; the performance of Denigrata Herself subverts any kind of normality. Performing black metal is the antithesis of "everyday normal performances," it is "specific abnormal performance," for which artifices like costume, corpsepaint, and instruments are composite aids in attaining a voidic space in which to perform. However, when sexist or misogynist engagements happen after shows with some male audience members, I am often glad of my corpsepaint, because it becomes my shield.

This artificiality does not necessarily extend to the music itself. I am tempted to offer a musicological analysis of black metal compositional formats, but I cover this in my upcoming monograph,[13] mostly because the subject is complex and needs a lot of analytical room. What I can say though is that the physical composition of black metal, the ostinati, the polyrhythms, the melodic and harmonic motifs, are musicians writing popular music, albeit with a subcultural and subgenre engagement. Remove the distortion, replace the screaming with clean vocals, and the musical categorization shifts.[14] I find my black metal composition to be an honest and open creative process that is free from artifice and is welcoming of my trauma and pain and offers me the ability to navigate it all. Performing black metal is "the [my] body's dramatalurgical presence,"[15] which "disrupts the status quo, uncovers the understory of hegemonic systems."[16] It is subcultural, musical and performative poiesis, a conscious subjective construction.

The process of creating black metal is an alchemical conjuration that reaches its claws into the abyss of the soul. There is no artifice in the musical engagement (the cultural one exists in a more fractured, painful way); you cannot stand before the altar of black metal and not be prepared to face your fear, your demons, and the trickery of your outward persona. In black metal, you simply cannot fake it "till you make it"; it just does not work, because in-depth subjective engagement is not easy, and when you compose, perform, and create art in black metal, you have to dig deep.

Lauren Roberts's article "Dark Moon Magick: Rooting into Womb Power" states:

constant change, like a swinging needle on a compass, is the only truth we can count on to lead the way. Just as the Moon takes a plunge into the darkness, we too can dive deep into our own inner world. Here we can examine what serves, what does not, and where our journey will take us next. This is where womb power lives.[17]

When writing for Denigrata, this is what I do; sometimes that womb power is a broken chordal structure that washes over bass drum–led blasts and sometimes it is a brutal riff that quickly traverses the fretboard over hammer blasts and sometimes it is just a pure legato scream. Whatever form it takes, it is a witchcrafting. It is witchcraft.

MALLEUS MALEFICARUM

The term *witch* is not a singularity but a complex and multifaceted ontology that has shifted and changed depending on historical context. Attempts to define the term *witch* encounter numerous problems. Certainly, in Europe, the weight of history for witches is significant; it has bled down the ages from the burning times of the fifteenth, sixteenth, and seventeenth centuries, supported by tomes such as the *Malleus Maleficarum* or *Hammer of the Witches* by the now discredited Heinrich Kramer (1487) and witch-finder generals such as Matthew Hopkins, all answering to the most notorious royal witch-hunter, James I of England and VI of Scotland. This extraordinary, centuries-long gender violence and genocide marked cunning women as dangerous.[18] These horrific events remain deeply embedded in our ancestral heritage and common narrative—a knowledgable woman is an aberration and must not be suffered to live.

In more contemporary terms, Russell and Alexander's *New History of Witchcraft* goes to great lengths to identify the variables caught up historically in the term's etymology and provide the following summary:

Historians distinguish between European alleged witchcraft, which was a form of diabolism—that is, the worship of evil spirits—and worldwide sorcery, which involves not worshipping spirits but exploiting them. The English word *wicca*, which appears in a ninth-century manuscript, originally meant "sorcerer," but during the witch-hunts it was used as the equivalent of the Latin *maleficus*, a Devil-worshipping witch.

Similarly, in Donald C. Laycock's *The Complete Enochian Dictionary*, the term *witch* is aligned with the goddess Babalon. Laycock writes, "Bab—power, ability, possibility; Babalon—Wicked; Babalond—Harlot." She exists as an anti-patriarchal apotheosis that perhaps, unsurprisingly, has come to represent a wild woman. Denigrata Herself's representation of the wild woman and development of the "wild woman as witch," alludes to the *maleficus*, which aesthetically ties in with much of black metal's imagery and symbolism. However, this could easily be performed as a construct, puppetry, or mimesis, as something created simply for performance purposes. What has surprised me is that this has not been a case of "I want Denigrata Herself to look like a witch, because it *can* be the female in black metal, and it looks cool," it has come from within as "a force, not an order. Witchcraft is rhizomatic, not hierarchic...[it] defies organisation, not meaning."[20] Simply put, Denigrata's music makes me feel powerful, I feel like a woman who acknowledges the weight of patriarchy's gender essentialism and chooses to disrupt it. I can step outside of myself, outside of my usual material cultural reality, and I can be part of something different, something other. When I step into the role of front woman, I step into an altered existence, one where I am in control.

As the front woman, Denigrata Herself impels the performance, and "in witchcraft it is the woman who initiates."[21] This matrifocal locus positions the active, free, and powerful notion of womanhood at its center; it is the antithesis for black metal and its excription of women and of metal and popular music writ large.

Matrifocal means "an emphasis on the feminine in modern paganism without it being a matriarchy."[22] This idea is relevant to Denigrata, because there are women and men in the band. However, there is a focus on Denigrata Herself and Manea in terms of composition and the artistic elements of the perichoresis. Both of us, particularly while filming and curating the video for "Kyrie Eleison," instigated a reimagining of ourselves in matrifocal, witchcraft terms. We did not want to present ourselves as hegemonic constructs of femininity, to be subject to the male gaze, and if we could not prevent this, we wanted to at least disrupt it by *code manipulation*. Burns and Lafrance offer this term as a way of understanding othered meanings in a piece of music, but, because of their study on women in popular music, it is also connected to the representation of female musicians. They state that "as with any interpretive reception of [socio]musical conventions, the conventional readings do exist, but they may not be intended to bear that conventional meaning in a given musical composition [or performance]."[23] I apply this to Denigrata Herself and Manea's ability to manipulate the masculine musical and aesthetic codes by consciously presenting ourselves as witches and deterritorializing black metal signifiers.

Figure 3. Manea, photo by ©Ester Segarra, 2015.

Figure 2. Denigrata Herself, photo by ©Ester Segarra, 2015.

Manea and Denigrata Herself certainly evince a folkloric depiction, as can be seen in Figures 2 and 3. Peter Grey's *Apocalyptic Witchcraft* manifesto states that "witchcraft is the art of inversion...it is revolution and of the power of woman."[24] An asomatous passage, manifested through Denigrata, marked the way. Grey adds "witchcraft is the recourse of the dispossessed, the powerless, the hungry and the abused. It gives heart and tongue to stones and trees."[25] This speaks to the pastoral nature of black metal, my autoethnography, and to my performance as Denigrata Herself. Aesthetically our representations differ; Manea wears a long grey wig with different corpsepaint; she concentrates on linear specificities around the eyes and mouth and whites out the rest of her face. Denigrata Herself wears a long black wig, antlers and corpsepaint that runs from blacked out eyes down the cheeks and bleeds from the lips. We offer two definitions of the same dark womanhood; we are both creatrixes and destroyers. We have been told at performances that we look like witches, so whatever image people have in their minds from popular culture is aligning with what they see in us. We did not start out with this in mind, however; it has developed as Denigrata has, finding traction and evolving along the way. It is a nomadic deterritorializing of hegemonic femininity, of black metal's masculine frame, and has found a home with the most patriarchally hated of folkloric female figures represented by and through us.

In Denigrata's video for "Kyrie Eleison," we both appear as glitches and clipped images, the camera only resting on us for a few seconds before cutting to a different shot. This adds to our transient nature as witches, existing at the edge, as Grey notes, "thriv[ing] in this liminal, lunar, trackless realm."[26] The band emerging from the water at the end of the video is antibaptismal, because, not only does the water represent a sacred liminal text, it is also us emerging from its waters, not us being immersed into it; through black metal witchcraft we name ourselves as sacred and become our own "apophatic liturgy."[27] Throughout all of Denigrata's perichoresis, we are crossing the borders between noise and silence, fluidity and stasis, life and death. Our use of corpsepaint, the act of looking like death in life, mirrors the cold dead landscape of the video. The presence of band members as witches alongside witchcraft symbolism serves to locate a specificity of occult femininity. In black metal this would usually be a masculine engagement only.

Interestingly, there is a polysemia to Denigrata Herself being perceived as a witch. Brenda Gardnour-Walter, an academic who writes for *Dirge* magazine, published an article titled "Goring the Stag: the Satanic Antlered Priestess" in which she compared Denigrata Herself's role and appearance with Kay Walsh, the protagonist from the Hammer House of Horror film *The Witches*.[28] She writes:

In the scrotophilic musical subculture of Satanic Black Metal, Denigrata Herself claims female authority. Performing as an antlered priestess, she gives voice to the feminine abyss. She is not a plaything for male desire, not a "groupie" or a "girlfriend." Neither is she a witch at her cauldron in the forest, waiting in puerile

obedience for the arrival of Baphomet or Beelzebub. Instead, she is
herself the Sacred Stag, the great Horned God, the ruler of the night.
It is she who commands the ceremony and begins the dark dance.[29]

Gardnour-Walter identifies some of the enduring problems for women in black
metal and in popular music in general; the categorizing of women as groupies
or girlfriends, never musicians. She also states Denigrata Herself is "not a
witch" who is subject to the rule of a male deity. Here I identify a difference in
understanding the notion of the witch that recalls Russell and Alexander's earlier
point that understandings of this female archetype vary depending on location
and time period. My understanding and engagement with Denigrata Herself as a
witch is specifically feminist, not as the great Horned God of the *Dirge* article.
Anne Theriault, in an article titled "The Real Reason Women Love Witches," writes:

These days, the terms *witch* or *witchy* cover a broad spectrum of
things—it might mean someone who practices witchcraft (who may or
may not align with a particular pagan or neopagan religion), but then
again it might not. In some ways, 2016's version of "witchy" might
seem to refer to more of an Instagrammable aesthetic choice than
anything else—wearing dark lipstick and crystal pendants, growing
cute kitchen herb gardens, and arranging household altars of dried
flowers and animal skulls. It's tempting to write these things off as
being merely superficial affectations, but to do so would be a grave
underestimation. Beneath all that glossy packaging hums the same
idea that has tantalized girls for millennia: the fact that to be a
witch is to be a woman with power in a world where women are often
otherwise powerless.[30]

While perhaps some audience members or those in the black metal community
might write off Denigrata Herself and Manea's on stage appearance as superficial,
as Theriault states, this would be an underestimation. The "universal as male"
demography and the masculine behavior of black metal can attempt to disregard
this performance,[31] but the music of black metal celebrates the blackened
crossing of borders. The summary on Black Metal Theory's homepage, the "not
black metal. Not theory. Not not black metal. Not not theory. Black metal theory.
Theoretical blackening of metal. Metallic blackening of theory. Mutual blackening;
nigredo in the intoxological crucible"[32] of its music and its theory, infers a dark
space that exalts transgressions.

The alignment of black metal and my performance translates to Denigrata Herself performing with power and transgression in a musical subgenre that does not want to give her any. The witch as transgressive archetype means that Denigrata Herself can be read as a powerful woman existing and resisting in a masculine closed network of signification.

ABJECTING THE CREATRIX AND DESTROYER

Peter Grey states that "witchcraft is unbridled sexuality. In witchcraft, it is the woman who initiates. We challenge man to be the equal of this woman."[33] Seeing it written so clearly, there is no way of engaging with feminism, witchcraft, and matrifocal black metal performance without acknowledging the role of abjection. Julia Kristeva's analysis is the fierce angry voice that Denigrata Herself hungers for. For Kristeva, abjection is fear and revulsion as a response to a signifying system of feminine processes (menstruation, pregnancy, birth, breast feeding, sex, body hair, body size, urinating, defecating, vomiting—I would add to this that knowledgable women evoke similar abjecting responses from the hegemony), the repugnance of bodily functions that prevent the patriarchally preferred clean and proper body. It is hegemonic horror of a woman's body as the point of origin and its ability to "disturb identity, systems [and] order."[34] The female body abjects and *is* abjection. A woman's body houses the void that is the creatrix and the destroyer, she "does not respect borders, positions, [or] rules." The abject lies in the liminal space between the object and the subject, and that liminality is a threshold. Kristeva's abject is not "the object facing me, which I name or imagine [that] makes me ceaselessly and infinitely homologous to it; what is abject... the jettisoned object, is radically excluded and draws me toward the place where meaning collapses."[35]

As domains of abjection, Denigrata Herself and Manea append and supplement each other's performative existence in the same space, but the abjection operates differently. Manea performs an essentialist and, therefore, more recognizable "feminine," because she is fully a performance of "woman" on stage. Her musicianship denotes historically ascribed feminine roles, that of keys and soprano, so any abjection experienced is the expected patriarchal abject of a woman being a woman. Interestingly, her abjection also occurs through her ubiquity *within* a normative feminine absence, she occupies a space where women historically are *not*, inside a visible and orthodox hegemonic musical form. Denigrata Herself fractures that abjection by expounding a "place where meaning collapses."[36] She is a front woman who performs the opposite of what is expected; she is a performative antithesis, an anti-poiesic apotheosis of womanhood, musicianship, and hegemonic systems of performance and representation. She is fully clothed in black, wearing antlers and corpsepaint, playing guitar, and screaming. She composes on a black B.C. Rich Warlock 1987 Class Axe series guitar. She screams a piercing, shattering sonic assault. While occupying the same tessitura as Manea, the delivery could not be more different. It is a sound a woman makes when she is angry and/or in pain, and I am both. I am a woman performing an historically male musical role; I am the front woman, yet I do not sing. I am a composite of hegemonically inscribed male and female gender essentialism juxtaposed in one representation and role. That in itself is an alchemical conjuration and crafting of creative purpose that comes to rest as a hybrid and a nomad. Denigrata Herself is not a singularity.

In psychoanalytic terms,[37] both women can be read as castrated and castrators navigating abjection-as-hegemonic-womanhood. Denigrata Herself and Manea function as Kristeva's "two-faced mother [who] is perhaps the representation of the baleful power of women to bestow mortal life."[38] We birth the creation of music; we are creatrixes regardless, and this can also be seen through our aesthetic representations. This is juxtaposed against the juridical hegemony that insists on constructing and perpetuating gender essentialism. Black metal is an extension of this dominant structure; as women are not the phallus, we must know our place or be reformed into the mother. This echoes Sonia Vasan's work on death metal, titled "Den Mothers and Band Whores: Gender, Sex and Power in the Death Metal Scene,"[39] in that women must be considered as sexual objects or as maternal figures that prevent subjective empowerment outside of patriarchal trappings and gender encodings, hailing women as code keepers, not code breakers. And, of course, they must not be in control of creating art objects.

Denigrata Herself and Manea's castrating capacity ruptures black metal's standard practice; their occupation of black metal space positions them as outsiders, interlopers in this masculine dominant discourse. The orthodox systems of black metal put up with women under a begrudged sufferance as girlfriends, sometimes fans, never creatrixes.

According to Kristeva:

What we designate as "feminine"...will be seen as "other" without a name, which subjective experience confronts when it does not stop at the appearance of its identity. Assuming that any Other is appended

Both women in Denigrata are abjecting performers that infiltrate black metal's
paternal interdiction, provoking it to face the "feminine as unnameable other."
Denigrata's gigs expose black metal's vain-gloriousness and its anxiety of
an "obsessional and paranoid structure,"[41] determining female black metal
performers as a bluff or a menace, jostling and maneuvering to conserve and
insulate itself against potential usurpation.

RESTORATIVE FEMINISM

Whether Denigrata Herself and Manea are seen as black metal simulations,
witches, or Satanic antlered priestesses, I claim this process as restorative
feminism, because through my application of this powerful othered female
archetype to my black metal performance I am able to exist and perform in that
space with a more thorough understanding of the overt and covert patriarchal
strategies and discourses that inform and inscribe it. The archetype of the witch
as performative mode means that Denigrata Herself and Manea can take up black
metal space not just as women that are understood in patriarchal terms but as
witches whose performance erodes and corrupts its masculine juridical laws. The
witch is our code manipulation and our restorative feminism.[42] Through the witch
as ontological representation, we bring feminism to black metal with an active,
matrifocal performance as fierce, terrifying women; "we are the witchcraft, the
practice of [it] is one of revolution and of the power of women."[43]

Gayatri Spivak wrote one of my favourite quotations, which epitomizes what
it means to be a feminist when we stand against the monolith of hegemonic
patriarchy. She states, "it is only when one takes a whack at shaking up the
dominant structure, one sees how much more consolidated the opposition is."[44]
Women are crushed underfoot by patriarchy, and the moment we raise our heads
and speak up, we are seized and confronted by the totalizing suffocation of the
precarious liminality of our prescribed existence. We are nothing more than a
rupture, a breach, a crisis in the masculinity-as-perpetuity ideological veil that is
draped over us. Well, I'm done choking on it.

We are witches performing black metal, witches crafting, witches embodying feminism as resistance. We are the feminine as unnameable other. We do not seek permission, nor do we seek glory. It is enough to exist, to create, and to perform. We have no expectation to be understood, least of all by a dominant structure committed to misunderstanding us and keeping us bound. Peter Grey writes, "witchcraft [does] not expect to be understood or welcomed by the herd or at the hearth. We have our own company to keep, our loves and customs,"[45] and if "the witch is simply the final form of the despoiled Goddess, her immortality, and ultimately the form in which she will enact her revenge,"[46] so be it.

We are a mutinous performance that conjures our abjection as weapons, our witchcraft as armour. We stand on stage, in corpsepaint and antlers, wild hair and raven's feathers, unafraid musicians offering our incantations in musical form. We are the *malefica,* and we offer the witch as restorative feminism in black metal performance.

Notes

[1]Peter Grey, *Apocalyptic Witchcraft* (London: Scarlet Imprint, 2013), 14.

[2]Hunter Hunt-Hendrix, "The Perichoresis of Music, Art, and Philosophy," in *Mors Mystica: Black Metal Theory Symposium,* eds. Edia Connole and Nicola Masciandaro (London: Schism Press, 2015), 279.

[3]Charmaine Sonnex, *Extending the Non-Contact Healing Paradigm to Explore Distant Mental Interaction Effects of Pagan Healing Spells* (PhD diss., University of Northampton, 2017), 129.

[4]Helen Tiffin, "Post-Colonial Literatures and Counter-Discourse," in *The Post-Colonial Studies Reader*, eds. Bill Ashcroft, Gareth Griffiths, and Helen Tiffin (London: Routledge, 1994), 96.

[5]See the works of Monique Bourdage, Laina Dawes, Rosemary Hill, Marion Leonard, Sonia Vasan, Deena Weinstein, and Sheila Whiteley.

[6]Ibid.

[7]Cavan McLaughlin, dir., "Kyrie Eleison," *Missa Defunctorum: Requiem Mass in A Minor*, YouTube, May 24, 2016, accessed March 28, 2021, https://www.youtube.com/watch?v=oVrOrbXk25Y.

[8]See the majority of second-wave black metal bands from Mayhem and Darkthrone through to contemporary examples like Behemoth and Watain.

[9]Fandom is another issue entirely, which theorists like Mikael Seralin, Niall W.R. Scott, and Karl Spracklen have dealt with expertly.

[10]Drew Daniel, "Corpsepaint as Necro-Minstrelsy, or Toward the Re-Occultation of Black Blood," in *Melancology: Black Metal Theory and Ecology*, ed. Scott Wilson (Winchester: ZerO Books, 2014), 44.

[11]Dramatalurgical: from the term *dramaturgy*, a sociological position that examines micro-social exchanges for the theater, developed in Erving Goffman, *The Presentation of the Self in Everyday Life* (New York: Anchor Books, 1959). I apply it here through the presentation of my performance "self" in the minutiae of social interactions at gigs, often where problematic engagements occur in relation to women taking up perceived "male space" on stage. My dramatalurgical presentation of a constructed subjectivity for black metal performance allows for subversion of gender essentialism but does not protect me from sexist social interactions.

[12]Daniel, "Corpsepaint as Necro Minstrelsy," 44.

[13]Jasmine Shadrack, *Black Metal, Trauma, Subjectivity and Sound: Screaming the Abyss* (London: Emerald Publishing, 2020).

[14]Lyrical content is purposefully omitted because that is an essay in itself.

[15]Norman K. Denzin, *Interpretive Autoethnography* (Newbury Park, CA: SAGE Publications, 2014), 54.

[16]Tami Spry, *Body, Paper, Stage: Writing*

and *Performing Autoethnography* (Walnut Creek, CA: Left Coast Press, 2013), 20.

[17]Lauren Roberts, "Dark Moon Magick: Rooting into Womb Power," *The House of Twigs*, July 21, 2017, accessed August 3, 2017, unavailable March 28, 2021, http://thehouseoftwigs.com/2017/07/21/dark-moon-magick-rooting-into-womb-power.

[18]There are examples of men killed for witchcraft as well. My hometown of Northampton, England, bore witness to this with its own witch trial in 1612, which saw the dunking method used for the first time in Britain; see Nicole Le Marie, "400 Years Since the Northampton Witch Trials," *Northampton Chronicle and Echo*, September 24, 2012, accessed April 23, 2019, unavailable March 28, 2021, https://www.northamptonchron.co.uk/news/400-years-since-the-northampton-witch-trials-1-4280929. However, in the overwhelming majority of documented cases, women were murdered for witchcraft. According to Tracy Borman, "They resulted in the trial of around 100,000 people (most of them women)"; see Tracy Borman, "James VI and I: The King Who Hunted Witches," History Extra, March 27, 2019, accessed March 28, 2021, https://www.historyextra.com/period/stuart/king-james-vi-i-hunted-witches-hunter-devilry-daemonologie.

[19]Jeffrey B. Russell and Brooks Alexander, *A New History of Witchcraft* (London: Thames and Hudson, 2015), 15.

[20]Grey, *Apocalyptic Witchcraft*, 15.

[21]Ibid.

[22]Sonnex, *Extending the Non-Contact Healing Paradigm to Explore Distant Mental Interaction Effects of Pagan Healing Spells*, 129.

[23]Lori Burns and Mélisse Lafrance, *Disruptive Divas: Feminism, Identity and Popular Music* (London: Routledge, 2002), 48.

[24]Grey, *Apocalyptic Witchcraft*, 16.

[25]Ibid., 14.

[26]Ibid.

[27]Niall W.R. Scot, "Seasons in the Abyss: Heavy Metal as Liturgy," *Diskus* 16, no. 1 (2014): 13, accessed March 28, 2021, https://core.ac.uk/download/pdf/196350365.pdf.

[28]Cyril Frankel, dir., *The Witches* (London: Hammer Film Productions, 1966).

[29]Brenda Gardnour-Walter, "Goring the Sacred Stag: Denigrata and the Satanic Antlered Priestess," *Dirge*, November 5, 2016, accessed August 3, 2017, unavailable March 28, 2021, http://www.dirgemag.com/denigrata-Satanic-antlered-priestess.

[30]Anne Theriault, "The Real Reason Women Love Witches," The Establishment, July 20, 2016, accessed April 23, 2021, https://theestablishment.co/the-real-reason-women-love-witches-647d48517f66.

[31]Rosemary Hill, *Gender, Metal and the Media: Women Fans and the Gendered Experience of Music* (London: Palgrave MacMillan, 2016), 4.

[32]See *Black Metal Theory*, accessed April 23, 2021, http://blackmetaltheory.blogspot.co.uk.

[33]Hill, *Gender, Metal and the Media*, 15.

[34]Julia Kristeva, *Powers of Horror: An Essay on Abjection*, trans. Leon Samuel Roudiez (New York: Columbia University Press, 1982), 4.

[35]Ibid., 2.

[36]Ibid.

[37]I talk more fully about Denigrata and abjection in Jasmine Shadrack, "*Mater Omnium* and the Cosmic Womb of the Abyss: Nomadic Interiorities and Matrifocal Black Metal Performance," *Metal Music Studies* 4, no. 2 (June 2018): 281–92, accessed April 23, 2021, tiny.cc/hzbytz.

[38]Ibid.

[39]Sonia Vasan, "Den Mothers and Band Whores: Gender, Sex and Power in the Death Metal Scene," in *Heavy Fundamentalisms: Music, Metal and Politics*, eds. Rosemary Hill and Karl Spracklen (London: Inter-Disciplinary Press, 2010), 69.

[40]Kristeva, *Powers of Horror*, 58–59.

[41]Ibid., 60.

[42]Burns and Lafrance, *Disruptive Divas*, 48.

[43]Grey, *Apocalyptic Witchcraft*, 16.

[44]Gayatri Chakravorti Spivak, "Can the Subaltern Speak?," in *The Post-Colonial Studies Reader*, 2nd ed., eds. Bill Ashcroft, Gareth Griffiths, and Helen Tiffin (London: Routledge, 2006) 16.

[45]Grey, *Apocalyptic Witchcraft*, 112.

[46]Ibid., 26.

Righteous Violence:

ZEAL & ARDOR'S APPLICATION
OF AFRICAN AMERICAN FOLK
MUSIC IN BLACK METAL

LAINA DAWES

The 2012 documentary series *One Man Metal* featured three reclusive black metal multi-instrumentalists who described how their disdain for human interaction compelled them to play all of the instruments on their albums and not perform their music in public.[1] For the musicians, individualism was defined as the desire to isolate from the external world and focus on individual needs and concerns.

From a musical perspective, this self-imposed isolation represents the subgenre of black metal as part of the music-making process and as a badge of authenticity. Underground black metal musicians often create in a manner so their music will never appear in mainstream media, using purposefully disharmonic and noncommercial methods. Therefore, black metal "becomes a means to both preserve and protect the subject against forms of social expectation and conformity that insist upon the repression of life's ugly, evil and destructive tendencies."[2]

Individualism in black metal also represents the rejection of any socially conceived institution or morality. It is created to oppose anything designed to control, such as organized religious institutions or the government, as they represent a "homogenous image of 'moral public goodness' and an idealized adaption to the subject of social norms."[3] Critiques of Christianity, politics, or anything that infers limitations on the ability for people to live their lives and, in some cases, end their lives in the manner they choose is a common theme used in lyricism and its accompanying imagery. The decision to retreat from societal norms is seen as the ultimate dedication to the music and to individualism over social conformity and is encouraged.

Zeal & Ardor was initially conceived as a one-man musical project created by multi-instrumentalist Manuel Gaǵneux, but in the past two years it has grown to include five additional members. As the Swiss-born, black/biracial musician also records under the moniker Birdmask, producing electronic, midrange rock instrumentals, his followers were surprised when he released *Devil Is Fine* in 2016, a hybrid of various underground musical genres on top of an industrialized black metal foundation. Accentuated by Gaǵneux's layered vocals, influenced by archived field recordings of rural African American folk, blues, and spirituals sung by African American prisoners, the album was critically, if not commercially, acclaimed.

The album seems inspired more by the mythological and aesthetic properties of black metal rather than any substantial effort to keep traditional modes intact through live instrumentation. The computer-generated blast beats, an essential element of black metal, are thin, and the guitar riffs lack emotional depth. The idea of a one-man black metal artist creating their own soundscape is interesting, and the sampling techniques imposed on the melodic and atmospheric nuances offer an alternative view of what black metal can be. However, the listener is left confused as to the meaning of the cumulation of musical ideas and is forced to rely on verbal clarification from the artist. In discussion with Gaǵneux, journalist Catherine Fearns describes the album's concept as imagining "American slaves rejecting the Christianity imposed upon them, and instead embracing Satanism as a form of rebellion," an idea that Gaǵneux later confirms in another interview.[4] The problem with this explanation is that the comparisons between Satanism and African American folk music Gaǵneux employs to make his point contradict each other on factual, spiritual, and moral bases.

This chapter explores the implications of assuming that Negro spirituals, field hollers, ring shouts, and black metal are all types of music that, in Gaǵneux's view, are musically comparable. By citing interviews with the musician, exploring the cultural meanings within music created by enslaved African Americans and steeped in meaning outside of its musicality, this essay will look at what happens when these elements are paired with a genre and culture that is often nihilistic and exclusionary. Also, what are the implications in the merging of two different musical cultures by a biracial man who belongs to a marginalized ethnocultural community that has been vilified by black metal listeners and musicians? The obligation, if any, for an artist to acknowledge the social and political structures that discriminate against cultural and religious minorities will be discussed, and the ethical responsibility to avoid the creation of music and visual or lyrical imagery that perpetrates racial inequality will be addressed.

One of the desirable traits of heavy metal is also one of its highest detracting factors. By consuming the music and adopting its cultural signifiers, black listeners who are more vulnerable to racial discrimination at metal concerts than other ethnocultural communities, can access stereotypical "masculine" power denied to them in their everyday lives.[5] Also, masculinity is felt to be at the crux of the heavy metal lyrical themes, which are perceived by Adam Rafalovich as "ideological representations of manhood, demonstrating individualism through extreme domination, or conversely, through extreme suffering."[6] The music's energy invokes and internalizes a sense of power, challenging the capitalist, hierarchal contract of power imbalances within mainstream society that black listeners are often forced to internalize—it gives them more ability than they have in the real world.[7] While it cannot be proven that these ideologies impact listeners by shaping their individual views or compelling them to change their perspectives on race, religion, and sexual identities, this essay will look at how the black metal music genre and subculture transmit ideologies that alienate black fans from actively participating.

Gaǵneux's reasoning for creating was born of his penchant for posting his musical ideas on 4Chan, an online bulletin board where people can post anonymously, which has led to racist, misogynist, and extreme right-wing content. After posting some musical ideas and asking for some feedback, he received two responses that stood out to him: "nigger music" and "black metal." Instead of being offended, he saw a potential musical connection between the two responses and decided to create a one-off musical project to explore the similarities that inspired him.

However, there is a sense that Gaǵneux was more interested in being a provocateur than in creating a timeless black metal album. When asked why he chose to combine the two genres he replied, "It started as a joke. Something about gospel voices singing Satanic lyrics just really cracks me up."[8] Many interviewers and album reviewers covering *Devil Is Fine* had limited knowledge of what they considered the "samples" Gaǵneux interwove within each song to symbolize. One journalist described Gaǵneux's army-like bellowing and singing of spirituals as "sacrilegious hymnals sung to the tune of African American slave anthems."[9] Others described them as gospel chants, not understanding that blending abrasive hollers, shouts, and the sounds of clanking chains with ethereal church hymns makes no sense. All acknowledged that the mostly unfamiliar music came from the African American experience during New World slavery but were unaware of the meaning of each musical art form.

In his essay "Of the Sorrow Songs," W.E.B. Du Bois described what he referred to as "Negro folk music" as "the rhythmic cry of the slave" that has captured the vigor and ingenuity versus the beauty of America (which he believed the country has little of to offer): "It has been neglected, it has been, and is, half despised, and above all, it has [been] persistently mistaken and misunderstood; but notwithstanding, it remains as the singular spiritual heritage of the nation and the greatest gift of the Negro people."[10] "Sorrow songs" represent the mourning to underscore the pain, suffering, and intergenerational trauma that was, and still is, experienced by African Americans. Often described as "spiritual songs," they note and transcend the insidious racism that its orators experienced. The music served as the only true documentation of the experiences of African slaves. Some, according to Du Bois, demonstrate the carefreeness and happiness of slaves, but most often, "they are the music of unhappy people, of the children of disappointment; they tell the death and suffering and unvoiced longing toward a truer world, of misty wandering and hidden ways."[11]

Instead of turning to historical references produced by African American historians to research the social, emotional, and cultural meanings behind the songs, Gagneux listened to the recordings of Alan Lomax. In the 1940s, with his father, John, he went to the rural Southern states to record what they regarded as "Negro folk songs." It is unclear if Gagneux was aware that while the recordings that were used to develop the Archive of American Folk Song at the Library of Congress have proven to be extremely important to historians, musical archivists, and ethnomusicologists, their recording process was disrespectful to the men they recorded. Both father and son had a clear idea of what they wanted and would manipulate and, at times, threaten musicians to comply with their musical demands.[12] Recounting a terse exchange between John Lomax and musician Blind Willie McTell, where Lomax attempted to get McTell to talk about songs centered on racist friction between whites and blacks (which if he had, would have caused a lot of trouble for McTell), Karl Hagstrom Miller writes:

Black musicians had to remain wary of such queries, carefully assessing the intentions of the white inquisitor, for more often white southerners made such requests to gauge black acceptance of Jim Crow and ensure that they were willing to play by its rules. The wrong answer could result in reprimand or violence. Thus, even as Lomax hungered to hear songs of protest, McTell could not be sure of his intentions and appeared ready to take Howard Armstrong's advice to get up and run.[13]

When they recorded in all-black prisons to capture the authenticity of field hollers and ring shouts, Alan Lomax would bribe correctional officers to threaten prisoners to perform. According to a WNYC Radio segment about Lomax's recording practices, he reportedly said, "[t]he black communities were just too difficult to work in with any efficiency, and so my father had the great idea that probably all of the sinful people were in jail. And that's where we found them—that's where we found this incredible body of music."[14] Other historians, such as Dwandalyn Reece, the curator of music at National Museum of African American History and Culture in Washington, DC, believes that the targeting of imprisoned black men and impoverished rural musicians perpetrated racialized stereotypes. "African Americans are criminals, are illiterate. They are not serious; they are not smart. That 'authenticity' is rooted in having that kind of vision of what an African American can or cannot be."[15] One could surmise that the lack of credit given to the vocalists in the archives (available online) was because group recordings were conducted without the time or care taken to get the names of the prisoners. There is irony in being inspired by the recordings by historians who, most likely, did not have much respect for a good portion of the musicians they recorded to enhance a genre that has a reputation for racial and religious intolerance.

However, Gagneux has acknowledged in interviews the meanings behind what he called "slave music" and felt that there was a correlation between that and black metal. "It's a form of rebellion. Even if slave music isn't defiant, it's still like the triumph of the will of the people," he said in an interview with Noisey, *Vice* magazine's online music channel. "I think there are parallels with, say, Christianity forced upon both the Norwegians and the American slaves, and I wondered what would've happened if slaves would've rebelled similarly to (established black metal bands) Burzum or Darkthrone."[16]

His definition of rebellion is a bit confusing, especially when he refers to a musical inspiration. Burzum is a one-man band founded by Varg Vikernes, who, in 1994, was convicted of arson and the murder of a fellow black metal musician. As a young man, Vikernes, along with other associates in the local heavy metal scene, questioned Christianity and the Christian churches that they felt overshadowed the importance of the stave church.[17] The medieval wooden Christian buildings, some of which were erected during the Middle Ages, are an essential feature of Norwegian culture and had rapidly shrunk from twelve hundred to thirty-one during the second half of the century.[18]

It is unclear what Gagneux's point was—was he suggesting that slaves should have violently "fought back" to strengthen their rebellion? The comparison between angry young white men who used arson and pseudo-Satanic nihilism and music created by kidnapped Africans forced into servitude, who were often tortured, raped, and murdered, is insultingly weak. For hundreds of years, African slaves on American soil used spirituals, ring shouts, and field hollers that serve as both forms of communication and as archival resources to document their experiences through the Middle Passage and the spirituality they were forced to abandon. Youthful rebellion from white teens, while violent, can easily be dismissed as looking for attention and cannot be compared to the resistance through innovative musical forms that humanized a demographic forcibly brought to America to serve as chattel.

The origins of African American musical culture that spawned ring shouts, field hollers, and spirituals not only emerged organically but out of necessity not rebellion.[19] The music served as a way to communicate messages unbeknownst to the owners and overseers, and the songs assisted newly enslaved Africans in making sense of their new surroundings. This music also served as a way to stave off impending insanity due to the laborious, backbreaking work in inhumane conditions, and for the first African population to descend upon American shores, the harmonies and the spiritual lyrics reminded them of cultural traditions from home. Songs that individualized the singer served as a precursor to blues music, as they humanized the orator, telling the listener that they embodied the same emotions, desires, and hardships, in defiance to their position as subhumans used to justify inhumane behavior. Through his suggested correlation between spiritual elements and the (suggested) Satanism within black metal's ethos, Gagneux does offer an uneasy unison within his romanticism of black metal culture. On *Devil Is Fine*, emotional and spiritual discomfort is embedded within both genres, as European black metal artists, such as Burzum, often use Satanism and paganism and employ their country's folk music as a form of nationalism. While it is unclear if and doubtful that he did this intentionally, the album flips the script; while he offers a similar mood that highlights black metal's underbelly of darkness, his focus interrogates the deepseated and, I argue, justifiable, anger in the historical narrative of the experiences of African American slaves.

The enslaved have a reason to be angry, but Gagneux offers that anger with a sense of resignation, most notably on the title track "Devil Is Fine" On the single, he posits a machismo aggression in his usage of call-and-response ring shouts. The lyrics "Nobody going to show you the way now/nobody going to hold your hand now/Nobody is going to lead you the way now/Devil is fine" serve as a powerful statement that belies black metal's traditional usage of survival of the fittest. Surrounding the desperation to hold onto a belief system offers a different take, as the "survival of the fittest" is not based on one's skin color or nationality but on the ability to endure the unimaginable suffering that one can only experience when their humanity is denied. Gagneux's application of the black slave narrative, coupled with the unsettling clink of the silver chains that binds the men together and the slow introduction of strings and plaintive piano chords, emphasizes the feeling of captivity, thereby accentuating the considerable effort to retain one's humanity. It is interesting, then, that his interview responses are so trite.

SATANISM AND TRANSGRESSION

Black metal is one of the most provocative music styles within extreme music—and one of the most profitable.[21] There are two waves of black metal, the first originating from young Norwegian and Scandinavian tape traders who favored the music emanating from both the early 1980s new wave of British heavy metal (NWBHM), traditional metal bands, and the American thrash metal scene. Spearheaded by a spate of black metal bands that emerged out of Norway in the mid-1990s, the second wave of black metal marked a significant change in the culture, both in increasing its popularity and in creating a distinct musical culture.

Influenced by American heavy metal musical subcultures, such as thrash and death metal, black metal is often mixed with more musically palatable genres, such as electronic music. Some bands have also made a concerted effort to incorporate their musical and national heritage by applying either a folk-inspired sound or integrating traditional tales about their country within their lyrical content.[22] This wave also introduced an ethos based on a critical view of Christianity (a response to the emphasis of the religion that was seen as obliterating indigenous Scandinavian and Nordic culture), Satanism, and nihilism and, most notably, in the case of European bands, nationalism that, if not pointedly right-wing, was extremely conservative.[23]

In an interview with *Revolver* magazine, Gagneux discusses why he wanted to compare Christianity to enslaved people and European black metal bands. "It struck me as odd that American slaves adopted the beliefs of their oppressors and masters in their very personal music. If they sang the spirituals truly for themselves, it's hard to believe that they incorporated Christianity into it. So [embracing Satan] seemed like an interesting form of rebellion, at least in my head."[24] Two things that are tragically missing in his observation is the limited autonomy that enslaved African Americans had in both the pre- and post–Jim Crow South and the fact that slaveowners often justified slavery by reinterpreting Christianity. However, instead of their notion that religious faith would have a calming effect, it had the opposite effect, as slaves used the tenets of the faith against their slaveowners, arguing that their freedom was guaranteed—or should be—in the eyes of religion.[25]

There is a tradition of Satan and evil within Christianity, as well as a well-documented relationship between Satanism and its use in all musical genres.

Jesper Aagaard Petersen writes that Satanism is cultivated within the modern era through "various actors calling themselves Satanists or describing their project as Satanic."[26] They all have different ideologies and varying levels as to how they present their views in the public eye, and Petersen believes that the "grey area" that exists between the perform-for provocativeness and the extreme has been manipulated for various reasons. *Devil Is Fine* toys with the grey area, relying on the fact that iconography sells more than the actual meaning. From a review and interview published in *Overblown Zine*:

Slavery, cultural appropriation, Satanism; Zeal & Ardor has certainly laid Gagneux open to criticism with his potentially controversial subject matter, but he takes a fairly light-hearted attitude. His fans are referred to on social media as "Servants," and his merchandise stands are decorated with guillotines, stocks, and shackles, as well as Satanic candles. At the concert I attended, I watched a fan being branded with the Zeal & Ardor logo. I ask Manuel how he feels about all this.

"That was an artist called Luca Piazzalonga. Actually, he comes from the same town we all hail from, and he is a fellow with a lot of energy, a lot of ideas, and actual capabilities to realize it. Off the cuff, he said I might do a little something for you...and I think I was drunk I just said 'yeah great idea,' and a week later he calls me up and says 'how about a guillotine?' and so we were kind of ambushed by it all, in the best sense of the word."[27]

Transgression is a way for people to indulge in what can be perceived as the beauty of death, experimenting with thoughts and ideas that are avoided in open discussions within mainstream culture, and this is common within many music genres.[28] Georges Bataille argued that transgression is a viciousness that is contained within a particular parameter—it is limited, as it is a "violence that exceeds closure while paradoxically remaining trapped within its limit."[29] The limits, he wrote, allow for the experience of fear, horror, terror, and evil without actually having to subject or commit to thoroughly delving into evil.

If we apply Bataille's theory that the limits of transgressive behavior allow people to apprehend things that are outside of their lived experiences, this might explain the actions of Gagneux's fan base—the excitement and danger in participating in something so subversive is part of the culture. The problem is what happens when the branding, the guillotines, stocks, and shackles used to restrain, torture, and kill people who are seen as chattel are divorced from the reality and have morphed into twisted entertainment? Gaĝneux's blithe dismissal of what his music has created in his followers is disturbing.

RACIAL AND RELIGIOUS INTOLERANCE IN BLACK METAL

As black metal has always been rife with rumors and innuendos about the social and political worldviews of musicians and their fans, these tales make the participation of black listeners and other marginalized groups more challenging, and the participation of others is seen as a threat to the origins of black metal culture. A concerted effort to maintain the authenticity of black metal as the formation of bands spread across the globe has meant that exclusionary practices on the part of both the fans and the musicians have been prevalent.

The ideologies emerging from black metal's second wave are from Northern European countries like Norway and Sweden, with demographics limited in social, racial, and cultural diversity. Common lyrical themes that, for example, emphasize the indigenous culture of European countries and utopian communities are similar to Nazi propaganda materials. They are not explicitly racist in sentiment but suggest a desire to encourage the "return" to an era when the country consisted of a "pure race."[30]

Norse mythologies, popularized by Vikernes in both his music and writings, have reinterpreted history, which has led to "some individuals in the white supremacist movement taking this idea further into esoterica by mixing Nazism with occult mysticism or pagan religions."[31] The second wave of black metal not only brought an emphasis on controversial ideologies but also violence. A handful of prominent Norwegian black metal musicians faced convictions for burning down Christian churches, and two of those artists, including Vikernes, served jail time for murder.[32]

In addition to falling under the subgenre of black metal, Burzum is part of the National Socialist black metal (NSBM) subculture. Artists labeled NSBM are perceived as having blatant racially intolerant views, which separates them from nonpoliticized black metal bands. There is little difference in musical style between the subgenres, as many self-identified NSBM bands also take musical elements from other extreme metal genres to create a sound that is more attractive to a broader audience. Regardless of the difference between NSBM and other black metal, Ross Hagen notes that both agree that Christianity "weakens and enslaves" people, and that people are either "weak" or "strong"—with band members and supportive listeners being strong and critics being weak.[33]

Unlike traditional heavy metal musicians, such as Black Sabbath, who have been vocal about the music's origins, there are Eastern European black metal bands that have purposefully abandoned the traditional developments of metal music by avoiding African American blues music within their musical foundation. Vikernes is an example of one of those musicians that erase African American involvement, believing that heavy metal is not from any music of black origin. This suggests that the music is created for white audiences.

The guitar, a predominant instrument in blues music, is perceived by Vikernes (and also by other reportedly fascist bands that choose to eschew the guitar) as illegitimate because of its cultural origins within the genre. Blues chordal structures are a foundational characteristic in early heavy metal music, as artists relied on the instrument's ability to create the structures and rhythms derived from African American musicians. In a casual manner, which is unsettling because of his use of racist epithets, Vikernes explained in an interview that heavy metal should be used to transmit messages that can educate people about "Aryan music":

The guitar is a European invention, just like the synthesizer. However, the music played on guitar is mostly nigger music—and that goes definitely for all metal music. I have nothing against guitars, as you might know, a lot of classical music is played on guitar. If I made any more guitar music, it would be classical music. So, it has nothing (or better: little) to do with the instrument in itself... Instead of primitive, degenerate, subhuman mentality promoted by the nigger (pop) music today, we can educate and "heal" our race with Aryan music, promoting Aryan ideals like honesty, justice, honor, faithfulness, strength, courage, respect, nature awareness, and so on.[34]

While it is safe to assume that their perspectives are unpopular, there have been no public refutations of their beliefs, which suggests that others do not see these sentiments as being barriers to blacks participating in extreme metal culture. I argue that the silence in resisting not only the above statements but similar opinions expressed by musicians, fans, and record executives is the primary barrier to access and opportunities within heavy metal culture. American musicians have stated more often that the removal of the traditional sounds was to test the boundaries of what music can be—to create something original that matched their own beliefs and to challenge their creativity.[35] For the genres in which there are traditional heavy metal signifiers within the sound, Kahn-Harris believes that "extreme metal reduces musical freedom still further until it appears so that it can be controlled."[36]

"I grew up with black metal and listened to it excessively as a teen because it is a very teeny angst kind of music—this exclusive stuff where you're not allowed to do this or that because of whatever [reason], so I thought I'd just spice it up I guess," Gagneux explained to Noisey.[37] His reasons for gravitating toward extreme music are substantially similar to many young men and women but, as an adult, he seems to have little awareness as to the racial implications of favoring music in which the musicians have tried to erase the musical and cultural contributions of his ancestors.

The issue with trying to discuss how subversive philosophies within extreme metal are alienating is complicated, especially when music is so widely available via online and social media outlets and accessible to listeners across the globe. As cultures are developed through shared specific beliefs, following consistent practices that represent what is thought to be the "culture" in its entirety is imperative. Jeffrey C. Alexander believes that regardless of why people adhere to a cultural phenomenon, such as extreme metal culture, fundamental conflicts will always exist.[38] Because cultural stereotyping is so pronounced in the larger society, it legitimizes his belief that there is political and social strife. In light of the rise of nationalism in both North America and Europe over the past few years, this is a somewhat naïve and obviously self-serving sentiment. As an artist, he has the right to explore different sounds and samples to create something unique, but I am incredibly skeptical when symbols of resistance within African American folk narratives are dismissed as a simple accentuation to create something different from everyone else, without taking its historical meaning into context. Regardless of the artist's perspective that the music should be separated from their personal views, how one views Gagneux's musical decisions or lack thereof in the development of *Devil Is Fine* cannot be dismissed.

In black metal, the emphasis placed on individuality leads to a refractive result, as "interest-bound" refractions tend not to acknowledge the differences of others.[39] Using a simplified value system to determine who is perceived as a legitimate fan is often based on the experiences of the individual. If experiences between group members differ and are highlighted, there is usually agitation that shuts down any opportunity to explore challenging intradynamics that threaten to disrupt the subculture. The resistance to discussing the alienation of black fans is symptomatic of refraction, as the larger population of listeners do not acknowledge that the participatory and behavioral traits now include women, black, and queer fans, but that transgressive themes are hindering heir participation.

CONCLUSION

With *Devil Is Fine*, Gaǵneux aims to show the world his talents through the lens of black metal by focusing not on the music per se but on the symbolism of what the subgenre means to listeners, which allows for a certain amount of variance to defy its common perceptions. The darkness and anger attributed to black metal culture are perfect for exploring the imagined black rage, which in North America is dismissed as irrelevant due to the reluctance to acknowledge its residual effects within institutional, political, and systemic social structures, or it is feared, which justifies discriminatory behavior. That is not that unique; several heavy metal artists, including Iron Maiden, have relied on history to shape their lyrical content and overall aesthetic. What Gaǵneux has offered is a political statement in itself—how music can serve as a fitting soundtrack to a racist and violent period in American history that prompts similar feelings of isolation, anger, and grief. The question is: Is anyone listening?

In reviewing the interviews and album reviews selected for this chapter, it is apparent that the journalists were more concerned about how black metal fans would receive an album that incorporated the music by African Americans than in how African Americans would receive it. For instance, in an interview with the website Toilet ov Hell, journalist Jimmy McNulty asks, "Okay dude, let's tackle ethnicity. You pull off a fantastic 'black guy' voice: it's strong, it's soulful, it's convincing."[40] There is an assumption that black fans of extreme music did not factor into having an opinion on Zeal & Ardor.

This is indicative of a larger issue that alienates black fans from actively participating in their local scene, and Gaǵneux is just as guilty of this. After explaining the meaning of the branding iron by noting that enslaved Africans were branded as chattel, he willingly notes that there is always one, hot and ready, at his performance for him to brand willing audience members, as though he was passing out candy. In a later interview, he admits (while also noting that the idea is stupid) that the branding became a marketing tool at the merchandise table, as people who chose to be branded would get all of their T-shirts, buttons and other promotional merchandise for free.[41] The blitheness of his response indicates that he is not connecting to the brutality of the New World slavery that dehumanized his ancestors and is primarily concerned with appropriating their music for his own purposes.[42] Gaġneux favors his role as a provocateur over prompting a much-needed conversation about the intersections between music, race, and identity. When asked by the Swiss online publication Alpkvlt if *Devil Is Fine* has "subversive power" because of his usage of a genre commonly associated with racial and religious intolerance, he responded, "to be honest, I was not primarily concerned about this effect—the provocation is rather a welcome flavor. I find black metal mainly sounding interesting."[43]

Gaġneux's follow-up album, 2018's *Stranger Fruit* (the title inspired by the iconic song performed by Billie Holiday about lynching in the American South) represents how the success of *Devil Is Fine* broadened his musical output. With the addition of five musicians, including two backup vocalists, *Stranger Fruit* is a well-produced, musically diverse album that further explores the various tones of textures within the black metal genre. However, the use of field shouts, hollers, and bluesy spirituals becomes paradoxical: what once had the power to raise awareness about black music and history within a predominately white and male music culture is trivialized, as the emphasis on clanking chains and stomping on the single "Gravediggers Chant" becomes a worn-out cliché.

There is a possibility that listeners will find that the symbolism, whether applied as a marketing tool or not, in *Devil Is Fine* and *Stranger Fruit* resonates with them, perhaps compelling them to delve deeper into how African Americans used these vocal methods as a form of communication, self-identification, and in defiance against their oppressors. What is troublesome is that they will discover an important aspect of black American musical history that the music's originator did not.

Notes

[1]Jordan Radaelli and Michelle Rabinowitz, *One Man Metal* (New York: Vice/Noisey, 2012).

[2]Vivek Venkatesh, Jeffrey S. Podoshen, Kathryn Urbaniak, and Jason J. Wallin, "Eschewing Community: Black Metal," *Journal of Community and Applied Social Psychology* 26, no. 1 (June 2014): 77.

[3]Ibid., 77; Michael Moynihan and Didrik Søderlind, *Lords of Chaos: The Bloody Rise*

of the Satanic Metal Underground (Port Townsend, WA: Feral House, 2003), 40.

[4]Catherine Fearns, "Interview: Zeal & Ardor—Swiss Metal Is Rearing Its Ugly Head Again," Broken Amp, August 18, 2017, accessed April 23, 2021, http://brokenamp.com/interview-zeal-ardor-rock-altitude-swiss-metal.

[5]Laina Dawes, *What Are You Doing Here? A Black Woman's Life and Liberation in Heavy Metal* (Brooklyn: Bazillion Points, 2012), 46-53.

[6]Adam Rafalovich, "Broken and Becoming God-Sized: Contemporary Metal Music and Masculine Individualism," *Symbolic Interaction* 29, no. 1 (Winter 2006): 22.

[7]Dawes, *What Are You Doing Here*, 46-53.

[8]Jamie Coughlan, "Zeal & Ardor Interview: 'I Kinda Yell Satanic Stuff in a Gospel Voice,'" Overblown, June 4, 2016, accessed April 23, 2021, https://overblown.co.uk/zeal-ardor-interview-yell-Satanic-stuff-gospel-voice.

[9]Kelly Mason, "Zeal & Ardor's Manuel Gaǵneux, Black Metal's Rising Rock Rebel," Chimera Magazine, June 2, 2017, accessed January 21, 2020, unavailable April 23, 2021, http://thechimeramagazine.com/2017/06/02/zeal-ardors-manuel-gagneux-black-metals-rising-rock-rebel.

[10]W.E.B. Du Bois, "Of the Sorrow Songs," in *The Souls of Black Folk: Essays and Sketches*, 4th ed. (Cambridge: Chadwyck-Healey, 1999), 3.

[11]Ibid., 3.

[12]Karl Hagstrom Miller, *Segregating Sound: Inventing Folk and Pop Music in the Age of Jim Crow* (Durham, NC: Duke University Press, 2010), 80.

[13]Ibid., 79.

[14]Kurt Anderson, "How Alan Lomax Segregated Music," WNYC, February 5, 2015, accessed April 23, 2021, https://www.wnyc.org/story/how-alan-lomax-segregated-music.

[15]Ibid.

[16]Kim Kelly, "The Real Story Behind the Spiritual Black Metal Blues of Zeal & Ardor's *Devil Is Fine*," Noisey, July 7, 2016, accessed April 23, 2021, https://noisey.vice.com/en_ca/article/6wqvnb/zeal-and-ardor-interview.

[17]Moynihan and Søderlind, *Lords of Chaos*, 82.

[18]Ibid.

[19]Shane White and Graham White, *The Sounds of Slavery: Discovering African American History through Songs, Sermons, and Speech* (Boston: Beacon Press, 2005), 9.

[20]Dawes, *What Are You Doing Here*, 56.

[21]Ross Hagen, "Musical Style, Ideology and Mythology in Norwegian Black Metal," in *Metal Rules the Globe: Heavy Metal Music around the World*, eds. Jeremy Wallach, Harris M. Berger, and Paul D. Greene (Durham, NC: Duke University Press, 2011), 181.

[22]Vivek Venkatesh, Jeffrey S. Podoshen, David Perri, and Kathryn Urbaniak, "From Pride to Prejudice to Shame: Multiple Facets of the Black Metal Scene within and without Online Environments," in *Educational, Psychological and Behavioral Considerations in Niche Online Communities*, eds. Vivek Venkatesh, Jason Wallin, Juan Carlos Castro, and Jason Edward Lewis (Hershey, PA: ICI Global, 2014), 371.

[23]Hagen, "Musical Style," 192.

[24]J. Bennett, "Slavery and Satanism: Inside Zeal & Ardor's Controversial Take on Black Metal," *Revolver*, August 31, 2017, accessed April 23, 2021, https://www.revolvermag.com/music/slavery-and-Satanism-inside-zeal-ardors-controversial-take-black-metal.

[25]Amina Gautier, "Reviewed Work: *Hell without Fires: Slavery, Christianity, and the Antebellum Spiritual Narrative* by Yolanda Pierce," *African American Review* 41, no. 4 (Winter 2007): 819, accessed April 23, 2021, https://tinyurl.com/jyvjra22.

[26]Jesper Aagaard Petersen, "Smite Him Hip and Thigh: Satanism, Violence, and Transgression," in *Violence in New Religious Movements*, ed. James R. Lewis (Oxford: Oxford University Press, 2011), 352.

[27]Coughlan, "Zeal & Ardor Interview."

[28]Keith Harris, "'Roots?' The Relationship between the Global and the Local within the Extreme Metal Scene," *Popular Music* 19, no. 1 (January 2000): 29.

[29]Joseph Libertson, "Excess and Imminence: Transgression in Bataille," *Comparative Literature* 92, no. 5 (December 1977): 1013.

[30]Hagen, "Musical Style," 192.

[31]Nicholas Goodrick-Clarke, *The Occult Roots of Nazism: The Ariosophists of Austria and Germany 1890-1935* (Wellingborough, UK: Aquarian Press, 1985).

[32]Moynihan and Søderlind, *Lords of Chaos*, 193; Keith Kahn-Harris, "'You Are from Israel and That Is Enough to Hate You Forever': Racism, Globalization, and Play within the Global Extreme Metal Scene," in Wallach, Berger, and Greene, *Metal Rules the Globe*, 215.

[33]Hagen, "Musical Style," 193.

[34]Chris Mitchell, "Interview with Varg Vikernes," Burzum Website, October 5, 2005, accessed April 23, 2021, http://www.burzum.org/eng/library/2005_interview_metalcrypt.shtml; originally published in *Metal Crypt E'zine*.

[35]Albert Mudrian, *Choosing Death: The Improbable History of Death Metal and Grindcore* (Port Townsend, WA: Feral House, 2004), 34.

[36]Keith Kahn-Harris, *Extreme Metal Music and Culture on the Edge* (Oxford: Berg, 2006), 34.

[37]Kelly, "The Real Story Behind the Spiritual Black Metal Blues of Zeal & Ardor's *Devil Is Fine*."

[38]Jeffrey Alexander, "Three Models of Culture and Society Relations: Toward an Analysis of Watergate," *Sociological Theory* 2 (1984): 292.

[39]Ibid. 297.

[40]Jimmy McNulty, "A Conversation with Zeal & Ardor (Manuel Gaǵneux)," Toilet ov Hell, June 16, 2016, accessed April 23, 2021, http://www.toiletovhell.com/a-conversation-with-zeal-and-ardor-manuel-gagneux.

[41]Michael Hann, "Zeal & Ardor: Meet the Black Metal Bluesman Who Brands His Fans," *The Guardian*, May 22, 2018, accessed April 23, 2021, https://www.theguardian.com/music/2018/may/22/zeal-ardor-black-metal-bluesman-brands-fans.

[42]McNulty, "A Conversation with Zeal & Ardor."

[43]Von Huz, "Die Provokation ist eher ein willkommener Beigeschmack," Alpkvlt, January 21, 2017, accessed April 23, 2021, http://alpkvlt.ch/die-provokation-ist-eher-ein-willkommener-beigeschmack; translation by the author.

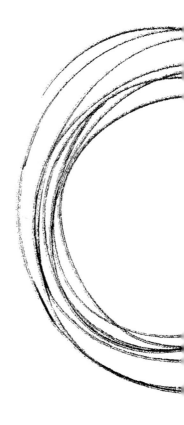

Queer Rot

JOSEPH RUSSO

> And no marvel, for Satan himself is transformed into an angel of light.
>
> —CORINTHIANS 11:14

The contention of this experimental/autoethnographic polemic is that contemporary ethnographic practice could stand to benefit from the interventions of black metal and queerness as genres of rotting form. Here, black metal and queerness are affective genres whose romantic end is to rot the discursive, conceptual, and bodily event of the category. I call these ends romantic, because the first question one must ask of a form that apparently seeks the dissolution of form is: How is openness regimented? How can the specificity and adherence to genre, vital and generative encounters with the world, emerge from deterioration? Queerness's history as a matter of scrutiny is brimming with divergences. Factional elements claim the function of queerness as a slippery dyad; it is by turns subjected/subjectless, generative/destructive, a matter of language, a matter of action, a matter of being. It is playful naïveté and serious wisdom, profane and sacred. I write of queerness as a genre in order to speak to these textures, for queerness is nothing if not a mixed genre. What I return to here and what informs the structure of this piece is Edelman's "the no, the not, negation in being,"[1] queerness as a genre with a goal to rot genres, to rot being in itself. Queerness's agency has been spoken of, and here its agency is always turned toward that antisocial thesis, unseeking the social.

Second, the turn to theoretical work on black metal proliferates a varied number of utilities. I have written elsewhere on the genres of black and death metal as rot genres.[2] In this sense, black metal and queerness have something in common; they are genres that fluctuate between seeking and unseeking. Berlant and Edelman have brought to the table the possibility of the negative as bound up within the social, the negative as a disorganization of self.[3] This experiment is also in line with the project of queer necropolitics,[4] and the ethnographic writing below attempts to face fully the frame of death-in-life, not only for queers but for the Southeast (SE) Texan scene in which I found myself as an ethnographer; a pocket of contemporary America rife with abandonment and negativity that proliferates in a mythos of life-as-rot. In this spirit of negativity, rot is a way of dwelling within disrepair and the necropolitical as a process.

This contention is also informed by a sort of playful bitterness aimed at the current state of the social sciences that reviles the training and deployment of ethnographic researchers as functionaries whose aim is to further the livelihood of an Academy that bases itself on the detection and critique of intact forms. It has become pertinent, as Stewart insists, to strategize methods of "sidestepping the dualist dead ends of modernist, humanist social science and its unfortunate affective habits of snapping at the world as if the whole point of being and thinking is just to catch it in a lie."[5] In this instance, the strategy is to enact a rotting in the very event of this piece of writing. To intensely, perhaps recklessly, melt the commensurable, distinct rigidity of ideas knowing that even this method, itself a well-practiced one, runs the risk of replicating what it rejects or just screaming into the void. It runs that risk with the pleasure enacted in an explosion of queer laughter or a shredded scream from a corpsepainted maw.

Form rots. Better, form is rot. Degradation assails it even upon the peaks of its most sacred limit. No air is so pristine as to ward off the degradation of form; it is at most waylaid for a breath's turn by something they call suspense—waylaid in the wallowing of the vitality illusion. The wanton lie of intact materials must be the peskiest fulcrum of thought. It governs, sweeps with cunning its devotees into the rush of its purposeful lie. It structures the group, the thought, the idea, the event itself. It is the illusion of this cohesion, this blooming rather than degrading of the Thing, upon which all gestures are based—from the building up of great societies to the careful moment of self-recognition. We see in the putrid mirror a thing intact, and not its degradation now and now and now. The trap of the ethnographer is twofold—it flattens the Thing into the viewed and, therefore, witnesses classified encounters: ways, flows, types, and genres. I wish to dwell in the space Alexander Galloway identifies between the flow/flux and the structure of forms.[6] Two genres within which this view is enacted are queerness and black metal—the genres, which became emergent in the fevered adolescence of my generation, and which seemed to entwine antennae, to speak without words—which is to say, I saw something queer in metal and something metal in queer. Rot here must be preserved as a mythic process—it must not be swayed by interventions of the laboratory or the church—the swarm of life that brings rot, the return of the body to the earth in some cycle of life—these are beside the point. It does not matter that maggots are alive or that we become dirt when the body gives way—rot is a structure that does something.

Despite the aspirational tendencies toward categorical absolutions, which in the humanities and social sciences are almost always superficial commitments to rot, what is attained in the end is only a reveling in shift, rot's more puritanical cousin. It is often called flux, in a wide swath of tracings from the Heraclitean river to the postmoderns. Much of contemporary academia is based in this marvel, a frankly self-congratulatory habit of finding things *here* instead of *there*, smug in the surety of the villain, the bad people somewhere, the big bad state, absorbing the nods and kneading of chins. Critique expends itself this way, upon the impasse of *knowing better*, and makes way for the most vibrant and persistent forms of talk—what they recoil from and call post-truth, not having the vision to realize their own hand in this manifestation. Our venomous and beautiful broken atmosphere: a rotting amalgam of fleshly stupidity, category fetishism, and endless bickering. This incarnation of modern leftism stops at the level of the debate, the public telling off, the strongly worded status update. And that cadre of the Academy, which emblazons itself with queerness as a mode of fashion, is content to locate and fetishize, content with the whiff of disruption. It has daddy issues with normativity, that great canard. We want it and see it everywhere, yet it does not exist. A stick in the gears for a moment and we have queered the text. The contributions of the best early queer theorists were that they understood play[7]—and play is debased in the self-seriousness that has become academic *rigor mortis*. Seeing queerness everywhere does nothing to rend the fabric of the category's fascism. But the task is not so daunting. Just to sit for a moment in the world that resides outside of this myopic purview, the Starbucks of easy queer leftism, is enough to know this brutality, which is preferable to an illusion. Here, rot is not flux. It serves an end. It conserves itself on being the unmentioned inevitable terror of the populace. Gestures evoke it, cinematic, aural gestures played out in the lived scene of people in the desperate climes and backwaters of this falling kingdom, this epicenter of rot that is no longer just America. America is masked beneath a visage of illusory intact form. The space of rot between the mask and the face beneath swarms with arcane processes. The early queer theorists vivisected the intact corpus, revealing pores, chasms, a body already in degradation. Rot was a sort of conceptual play for them, an almost mystical engagement with showing all manner of bodies in trouble, and it was done with the smile of a trickster god, a jester lifting up the robes of the king to reveal skinny legs. But the trick, repeated ad nauseam, loses its smile. "Everything we can know is full of interesting holes" is not the same thing as "everything is everything."

Ethnographers were perhaps the most blatant of form seekers. So, it is with reluctance that they admit into their taxonomic collections anything that unseeks. Fixing lived reality into genre while playing about with form. Putting culture in places—but what is a culture if not a fetid and rotting specimen? And for so long, culture was *elsewhere*, and it was thriving. Even as we stomped on it with our rifle butts. The subjects of these explorations were "resisting," and they were "coping," and they were "innovating"—they were doing and generating and being and growing under and despite the imperial lash. And now the good benevolent ethnographer wants to help them decolonize, as if the dull infection of the colony was not gift enough. But having returned home to the locus of rot that is the American scene, they find something now to see there: it is fundable thought. Trumplandia scowled them into this interest, but no matter. Here the genres bewilder us if we spend time looking. Black metal, like queerness, is a genre of the unseeker, dripping ironically with a fascistically implemented aesthetic regime. It mocks our efforts over the blastbeat. A genre that hides its gaze from us under heavy black manes. A genre bound up in the bad feeling of American mythos, a feeling that obsesses our youth even still, our youth whose gazes are fixed upon the altars of bad feeling, the rotting ciborium that contains the worst communions, the filthiest wafers of loss and degradation. Black metal is a genre of the unseeker, at least at the surface of things, and for this it is troubling in the once rampant parades of obsessed youth, who the hysterical nightly news had suicide pacting all over God's country.

Cyclical blackening, no explicit politics, no punk rock indignation. It all came out later in the parasitic attachments of white nationalist homoeroticism to black metal. But at its core a gesture toward the void, the unseeking place. Ouroboros of rot—the play between rot as content and rot as form. A chant of depredation enacted in black metal by a rotting, a yowling beast song, a voice in aural disrepair. Shredded—what better predilection than through this form, aestheticized in the erotic sylvan, blackened, dressed in the tropes of various Dionysian revelries, abstract Vikings, and such. Masculinity unbound in an ahistorical travesty. What better manner of play than in the felched sprawl of the exurban strip-malled byways of our barren Midwest, our fecund Deep South, our fentanyl-aspirated New England, our voided palm West Coast? What better parasitic attachment than the thing obscured from its source in some abstract Norse and brought to the rot zone, the biggest and festering beast? That is America. This is a shot in the dark, an experiment with form that with trepidation jumps onto the great bucking back of Texas, a wayward parasite, to find what it wants there: a scene proliferating in the symbols and symptoms of queerness and black metal, a scene replete with vultures, the material blackening of racist legacy and social death, bodies funneled mercilessly through refinery logics, the place-as-tomb, a regional event composed of all of the elements these genres worship. They say everything is bigger in Texas. And this is undeniably true of the sky, the bodies enthroned upon Rascals ferrying them through parking lots, up and down supermarket aisles. Bigger putrefaction, more to rot, and more pockets to find rot in. In Texas, when an utterance requires reverence, it is followed by "I tell you what"—the utterance is also bigger.

Sepulchral madness, cabin fever of forests, finds its home in the Piney Woods. Lousy with rot, the sloughing off of old fleshliness, remnants of the pine beetle scourge. A tree here is a thing heavier than a placeholder for life. A tree here is a scarred and treacherous husk. The forest floor strata: loblolly needles, nutria rat corpses, kudzu detritus, creek matter. Decay retches the meager scene out, leaving bits in the esophagus scorching the lining in digestive acids. A trail from the mouth to the gnarled fecundity. Remembering the flatulent loam, halfburied rusty scythe, on this earth where no cotton would grow. The farted imprint, not memory, of the escaped slaves, shady merchants, the obliterated cannibal Karankawa, banished Caddo. A neverland of shadesong in the kingless days before that diarrheal spume burst forth from Spindletop: oil.

And then the coming of the long dead barons, the uproot and the upswell: Lucas, McFaddin-Ward, Dowlen, Lutcher-Stark, King Vidor. In Exxon blue, in radiation rose. The fisting of the land into treacherous flatness, the making of the beige city of Beaumont, America's gaping gusher. Boomtown—the place where industry forced the rubes to mix with the blacks who came for work and were shunned off of the tight, contracted bus routes, sat steadfast at lunch counters in places called the Pig Stand, now demolished, debased with condiments, hands held to braziers, spat upon. Lynching was an American pastime and in the old photographs showing the rabble smiling after the deed, no eyes glint as bright as a young white Texan man standing beneath a hanging black corpse, facing the camera with hat cocked in abandonment, a sexual gleam. And later the great white riots burning down the black neighborhoods in the 1940s, the gnarling in of the black community in the face of treachery, murder, torment. The cloistered Pear Orchard, a black neighborhood in Beaumont, where whites were admitted under supervision of escort. The great turning away from the rot of the boomtown factory deaths, already beginning to kill off the warring factions.

Beaumont, home of the largest Dalmatian-spotted fire hydrant. The Rat Pack had their own tunnel from the hotel to the theater back in the 1950s—this fart joke of there once being a rabble here who chased down celebrities. Where Ms. Barbara Lynn stood up and warned us in 1962 not to lose a good thing, strumming a left-handed Stratocaster, incanting the deathways of her gnarled Texas. Now the downtown is intact and peopled by zombie absentee commuters and the steadfast old queer gangs that endured the firebombing of their moldering nightclubs and whose drag queens fall from roofs, fight dogs in the street, and regale each other with vicious nicknames and betrayals, redneck Genet. One has fingernails that are a meter long, another tells and retells a story of her childhood friend, raped with a sanding drill bit by a group of men after he batted an eyelid wrong at his daddy's friends, perforated into a hobbling howling jackal child. A corrective bleeding out in the Piney Woods somewhere.

They recall the young golden Texan boys who were taken in the streets to be dealt with elsewhere, corpses found by an old psychic lady in a muumuu way out in the swamprot, reading glasses on a chain down far on her nose, a Charon librarian pointing an old finger to the spot where he had been stuffed, stomach full of cattails and gator-gnawed. The rouge thick on her jowls, she found all the kidnapped queers in those days. Their signal to her was a rosebudding rectal firework in the miasmic factory sky, a terrible oracular laughter in which she caught herself in the evening in front of the TV watching *The Golden Girls*, sudden gasping at the peripheral presence of a man in the shadow of her dining room with a cigarette hanging from his mouth. He whispered to her, George Jones lyrics or obscure laments or sometimes the precise coordinates of their floating or sunken remains. It was unclear if he was the murderer or the victim, being a blurry redneck avatar.

Now queer militia dreaming inhabits these forests abutting the rice fields, secreted away in the embarrassment of morning, cattle egrets grazing out in the mist—its totem an askew stack of cans of Keystone. The trainees are evening initiates, townies gritting their teeth, days cuckolded in cubicles, hanging IVs in the rear of Acadian ambulettes, forced grins inherited from dead aunts (the higher the hair the closer to God) through the venom at corpulence of suffering uncles, under a duress that something like "normativity" barely gestures toward. Venom is a sticking hate, is big, Texas big, the putrefaction of their days unfolds before them like no partygoer could ever fathom, here at the edge of what can be lived. The rural is in this sense not a place but a zone of rot, conceptual only in speaking it but in its basest truth a felt zone. Cities can be rural. Myth is not mere untruth but imbued with felt states, and this zone is the state of the knowledge of pestilence. On the weekend evenings thick with miasmic fog from the Goodyear plant they shoot bottles, trees, targets, sometimes each other. Jesus take the wheel. Back between Fannett and Cheek (and how precise is its naming, a Skoal scar branded in the mouth—"Uncle Jimmy had half his face taken off after that cancer took his tongue and that face was just a-floppin' like an empty rubber mask, brother, I tell you what."). Now they gather in Cheek, TX, and shoot each other with rifles and rut with tobacco spit slick on their dicks—sloppy communion unfurled beneath banners of blight. Green sky, green smoke. Swamp beasts chuck-chucking out in the dark parts, loupgarou specters just over the Louisiana border, the gnashing.

Human life costumed in fleshsacks in clumsy choreographed drudgery—enraptured by some waltz out of the leprous shell of armadillo roadkill across Texas to the sodden flat pocket of the Golden Triangle's abominations, brazenly necrotic. An agape maw of particulate matter blasting forth out of refinery stacks, rectums of industry spouting into good Texan lungs mixing with the dreadsmoke of cowboy killers, burnpiles stoked with Carolina curs and woodpile cats hung from tails in live oaks, buried up to their necks in the clay and yowling heads razed clean by

John Deere's rotor for a teenager's rasping laugh, a semi-erection. The cajoling of buddy's bulges, the play of not wanting touch, a dirtstache slick with Monster Energy drink, just for a moment behind the loblollies this ritual of madness, the dithyramb of accursed brotherhood now spent, cum gives way to nothing. Englazed orbs stagnant in skulls, reclined on futons, filthy sneakers, PS3 in the basement. It gets to where you do not know what is killing you, brother, I tell you what. The mechanized laughter of Peepaw's tracheotomy speaking valve.

The perforation, both of the body in sex and the safety net of the phobic mind, is the beginning of queer rot. The bad and true event of its anality—the very thing they all try to escape in their rushing toward it. The bringing forth of anality to the public scene—what a great shame. Genet knew it well, the fucking back up the ass of the most base and fecund of matters. Homoeroticism is the very structure of the social in this regard, one big farce of grabass masked as territorial barnyard bungling. What is a fudgepacker but the sacred naming of that institution—it is a name of recognition, an accursed name but all the same a welcoming home. The fudgepacker is known. The act transcends sociability; it assails bodily those who recognize it. It is a rectal knowledge. It remains mythic—the cock's encounter with shit is a matter of chance, unplanned in general, and, as a matter of course, often avoided. The urethral and the fecal try not to meet in the well-planned anal event. All the same. This is why the fudgepacker is a sort of mythic trickster and reigns over the imaginations of all boys whose venom conceals a deep want. All men, all boys, want to be fudgepackers.

The gnarl is every relation here. Strange time reigns. Things did not happen "when" but "whenever." Tethered always to the screeching pain of daddy's abscesses, mama's dark spells, echoic chamber, perpetuity of calling back—the tart mouth of sociological "phenomena" insufficient. The void is not just a place to find no culture. It is a place to tether one to the act of wallstaring, the sick bed, the ritual of panhandling out on the frontage turnaround. Region is kingdom. One is branded, I tell you what. It is a gnarled synthesis with the regional folkloric form, the Texas tall tale, which always dwells in strange time.

Whenever old Bill Thibodeaux pulled the twenty-foot gator out of Cow Bayou, whenever the lightning struck that live oak and it was filled up with guinea hens that flew every which way, whenever Mother Hudgins walked off into the cypress woods, before the war that was, and didn't never come back, and couldn't nobody tell why. That was when they still had spiritualist meetings at the First Baptist church

on Wednesday evenings and they'd have actors appear hanging in the doorway as ghosts. Ladies in old lace gloves covered in powder that'd wail and cry leaning on a torn parasol, old plantation schoolmasters in monocles that stood and grimaced holding a Bible. And boy did the people eat that up, poor saps. They'd pay to get in. Whenever I went up there last though that church was in bad shape. Hurricane got into it.[8]

"Whenever they was first getting' together she caught him fuckin' that dog, I swear to fuckin' God, brother. She come in, and he's just fuckin' away at that dog; hurt the little fucker too man it was a little dog. Stayed with his ass too." Followed by a rasping laugh, wide-eyed. A canine gaping. And mama at the stove, "What the fuck y'all talkin' bout—Christ but y'all are some nasty motherfuckers!" Ro-Tel tomatoes and green chilies burning in the pan. She turns up her Annie Lennox. Story here is the covenant with the gnarled relation; gnarled into rot it is a promise to bear witness, no balm in Gilead, no sleep for the wicked, no happy ending. Just wallow in the hard luck, sit with it. Ain't no gettin' away from it. Kingfisher off in the cypress knees demonspitting "chkchkchkchkchk," a bad cackle. The cypress gnarls in a knee, sprouted from swamp, abrading every surface of itself together. No beginning, no end. Keep us wallstaring at some Spencer Gifts blacklight poster of a wizard on a toadstool–smoking hookah. Black metal records from the 1990s, scratched CDs, covered in Nederland schwag. Drug dealers that lived in one-room shacks, barely outhouses, with nothing but beds and six or seven ball pythons.

A great, heavy symbol of Texas is old-timers sitting around talking shit. Pestilential hexing—the glee of speculating about Hillary Clinton muslimlicked on some slick linen in one of them fancy Yankee hotels. Ventilators thrumming. Through the hiss of his snot-flecked cannula, one of these sunbaked tortoises aspirates: "That's what'll get you, brother, that ventilator, I tell you what. Keeps you breathing while you rot. All of us in here will go that way, I tell you what." They address the incommensurability of their being presently seated in a clean and well-lit lobby by making vivid the humble and mudbaked origins of their lost domains. The pantheon of ancestry gets conjured like somebody bringing a powerful creature into play: "Well, that was Uncle Van lived out in the Devil's Pocket in a yurt. Motherfucker was so drunk on that shit he pulled from the still he'd drive to town on a car didn't have any wheels. Just a whole buncha sparks flyin', and here come Uncle Van. Took him two days to go and come back. Ran all over these pig trails. Grew all his own food too. Pokeweed salad and shit. Tough old motherfucker. Real clean though." Devil's Pocket is one of them big places out in

Newton County nobody knows where it starts or ends. Swampy and piney and filled with old haunts and sedge and sweetgum, bad roads that lead to the end of your fucking life. They say a meteor chunked out the Pocket back during settler times, and the whole damn place filled up with moccasins. A puddle of writhing balls of snakes fucking. Bears gang rape deer out there, and it is always nighttime. Way back, there used to be the Dog People out in the Neches River Bottom, so called because of their roving packs of curs. The big city for them was Woodville. They're all gone now, sunk down maybe under the River Bottom, waitin' it out til some future summons. Crickets clickin' in the ferns.

The plumage of swamp birds caked in the mud of this gnarled pageant. The retinue of gallinule, lilyhopper, rail, bittern, anhinga (swamp turkey, secret crow)—all of the cattail marsh skulkers. An enlarged throat sac, the subsonic wave of the bittern's song. Blast of deep. Bereft of sirenians, the Texan swamp is patient in its sick plenty. No southeast Texan sky, the zenith of which comes all the way down to one's knees, realizes full composition without an obligatory vulturine rotsniffer maintenance team, locked in perpetual glazed gliding vigilance weaving on the thermal drafts. One might count three hundred in a day, a whole wake of them, mixed flock of Black and Turkey, vortexing half a mile up, all for some gibbet buried down in the rot. And then perched silent on the latticed steel transmission towers. The Blacks scan for kill while the Turkeys sniff, make veering descent athwart the drafts, alight with ungainly hops and hiss to one another across the dusk's hum. The windfall being dogs, roadkilled big curs, some with collars. On a summer morning, one might lay intact, baking in a ravine. By afternoon they have dragged its gleaming viscera spiteful across the farm-to-market road. And the next morning just a clean femur bone in the ditch. And no collar. Has it been spirited to some vulturine altar? This is no aberration but the final debasement in a series of canine torment common to this place of old ways. It is a form of stewardship to harm one's curs, strap them glorious with frayed twine to the wide tow hitch of some lowboy and barreling breakneck down the road, gravel pelting them. One swerve and the arrangement goes into an elaborate last rite, a dog dragged for a ways and left by a coveralled clodhopper gumming a pipe. His master's voice in his skull with each bounce on the highway's shoulder. Bad. Dog. Bad. Dog. Down. Down. And then the vultures. What excoriates the vengeful vulturine deities, Coragyps or Cathartes, the ditchgods, is the hunger of the rotsniffers for Jim Bob or old Buzz, the want their gaze enacts in staring upon the odorous ham that is the body of a fat or even grizzled refinery operator, bound in Nomex coveralls and exuding pubic stink and beersweat. But how rare this feast, as the man has others who watch out for him, apparently, scandalized by the very same to befall him upon his frontage roads, his turnarounds, the curve of his parking lots even.

144

Especially there, for people gather there and let no man rot for longer than is tasteful.

Everything falls to a strip mall parking lot at sunset. A big tired man in a suit, an engorged Gailard Sartain with mellorine cheeks, might pour himself laboriously from an F-350, all that rot ramping up, under the hungry vigilance of the vulture sentries. The shell of life ushers him from space to space, from the truck to the bank or the grocery, keeping his big softness like a meat core hidden, protected, propelled on the weak slipstream of his groundchuck farts. And even that flash of vulnerability, the sidling incomprehensible drunken bear shamble from the parking lot, is curtailed by a trip to Sonic where one reposes, curt Buddha, after pushing a button, and wheezing from even the strain of that. They invented carhops for this purpose, eager teens on roller-skates, now with neon rubber bands on their teeth, names of Jayden or Brayden or Graydon in this 1950s pantomime. They chew your food for you and bring you drinks called Oceanwaters.

Accrual chafes at the bodyhusks, the hard-luck stories narrating the stubborn, dogged throwing of the unfortunate flesh sack into things, coming up against the impasse, the line past which things become intolerable. But nothing is intolerable, as it turns out. The great dynastic white trash families wield accrual in the arena of suffering. The exposure of the bodyhusk, the "look what has become of me," the places of rupture, atrophy, calcification, jaundice, blackening, death, rot. The gathering of husks hitched to oxygen tanks, strapped to Rascals. The gathering up of wounds and ailments worn like fat broaches upon the convex hurt chest adorning the ribcage. The scarred warrior hick, demented on Dilaudid, sporting stubs. The gnarl's home is a carapace of hurt. Nails perforating the flesh, roofs crushing skulls, lovers swept off down at Crystal Beach on a bed of brown kelp or sitting on a sofa in the warm Gulf wash. All the Candyman's half-buried boy victims, rectums and urethras perforated by glass pipettes and needle-nose pliers, buried out on High Island in their bellbottoms and heavy bangs. Only the vision of the red-eyed Roseate Spoonbills, the carotenoid pigment of a krillfed avian eye, can scan for them now. Their last moments in a rape van in 1971 thinkin' they was gonna get high on dope before being strapped to the rack and fiddled with to death. And what were they doing out there? "Hell, they was all fucked up. Now they rottin' somewheres." (rasping laughter, hacking cough)

Notes

[1] Lee Edelman, "Against Survival: Queerness in a Time That's Out of Joint," *Shakespeare Quarterly* 62, no. 2 (Summer 2011): 149.

[2] Joseph Russo, *"Perpetue Putesco—Perpetually I Putrefy,"* in *Hideous Gnosis: Black Metal Theory Symposium* I, ed. Nicola Masciandaro (Charleston, SC: Create Space, 2010), 93-105, accessed May 21, 2021.

[3] Lauren Berlant and Lee Edelman, *Sex, or the Unbearable* (Durham, NC: Duke University Press, 2013).

[4] Silvia Posocco, Adi Kunstman, and Jin Haritaworn, eds., *Queer Necropolitics*, (London: Routledge, 2014).

[5] Kathleen Stewart, "In the World That Affect Proposed," *Cultural Anthropology: Journal of the Society for Cultural Anthropology* 32, no. 2 (Spring 2017): 196.

[6] Alexander Galloway, "The Swervers vs. the F*ck-Annies," Culture and Communication, May 22, 2017, accessed April 23, 2021, http://cultureandcommunication.org/galloway/the-swervers-vs-the-fck-annies.

[7] Cf. Sedgwick's "weak theory," Berlant and Warner's "queer commentary," Edelman's "antisocial thesis," Bersani's "antirelationality."

[8] The quotations herein are an admixture of my informants' words and my own poetic stylizations of the *mise en scène* of big Texas—a place where I began, at a certain point and with pleasure, to lose the self I once thought I held. In other words, these are the mutual co-rotting of voicings in ethnographic time.

Elijah Burgher
Venereal Machine (Solar Phallic Princess), 2019
colored pencil on paper, 69 x 51 cm
courtesy of the artist

Francine B./Witnesstheabsurd
A New Idol, 2019
digital painting
courtesy of the artist

Doom Donkey:

MICK BARR'S DRONE OF INFORMATION AND *THE RAINBOW SUPREMACY*

ALIZA SHVARTS

I

Consider the figure of the donkey, the beast of burden, the working animal.

In a peculiar passage of *How to Do Things with Words*, J.L. Austin uses a hypothetical scenario of shooting a donkey to parse what he defines as the two main types of performativity: *illocution* and *perlocution*. Illocutionary performativity refers to the kind of utterances where to say something is to immediately do it, as in Austin's famous example of the marriage vow: to say "I do" is not to describe the action or state of marriage; it is to marry.[1] With perlocutionary performativity, on the other hand, the utterance produces extended action over time, as with a warning, a promise, or a plea.

In his hypothetical scenario, Austin identifies a specific type of multiplicity that arises at the convergence of an illocutionary command and its perlocutionary effects. Not only is there a temporal distinction between the immediacy of illocution and the extended action of perlocution, but there is also an internal and external expanse of actions in perlocutionary performativity itself: an endlessly divisible field of physical action that can be parsed into what Austin describes as "minimum physical acts."

The act of shooting a donkey, for instance, can be parsed into endlessly smaller movements—pulling the trigger, moving a finger, the parting of the lips.

As Austin concludes:

There is no restriction to the minimum physical act at all. That we can import an arbitrarily long stretch of what might also be called "consequences" into the nomenclature of the act itself is, or should be, a fundamental commonplace of the theory of our language about all "action" in general. Thus if I asked "What did he do?" we may reply either "He shot the donkey" or "He fired a gun" or "He pulled the trigger" or "He moved his trigger finger," and all may be correct.[2]

This idea of "minimum physical action" extends the speech act through an unrestricted chain of subsequent actions—"consequences." Though these minimum physical acts also inhere *in* the speech act. Any speech act can be divided into noises, and "the production of noises," Austin goes on to explain, "is itself really a consequence of the minimum physical act of moving one's vocal organs."[3] Such movement can itself be deconstructed into the flows of breath, the circulations of blood, the pulsings of the nervous system—the background activities that maintain and reproduce life itself. The utterance is always already situated in the hum of something already happening: a vibratory ground.

This is to say that the speech act not only produces an unrestricted succession of minimum physical actions but also arises from them, remaining attached to the sounds or noises that compose it. These, in turn, remain attached to the movements of a physical body. Here we can begin to see the distinction between illocution and perlocution breaking down: illocution—that instance of speech's immediate action—remains attached, perlocutionarily, to not only its *later* effects but also the *prior* conditions that produce it. Or, to put it another way, the illocutionary speech act always has perlocutionary dimensions, for speech acts set in motion a chain of actions extending beyond the time of the utterance, which enacts itself through a lineage of past provisions and future repercussions.

Though perhaps a bit dry and technical at first blush, this perlocutionary logic disassembles speech into noise, and noise into physical movement, which makes it useful for the analysis of metal—a genre similarly concerned with the permeable relation between sound and the body. In metal, sound's physical action is often achieved through intensity: reverb that shakes the bones, speeds that quicken the heart, volume that prickles the skin. Even when the music fails to achieve such effects, the aesthetics of metal—its preoccupation with darkness, heaviness, and brutality—invoke a sensate imaginary, one centered on the question of what a body can bear. The body becomes the bearing ground for both physical intensity and aesthetic pleasure. "Bearing," thus, becomes a matter of duration—of withstanding—as well as *generation*. In the performance of bearing intensity, metal as a genre is born and borne.

At its best, metal allows us not only to experience disassembling, but also to consider what is at stake in the maintenance and transgression of distinctions. In metal, as in the perlocutionary performative, speech, sound, and force converge. To be clear, Austin would not consider metal—or any other kind of aestheticized speech (such as theater or poetry)—to be performative, for its aesthetic remove prevents it from "acting" in social contexts in a real, everyday sense.[4] Yet Austin's theory of speech action is useful for the analysis of metal insofar as it complicates the distinction between language, sound, and force. Like metal, Austin's theory of speech action also seems to rest on a strange, privileged subject, or, perhaps more accurately, an abject: the beast of burden, the long-suffering working animal.

II

Consider now that the donkey in Austin's example is, pointedly, a female donkey, and that the utterance at the center of his brief analysis—"Shoot her"—interpellates not any specific donkey, but the general condition of the female load-bearing animal. The perlocutionary condition is a reproductive one, one that both creates outcomes and perpetuates possibility. As Austin writes:

The perlocutionary act may be either an achievement of a perlocutionary object (convince, persuade) or the production of a perlocutionary sequel. Thus the act of warning may achieve its perlocutionary object of alerting and also have the perlocutionary sequel of alarming, and an argument against a view may fail to achieve its object but have the perlocutionary sequel of convincing our opponent of its truth ("I only succeeded in convincing him"). What is the perlocutionary object of one illocution may be the sequel of another.[5]

In perlocution, the end of the performative act—its object—blurs into the perpetuation of performative force: the "sequel." The dual production of objects and sequels constitutes a rhythm by which performativity reproduces itself; it is an expression of force that simultaneously maintains the possibility of (future) force.

In this sense, the perlocutionary performative exemplifies a distinction between making and bearing. Rather than resulting in a finite act or event, perlocution carries with it a maintained potential for action and is itself the conduit for that potentiality: the packhorse, the passage. The mechanism of perlocutionary force works through two kinds of pluralizing differentiations—one that is internal (infinitesimal subdivision of the act into prior acts, sound into the vibration of vocal chords, etc.) and one that is external (the infinite chain of consequence). Highly reproductive, perlocutionary performativity becomes itself not through disappearance but through duration.[6]

Austin's notion of perlocution, insofar as it operates through an endless process of generative differentiation, resembles what Marxist feminist theorists have described as *reproductive labor*. Often counterposed to productive waged labor, reproductive labor consists of those unwaged maintenance tasks (biological, affective) that reproduce the capacity to work—maintenance of the body through cooking and cleaning and the maintenance of the workforce through the reproduction of children, etc. Like the perlocutionary speech act, reproductive labor is characterized by its extensity. Unwaged, it goes unmeasured, camouflaging the domestic work of the (historically) female laborer as endless and effortless "care."

Such reproductive work is governed by the marriage contract that exists in continuous relation to the labor contract.[7] Some feminist scholars have noted that both the marriage contract and labor contracts are framed against another kind of work, again usually not recognized as such: the nonconsensual and noncontractual state of slavery, which was foundational to the development of capitalism. It is this that Eve Kosofsky Sedgwick has in mind when she revisits the scene of Austin's speech act *par excellence*, the marriage vow, to consider the spatiality of the performative, literally what happens around the performative, or what she terms the "periperformative."

Specifically, Sedgwick writes:

the cluster of ostentatiously potent linguistic acts that have
been grouped loosely, since J.L. Austin, under the rubric of
"performatives" must be understood continuously in relation to the
exemplary instance of slavery. They must be understood already by
philosophers, linguists, and gender theorists in relation to the
exemplary instances of courtship/marriage and of juridical acts in
a general sense.[8]

The spatial performance of the marriage vow is structured through force of the marriage contract, and such performance of contractual and consensual relations is itself undergirded by the noncontractual and nonconsensual relations that are its historical context of possibility. Or to say it another way, the noncontractual and nonconsensual of the legacy of trans-Atlantic slavery structures the marital speech act "I do," insofar as the performative force of speech is made possible by the material histories that render the utterance effective (or, in Austin's parlance, "felicitous"). For Sedgwick, it is this material and historical legacy that both enables and inheres in performative force—which in instances such as the marriage vow, relies on the juridical, national, and social contexts to act.

Through this lens, the presumed male actor in Austin's text takes on new resonance. The "he" that speaks, acts, and shoots is not simply a default subject of the sentence but the historically produced subject of power. He speaks with a voice coincident to the "voice" of political agency. He acts in a social and legal sphere configured to legitimize and enable his actions. He shoots with the moral assurance that there is an absolute distinction between his life and the bare life that he wastes. The actor that appears in Austin's text has been well defined through Western philosophical, juridical, and religious traditions; yet perhaps more mysterious and more compelling is the occluded derivation of the animal at the other end of the barrel. He shoots; she dies. He owns; she breeds. He speaks; she makes noise. If he is the Western subject, then she is the "mule of the world."[9] For those of us at odds with the subject who holds the gun—unable to mouth his utterances, unconvincing when miming his acts—we might align ourselves with that female animal and find some kind of kinship in the sounds she makes.

III

Consider now a drone. Drone is the sound of labor happening, its minimum physicality, the hoofbeat of endless industry, the vibrational ground that bears the burden of bearing forth. Drone trills the body, becoming a useful way of feeling through the impasses of subject and object through movement, through difference and repetition that constitute its speeds and traversals. Drone offers a way of understanding passage, action, and perhaps even agency outside the enclosure of the subject. It actively negotiates music and noise, making palpable to the listener what it feels like to move in and out of meaning or legibility.

As a sonic materiality, drone is an enfolding wherein productive and reproductive labor become indistinguishable again. Marcus Boon characterizes the sustained and supportive quality of drone as that "which sustains a particular set of vibrations and sound frequencies in time, has a very close relationship to what we are, to our environment, and to the unseen world that sustains us."[10] Through its extreme vibrations, the drone opens up; it invaginates to create overtones, internal pockets larger than the whole. In drone, you feel the intensity of duration, of boredom, the way in which we remain discrete bodies, each subjected to, each enduring, each surviving, sustaining, and consolidating our figural singularity through this intense sound. At the same time, this intensity is enfolded in an extensity, a formlessness, or, more precisely, a spreading form or expansive arena to which we are given in common. This contraction and dilation into intensity and extensity is reproduction's frequency, the vibrational rate of differentiation.

The drone is both the sound of labor and a type of labor—a minimum physicality. In Austin's sense of the phrase, *minimum physicality* refers to the deepest reach of the perlocutionary performative, its vibrational germ within the body, the life-sustaining functions of breath and blood that are the seed of the utterance. The body's own labor of self-maintenance is contiguous with the more general notion of social maintenance and reproduction. Such reproductive labor is itself a minimum physicality (or background noise) in relation to the recognized work of waged labor.

Yet if drone has a relationship to reproduction—to the notion of maintaining, sustaining, and bearing forth, it also bears a relationship to its opposite: to stasis, to impasse, or what in a more "metal" parlance we might understand as "doom." Drone and doom are both genres of metal. The former is characterized by long durational tones, the latter by lower, "heavier" sounds (meant to evoke heavy emotion), and, as such, the two often overlap. Though perhaps more compelling than their delineating function as compositional categories is their conceptual connection. Drone extends toward a horizon, offering a vision of the future. Doom contracts, seeing in that same infinite horizon a bleakness rather than a promise. Or, to put it another way, doom illuminates how promises are already bleak and, conversely, how bleakness offers a kind of promise.

In philosophy as in music, drone names a type of doom, one that manifests in endless action. Stripped of affect, both "doom" (from the Old English word *dom*, meaning judgment, as in a legal judgment or sentence) and "promise" describe temporal expanse. Both function by holding us to a chain of consequence. Perhaps for these reasons, drone sounds have a strange relationship to speed and frequency. Some drones are created through long, sustained notes. Others are produced through high frequencies or incredible speeds: hums of rapid movement that creates an atmospheric effect. As both extremely fast and extremely slow, the drone is an operation of passage, of bearing, of birthing. It sounds not only that gendered social and sexual labor that reproduces the work force, but also that lasting engendering and racializing violence forged in the many berths and cargo holds carrying people to the "New World," where stolen lives and labors became the bearing ground of empire.

IV

Avant-garde metal musician Mick Barr—whose virtuosic guitar work is matched by his prodigious output—plays notes so quickly as to produce an effect of slowness. He produces a vibratory effect through speed rather than volume, cycling through notes so as to create what feels like a blurred internally differentiating sound. His drones are "a sort of a calm that can come in the midst of the most chaotic, overly composed music";[11] yet they are also the product of intense labor, not just the strumming of the fingers and vibration of the strings at the scene of performance but also an embodied repertoire built over years of practice. "I'd write a hundred riffs," he explains, "and then I'd put them all together, and then I'd memorize it, then I'd play it a lot so I could do it without even thinking about it anymore—and then I'd play it live, and it would take on a whole different thing."[12]

It is difficult to write of Barr's oeuvre, because he is so prolific, so wildly collaborative. His work inspires a critical view that is at once macro and microcosmic: one that takes in the atmosphere of his practice, reading it like a weather pattern, yet at the same time sees these larger trends borne out in the individual example, the compositional choices of a single song. This perhaps has to do with Barr's way of working, which he describes as having a ritual or devotional quality:

I got inspired by the whole legend of John Coltrane, who practiced all the time. It was a very spiritual thing for him—to practice all the time, to hone in. I don't know why, but I sort of fell into that approach, almost became a monk with that. That was my sole focus. That was my entire existence...It was slightly fractal; everything kept expanding.[13]

The fractal holds the promise of internal subdivision—of complexity maintained as you go deeper, look closer, hone in. It is an apt image for Barr's sound, which sustains a self-similar complexity at different resolutions of listening. It is in the interplay between a micro and macro listening that we can hear Barr's specific quality of drone. It emerges from the vibrancy of single notes blending into a continuous unfurling sound. From this same perspective, we can hear a doom in his work too, the way his hard labor occludes itself in the lull of listening, in the way virtuosity exhausts, if not the fingers, the ears, in which the discrete sounds meld.

What is "heavy" about Barr's metal is what he describes as "the sheer weight of information." This phrase is not only accurate compositionally, describing the musical density he achieves through his hundreds of riffs, but also provocative philosophically, conjuring an image of a mind, a body, laden with the burden of its own proficiency, with the weight of knowing. When you listen to Barr play, you are quelled by the certainty of a person who knows. Even when he introduces not-knowing into his performance through his experiments in improvisation, his inexorable competence carries through, played out in the improvised interchanges with the other musicians.

What Barr's music allows us to access is the thought that sound, vibrational movement, is not an abstract materiality but a formal operation of fecundity, born of and borne through the laboring animal in front of us: the musician. The experiential effect of speed—that calm in the midst of chaos—obscures the labor required to produce that speed, that is, the sweat of practice and performance. Unlike other kinds of metal that seek to reproduce the sounds of industry, Barr's compositions portray this other, subsumed legacy of work, one not recognized as such, which is to say his music deals in the aesthetics of maintenance work or reproductive labor—a feminine inheritance that distributes itself unequally among all bodies. This is not to say that Barr's music is feminine in any identificatory sense. After all, Barr does not identify as female or femme, and there are no overt references to gender or gender play in his performances. Yet he brings into audibility the sounds of the female laboring animal that are usually subsumed, excluded, silenced, or dismissed as "mere noise." In this uniquely labored sonic materiality, we can hear that legacy of the feminine normally occluded by the masculinist model of production and authorship. We hear it, even if it is not named, and it is this material rather than identity-based element that makes his music available for a queer feminist listening.

One of the salient features that parses productive from reproductive labor is the interval: the former is measured by the regular interval of the hour so that it can be waged, the latter is seemingly endless, spanning all hours of the day and night, perhaps only confined by the interval of a lifetime. In Barr's play with intervals of speed and slowness, he gives sound to that which is hard to hear, the human that dissipates into an atmospheric surround from which other things are born. We can hear this "drone of information" clearly in his song "Breinclouds" (2008) released under the moniker Ocrilim, which is an almost hour-long composition of repeating, high-end, electric guitar riffs. As they shift speeds, they create a dizzying, cycling effect. The guitar flutters, almost sings, recalling the airless space of a video game arcade and its electric chorus of noises. The speed makes the sonic information feel impenetrable, an effect compounded by the interludes of brief slowness or staccato, wherein the silence between notes creates a vacuum-like pull, making you aware of how your ear has come to rely on and anticipate the acceleration of sound. These moments demonstrate how the weight of information works on the listener not only through its presence but also through its absence.

Another work, *Octis/Ocrilim* (2005), cycles between fast riffs and longer droning notes. The title makes reference to the relationship between Ocrilim and his other oft-used moniker, Octis. "Ocrilim is Mick Barr overthinking," Barr has explained, and "Octis is Mick Barr underthinking. These names mean nothing when a live show is concerned. Come see Ocrilim and you may be forced to watch Octis."[14] In the song, these two different temperaments perhaps correspond to regular intervals of fast and slow play, but what begins to feel more meaningful over the thirty-four-minute composition is how the difference between the two—though maintained—begins to sound less like a binary than an extension and contraction of a singular gesture. The notes in the riffs are played so fast that they are difficult to distinguish, while the buzz of the long-held notes takes on a granular quality, as though the sound is disassembling over time into discrete units. Both are drones in their own right.

"Infamin" (Ocrilim, *Infamin*, self-released, 2013) plays similarly with speed and slowness, though this time the slow plucking and fast strumming of the guitar contrast with Barr's voice. The voice, in the extension of the metal scream, becomes raspy and the guitars melodic—almost as though the latter was "speaking" against the "noise" of the former. The human becomes atmospheric, the hiss of the voice dissipating against the more solid strums of the guitar. The first lines, which do not come in until almost halfway through the ten-minute song, also bring to mind dissipation. They go "let the sands sink/and let the lands drink," conjuring an image of sand disappearing into the ocean and the land absorbing the sea, which is to say an image of melding, difference dispersing, dry land and wet waters intermingling to become one. In the final line, "the fire dims and flickers," this dissipation between opposite elements is reimagined as the potentiality of a third. Whereas earth and water are two opposites placed in binary difference, the singularity of fire produces its own internal differentiation, a waning and surging, dimming and flickering, that, unlike the mixing of land and sea, never reaches equilibrium.

V

My favorite published interview with Mick Barr begins with his proclamation: "Black metal in all its permutations remains the sacred music of Satan. A way of expressing whatever that means to whomever is performing it."[15] It is a statement that is not quite literal, not quite ironic; it speaks to a shared affect, a shared stance of opposition among a community of listeners that is not simply reactive but generative of an aesthetic imaginary.

Metal, even for a technical virtuoso like Barr, is a mutable compositional category, one fed from multiple sources:

It's a presentation of music—that's all metal is...I don't just listen to metal, I listen to literally everything (minus a few key things) and it's all in there. Everything is an influence, even if you don't want it to be...As for metal, that's the presentation of music that I've always felt the most—I guess it's a little bit of a comfort.[16]

Yet even for him, black metal seems to stand out as an exemplary, even intoxicating, form. In addition to his numerous solo and collaborative projects, Barr has played in the black metal band Krallice since 2007. He describes his turn to black metal as a return of sorts: "I first heard Darkthrone in 1997 and it kind of threw me for a loop. Overpowered whatever I was interested in at the time. Black metal seemed way deeper than anything else, and I kind of got addicted to it. Hunted down whatever I could with whatever money I could find and eventually I had to deliberately force myself to quit for a while."[17]

Just as memorable as black metal's sonic innovations—its shrieks, tremolos, and corpsepaint—are its narrative ones, its themes of Satanism, paganism, suffering, and bodily extremity. These themes constitute what is "black" about black metal: the horror of reproductive labor—from its origins in primitive accumulation to its manifestation in the monstrous maternal—as imagined from the perspective of the white male European.[18] More than other genres of metal, black metal is historically oriented. To say that it is the "sacred music of Satan" is to implicitly recognize the way in which it is bound up with that originary moment of Christian colonization within Europe and the consolidation of the Church's power through inquisition and burning women as witches, brides of the devil. Satan's music, then, is not only one invested in iconoclasm, in the refutation of convention and propriety—that would be somewhat simplistic, even trite. Rather, what gives this music its sharp edge is its unconscious connection to the trauma of reproductive discipline—a trauma of the feminine laboring animal to whom we are all indebted.

Black metal is at once a music, a stylistic, as well as a collectively produced, image of our relationship to the history of capitalism. It renders this image through hyperbole and superlative, which in their most nuanced and sophisticated forms become a critical encoding. "Black metal in all its permutations remains the sacred music of Satan"—*forever and all time, categorically and without exception*. Black metal glints through this superlative sheen, catching some of us in the eye with a knowing shared disposition. At its most base level, we might call this disposition rage or hate, a wild reactivity unfortunately channeled into the hypernationalisms, hypermasculinisms, and heteronormativities that characterize some sectors of the subgenre. Yet these blunt forms seem to me to miss the point of black metal's transgressive potential, one that resists capture and codification by such complicit stances. Rather, what catches some of us (at least what catches me) is a shared sense of being caught in perpetuation, in a perlocutionary extensity of reproductive acts to which there is no end. It is a shared sense of doom, worn without hand-wringing, because to dwell in the tussle of such feeling is to miss the totality of the point. It is something summarized in a strange idea, which I turn to by way of conclusion: the idea of a "rainbow supremacy."

I take this term from the title of a strange collaborative improvisational album Mick Barr made with Nándor Névai. *The Rainbow Supremacy* (2009) was made on the spot as part of a free metal jam session and takes its title from the first line of the first song, which Barr describes both him and Névai immediately saw as apt: "He went into the booth to do a vocal and that was the first thing that popped into his head...It just fit perfectly."[19] "Supremacy" repeats a second time a couple of minutes in as if to revel in the brutality of the word, this time correlating to a surge in guitar. The album itself consists of two tracks and a bonus track, which all together are only about thirty minutes in length.

The songs show off Névai's range of vocal styles, from screams to whispers, militaristic shouting, guttural growling, high-pitched animal howls, throat singing, and maniacal laughing. Barr's shredding is punctuated by interludes of slowness, which he often uses to an accelerating effect, and Névai's percussion acts less as a constant driving force and more as an autonomous third element in the composition. Both musicians know how to let silence unfold between them, often letting one or two beats separate their interludes so that the collaboration seems almost like a conversation. The album feels like an intimate thing, a mutual recognition of skill between two accomplished performers, rather than a composition oriented toward an audience. Yet despite this intimate quality and the musicians' clear musical skill, what I like most about *The Rainbow Supremacy* is its felicitous title.

What is a rainbow supremacy? There's a reading of the phrase in which we could recognize it as perhaps just homophobic—a reactionary response to the saturation of rainbow flags that, as Névai describes, surrounded him when he lived in West Hollywood.[20] The phrase is composed of a double superlative, *rainbow* referring to the totality of color and *supremacy* denoting the state of being supreme, the greatest, the utmost. There is, of course, another dimension to the phrase that puts the words in opposition. Rainbow suggests the symbol for gay pride, and *supremacy* for many of us carries with it the imprint of its oft-used modifier *white*. But more poignant than that juxtaposition is the awareness that it is perhaps no juxtaposition at all, that gay pride and white supremacy are not mutually exclusive; indeed, the two overlap neatly in homonationalism, for nothing about sexual object choice inherently prevents the folding of gay identity into the otherwise unchanged ideologies of the state.[21] While each of these readings are oppositional, it is this third reading that achieves metal-ness in its fullest sense; it goes beyond the merely reactive or oppositional to embrace the relentlessness—the ruthlessness—of hegemony's true function. As a doubled superlative, the phrase seems to point to the dry humor of its own hype. Its hype is wielded within a metal parlance to point to the brutality of "best." In an idea like "rainbow supremacy," you hear the undertone of domination that attends narratives of empowerment or positivity.

Rainbow supremacy as a term is shorthand for a rarified kind of metal ethic, one that resists the catharsis of resistance for something more durational, more entrenched, more doomed. It sounds a squared superlative that fulfills, exceeds, and exhausts metal's terms of value and legibility and, by extension, the terms of value and legibility that structure our shared social world. It resounds in the sonic saturation of Barr's "drone of information," in his virtuosic capacity to bring the listener into contact with the sound and labor of extensity. To this extent, it resonates with the queer listener—or at least resonates for me—as expressing an impasse I recognize: the exhaustion of both empowerment and critique. In the droll hyperbole, nothing is solved, but something is shifted from the register of knowledge to the register of play. "Rainbow supremacy forever, man, that's great."[22]

Notes

[1] J.L. Austin, *How to Do Things with Words*, eds. J.O. Urmson and Marina Sbisà (Cambridge: Harvard University Press, 1975), 6.

[2] Ibid., 107-8.

[3] Ibid., 114n1.

[4] Ibid., 104.

[5] Ibid., 108.

[6] Here I make reference to the contested thesis in Peggy Phelan, "The Ontology of Performance: Representation without Reproduction," in *Unmarked: The Politics of Performance* (New York: Routledge, 1993), 146-66.

[7] "[C]onsider marriage, which posits itself as a 'work contract' (and relation) between the non-directly waged female houseworker and the waged male worker. This is the fundamental work contract of the female labor force. Even though it is more often seen as a non-work contract by the man and woman who make it, in fact this latter misconception is necessary, since it can only function as a housework contract for as long as it appears as a non-work contract"; Leopoldona Fortunati, *The Arcane of Reproduction: Housework, Prostitution, Labor and Capital*, ed. Jim Fleming, trans. Hilary Creek (Brooklyn: Autonomedia, 1995), 59.

[8] Eve Kosofsky Sedgwick, *Touching Feeling: Affect, Pedagogy and Performance* (Durham, NC: Duke University Press, 2003), 89-90.

[9] Zora Neale Hurston, *Their Eyes Were Watching God* (New York: HarperCollins, 2000 [1937]), 17.

[10] Marcus Boon, "The Eternal Drone: Good Vibrations, Ancient to Future," in *Undercurrents: The Hidden Wiring of Modern Music*, ed. Tony Herrington (London: Continuum Publishing, 2002), 65.

[1] Aliza Shvarts, interview with Mick Barr, November 2017.

[12] Ibid.

[13] Idem.

[14] Idem.

[15] Al Necro, "Interview: Mick Barr from Krallice," Echoes and Dust, December 2015, accessed April 25, 2021, http://echoesanddust.com/2015/12/interview-mick-barr-from-krallice.

[16] Ibid.

[17] Brandon Stosuy, "Show No Mercy," Pitchfork, August 6, 2008, accessed April 25, 2021, https://pitchfork.com/features/show-no-mercy/7520-show-no-mercy.

[18] See Aliza Shvarts, "Black Wedding," *Brooklyn Rail*, February 5, 2015, accessed April 25, 2021, https://brooklynrail.org/2015/02/criticspage/black-wedding.

[19] Shvarts, interview with Mick Barr.

[20] Aliza Shvarts, interview with Nándor Névai, December 2017.

[21] For more on this, see Jasbir Puar, *Terrorist Assemblages: Homonationalism in Queer Times* (Durham, NC: Duke University Press, 2007).

[22] Shvarts, interview with Mick Barr.

Sarah Horrocks
The Transfiguration of Three Queens, 2018
ink/digital coloring
courtesy of the artist

Sarah Horrocks
Goatlord, 2018
ink/digital coloring
courtesy of the artist

Flamboyant Atrocity:

HOW TO ENHANCE DEAD'S DEATH DEPICTION

ÉLODIE LESOURD

I am the beast with a contorted grin, contracting down to
illusion and dilating toward infinity, both growing and
dying, delightfully suspended between hope for nothing
and despair of everything, brought up among perfumes and
poisons, consumed with love and hatred, killed by lights
and shadows. My symbol is the death of light and the flame
of death. Sparks die in me only to be reborn as thunder
and lightning. Darkness itself glows in me.

— Emil Mihai Cioran[1]

Figure 1. Steven Shearer, *Blackhearts*, 2006, oil, ballpoint pen, tape
on inkjet, framed, 27.5 x 34.5 cm. © Courtesy of the artist, Galerie Eva
Presenhuber, Zürich.

He is a beast, a wild and discreet feline, whose decadent and blazing journey has only been observable during short and powerful moments. As a singular phenomenon in the history of music and underground culture, Per Yngve Ohlin (1969–1991) is the incarnation of this body full of fire and death, bathed in a permanent excessive intensity, to the limits of mankind. Does this body, lying eternally in a postmortem life under the glazing of a too well-known picture, allude to something other than his own annihilation; can this *transi*, presenting continuously his morbid and destructive side as a last spectacle, find a transfiguration?

Per Yngve Ohlin's figure, known as Dead, is trapped in an *ad infinitum* appearing apparition. His voluntary death, turned into an impossible icon, keeps on splashing minds, and repeats itself in the violence and the atrocity of its representation.

His gloomy voice, indisputable testimony of his incandescent presence in the band Mayhem, can be heard on the *Live in Sarpsborg* recording; but it is his corporeal envelope that is fixed on the artwork of the bootleg of this same show, entitled *The Dawn of the Black Hearts*.

The image, as unsettling as it is problematic, raises numerous questions about its reception, its ontological definition, and its possible aesthetic understanding by other fields.

Could it be possible to contemplate an acceptable approach to this image, to go beyond the spectacular, to go outside of the inertia of our look? Admitting that the cadaverous vision activates repulsion as much as fascination is an age-old evidence. In the specific case of this cover art, there is a story—become myth—which determines and crystallizes the very core of black metal and its heroes. But a sensitive element removes this object from its codified milieu: it is a color photograph. This quale potentially plunges the image into an unbearable condition, a theater of cruelty. Does the rise of the color imply the rise of the horror to which it refers? Is the color the motive of the transgression? Can the cadaver, exposed by the photographic act, be submitted to our vision, with impunity? It seems that a potential way of acceptance and sublimation could be art. If the voyeurism dissecting Dead's body was substituted for an aesthetic pleasure, if the raw and horizontal real was transformed into an *ars moriendi*, then could Dead's figure be freed?

Black metal, an excessive movement with unappeased transgressive dynamics, persists in pushing the limits. It produces moments of alarm leading on to a necessary catharsis. In existential darkness, it vomits a somber music that a precise visual cartography leans against. One of the most striking images of this movement is certainly the obscene photograph taken by Euronymous of his destroyed friend. Reduced to a square format to become a cover art, it is, at the origin, an analogue color image, taken among others, developed by successive baths after an abrupt shooting. This photograph, plunged into the banality of its medium, disconcerts due to the subject it stages but also because of its chromatic nature. Indeed, the question of the color has to be considered as one of the ambiguous elements of this sign.

CHROMOGRAPHIC CORPSE

The popularization of the color photography—from its commercialization during the fifties to its recent dematerialization—turns this medium into a trivial communication tool, trapped by a progressive deconstruction of the viewpoint. But the color is not self-evident. During the 1960s, both professional and amateur photographic practices agreed on the use of color, even if, at the beginning, the former had rejected it. Incidentally, it stays aloof from the photo features that privileged the efficiency, the simplicity, and the realism of the black and white. War photojournalist David Douglas Duncan voluntarily throws out the color, considering it inappropriate: "I've never made a combat picture in color—ever. And I never will. It violates too many of the human decencies and the great privacy of the battlefield."[2] The color was frightening, notably for technical reasons but also because of its supposed illusory and artificial nature: "For me, color is an artifice, a cosmetic (like the kind used to paint corpses)."[3]

However, it seems to give access to the realism—almost intolerable—of the image. It gives a genuine trace, and proves the phenomenal quality of the objects, defining itself as a natural element. Most importantly, it catches the eye; it makes an exhibition of itself and inspires an almost exhibitionist dimension to the subject. It is, by itself, uncommon to black metal typology. Clear contrasts, harsh confrontations between the black and the white, are the lexicon of a constant tension, set up as a distinctive marker of this scene. This choice of a limited palette, sign of radicalness, allows us, first and foremost, to reach a kind of aggressiveness, to sharpen the cutting edge of the image, to affirm a power through austerity. The disenchantment of the world expresses itself by its chromatic negation—the opposition becomes a norm, the lack of tints tries to scare, to turn blood to ice with its monstrous coldness. In *The Dawn of the Black Hearts* cover art, the color plays this part, precisely. It staggers by its violence, frees the terror, petrifies with its crudeness, enhances the dramatic excess. Black metal could agree with Cioran when he gives to color the power to shock: "To hate all the colors: they awaken spiritual states which end fatally in melancholy."[4] Why such an impact? Can the quality of a thing (described as secondary) overflow the thing itself?

In the real world, the categorization of color's nature oscillated for a long time between an objective physicalist vision and a more subjective approach. This is a complex phenomenon, because it combines at the same time physical, psychological, and cultural factors, and it depends on a key element—light— precisely the one the lucifugous characters of black metal avoid. Then, all the different theories of colors followed, delivering a learning and a comprehension of their uses, in painting notably. Thus, it is easy to understand that the image creates some shock by oppositions of contrast principles (domination of clear colors toned down by dark areas), complementary colors (strong red repeated three times in the scene, giving rise to visual leaps by the discreet apparition of a green, but also by the balancing presence of the blue below, played again sporadically by jacket's buttons), the harmony (warm tones in the majority) and the balance of strengths (black masses cutting the image longitudinally). Some terms recall it (harmonies, tones); it exists in some correspondences between colors and music from a fundamental viewpoint (the seven categories, two wave-like phenomena, etc.) but also in the perception field. It is, indeed, feeling perceived during the vision of the mimetic transfer from the photographed color to what it is supposed to represent. The color, through its realism, creates a denotation of elements that becomes comprehensible and sometimes shocking. The *Body Farm* (2000–2001) series by the artist Sally Mann is similarly exemplary: the black-and-white prints invite us to a kind of transcendence, contrary to the harshness of the color ones.

The red, in every shade, exploding in the heart of Dead's image, is not simply red; it is not a self-referencing color but a descriptive, local one. Because of the analogy principle, we only see blood. The *power-quality* of the red is limited only to a representation of the blood,[5] and no other interpretation of this tone could be possible—it is not red anymore; it is blood.[6] In Jeffrey Silverthorne's black- and-white photograph of a young man (recalling Dead at a certain point) with a disheveled jeans jacket, blood is only a gentle potentiality. The spurting colors of *The Dawn of the Black Hearts* indicate an unequivocal reading (even if some interpretations stay delicate, like the black traces in the neck), reawakening the affects and exhibiting the abjection of a captured real; they impose the unbearable of a violently ended life and generate a silent violence. The chromatic power over perceptions is immense, and its properties confer the impression of a direct, unfiltered experience. If Matisse declared himself to "feel through color,"[7] does it imply that this quality is enough to arouse a sensation? In the case of this cover art, the atrocity passes by the problematic representation of a corpse.

If art—pictorial or sculptural—finds possible ways to aestheticize the representation of death, first dry (symbolized by the skeleton), then damp (with the features of the carrion),[8] it sinks into an unsurpassable obscenity when it tries to objectify itself through photographic image. The photograph of a cadaver, documentary or artistic, is an affirmation of death itself, of its reality. Even when the scene is rationalized, correlated to a metric—like in Alphonse Bertillon's judiciary pictures—the presence of the dead body projects the scandal of its violence. The corpse is considered as that which "occasions the greatest concentration of abjection,"[9] because it shakes our points of reference and distorts our ego. The materialization of death with the appearance of remains provokes a crisis of the presence, because the undecided ontic status of the subject takes itself away from its primary identity. The cadaver is not the person anymore but is also not a thing; it is "someone [who] is what is still present when there is no one."[10] This trouble—the oscillation between life and its disappearance, real and unreal, presence and absence—causes dread and intensifies it with the nature of the image that destabilizes by its excess of reality. The image doubles the real, the dead doubles the living; this repetition of duplicities emphasizes the impossibility of a sign that cannot be seized. Furthermore, the photograph, the *that-has-been* of Roland Barthes, is a cut, a mutilation of the body, so much so that the violence of its representation keeps on playing that of the scene itself again and again. In the case of this cover art, the atrocity goes through the vision of the shapeless. The dead body, slipping to the carrion status with fluids and organs spreading all over, is unqualifiable, and, under our eyes, "a disgusting liquefaction, something for which no language has a name, the naked apparition, pure, simple, brutal, of this figure that it is impossible to gaze at face on, which hovers in the background of all the imaginings of human destiny."[11] The inside is outside; the invisible is visible. The major disfigurement, provoked by the alteration of an entirety, raises moral questions about the exhibition of such a brutality. The view of those necroscopies, falling within a certain voyeurism, causes repugnance but can also fascinate. How to deny the visual impact and the aestheticization of the famous Robert Wiles photograph,[12] or some close-ups, like the hand sensitively given up on a bloody bed from Patrik Budenz's *Post Mortem* series? If an anonymous body, faceless, photographed at the morgue, can have some qualities, what happens when the depicted corpse is not that of an unknown person? The cover art of this bootleg (which is not the only cover art of a record showing a truly morbid scene)[13] unsettles especially because it reveals, obscenely and intrusively, an annihilated face, that of Dead.

Among the musicians of what is known as the second wave of black metal, Per Yngve Ohlin is the one who concentrates inventiveness, radicalness, and brutality, and by his lightning presence—barely three years—participated in determining a style. His semantic field is death; from his limitless effusive fascination (initiated by his near-death experience when he was a child in Sweden, continued with the choice of his name and of his cadaveric appearance) to the euphoria of the damnation, it becomes a supreme manifestation of freedom. The photograph exposed by *The Dawn of the Black Hearts* freezes in ultimate deference Dead's fantasies: to sicken his audience, to reach eternal life (or death), to live in Transylvania as a final resting place.[14] He lived in an excess of intensity, colorful, as most of the images taken when he was alive show, bathing in a chromatic revitalization.[15]

His last portrait is the emanation of his hysterically colored flamboyance, from where springs the ugliness of the shapeless. The image brings a romantic liking to suicide. As a canonical figure of the history of the underground, Dead seems to possibly find a kind of salvation in art limbo; it may be possible to look differently at this image, to make it tolerable.

THE ART OF BEING DEAD

Dead was trying to overstep the norms; his extreme attitude during concerts led to scarifications—more than a self-sacrificial spectacle, it recalled the Mesoamerican devotional manifestations surrendering blood to the balance of the world—and established his desire to get closer to death. On April 8, 1991, inclined toward a final impetus, he resisted no more, and chose death to banish death itself.[16] This voluntary death, by the radical ostentatiousness of its image (metabolic deterioration, presence of weapons, body posture), is also significant for the outrageousness brought to the look. Its transgressive dimension also comes from the lethal gesture, considered for a long time as a diabolical act, a prohibited criminal deed. The suicide, sometimes sensed as an expression of freedom, a self-accomplishment, sometimes as the influence of a disease (Dead would have been diagnosed with Cotard delusion), inflicts upon the living the torments of its motives, the intolerable ethical judgment; but it is also a matter of meaning, a fundamental question for philosophy.[17] The suicide, *mortem sibi consciscere*, *autophonos*, or *authentès*, is taboo, and has always raised sociological, moral, and religious issues. From Durkheim to Baechler, from the Cyreneans to Schopenhauer, some of the comprehensive solutions given by the thinkers enable us to look differently at this lethal desire: "What greater wealth than the suicide each of us bears within himself?"[18] If Cioran broaches suicide as a possible refuge, removing all negative parts of it, even considering it as a religious act saving us from the "debauchery of life,"[19] would its romantic resonance soften it? Mostly, it seems possible to generate a certain calming from the infamy of this photograph. Excluding all glorification principles, art can potentially aestheticize such an act: like the numerous pictorial representations of Nero, Cato the Younger, Cleopatra, Seneca, or Socrates, John Everett Millais's peaceful *Ophelia* (1851–1952), the dark and unexpected *Suicidé* (c. 1880) by Édouard Manet, or, more recently, the poetically geometric photographs by Enrique Metinides showing a May 25, 1971 suicide attempt, or the intoxicating abstractions by Rob Pruitt, gathered together under the title of *Suicide Paintings* (initiated in 2013). Art allows us to introduce a distance to the troublesome and submerging reality; it provides the experience of the sublime. The paradox of negative emotion gives access to the transformation of pain into pleasure, ugliness into beauty. Thus, to exorcise blasphemy, art offers itself as the last sacrament.

The contemporary penchant for icons can be evaluated by the extreme hijacking of a subject by popular culture. Dead, through his dazzling apparition, aroused a strong and tenacious fascination and has been swallowed up in various forms: fan art, dolls (Visnes Dolls), soap (Dead hand soap by Corpsepaint Soaps), fake memorabilia, notably in the form of the bloody T-shirt worn on his suicide, caricatures, memes, part of his skull sold at auctions, museum recognition,[20] etc. Drained of its essence, the figure still keeps a powerful aesthetic potential, of which some artists succeeded in being the interpreters.

In a surprising *kairos*, with the advent of this Norwegian musical movement, contemporary art noticed referents that it has been able to move and deconstruct to give to black metal the extent of its existing field and to turn it into a new aesthetic category. In this momentum, Dead found numerous possibilities of incarnation, spectral apparitions like a revenant haunting the world of the living ones forever.[21] With Mayhem, he delivers his morbid visions in lyrics and drawings, as well as through scenic performances of torrential density; he inspires teenage ardor and enigmatic force in the works of Martin Bladh, Aaron Metté, or Georgi Tushev. Starting with portraits, they move the signifier thanks to symbolic interpretations or disappearance of the idol. Others questioned his sepulchral representation, including Seldon Hunt, who, using the *Live in Leipzig* cover art of 1996 in a 2013 drawing,[22] deconstructs the gothic macabre aesthetic and gives tangible form to the foreshadowed tempest, tearing the logo apart, inverting values, dissolving the face of the singer. Thanks to art, the body is brought into another space,[23] becoming utopia (utopia already called in the invention and use of the corpsepaint). This collapsed body on the bootleg also requires the absolution of his insult: his transfer, nay, his surpassing, in a double irreverence—that of the image, and that of its appropriation by art—seems to dig itself out the decadence of the shadows.

"Music is a tomb of delights, beatitude which buries us,"[24] and Dead buried all his being in it. This photograph is his open gravestone, profaning his dead body as much as glorifying him. When Euronymous, Mayhem guitarist and cornerstone of the guts of the genre, discovered the suicide at the end of that April weekend, he believed in photography as an objective capture, an incantatory negation, even a remedy to the excess of reality exposed to his eyes. As a disillusioned resurrectionist, he steals this cadaver to benefit from his mystery, after having enjoyed his contemplation: "I have to admit that it was interesting to be able to examine a human brain in *rigor mortis*."[25] In 1995, the Colombian label Warmaster Records, headed by Mauricio "Bull Metal" Montoya (former drummer of the band Masacre, to whom Euronymous had sent a print), spurted Swedish blood onto the face of the world. This deadly spectacle revealed itself through the edition of three hundred vinyl copies of eight tracks recorded during the show in Sarpsborg, on February 28, 1990 (under a catalog number already marked by the opposition, as it was Anti Grishnackh 001). The title, coming from lyrics written by Fenriz for Mayhem,[26] appended in golden letters, mirrors the band's name, enlightening the top of the image with the same brilliance. The photograph, captured in an impetuous gesture, presents itself in an average quality, with dull tints. If the hyperfocal distance of the disposable camera levels out, or even flattens out, all of the elements on a single plane,[27] the instantaneity of the shot, from a technical point of view, gives to the image an incomparable authenticity. The following versions of this live recording will extend to accentuate the sensationalism of the imagery, especially by pushing intensity fluctuations and color changes of the textual parts (black, then red, and modification of the title font), and by removing the article "The" from the title, pointing out the impossible designation of the object.

Whatever may have been the variations of this representation, the discords of its reception are the only aim—the scene itself had been organized with the goal of emphasizing its damnation. Staging death, like von Kleist or Mishima did, is an address to the world, a new form of ritualization. For Euronymous, the aim was firstly photographic (and ritualistic, by preserving some relics). Despite its incongruity (the peak of the gun is hidden by the arm, the jacket is partially taken off), the composition confers to the image a repeated triangular display, organic (from the brain to the heart to the hand), or material (knife, gun, jacket). The scene is flamboyant in its suffocative visual complexity. The exuberance of the body, in its curves, counter-curves, flame-like lines and meanders drags the eyes by the ardor of its sparkle to an infernal movement, as in the richest moment of the Gothic style. This "sleeping beauty" on an almost lascivious position, recalling the numerous languid Venuses of art history, seems to be doomed to inertia yet. If the open mouth seems to let a last breath escape, the look aiming at the sky and the contortion of the limbs (distinctive traits of death appearance, encountered also in *The Death of Dido* painting by Rubens) assign to the deceased a brutal materiality of the instant. The transcendence, drained from the scene, probably encouraged some artists to glorify the swan song: hasty reappropriations—including the luxuriant painting with garish colors hanging over the canvas, like blood, by Benjamin Eliasz in 2010, or *Topp Tiles* by S. Mark Gubb in 2011, inclining towards the decorative aspect recalling *azulejos*—keep the anecdote dormant and struggle to go beyond the subject. Other more distanced reinterpretations transform the sign, as Lisa Lie and Erik Tidemann attempted with the *Skogsunderholdning: Talk Softly but Carry a Big Stick* performance in 2007: by confronting occultism and reality, they reuse the bloody T-shirt with the "I ♥ Transylvania" design worn by Dead. While the horrific and terrible aesthetic can be a source of pleasure, Steven Shearer desacralizes the abjection, notably by extracting the figure from the monstrous scene (as in *Untitled Drawing*, 2010), but

Figure 2. Steven Shearer, *Untitled Drawing*, 2010, ballpoint pen on paper, 11.5 x 8.8 cm. ©Courtesy of the artist and Galerie Eva Presenhuber, Zürich.

mostly by repeating the representation as shown by various works since 2006. For example, the black, vigorous, and prominent outline in the *Fuck Off* (2010–2014) drawing is counterbalanced by the appeasement and the sensitivity shining through his *Untitled Drawings* (2008).

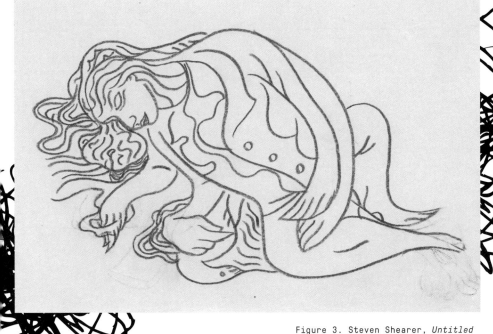

Figure 3. Steven Shearer, *Untitled Drawings* (detail), 2008, crayon on Japanese paper, 1 of 7 drawings, framed drawing: 10.5 x 15.9 cm. ©Courtesy of the artist and Galerie Eva Presenhuber, Zürich.

We can see here all the flamboyance of a languid body, burning with softness, with undetermined and infinite curves, mixing in an ox blood red the organic with the imagined. The work *Last View (Dead)* (2012) by Graham Dolphin also suggests respite: it depicts what could have been the last view of the singer and proposes a very redeeming off-screen. Finally, completely leaving aside the explicit reference, the work *Pagan Postcards (Mayhem Excerpt #3)* from a 2011 series by Johan Bergström relieves the viewer. The perfect melancholic coloring of this Norwegian landscape reflects the astounding reality of its words, "Only silence can be heard,"[28] and confronts us with the oblivion of disappearance.

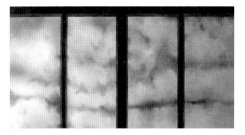

Figure 4. Graham Dolphin, *Last View (Dead)*, 2012, graphite on paper, 90 x 130 cm. ©Courtesy of the artist and David Risley Gallery, Copenhagen.

Figure 5. Johan Bergström, *Pagan Postcards (Mayhem Excerpt #03)*, 2011, pigment print, 43 x 59 cm / 65 x 89 cm / 100 x 137 cm. ©Courtesy of the artist.

Photography is, by its essence, the capture of what is gone; it keeps the trace of what no longer is. The taboo of death is also the one of its representations, because "[i]f the photograph then becomes horrible, it is because it certifies, so to speak, that the corpse is alive, as corpse: it is the living image of a dead thing."[29] *The Dawn of the Black Hearts* cover art is shocking by its nature, history, and presence. Although it is outside of the usual black metal codes, it submits color to a new typology of horror by reinvesting it with a transgressive burden. If Dead, always aiming at outrageousness and chaos, wanted to stir up disgust—"I want people to feel disgust when they see us live"[30]—the exhibition of his dead body is certainly the final statement of his desire to provoke, his ultimate work of art. Does the transgressive part of the image come from its subject, the gesture that initiated it, its content, its diffusion—all the more so as a certain sociology of reception can multiply the perceived feelings? Is an image more shocking when it is a raw documentary photograph or when we face an artistic gesture meant to transform the vision? Does the reality invite us to its own escape? Is art the place for this break?

The body, blocked up under the varnish of the inks, this "lake of blood haunted by bad angels,"[31] turns the figure into an eternal icon, a Peisithanatos who invites us not to our own death but to consider life in a different light, to confront and to accept our own void. It is more the evocative power of Transylvania than the Scandinavian mythology celebrating Odin for his brave suicide, which inspired Dead. Cioran, born in Transylvania, more than allows to shine a light on experiences lived by Dead; he could have been his very inspiration—first, by considering the suicide as an escape: "Look, don't be desperate, you can kill yourself whenever you want";[32] then, by arousing the possible negation of his condition: if "man can also be *not-man—that is, something other than himself— then I am not-man*."[33] The French-Romanian thinker forecasts the decline of humanity that Dead felt: "I am not a human being. This is just a dream, and soon I will awake,"[34] or "I am a mortal, but am I human?...A human destiny, but nothing human inside."[35] Going out of oneself, more than in negation, through disinterest, gives access to the ultimate aesthetic experience; where the cadaver disappears for itself, the beauty looms, and where our fleeing being finds a consolation in art. Extinguishing passions to learn to die.

Figure 6. Élodie Lesourd, *Synopsie (blackSheart)*, 2019, print on paper, aluminium tape on paper and on floor, 260 x 580 cm (on the wall). ©Courtesy of the artist.

Notes

[1]E.M. Cioran, *On the Heights of Despair*, trans. Ilinca Zarifopol-Johnston (Chicago: University of Chicago Press, 1992), 56; originally published as *Pe culmile disperării* (București: Fundatia pentru literatura si arta Regele Carol II, 1934).

[2]Quoted in Max Kozloff, "Photography: The Coming of Age of Colour," *Artforum* 13, no. 5 (January 1975): 34; David Douglas Duncan said this in 1968.

[3]Roland Barthes, *Camera Lucida*, trans. Richard Howard (New York: Hill and Wang, 1981), 81; originally published as *La chambre claire: Note sur la photographie* (Paris: Gallimard, 1980).

[4]E.M. Cioran, "The Book of Delusions," chapter 5, *Hyperion* 5, no. 1 (May 2010): 79; originally published as *Cartea amăgirilor* (București: Editura Cugetarea, 1936).

[5]"Qualité puissance" is an expression that Gilles Deleuze used in his class on cinema at Paris 8 Vincennes–Saint-Denis University, January 11, 1983. All the uncredited translations are by the author.

[6]An inversion of Jean-Luc Godard's famous quote.

[7]A statement recorded by Gaston Diehl, June 1943.

[8]Hicham-Stéphane Afeissa, *Esthétique de la charogne* (Bellevaux: Éditions Dehors, 2019).

[9]Julia Kristeva, *Powers of Horror: An Essay on Abjection*, trans. Leon S. Roudiez (New York: Columbia University Press, 1982), 149; originally published as *Pouvoirs de l'horreur: Essai sur l'abjection* (Paris: Seuil, 1980).

[10]"...ce qui est encore présent quand il n'y a personne"; Maurice Blanchot, *The Space of Literature*, trans. Ann Smock (Lincoln: University of Nebraska Press, 1982), 30; originally published as *L'espace littéraire* (Paris: Gallimard, 1955).

[11]Jacques Lacan, *The Seminar of Jacques Lacan*, Book II: *The Ego in Freud's Theory and in the Technique of Psychoanalysis, 1954-1955*, ed. Jacques-Alain Miller, trans. Sylvana Tomaselli (Cambridge: Cambridge University Press, 1988), 231; originally published as *Le Séminaire*, livre II: *Le Moi dans la théorie de Freud et dans la technique de la psychanalyse (1954-1955)* (Paris: Éditions du Seuil, 1977).

[12]Mortuary portrait of Evelyn McHale, shot

four minutes after her suicide, on May 1, 1947. The image was later colorized, inspiring, among others, Andy Warhol, for his 1963 work *Suicide (Fallen Body)*.

[13]For instance: Carcass, Nailbomb, Pissgrave, Numenorean, etc.

[14]The expression "to travel to Transylvania" became a metaphor evoking suicide.

[15]Photographs shot by Øyvind Ihlen at the rehearsal studio with fake blood or those shot in the basement of Øystein Aarseth's father's house in Ski, etc.

[16]Vladimir Jankélévitch, *La Mort* (Paris: Flammarion, 1966).

[17]"There is but one truly serious philosophical problem and that is suicide"; Albert Camus, *The Myth of Sisyphus*, trans. Justin O'Brien (London: Hamish Hamilton, 1965), 11; originally published as *Le mythe de Sisyphe* (Paris: Gallimard, 1942).

[18]E.M. Cioran, *A Short History of Decay*, trans. Richard Howard (New York: Arcade Publishing, 2012), 37; originally published as *Précis de décomposition* (Paris: Gallimard, 1949).

[19]"L'égarement qu'est la vie"; E.M. Cioran, "Le crépuscule des pensées," French trans. Mirella Patureau-Nedelco and Christiane Fremont, in *Oeuvres* (Paris: Quarto Gallimard, 1995), 490; originally published as *Amurgul gândurilor* (Sibiu: Tipografia Dacia Traiana, 1940).

[20]The Rockheim Museum in Trondheim, Norway, holds written lyrics by Dead.

[21]Among the Diolas of Senegal, voluntary death upsets the living, as it allows ghosts to persecute them; see Martin Monestier, *Suicides: Histoire, techniques et bizarreries de la mort volontaire des origines à nos jours* (Paris: Le Cherche midi, 1995).

[22]Published by Avantgarde Music; the 1993 edition, released by Obscure Plasma Records, had a different cover.

[23]"[C]'est le cadavre qui assigne un espace à l'expérience profondément et originairement utopique du corps"; Michel Foucault, "Le corps utopique" (radio lecture), December 7, 1966, *France Culture*; accessed April 25, 2021, https://www.youtube.com/watch?v=NSNkxvGlUNY;

published as Michel Foucault, "Le corps utopique," in *Le corps utopique—Les Hétérotopies* (Paris: Éditions Lignes, 2009). "[I]t is the corpse that assign[s] a space to the profoundly and originally utopian experience of the body"; Michel Foucault, "Utopian Body," trans. Lucia Allais, in *Sensorium: Embodied Experience, Technology, and Contemporary Art*, ed. Caroline A. Jones (Cambridge, MA: MIT Press, 2006), 233.

[24]E.M. Cioran, *Tears and Saints*, trans. Ilinca Zarifopol-Johnston (Chicago: University of Chicago Press, 1998), 8. "La musique est un tombeau des délices, une béatitude qui nous ensevelit"; E.M. Cioran, *Des larmes et des saints*, French trans. Sanda Stolojan (Paris: L'Herne, 1986), 95; originally published as *Lacrimi si sfinti* (București: Editura Autorului, 1937).

[25]Extract of a note by Euronymous on the back of the vinyl edition.

[26]The text was titled *Dawn of the Black Hearts*, but Euronymous refused to use it.

[27]Cameras in fashion during the 1990s; they have received a surprising resurgence of interest recently.

[28]Lyrics written by Dead for the song "Buried by Time and Dust," on Mayehm, *De Mysteriis Dom Sathanas* (Oslo: Deathlike Silence Productions, 1994).

[29]Barthes, *Camera Lucida*, 79.

[30]Dead, interviewed in *Putrefaction Zine* no. 3 (1990): 28.

[31]"[L]ac de sang hanté des mauvais anges"; Charles Baudelaire, "Les phares," in *Les Fleurs du mal* (Alençon: Auguste Poulet-Malassis et De Broise, 1857), 24.

[32]"Écoutez, ne soyez pas désespérés, vous pouvez vous tuer quand vous voudrez"; E.M. Cioran, "Entretien avec Leo Gillet," in *Entretiens*, ed. François Bondy (Paris: Gallimard, 1985), 95.

[33]Cioran, *On the Heights of Despair*, 69.

[34]Dead's suicide note: "Jag är inte en människa. Det här är bara en dröm, och snart vaknar jag."

[35]Extract from "Life Eternal," lyrics written by Dead on April 8, 1991.

Stephen Wilson
Homogenesis, 2021
digital illustration, 13.97 x 21.59 cm
courtesy of the artist

Bizarre Black Metal

DANIEL LUKES

A key, yet underrated, component of second-wave black metal's sound, aesthetic, and philosophy, despite the genre's overt subscription to black-and-white paradigms of starkness and glumness, is a spirit of the carnivalesque.

This element is clearly discernable in bands falling under what we might term the "bizarre black metal" or "weird black metal" umbrella. Channeling and splicing industrial electronica and noise, baroque and symphonic prog rock, and cosmic, sci-fi, and surreal themes—modernist, avant-garde, and futuristic bands as diverse as Arcturus, Ulver, Covenant/The Kovenant, Dødheimsgard, Fleurety, Sigh, and many others unshackle black metal from its grim and icy valleys to go stargazing in "spiritual black dimensions" and dance through "bizarre cosmic industries." Bizarre black metal bands such as Impaled Nazarene, Tsatthoggua, and Vondur take the nominally asexual and self-serious genre down camp and comedy alleys and Sadean gutters in an orgiastic war dance of suicidal self-abandon and joyful karmageddon. The carnivalesque opens up black metal's infinite black hole, shitting out glorious rainbow shards of black metal futurities and possibilities along the way, to populate a valley full of black metal's splurging colors.

Two main currents of second-wave black metal can be identified, starting in the early 1990s: the grim and frostbitten variant that skews toward the minimalist (Darkthrone, Burzum, Immortal), often evoking large expansive landscapes devoid of life (human, animal, or vegetable) and populated by frozen forests, glaciers, ice storms, and their attendant demons, and the symphonic variant: opulent, synthesizer-saturated and layered: bands such as Emperor, Cradle of Filth, Dimmu Borgir. Symphonic black metal bands are often over-the-top excessive and abundant, in a sense that recalls the Bataille of *The Accursed Share* (*La part maudite*),[1] expressing the too muchness and overabundance of life's vitalistic spread in all its piping diversity, rather than a sense of paucity or lack. Between these two poles of the black metal spectrum—paucity and excess—there is a strain that traverses and infects both of them, that of the carnivalesque, circus, or clown black metal, which I will be addressing in this chapter under the banner of bizarre (or weird) black metal.[2]

Bizarre black metal is not so much a subgenre (though it can be a subgenre) as a mode or approach that both diverges from canonical and hegemonic black metal paths and yet imbues those very paths with a spirit that flickers and disappears at will, like the archetypal trickster. Even the most ostensibly dour and po-faced of the black-and-white black metal set, who rail at the unrelenting bleakness of a world crystalized and smeared with the cascading ash of crushed and crumbling empires, may, at closer analysis, be seen as performing a little dance of the camp and the grotesque, the downturned black metal mouth in actuality an upside-down crooked grin. Immortal, for example, whose postures have always invited equal awe and ridicule, and who, for this reason, I would say, in addition to their stark and iconographic corpsepaint, have become *the* memeworthy face of the genre. Immortal's campness is beyond doubt and is very much visible in their "Call of the Wintermoon" and "Blashyrkh (Mighty Ravendark)" videos and in a certain knowing and winking approach to the genre's conventions, including that very memorable photoshoot with extended "invisible orange" hand gestures and drummer

Horgh ostensibly sticking his gut out. When Immortal go prancing in the forest, it is fabulously silly, and it would be ridiculous to deny that silliness is one of the key pleasures of black metal, however much it may be disavowed. The "Call of the Wintermoon" video speeded up and set to the ludicrous Benny Hill theme tune completes the picture. The line that goes "You might say I'm demonized"—from "Grim and Frostbitten Kingdoms"—is, for me at least, possibly the quintessential black metal lyric, the delicacy of the "you might say" perfectly poised against and the classic Satanism of "I'm demonized"—joyfully contaminating, diluting, and queering it. You *might* say I'm demonized. Then again, you might not. Who's to say, really?

On some level, black metal is notoriously asexual or presexual, in that it presents a desexualized male figure who sublimates his frustrated teenage horniness in a preadolescent *Dungeons and Dragons* or *Lord of the Rings* world of male goblin demons. In the world of black metal, sex is generally left out of the picture, and this provides comfort from the demands of sex. The exception to this (proving the rule) is when sex is introduced into the picture as rape in the context of Sadean symphonic or ritualistic black metal bands such as Cradle of Filth, Impaled Nazarene, and Belphegor. If grim and frostbitten black metal represents a denial of the sexual body in favor of the pure transcendence of the becoming mineral ice storm as a way of fleeing the sufferings and achings of the lonely flesh, symphonic black metal presents itself as especially grounded in the flesh, a horrorflesh of erotic excess à la *Hellraiser*. Cradle of Filth's *Midian* (2000) mentions "lips" eight times ("a mask of rich red lips," "new lusts eclipsing lips," "lips attuned to symmetry," "wet lips nailed to cemetery coldness," "familiar lips licking dry a witch's itching stitches," etc.).

Symphonic black metal and lo-fi can certainly overlap, such as in Emperor's *In the Nightside Eclipse* (1994), which combines a raw, lo-fi production with its symphonic aspirational grandeur, with the paradoxical result of being grounded in limitation and smallness, yet dreaming of and reaching for the stars. If black metal is constantly in tension between the poles of excessive black metal and minimalist black metal, bizarre black metal flits between the two, unfurling black metal's innate weirdness, belying its inability to take itself or be taken seriously, despite what the po-faced brigade may want to argue. Bizarre black metal tilts the symphonic sublime into the ridiculous, with its delusions of aristocratic highness brought into absurdist little dances of the grotesque. The jaunty, waltzy "Trollberg" on Troll's *Drep de kristne* (1996, a Nagash side-project), with its time signature combination of 6/8 over 2/4, with triplets on the ride cymbal, is synth-drenched silliness, a gothic ballroom number conjuring up a feel of castle dancing.

It quite possibly is the best thing Troll have ever recorded, because it forgets all about black metal for a moment only to cast black metal as a charade, a bit of troll mountain fun, fantasy role-playing and a dance. On Encyclopedia Metallum, Noctir writes that "Trollberg" "is totally ridiculous and tries to add some sort of folk feeling...[a] goofy song."[3] Black metal teeters on an edge, and bizarre black metal pulls it down into strange and dark waters, getting it wet and undignified in the process.

SEND IN THE CLOWNS[4]

Despite its protestations, black metal is pop music of a sort; just listen to Darkthrone's "Transylvanian Hunger" and tell me it isn't a great pop song. However strongly black metal may define itself against The Beatles, what I'd like to look at is how black metal digests and works through The Beatles, just like everyone else has to contend with them in one way or another. Not just any old Beatles. In the way that "Eleanor Rigby" can be seen to predict depressive suicidal black metal ("All the lonely people/where do they all come from?"), here we will look at how the clowncore Beatles of "Being for the Benefit of Mr. Kite!" prefigures circus black metal.

We can place the song as a beginning point of carnival or circus rock; its genesis originates from the contents of a nineteenth-century circus poster bought from an antique shop and in John Lennon's possession, the lyrics being all elements or adaptations of the various circus acts listed there. Circus rock takes the circus performance and atmosphere as its world, recreating rock music through that prism: the carny atmosphere, the traveling show, the barker and announcer of the great delights that await under the big top, the clown a central figure, of course. One early example is *The Rolling Stones Rock and Roll Circus* (1968), a show performed on a replica circus stage at Wembley Stadium, featuring The Rolling Stones, Jethro Tull, The Who, Marianne Faithfull, John Lennon and Yoko Ono, and Eric Clapton. The Beatles begat Pink Floyd who begat King Crimson (with their futuristic, Twenty-First-Century Schizoid take on the carnival, and the space carnival, a subroutine of space opera, that would loop back into black metal as cosmic circus black metal), who begat Ozzy Osbourne, Screaming Lord Sutch, Frank Zappa and Captain Beefheart, The Residents, Devo, Foetus and J.G. Thirlwell, Oingo Boingo and Danny Elfman,[5] leading to Mr. Bungle and Faith No More in the context of funk metal and comedic thrash, particularly fertile in the Bay Area and beyond: Thought Industry, Primus, Mordred, Gwar, Green Jellÿ, Lawnmower Deth, Big Dumb Face.

Mr. Bungle in particular are a sort of ground zero for circus rock in the modern era, influencing Korn and nu metal (Korn refer to a "Bungle chord" they used in their early days), System of a Down, and Slipknot and their various offshoots and soundalikes (Mudvayne, Motograter, Mushroomhead, and the genre still going with bands like Sunflower Children, Amerakin Overdose, and Kissing Candice). The 1990s were a golden age of circus metal, in which we have sad or angry clowns: the sad Pierrot, like Marilyn Manson,[6] and the evil clown—Louisiana band Acid Bath used a self-portrait by serial killer John Wayne Gacy of himself as Pogo the Clown. Mark Dery analyzes this figure, which is a horror movie trademark, in his essay "Cotton Candy Autopsy: Deconstructing Psycho Killer Clowns."[7] Eighties and nineties alternative rock was rich in clownery, from Butthole Surfers, Clown Alley (and their 1985 abum *Circus of Chaos*), Melvins, Cows, and the Amphetamine Reptile scene to Ween, Pigface, and industrial rock. Or bands with names like Pigmy Love Circus, Tumor Circus, Nero Circus, and Circus of Power. Pop-punk band Pennywise took their name from the evil clown in Stephen King's *It*, and NOFX's Fat Mike has an alter ego named Cokie the Clown. There is horrorcore circus rap, spearheaded by Insane Clown Posse, whose *The Great Milenko* (1997) digs deep in the clowncore well, and whose followers, the Juggalos, are also a kind of parallel world black metal type in their own Insane Clown Forest. Even Kiss had their clowncore record, 1998's *Psycho Circus*—and so did David Lynch: 2011's *Crazy Clown Time*. In 2018, we saw the emergence of saxophone, keyboard, and drum duo Clown Core, who made a splash with the video of their song "Hell," performed in a porta potty. Pink titled her 2008 album *Funhouse* and Katy Perry's 2020 album *Smile* has her in a sad clown costume on the cover. So many rock 'n' roll clowns and circuses over the years!

Oingo Boingo's American new wave take on The Beatles brings ska into contact with goth, and Mr. Bungle add in death metal. Bungle's self-titled debut album, produced by John Zorn, is a ska-funk-metal prog carnival, with the occasional foray into death metal growling and grumbling and a juvenile, scatological quality. "Carousel" is a representative song, self-consciously configuring rock music as a roundabout, a show: "If you want to know what's behind the show/You ride my carousel and enter life's jail cell/Love and blood begin to meld, you've lost the self that you once held/Merry go round your head—awake, asleep, alive, or dead." Like The Beatles' *Sgt. Pepper's*, it is rock as self-consciousness, a show within a show—another type of show constructed from an earlier art form. Here, a tangent could be rock's minstrel show roots, on the topic of which Drew Daniel's essay "Corpsepaint as Necro-Minstrelsy" does a great job of tracing the glitchy lineage between blackface minstrelsy and black metal corpsepaint.[8]

Mr. Bungle's second album *Disco Volante* (1995) represents a qualitative jump for the band, who go far and deep into progressive, avant, and musique concrète territories; the album is named after villain Emilio Largo's boat in the James Bond film *Thunderball*, which is, in turn, Italian for flying saucer (literally "flying disc"). It lives up to the multiple and layered meanings of its name (disco as in discotheque, where records are played), and digging deep into noise rock, musique concrète, ambient, it's funk metal in the context of a cold alien and underwater world. *Disco Volante* is an abstract and retrofuturistic science fiction adventure, creating a deep and immersive environment where everything is sunken and genre distinctions have lost their meaning. It feels like an artifact from a previous future, a work of underwater necromancy that time has flattened and in which oceanic pressure has melded together things previously separate. *Disco Volante* is of the genre of the miscellany, the anthology, the almanac, a maritime motley of discordant and barnacled cultural refuse; its final track "Merry Go Bye Bye" jams together The Beach Boys and death metal aliens in a sci-fi alien trip to the stars, where we're all going eventually in the form of stardust. Mr. Bungle's 1999 *California* also embraces The Beach Boys, in an even more terminal way, not least for being their last record—for the following two decades at least.

NEGATIVE KINGDOM AND THE SOFT BLACK STARS

Of course, black metal is not immune from the allure of the circus call, and there is a carnival developing at the heart of the black metal scene. Ulver and Arcturus, the projects of Kristoffer Rygg, are obvious candidates for analyzing black metal's carnivalesque and can certainly be compared to the work of Mike Patton and Mr. Bungle. Arcturus in particular are one of the architects of black metal's carnival bizarre, starting out as melodic black metal with a stargazing bent, with *La Masquerade Infernale* (1997) they abandoned their Norse medieval vibe and adopted a swashbuckling, prog-manic development. Rygg's melodicism is all over this album, which stomps through proggy carousels of piratic nonsense, welding black metal infernalities to gemstones of ironical glee, harking back to an eighteenth- and nineteenth-century aesthetic, visible in the cover art, with its robes, mask, and blunderbuss. The high point of this album is Simen Haestnes's shrieking on "The Chaos Path" (he would become the band's singer after Rygg departed). Arcturus is a prime representative of black metal that jauntily brings in the circus organ, foregrounding black metal as a form of black clowning. Rygg named his label Jester Records,[9] and the band went by the name Arcturus and The Deception Circus for their remix/compilation album *Disguised Masters* (1999), which featured an early example of rap/black metal crossover, "Master of Disguise (Phantom FX Remix)."

Arcturus arguably reached their pinnacle with *The Sham Mirrors* (2002), which streamlined their sound into a compressed cosmic prog black metal pop sound on a one-way trip to the stars, in which black metal arguably appears as the key to human self-annihilation. This album appears to weave a science fiction fantasy about extinction, in which the music itself plays the role of humanity's trace persisting as an echo in the universe after it has gone, and black metal is its letter to the future. It is a cosmic voyage that ends in disaster and transcendence: humanity wiped out and transmogrified into something astral but evanescent, a piece of culture, a ghost transmission that speaks to itself in digital circularity, a closed-circuit swansong for humanity's lullaby.

The works of French band Spektr complete this thought, making black metal into a spidery static trace. Unlike Spektr, much cosmic black metal is not minimalist and spectral but rich and sumptuous, and *The Sham Mirrors* is a fairly flawless example of excessive cosmic bizarre black metal, the circus in space; instead of being raw and grainy, it presents a pristine surface of electronic goggling and squelching, heavily processed and compressed guitar sounds resonant of the flashiest industrial metal, and, above all, the soaring vocals of Rygg, who turns in a maestro performance. *The Sham Mirrors* works and wows through excess; it is all too much, deliberately and ostentatiously so. The closing track "For to End Yet Again" is a glorious funk metal cavalcade with Pattonesque vocals that slip and slobber all over waltzy drunken odes to future regenerations, cyclical reconstitutions of the monadic self, biomatter separated Babel-like by walled-off consciousness in cells: the negative kingdom of space.

Cosmic black metal also flourishes within two paradigms, the minimal and the excessive, raising the question of how to faithfully sonically represent outer space. The cold, ghoulish expanses of Limbonic Art, Darkspace, Mysticum, and Mare Cognitum, which project gloom into the bitterly compressed places of deep space black metal. Godlessness blooms in these darknesses: the dead crackle of radio-transmitted extraterrestrial movements transmits mechanical assemblages of the universal paradigm. In space, no one can hear you scream, but the grindings of the planets, the rock and ice and sheer minerality of the expansive dimensions of the outward reach into the black void and echo backward: an abyss that undulates in rubberized blissful horror that can only be placated by starsong. Thus, the space metal arias of Covenant/The Kovenant's *Nexus Polaris*: ultramelodic cavalcades that gallop and trample the stars in souped-up technological chariots, jalopies of digital flame that warp, and disrupt star-kissed corridors, the stars themselves a bejeweled crystal world that pulses in wicked agony and sighs of sweat-drenched surrender of the mutating human flesh.

Nexus Polaris presents a welcome feminine black metal spirit, with its cover art of a cosmic goddess triumphant, in saturated blue airbrush art, and Sarah Jezabel Diva's soaring vocals, which elevate the chuggingly compressed industrial/black-thrash riffage into the cosmic realms of the beyond. Along the lines of forward-thinking mutoid black metal that never repeats itself, Covenant's next release would see them morph into the Kovenant, who with *Animatronic* would present a sheerly cyber-goth industrial metal face, with vocalist Lex Icon, formerly Nagash of Dimmu Borgir, getting more visually into the role of Marilyn Mansonesque goth androgyne, replete with silvery dress and pigtails. The album is a love it or hate it fan favorite, recalling Rammstein spliced with a black metal pop folk melodicism, once more elevated by operatic female vocals (Eileen Küpper), and a daring, if forgettable, cover of Babylon Zoo's "Spaceman." On their follow-up, 2003's *S.E.T.I.*, the Kovenant continued to go even more cyber-spacey industrially, jettisoning their black metalness altogether, to far less interesting results, and the follow-up album *Aria Galactica* remains unreleased.

MODERNIST BLACK METAL

One of the traditional journeys of black metal is from medievalism to futurism; second-wave black metal situates its events within a fantastic medieval framework, a world building of fantasy darkness and aristocratic cruelty. Satyricon's *Dark Medieval Times* and Covenant's *In Times Before the Light* speak of a hellworld built upon a "Dark Ages" cultural ideology filtered through occult Satanic horror, not unlike that of manga *Berserk*, in which the "Apostles," the leaders of the Christian church, are helldemons in disguise. Black metal travels through time to the modern day: from *The Shadowthrone* (1994), with its Viking folk pop songs and its flights over peaks and valleys, swooping over forests and fjords and peaking in particular in the soaring call and response folk melodicism of "Vikingland," and Satyricon's next album *Nemesis Divina* (1996), altogether heavier, thrashier, and more "metal." Satyricon shift gears with *Rebel Extravaganza* (1999), which is a dive into urban and dystopian landscapes, with a bare-bones industrial-tinged sound, which has remained a mark of their music for quite a while now. *Rebel Extravaganza* is central to black metal's modernist movement, a trend toward the abstract and the futuristic running throughout alternative metal and culminating in nu metal and emo.

Satyr's label Moonfog Productions positioned itself as a leader in forward-thinking black metal, namely, the idea that black metal itself was subject to evolutionary forces, a genre under some kind of obligation to evolve and climb out of its self-imposed gutter, reinvent itself, and try to become radically different each time.[10] Moonfog signed bands like Dødheimsgard, Disiplin, Gehenna, Khold, Thorns—and also stalwarts Darkthrone, who never underwent a modernist renovation but remained staunchly traditionalist in terms of working within a recognizably classic metal framework—and some side projects (Neptune Towers, Wongraven). *Moonfog 2000—A Different Perspective* was a taste of this: a label sampler that, down to the graphic design, fomented a modernist, futuristic, abstract aesthetic, even spilling into cyber, electro, and industrial styles and sounds; Satyricon themselves embraced the cult of the remix for the *Megiddo* EP (1997), on which they previewed their new industrial sound.

The key band on this mix was Dødheimsgard, with their 1999 album *666 International*, which is explored in detail in this book's oral history chapter, on pages 193-206. Beyond Moonfog there was a plethora of black metal bands branching into the modernist and industrial void: ...And Oceans, with their electro dance black metal release *A.M.G.O.D* (2001), Source of Tide with *Blueprints* (2002), Manes with *Vilosophe* (2003), etc. Where did modernist black metal go? It had many fates: it petered out and disappeared and was replaced by a triumphant traditionalist black metal movement in the 2000s; it exited the genre and left black metal behind, as in the case of Ulver; it folded its modernisms back into a black metal—the case of Satyricon; and it filtered through to our time, with the development of post-black metal and blackgaze.

Satyricon streamlined their sound into a kind lean and minimalist black 'n' roll, exemplified by the song "Fuel for Hatred" (2002), whose video saw Satyricon team up with Jonas Åckerlund for a very rock star feel (including sunglasses!): black metal had finally found its way to Sunset Strip circa 1980s, long before the *Lords of Chaos* movie. They spent the 2000s and 2010s perfecting their formula, putting out solid and convincing albums with tight songwriting, especially *Now, Diabolical* (2006) and *The Age of Nero* (2008), the industrial influence not so obvious but folded into their sound in terms of a kind of discipline and minimalism, replete with a flair for pop economy and for addictive and memorable choruses.

Black metal also goes to chiller places: cool urbanity replaces rural jaggedness and hostility, the howling winds of the forest at night in the snow and the dripping ice are traded for the clean exactitude of a techno, disco ambience. Kristoffer

Rygg's current main project Ulver's *Perdition City* (2000), sometimes decried as "black metal goes trip-hop," illuminated how one could slip out of black metal so easily, quit it for good, while also never quite leaving it fully behind. By moving beyond it in radical cuts, Ulver opened up black metal by erasing its most obvious elements, its basement convulsing and headache din, while preserving its sense of melancholy, hopelessness, and emptiness, and opening up a post-black metal field of pop, rock, and electronica, illustrating how it is possible to push the limits of what black metal could be in any direction.

Rygg was able to transcend black metal—no easy feat. Ulver keep going, embracing pop and ambient in a consciously *avant* way, playing with geopolitical symbology: the white and red and the red cross imagery of *Blood Inside* (2005), the Osama bin Laden prophet in swirling bullet storms in the video of its lead single "It Is Not Sound," and *The Assassination of Julius Caesar* (2017), which you could describe as the best album Duran Duran never made.

WHEN ALL GOLDEN TURNED TO SHIT

It's important not to be too rosy about black metal's carnivalesque and remember its ugly side. Bizarre black metal is also Beherit and Impaled Nazarene and Vondur and Tsatthoggua: a grimy black metal carnival of the gutter that can be menacing, sexualized and rapey, and kitsch pornographic black metal. Finnish band Impaled Nazarene are fairly unique, exuding in their early releases an overriding aesthetic of grimy punk disgust, in particular on their debut *Tol Cormpt Norz Norz Norz*. Their 1996 album *Latex Cult* suggests a different type of partying like it's 1999, a cyber-fetish death orgy at the end of the world, in which all rules are suspended and a terminal carnival of sex and death reigns, exploding into an ejaculatory burst of sound. It is more Merzbow than Mayhem, the reverb squeal of Jimi Hendrix extended out infinitely in an endless orgasm. But look a little closer and Impaled Nazarene reveal themselves as right-wingers, the Finnish flag nationalistically draped over their artwork, and fascistic sentiments expressed in their music: the lyrics of "Winter War" ("20,000 Communists dead, we'll do it again"), a track that reprises Boyd Rice's "Total War," and "Ghettoblaster," with its images of rats and genocide recalling Nazi hatred of Jews. Not to mention the homophobic song from 2000, "Zero Tolerance" ("Why should we tolerate pansy faggot shit/Not even in an animal world, male sucks male dick"). For a band built on a Sadean orgy of cruelty aesthetic, this rote homophobia is somewhat depressing.

Finnish band Tsatthoggua put out two albums of bizarre fetish black metal in the nineteen: *Hosanna Bizarre* (1996) and *Trans Cunt Whip* (1998). Though musically quite conventional, *Hosanna Bizarre* stands out for its sadomasochistic artwork, featuring a hooded gimp dominating a woman in a white dress and corpsepaint, who on the back cover is dominating him. Vondur, yet another Finnish band, pursues a kind of *Star Wars* galactic black 'n' roll, with the album *Striðsyfirlýsing* (1996), which features cover art of Darth Vader doing what looks like an invisible orange gesture, and the EP *The Galactic Rock 'n' Roll Empire* (1998), which includes covers of Bathory, Judas Priest, Mötley Crüe, and Elvis and a confederate flag adorned with a golden flaming inverted cross and lavish Vondur logo on the cover. When I interviewed Trey Spruance of Mr. Bungle in London in 2000, we discussed Vondur, which I called more of a joke band. Spruance disagreed:

Is it though? I mean, think about those people man, they are fucking fucked up...I take that as really serious in a certain way. I think that those guys are really serious. They're making a masquerade out of the commodification of black metal. It's a pretty serious thing to do, you know. They were right to do it. I'm totally on Vondur's wavelength on all of that.[11]

Black metal as carnival is also Peste Noire and their accordion-wielding nationalist troubadour black metal. Peste Noire freely enters and exits black metal, blurring an understanding of the boundaries of the genre, with extensive forays into folk, punk, noise rock experimentalism, Tom Waits drunken rambling clochard lunacy, even rap and trap music. Sad irony that one of the few explicit attempts at a black metal/hip-hop crossover (their *Peste Noire—Split—Peste Noire* album, 2018) is a right-wing and racist one, adorned with blackface artwork. What Peste Noire represents is the extent to which far-right politics has embraced clownish and carnival cultures as cover for political violence: joking and behaving buffoonishly—fascist clowning—is a way of disarming your po-faced enemy who does not take you as a serious threat and lets their guard down.[12] With their putsch imagery and would-be-Death in June costumes and performative madness in the school of Antonin Artaud and the theater of cruelty, Peste Noire stands out from NSBM, which tends to be musically and aesthetically very dull and formulaic (with its black-and-white photos of World War II and swastikas, its trad black metal visual aesthetic, and its music in the "brutal" tradition of Marduk or full of folk and triumphant prog flourishes) and makes use of the carnivalesque as a recruiting and organizing ground for neo-Nazis, via the band's associations with the Militant Zone label, the Asgardsrei festival, and the Azov Battalion. Underestimating the creative abilities of fascists is dangerous. Ah, how easy that would be, if one could equate aesthetic creativity and freedom with political progressiveness!

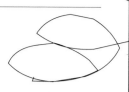

There's so much carnivalesque black metal to talk about; you could write a whole book. There is Sigh, with their psychedelic and prog heavy metal operatics, including saxophones; there is Abruptum's esoteric abstract black metal noise and Furze's deconstructed black 'n' roll; there is Fleurety and Zweizz and the projects of Svein Egil Hatlevik; there is the post-black metal of Solefald and In the Woods... and Borknagar and Vintersorg and folk black metal; there is Finntroll and Mortiis and Trollheims Grott and the subgenre of troll black metal; there is Charmand Grimloch's keyboard-drenched psychedelic black metal Tartaros; there is Evol and Opera IX and Aborym and weird black metal from Italy, including Inchiuvatu front man Agghiastru's host of Mediterranean scene bands and projects; there is Blut Aus Nord, recently embracing a psychedelic world of color on 2019 album *Hallucinogen*;[13] there is the industrial pink black metal dirgery of Fullmoon Bongzai and their 2008 album *Noisense*; there is Pensées Nocturnes and their circus-themed 2019 album *Grand Guignol Orchestra* or Mr. Bungle's Trey Spruance producing Imperial Triumphant's *Alphaville* (2020); there is Lifelover and the whole field of post-punk black metal crossover, including Beastmilk, Vaura, Penance Stare, Botanist, and the opening up to post-black metal, blackgaze, and lush black metal. The future of black metal is wide open, whether it is The Soft Pink Truth's disco irreverence, Deafheaven's black metal sounds of the summer, or Oranssi Pazuzu's black metal psychedelia. The carnivalesque is one of the ways black metal opens up to the world, and there is no going back.

The note I'd like to end on is black metal as self-care. Beyond the grim and harsh sounds and reputation, beneath the static fuzzing harshness, is a soft core, a grim beating heart of forgotten self-love. Black metal is taking care of yourself so you can take care of others. It is laughing so you don't cry, and its carnival is where that laughter most clearly rings out and echoes forth. What better to encapsulate this than the image of black metal as laundry: the black metal washing machine. *Terrorizer* magazine famously used variations on the phrase to describe Swedish band Marduk: "Not for nothing did our former editor dub them 'washing machine' metal. Just go to a Marduk live show and feel those endless blast beats, repetitive grinds and swirling heads lull you into a comatose trance,"[14] writes Keith Kahn-Harris in 2001, concluding that the album he is reviewing "will certainly see me through to the next slice of silliness from the black metal washing machine." This description is beautiful, because it contains affectionate mockery of Marduk's stiff rigor and refusal to budge from their self-serious war black metal template and brings out an inherent quality in the music

Figure 1. The Black
Metal Woolite meme.
Author unknown.

that is soft and mundane, which the music aggressively disavows (and this innocently before Marduk were known to be Nazis). The second image is the "Black Metal Woolite" meme, which features a black Woolite bottle, with images of Immortal on it, of course: "Most effective with evil washing maschine—Makes black from everything!" Third, we have the genre of YouTube videos of washing machines "playing" black or death metal—performing their percussive spins, which are akin to blastbeats, with a black or death metal track layered on top. Black metal is laundry, because black metal is self-care and catharsis: a laundrifying catharsis of all manner of unpleasantnesses, a hot bath of catharsis for feelings, round and round, until the soul is individually and socially cleansed, until next time. Black metal is community—a communal laundry—and must be open to everyone...

Notes

[1] Georges Bataille, *The Accursed Share: An Essay on General Economy*, Volume I: *Consumption*, trans. Robert Hurley (New York: Zone Books, 1991); Volume II: *The History of Eroticism*; Volume III: *Sovereignty*, trans. Robert Hurley (New York: Zone Books, 1993).

[2] Some black metal commentators use the term *weird*, including Dayal Patterson in his two chapters "A Turn for the Weird, Part I and II" in *Black Metal: Evolution of the Cult* (Port Townsend: Feral House, 2013), 414-27. In a review of Ulver's 1999 album *Themes from William Blake's The Marriage of Heaven and Hell*, Nick Terry refers to 1997 in black metal as "that Fabled Year When It All Went Weird," *Terrorizer* no. 63 (1999): 49. My choice of "bizarre" over "weird" is influenced by the song by Covenant/the Kovenant "Bizarre Cosmic Industries" —and alliteration.

[3] Noctir, "Review of Troll, *Drep de kristne*," *Encyclopedia Metallum*, November 3, 2012, accessed April 25, 2021, https://tinyurl.com/eey47m76.

[4] The title of this section references the 1973 song by Stephen Sondheim.

[5] The influence of Danny Elfman on symphonic black metal is huge, and you can hear it especially on Dimmu Borgir, *Death Cult Armageddon* (Nuclear Blast, 2003).

[6] In 2009, Trent Reznor said that Manson had become "a dopey clown"; Daniel Kreps, "Trent Reznor Says Marilyn Manson Has 'Become a Dopey Clown,'" *Rolling Stone*, June 2, 2009, accessed April 25, 2021, https://www.rollingstone.com/music/music-news/trent-reznor-says-marilyn-manson-has-become-a-dopey-clown-73520.

[7] Mark Dery, "Cotton Candy Autopsy: Deconstructing Psycho Killer Clowns," in *The Pyrotechnic Insanitarium: American Culture on the Brink* (New York: Grove Press, 1999), 63-86.

[8] Drew Daniel, "Corpsepaint as Necro-Minstrelsy, or Toward the Re-Occultation of Black Blood," in *Melancology: Black Metal Theory and Ecology*, ed. Scott Wilson (Winchester, UK: ZerO Books, 2014), 26-49.

[9] "The name Jester came up in the midst of Arcturus's cabaret/opera excursions, so we thought it was humoring, also as the music we were creating was becoming so strange and unpredictable, the jester seemed a fitting symbol for what we do"; Rygg speaking to Einar Sjursø, "Ulver: Lone Wolves," *Terrorizer* no. 63 (1999): 29.

[10] The term *modernist Black Metal aesthetic* is used to refer to Moonfog in a 1999 Satyricon cover story; Nick Terry, "Satyricon: The Art of Rebellion," *Terrorizer* no. 70 (1999): 16.

[11] Transcript of an interview with the author.

[12] For a discussion of the clownery of the fascist demagogue, see Theodor W. Adorno, "Anti-Semitism and Fascist Propaganda" (1946), in *The Stars Down to Earth and Other Essays on the Irrational in Culture* (London: Routledge, 1994), 218-31.

[13] Ironically, Vindsval of Blut Aus Nord uses the image of the circus to describe the kind of formulaic black metal he *disassociates* from: "If black metal is just this subversive feeling and not a basic musical style, then Blut Aus Nord is a black metal act. But if we have to be compared to all these childish Satanic clowns, please let us work outwards [from] this pathetic circus. This form of art deserves something else than these mediocre bands and their old music composed ten years before by someone else"; Chris Dick, "Blut Aus Nord," *Decibel* no. 26 (2006): 28.

[14] Keith Harris, "Marduk: *La Grande Danse Macabre*," *Terrorizer*, no. 88 (2001): 66.

DØDHEIMSGARD'S
666 INTERNATIONAL:

An Oral History

DANIEL LUKES

Dødheimsgard's *666 International* (Moonfog
Productions, 1999) is that unique black metal
album that boldly went where no black metal
had gone before—or has gone since. A strange
journey to the stars and beyond, it welds
together industrial, electronica, and prog
metal, using black metal as a launchpad from
which to transgress, expand, and alchemically
transmogrify the parameters of the genre.
The album sets out on a cosmic and
psychonautical journey to explore a plethora
of interconnected themes: war and love, sex
and death, mystical alienation, harshness in
beauty. Its very harshness is legendary; it is
one of those works that takes up black metal's
challenge to be everything other, running with
it all the way to warp speed and beyond.

This oral history gives voice to the main actors involved, in an attempt to piece together the puzzle that is *666 International*.

THE CAST:

Aldrahn (Bjørn Dencker Gjerde): Blue

Apollyon (Ole Jørgen Moe): Purple

Mr. Fixit (Yusaf Parvez) aka Vicotnik: Red

Czral (Carl-Michael Eide) aka Aggressor: Orange

Magic Logic (Svein Egil Hatlevik) aka Zweizz: Pink

Bjørn Bogus (Bjørn Boge): Green

Ginger God (Ginge Anvik): Beige

Bernt B. Ottem: Turquoise

Esben Johansen: Yellow

ALDRAHN: It was a product of the time and the environment we were in. All of us experimented with all kinds of things, both physically and mentally. Some more extreme than others, but still we were young people in search of something. The outcome that was titled *666 International* had baggage loaded with grime at its core. An artistic adventure that held many profound moments of freely expressing our minds and, thus, outliving the very core melody of what black metal was all about.

APOLLYON: I met Vicotnik in, maybe, 1993 or was it 1992? I enjoyed his company, and we hung out a lot. He was basically living in the rehearsal room for quite some time, and I slept there more than once myself. Head inside the kick drum. I think I knew already that I was gonna be part of Dødheimsgard when they released the first album. At least me and Vicotnik had talked about it. I was in the army that year though, in 1994, way up north next to the Russian border. I think I joined the band right after I came back down to Oslo. For some reason, they had kicked out Fenriz, or he had quit. I guess he wasn't able to be as devoted as they would've liked him to be or whatever. He had tons of projects around that time anyway. In retrospect, I admit that I was truly bummed by missing my one chance to play with him. Not in a gay way—more that he oozed musical skills, devotion, intelligence, and authority. Darkthrone are from the same place as I am, so I had admired their work and personae ever since I first saw them live in 1988–1989, and I still think they're the most important metal band to come out of Norway. I don't even think black metal would have become what it is today if it wasn't for them. Not that black metal is so great today but, you know.

CZRAL: I remember that in the beginning I was supposed to play guitar on the album, and Ole (Apollyon) was supposed to play drums, so I learned most of the guitar riffs, and then we decided that I was going to play drums. So it was quite a lot of work. I didn't start playing until we were in the studio. We didn't have time to rehearse the drums very much. My involvement in the album was just functional; I did the drums, and that's it. All the artistic decisions were made and the writing done by Yusaf and Bjørn. Bjørn also had a lot to do with the aesthetics, the make-up and the photo session. I think this was the pinnacle of the cooperation between Bjørn and Yusaf. I didn't provide any material for the album. I only wrote the outro song, the little snippet with the classical guitar thing—but I wrote nothing else on the album.

MR. FIXIT: Well, Carl-Michael was my best friend; you have several best friends, but I guess he was...he is one of them. So, having been making music for a few years already, I helped him with the guitar sound of the first Virus album. We have a tendency to bring each other in, like expertise or help, because both the musical collaboration and the personal relationship were so close. It becomes your go-to person. As a drummer, Carl was miles ahead of almost any other drummer at the time; here in the Oslo area you have Hellhammer (or Jan Axel) and Fenriz, but Fenriz Gilve didn't want to play technical drums, and Carl-Michael, those were the three most accomplished drummers here at the time. Carl was really the drummer to bring in, because he could think and accomplish at the same time. We just did it on the fly.

APOLLYON: I seriously cannot recall how it all went down, but it was around then that Vicotnik and Aldrahn became something like the Toxic Twins. There was loads of psychedelics going on and weed, which I really disliked at the time. (I found that it only led to niceness and silliness. I later had a long period of silliness of my own.) I was more pro-speed if anything, but preferably nothing at all. Many of us were into techno, but some lived it more than others. So we started to drift slightly away from one another. I don't remember just how, but it was suddenly decided that we were gonna record the album just riff by riff and then glue all the parts together. Carl-Michael (Czral/Aggressor) recorded some drum patterns for the riffs we had ready, and then they played around with those recordings in the studio, creating new beats and processing them. I was gonna play bass. Typically they would ring me up from studio and ask if I wanted to come down and play bass on one or two riffs, and many times I asked if they could just play it themselves. I was a bit anti the whole process, I guess, and already had half a leg out of the band. I am sure it all went according to Vicotnik's vision though, just that I wasn't in on it and didn't bother to disagree.

CZRAL: It was tight and small, recording in the studio, I remember. The drum room: there wasn't room enough for a really great big drumkit in there. I remember we did it at Bjørn Boge's. Bjørn Boge is the guy who recorded it. He's like an old mentor for both me and Yusaf. He was the head of a place called Stovner Rockefabrikk, which was a recording studio, and there were rehearsal rooms and everything. Me and Yusaf, we used to work there in the beginning, this was in 1993–1994, and Bjørn Boge, he's a very professional musician, he had been in quite a big rock band from Norway. I think they did like three albums or something in the 1980s. He's a fantastic musician and a very good mentor. He played the bass on the last song with my classical guitar thing. He's sort of still a very respected guy. I still look up to him, and I still feel that I learned a lot from him in regards to music and how to perform and how to play well. We learned a lot from him.

MR. FIXIT: It is a bit coincidental that the album turned out the way it did. When I wrote the songs for the album, they were more similar to *Satanic Art* (Moonfog Productions, 1998). So there is really a missing link; there should have been an album that was more similar to *Satanic Art* before we developed even further. The songs had about 70–80 percent blast beats and 20–30 percent higgledy piggledy and experimental stuff. But in the end, in the studio, we kind of changed the formula. There were so many players involved in the album: really a lot of choices there. I called Carl-Michael into the studio to do the drums. Then we just did it almost riff by riff, rearranging them and making different beats for them than initially intended. There's no way any of us could have stood before the album was recorded and figured out how it would sound like in the end, because stone by stone we were taking decisions that really ended up making a mark on the product. The only thing that's really similar from start to finish is that the riffs are the same—the guitar riffs.

BJØRN BOGUS: It's very important to understand that the whole album is a collage. The entire album is a collage. It's not one track sort of played as a song. I think we had something like sixty-five different parts or something. Sometimes I didn't even know what song we were working on. And this guy called Ginge—he was fantastic dude—he was doing more ambient techno, not this music at all, but he was a master at editing, and Yusaf had gotten in touch with him, I don't remember how. We just gave him the drum tracks and this chart of time signatures and lengths and he actually chopped them up and spliced them together again, and Yusaf sort of just said, "Do whatever you want." There was no sort of *red line* through the whole thing.

Yusaf slept in the studio, and all the guys were coming and sitting out in the kitchen and smoking whatever and drinking, and it was like a very dysfunctional family. It was amazing. I knew the guys, and there was something weird going on when you put certain people in a room together. On a one on one basis, they can communicate, but when you put them together in the room it is all mayhem. Sometimes also very funny. I mean, these guys have a tremendous sense of humor. It was very important for me to stress that I didn't want to work with this dark, gloomy, very serious black metal. "We want to kill everyone." Come on guys, it's just music. There was this TV series in Norway called *Barron Blod*. It mocked the black metal thing. It was a very famous comedian, and we were laughing our ass off. I think there were some rather famous metal musicians doing it, but the singer, he was a comedian. And if you don't laugh at *Barron Blod*, I cannot work with you, because we need this distance. I mean, some guys are really hardcore Satanists, and no.

The whole idea with Dødheimsgard was just like, you know, giving the whole black metal scene a big "up yours" thing. Yeah, they wanted to be different. They wanted to piss people off. The way they dressed on the album cover, and they were so sick and tired of this uniform. More and more albums were like the McDonalds' of metal. Everything started to sound the same. It was just like, no, let's do something very, very different, and I said yes. Yusaf and Bjørn were sitting out there in the kitchen like an old couple—they're great friends, and they hate each other—and there was just, like, a lot of strange stuff going on out there, and I was working on other things, and, "Hey, guys, don't kill each other; it's only rock 'n' roll, you know," and something really good came out of it. I mean, the lyrics are totally surreal, but there's still something about it that, for me, completely suits the music. It's just gibberish, but the music is also sort of the same thing. It's coming from everywhere. It's going nowhere. It's just surreal. And there was only one sort of dogma for me. I said, "I hate these albums where you cannot hear the lyrics." I want the lyrics and the lead vocals to be not necessarily so clear, but they should be understandable, and they should be loud. People need to understand it to be able to connect to it. You need to have some kind of dynamics.

That was when Svein Egil came up with his parts. I was working as an engineer in the big congress center in Oslo at the time, doing speeches and stuff, and at this hall, we had a wonderful grand piano. The problem was that in daytime there was no chance in hell to record, because it was occupied all the time. I was able to use it at like three or four o'clock in the morning. Luckily, the ventilation system was turned off, so there was almost no background noise at all. We could do these acoustic piano tracks in that hall, and it was really cool, because Svein is not a very technical player, but he was listening to a lot of Erik Satie, this totally different kind of music, and I really loved it. I said to him, one of these tracks sort of reminds me of a tiny ballet dancer, everything is cool until she turns and she has a knife in her back, stuff like that, you know, sort of painting mental pictures. There's one of the keyboard pieces where it's all in the distance, and it's coming closer and closer. This is more like the Hunchback of Notre Dame is sitting in the church playing his stuff, and you enter the room, and you're walking toward him. Then we have this: imagine along the road in the countryside in Poland, and there's a guy sitting playing the piano in some kind of beer stoop; it's a Thursday afternoon, no one is listening, he's just sitting there. Okay, that's the impression we want to give. Let's make it grey. Let's pretend that this is an astronaut, sort of being dropped off with a spaceship, and he's just, you know, going off into the distance.

Of all albums and stuff I've done in the studio, I think this one may be the one I'm most proud of, because we sort of fulfilled the vision. We wanted to create something different, and we wanted to piss people off. People expecting the regular metal stuff will get ten seconds of it, then something else comes up that will totally put them in another place. I read some reviews, and I love them. People love it, or they hate it.

MAGIC LOGIC: I think the way I perceive it now and also, to a certain extent, the way I perceived it then was that there was a lot of willingness to just try different things, mostly because of this certain type of new technology being accessible:

the computer technology that you could use for editing, moving things. But nobody in the band really had any competence or skills using this technology, so we had this external guy called Ginge Anvik who did most of the electronic-sounding drums. I guess to the outsider, it has to be impossible to distinguish what's keyboards and what is samples and what is guitars with effects and what is what, and I think that's a good thing; it's good if it stays that way. Even though there was no explicit description or explicitly formulated idea of what this album was going to sound like, at least there were ideas about what it was *not* going to sound like, with Yusaf being the gatekeeper. He was kind of the director of the band, like how you make a motion picture. I remember very specifically Yusaf saying, "I want it to sound like a factory." That kind of makes you think of industrial music, but it doesn't always sound like a factory either; sometimes it sounds like a spaceship, sometimes it sounds like something else, and you have these like piano interlude things going on.

GINGER GOD: I think this was a "hand of God" moment. At the time, I was totally broke and had few illusions left about making a living in the music industry. As I had a religious upbringing, I have a lot of friends who had just become priests, and after a dinner with one of my clergy friends, I was lamenting my grim vision of my future. She said, "I'm going to pray to the Lord and ask him to get you a job." I don't know exactly how long it took before Bjørn Boge called me and told me he had this band of Satanists he'd been recording who needed some work done. They had killer riffs, but the drum track...it needed something. He asked if I'd be willing to play around with it and see what would come of it. I was pretty much given the freedom to do whatever I wanted, but I think Boge mentioned they were after something industrial-sounding.

My clearest memory was when Yusaf and the guys came to my flat to listen to some stuff. I'd just become a father a year before, and my one-year-old kid, who had just learned to walk, was staggering around the apartment when the doorbell rang. The only dealings I'd previously had with black metal was being on the same boat as Dimmu Borgir on my way to play a gig with my band SubGud at the Roskilde festival. From what I could tell, the Satanists spent most of the time on the ferry in the cosmetics department of the tax-free shop adjusting their pony tails. However charming I thought it was, it kind of confused me about black metal's image. Anyway, I thought it was cool, and from then on we just called them "Dimmu Borghild." Apart from that, I'd never had anything to do with black metal and wasn't really sure what to expect. Actually, being the son of a missionary, albeit a *very* agnostic son of a missionary, the mere thought of having dealings with black metal was enough to lead to eternal damnation in the eyes of my parents and to possible severance of my inheritance. My flat was on the fourth floor, I buzzed them in, opened the door and stood waiting listening to their chains jingling all the way up. The first thing Yusaf did when I let them in was to totally charm my one-year-old, squatting down with him and patting him on the head. After that things went pretty smoothly.

This was my first serious meeting with black metal. I hadn't spent any time trying to understand black metal and knew no one in the community. I suppose what prompted Boge to call me might have been my involvement with Seigmen. Some of the stuff we did together had been labelled "an occultistic abomination" by Norway's largest Christian newspaper—maybe that helped. I was totally green but very curious to understand what the guys were doing. I spent a lot of time just listening to their tracks and was really taken by both their energy and their attitude. It seemed to me these guys had their own thing going on, and that they wanted to stretch the conventions a bit. So I started hacking into the drum track, chopping, stretching and adding stuff you'd be more likely to hear at a construction site than on a black metal album, and the guys were totally cool with it. Bjørn Boge incorporated it in the mix, and it became something I'm really proud to have been a part of. It didn't go down very well with my parents, of course, but I kept my inheritance. Forgiveness, I guess. I remember going to see them play live at Rockefeller a while after the release. They were dressed up in evening gowns and gas masks. How cool is that? They were totally ahead of their time.

The alias "Ginger God" is probably because I *am* a ginger, and also that my band at the time was SubGud—Gud meaning God in Norwegian. I'm not sure if I told them that our collaboration may very well have been a sign from above or below— whatever suits your conviction. I met the priest that had contacted her Employer about giving me a job not very long after we'd finished the work on the album. She eagerly asked me if I'd landed a job. After a minute of awkward silence, I answered "Mmmmmmnyeees...but you're probably not gonna like it—the Lord works in mysterious ways." She is still a priest, and I haven't really had any signs of the existence of an omnipotent supreme being neither before nor after this. But if there is a God, I'm pretty sure She has *666 International* on repeat.

CZRAL: It's a very chaotic album, but there's a red thread that runs through it.

ALDRAHN: The conceptual idea, if there was one, was that of an opening of sight in new directions of esoteric trust. A dismantling of previous convictions and narrow-minded patterns of viewing the world. Earlier on, I was stuck in a quite small room of thoughts and viewpoints concerning the mysticism of life. I think it's safe to say that discovering the myths and mystics of the ancient world held great interest for someone already hugely passionate about the Norse mythology and pre-Christian beliefs. It became a symbiotic union and led to an outcome quite different from what we had done before. The fact that Vicotnik is of Indian heritage was probably also a key factor in the inspiration to merge into this world of symbols. It was also a way to break with the standards of black metal, even though that itself was not a conscious choice. It just happened that way. All the lyrics on that album came as a result of some years tripping on LSD. They portray different experiences I had while tripping and also a lot of the contemplation and reflection I did on each trip.

Chaos is the ground floor of life and has always been a motivating factor for writing lyrics. When chaos opens up, and you can taste the molecules and read the atoms that bind all form, and you can see the sounds, literally speaking, that creates a flow of immense pen power. It is the battle of all ages. Pure present awareness against its adversary, the ego, which constantly distracts its maker away from the moment and into illusions and bewilderment. I think polarities are necessary for us to have a keen experience of things, and in this way the adversity of existence is also a necessity for humans to have a clear vision and experience of themselves in true being. I wanted to point out that human beings consist of feminine and masculine polarities within themselves, and that the feminine characteristics are the prudence of life and the creative source, closest to what we can call divine. The symbiotic union of the two makes for a whole, not only between the two but also inside the one. It is through eroticism and sexuality we come closest to what we may call the spiritual source, if we understand how to use it right. I'm talking about the upward or downward movement of the Kundalini.

It tells a story of someone searching for something—the truth maybe. Who knows? The *red thread* of thoughts leads us to a place of great wonder that may have little to say but be more of something to marvel at like a child would at the first sight of life—though in a murky and slightly twisted way. It keeps us locked inside a labyrinth of dreaded portraits of a soul in anguish but at the same time offers promises of release through death, not carnal death but a death of self. A splintering of the human codex and manmade concepts for the ongoing arrival at a place where everything is abundant and beautiful. In this sense, it is outside of time and space and speaks from a place of deathless light. In other words, it is a product of sheer creativity with few or no thoughts about fitting into or even being compared to the culture from which it descended.

At that time, Satan to some degree represented a character bound to the splintering of regulations and standards, some kind of alternative identity. Satan was a personification of a free spirit or a savior, like in the children's books, when the villain portrays himself as a mentor. Satan was an idol, I'd say, and also an important aspect of life to delve into, because it took me quite far on my internal journey as a being, and even though it led me astray and into much confusion, it also helped me understand elementary aspects of life.

MR. FIXIT: I think we were still a bit in that "dominance" mindset around that time, but it wasn't only about that. We kind of threw out a lot of the black metal clichés, and I guess it was the starting point of trying to be honest; we hadn't really gone about it in an honest way. Because, you know, finding yourself, you want to flaunt it, you want to show off, you want to bring all your feathers to the foreground. You are allowed to show vulnerability and disease and not functioning and stuff like that, which is in deep contrast to true black metal and the portrayal of the kind of warrior king who destroys things with his bare hands while sitting in his mother's basement playing guitar.

As a social revolt, it was rewarding, in the sense that we were all outsiders long before we started being black metallers, because we were misplaced kids in the schoolyard and were kind of embracing and being proud of that, and at last had an outlet where those things are allowed to shine. There's a big difference over here in Norway now. If you really compare it to the 1990s, you know, you can have whatever style you want. I'm sure black metal played some role in that.

Norway is about ten to fifteen years behind Sweden. I grew up in Stockholm for my first ten years. My father was a first-generation Indian immigrant. So my family didn't always understand the choices I made; that was the risk of being an outsider both at home and in society. There weren't many immigrants in Norway at that time, especially not in small towns, and I came to a small town, and we were regularly maybe one immigrant per class. I know I had an easier time than many others, because my skin tone is familiar, but I always had a strange name, at least in these parts. But you learn the ropes, and you also have to make a choice about whether you want to grow from it or be a victim. There's no really good reason to be a victim, because it is all in your mind. It's not like somebody actually locking you in a cage and throwing away the key. You're just making mental cages, which you can break out of.

666 International celebrates your freedom as a human being and of the species: embracing your beast worldwide; everybody should embrace their beast worldwide.

BERNT B. OTTEM: After graduating design school in Oslo in the mid-1990s, I got to work a lot with projects for the Norwegian pop music industry through my first job with KRAN Design. In 1996, I started working for Union Design, which had Moonfog Productions as a client. Moonfog Productions was a Norwegian record label founded by Satyricon front man Sigurd Wongraven. The label specialized in black metal. Because of my previous experience working with the music industry, Union Design included me in a small group of designers working closely with the label. During my three years at Union Design, I worked on numerous projects for Moonfog Productions: Satyricon, Darkthrone, Gehenna, Isengard, and Wongraven. In 1999, I decided to leave Union Design and move to my home town of Tromsø in northern Norway. I did, however, stay in touch with Sigurd and continued to do projects for Moonfog from Tromsø. Sigurd called me about a new Dødheimsgard album, and he sent some photos of the band members for me to start working with. The photos were not good, so we decided to arrange a new photoshoot with Oslo-based photographer Esben Johansen. Esben brought the band to a cellar in an old apartment building in Torshov, Oslo, and delivered a set of fantastic photos that were much better suited for the album.

I actually didn't meet the band until after the release of the album, at a Moonfog Christmas party! During the design process I worked solely with Sigurd, as I did with most Moonfog projects. Sigurd is an extremely focused and demanding design customer. We somehow found a way to collaborate that really fueled the design process. We wanted an industrial look for the album cover and a darker feel for the inside booklet. Combining Esben's photos with futuristic typography and elements of gothic typography we hopefully put the listener in the mood for repeated runs through the album.

ESBEN JOHANSEN: It was pure luck that I got to be the photographer for the album cover, since I was basically straight out of college. My photographs from college where dark and sometimes dystopian, so my portfolio looked very different and wasn't really great for commercial work. I didn't get a lot of jobs from showing my portfolio around to agencies, but I did get the attention from a real creative designer by the name Halvor Bodin, working at Union Design. Halvor suggested me for this project to another astonishing designer called Bernt B. Ottem, who had previously worked on several black metal bands' album covers. Later I also got to contribute a photo to Darkthrone's album *Ravishing Grimness*, which Bernt was designing.

There was one photograph in particular from my portfolio that stood out for Bernt, and this was the image I took inside a factory that was lit with hard light that cast a lot of shadows and made the minimal colours pop out. The whole scene had monochromatic colours except from a pool of blood running down a drain. The funny thing is that everybody thinks it's from a slaughterhouse or somewhere a murder has happened, but I can reveal to you right here that the photo was taken in a factory that makes black currant juice and empties their tanks at the end of the day.

The photoshoot location the band chose was a cellar in an old building in Oslo. What I remember most vividly was the boys showing up to the photoshoot in their regular clothes: I didn't know what to expect, since I knew little about the black metal world. They looked like economics students, and it was great to see the transformation they went through to get into their "real" characters.

MR. FIXIT: I asked Satyr if he could get in touch with some art people, so he found me this photographer, and he showed me the photo, and I said, "Man, shit, this looks familiar." It's actually a factory in my hometown. The photographer also grew up there, so we shared a lot of common memories. We were both escapees so to speak: we both ran from this small city at some point. It was a different album cover than most of the covers of the day. It's also a bit evocative, in the sense that you don't really know what it is. You said you thought it was an airport. You made the correlation between the title and the picture. You painted your mind picture on that basis. It kind of becomes the listener's art and stays that way. You don't know if it's blood on the floor or juice or whatever. To this day, sometimes I look at it, and I find new details in the corner somewhere on the cover that I haven't really seen yet, so the depth is in the whole composition.

APOLLYON: Yeah, I was nowhere near happy with the outcome. I thought we started out with many cool riffs and ideas though. I probably haven't listened to the whole album since it came out, but I found it extremely audible that it was just loads of pieces glued together in the mastering, with every part having a different sound to it. I thought the drum sound was crap and found the vocals hard to swallow most of the time. I also never liked that kind of progression, where the bass and drums play alone with the vocals a long while before the guitar kicks in. Like on that "Ion Storm" song. Must have been something someone had picked up from Marilyn Manson or whatever—if he had been invented yet. Vicotnik plays all the guitars. I guess several of the riffs have dozens of layers of guitars on them. Not that there's anything wrong with that. The only song I was satisfied with was the hidden one, where the producer plays his legendary fretless bass. I liked it, because it had some consistency to it—it's atmospheric.

For me, the album is just ruined by the production method and drug use. I think it was my first encounter with "copy/paste" in music: play a riff perfectly once and paste it onto the rest of the track—not very soulful. It certainly stands out in the DHG catalog but, to me, only as the most messy release. I like weird when it's genuine, not when it feels forced. Like *Twin Peaks*. I never liked it. No substance. Only weird for the sake of being weird. I think *666 International* has a lot of *Twin Peaks* in it—I am aware there's a sample on *Satanic Art* as well. It's not for me though, but a lot of other people like to be confused. So many times where other people see genius, I see wasted potential and some guy tripping on mushrooms. Obviously, I had no influence on that album at all apart from playing some bass and, if I am not mistaken, Czral used some of my drum patterns for the riffs that were ready before we went into the studio.

Right after the release, we went on tour with Dimmu Borgir and Dark Funeral. We had the drums from the album on minidisk! The guys had bought all their stagewear in the women's department at H&M, and the Dimmu fans were anything but happy. Neither was I. Our first soundcheck came four weeks into the tour. Most of the time, we didn't even have the minidisk drums in our monitors, so at best it must have sounded totally chaotic. When nobody ends the song at the same time and the drums are still playing or stopped half a minute ago, it's difficult to fake. So I convinced the others to change the setlist to older songs up until *Satanic Art*, and I switched to drums, and the second guitarist switched to bass, and we played like that the last shows, and I must have quit the day after we came back home. Worst tour of my life concert-wise. I thought we sucked live. Very wobbly. As people, we had some kind of chemistry going on, but as musicians it was not at all where you would want things to be. We kept fucking up the riffs; typically, someone would be half a bar behind the rest of the band, and then we would fight over whose fault it was after the show. I had great and memorable walks with Zweizz, the keyboardist, and the bus ride with the openers Evenfall from Italy/Austria was also quite enjoyable. Especially the Italians were very confused about Vicotnik insisting on blasting Modern Talking on the bus stereo every night, but they didn't dare to complain and certainly didn't get all the layers of irony.

MR. FIXIT: Shit. Completely shit. A lot of people probably didn't know what to think of the live shows and were appalled that it wasn't recognizable. It made sense to me that it didn't make sense to anybody else. It makes sense to me to take that other role, especially the group of people I hung around with that always kind of strived ahead instead of just staying in place: it's art. It should be alive. How many albums can you release with the same kind of look, sound, album cover, etc., etc. without becoming a stale piece of shit?

ALDRAHN: *A Umbra Omega* (Peaceville, 2015) was a late continuance of *666 International*. It was an intriguing album to be part of and a keen ventilator for me after many years in artistic hibernation. I still deem *666* though to be the crystal palace of the DHG journey.

MR. FIXIT: I didn't follow it. That was my solution. It was never my intention to follow *666 International*. Even when I started writing songs, right after the album was finished, they were completely different.

CZRAL: I quit, I think, even before we did *Supervillain Outcast* (Moonfog Productions, 2007). I don't remember. I might have quit straight after the recording of the drums or right before. I don't remember why, really; maybe I thought it was a bit too much work or something like that. To be honest, it's been a while since I listened to *666 International*. I have to sit down and listen to it again and take it in again. It's been out of my system for a while. I should really listen to it. It's a great album. It's fantastic.

Figure 1. Poster for 666 International, photo by ©Esben Johansen (1999).

Svein Egil Hatlevik

ARTIST PROFILE

DANIEL LUKES

Svein Egil Hatlevik is one of the key players of weird black metal: he is one half of Fleurety, who have carved out their crooked path through and beyond black metal since the early 1990s; he played the uncanny keyboard parts on Dødheimsgard's *666 International*; and his solo project Zweizz is one of the pioneers of pink black metal, with the abstract, electronic, genre-defying *The Yawn of the New Age* (2006).

Hatlevik has many other projects, including raw black metal band Umoral and industrial black metal outfit Stagnant Waters, and, alongside Vicotnik from Dødheimsgard, he has now joined a reformed Strid on drums. We caught up with him over Facebook Chat, to discuss his musical trajectory, weirdness in black metal, and coming home to 1980s pop.

EARLY DAYS: FROM KISS TO HELVETE TO FLEURETY

I remember when I was five years old, the first record that my parents gave me was this Kiss *Paul Stanley* solo album. I originally wanted the *Gene Simmons* one, but my dad decided that was too scary for a five-year-old kid, this guy with the demon makeup and blood coming out of his mouth, so he went for the star boy instead of the demon record. The second album my parents got for me was a *Winnie the Pooh* stories on vinyl, so I guess it kind of starts from there. Growing up and being a kid in the 1980s, I was listening to Iron Maiden and W.A.S.P. and AC/DC. Then toward the end of the 1980s, Public Enemy: hard beats and samples, hip-hop. I didn't really discover Public Enemy through Anthrax. I already listened to Public Enemy and Anthrax, so it was in the Zeitgeist that these two things should collide or merge at the time.

I come from this area of Norway—Ytre Enebakk—which is not very far from where Mayhem and Darkthrone and all these bands were doing their thing; it was a word of mouth thing going on, from other people who are interested in metal, kids in the neighboring municipalities. You hear these rumours: "Oh you know what this guy did? First he slit his wrists, then he slit his throat, and then he wasn't fast enough so he shot himself in the head." It was, like, "Wow, this is really fucked up." We were already interested in death metal, then you discovered this record shop, Helvete. "Slag i slag" ["in rapid succession"], you say in Norwegian. Things go very quickly when you're thirteen, fourteen, fifteen years old. I think I remember the first time I ever saw Øystein Aarseth—Euronymous—he was wearing this cape and makeup and stuff, handing out flyers outside a Sepultura concert in Oslo. By then, we actually knew where the record shop was, so we went there.

In ninth grade in school, in the Norwegian school system, which would be the last year of junior high school in the Anglo-American system, we had this project in the religious studies class. Alexander Nordgaren (who is also in Fleurety) and I went to Helvete to do this school project. We had this assignment to interview a person who belongs to a nonmainsteam religion, i.e., not Lutheran, which was our dominating and state church in Norway at the time. We went to interview him for our school project because he was a Satanist, so we got the best grade, an A.

So everything goes very quickly from there. You go to this record shop and buy this newly-released record called *A Blaze in the Northern Sky*. It is very different from the American or Swedish or British types of extreme metal that is available at the time, or even Bathory or Celtic Frost. This is kind of like April 1992. When you go back some weeks later, and you can buy the first Burzum album, May or June 1992. By the end of the summer, you throw away all your non-black undergarments, and everything is all about this type of music. It's very quick, so I think that's the kind of development a lot of people in my generation had, meaning the generation later than Emperor or Burzum or Darkthrone or Mayhem; it's a very short time frame between each generation, because everything goes so fast.

I started playing the drums when I was about thirteen, fourteen, I think. Basically, you just start playing whatever song is possible for you to play. Then there's this other kid living down the block, and he knows the Anthrax riff, "I Am The Law," and, basically, you come together, because you like heavy metal, and after a while you transition from the other people who you were playing thrash metal or Metallica cover songs with; you can't really play with them anymore, because they don't understand this new thing. They don't get it. Alex and I, we started this band together in late 1991. We didn't really have a band name. We had a notebook with twenty, thirty, fifty different suggestions for band names, and they're all like along the lines of "Morbid Death." We found this band name sometime during the course of 1992; we landed on this Fleurety name after having found this diagram of different demons in *The Lesser Key of Solomon*, this black book, a grimoire, so we stuck with that ever since.

THE CENTRAL PARADOX OF BLACK METAL: CONFORM AND BE ORIGINAL

Euronymous was a kind of strategist and figurehead of the scene, and there were two rules, seemingly conflicting: You had to conform and you had to be original. You had to conform to the dark lifestyle, you had to wear black clothes and spikes, and laughter and you were strangers. On the other hand you would not be taken seriously with a copycat and unoriginal band. So when it comes to Norway, a lot of the success of the Norwegian bands depend on these conditions that made people have to work hard to develop their own style within a very strict framework.[1]

If you take that paradoxical quality about it, and extrapolate from it, it kind of also follows that—if that's where you start—you will just continue being ambiguous about it for perpetuity. I'm not gonna mention names, but let's imagine this specific record is the birth of generic black metal. It has no qualities; it's only form. There's nothing inside there. It's just a form. I can hear myself very easily say that about a lot of bands, really, but, on the other hand, if you ask this question: "Are you trying to be consciously weird or trying to be consciously eccentric?" I'm often thinking, "Come on, man, give me a break." It's not about that, but it's kind of like, everything starts with a paradox. If something starts with a paradox, if it's going to stay interesting, it has to stay a paradox.

If you land on either side—"Let's make this weird music that outweirds everything else"—it's kind of straying from the original goal. Also if you go to the makeup store and you buy the white and black makeup. Then you go to the internet—I went to this internet page some months ago to see what types of spikes were there, because I was considering buying spikes for whatever reason; I haven't considered doing that in twenty-five years, but I was considering it a couple of months ago, and I saw you have this model of spike called Gorgoroth and one called Arcturus and one called Burzum and one called Mayhem. So there has to be this tension, and when you've been doing that for certain number of years, I guess this kind of tension is kind of internalized, and you don't really think about it anymore.

For instance, I took a long break from playing the drums when I was eighteen or so. Then, when I turned thirty-three, thirty-four, thirty-five, I discovered that I missed drumming, that I wanted to be...to have this activity in my life. I was thinking, "What the hell can I do now?" All the other players in the field have been rehearsing these techniques since they were thirteen. I have to do some thinking. How can I play these drums in a way that's interesting? It can't just be like regular rock drums. But there's also no point in trying to bridge the gap between me and all the George Kolliases out there. When you start working in that field you kind of end up playing something that people will perceive as weird or at least different from what they've heard before. We recorded this most recent Fleurety album in

2014, and I picked up my drum sticks again in 2011–2012. So I spent a couple of years fairly intensely trying to write drum patterns that would be different from what I heard in comparable styles. The point is, I think that this paradoxical quality of this music has kind of become internalized. It's not like you sit down and I want the weirdness/tradition ratio to be 70 percent weirdness and 30 percent tradition.

I think every kind of subculture has these conflicts, like punk. "These are keeping it real, and the other people are sellouts and blah blah blah." Every kind of art form has to at least try to resist in some way this commodification, because an artwork is not a commodity. It might not be impossible to continue living as an artist, unless your artworks to some degree become a commodity. This is not, I guess, unique to black metal: every type of culture has to struggle with this balance between art and commodity.

PINK BLACK METAL: FROM DØDHEIMSGARD AND FLEURETY TO ZWEIZZ

To me, Zweizz continues, chronologically and methodologically, from where *666 International* stopped and where Fleurety's *Department of Apocalyptic Affairs* stopped. At the time, in 2002–2003, Dødheimsgard had become a band that was really working in the rehearsal studio and sounding like a proper metal band. The two main reasons I quit were, first of all, I had no idea how I could contribute to those songs. When I went to the rehearsals, and I heard them play, I thought, "Why the fuck should there even be keyboards or electronics here?" This insecurity, having no idea how I saw myself contributing to this, then developed into me thinking that there shouldn't really be electronics for this record, so I just pressed the eject button. A lot of the material on the Zweizz's *The Yawn of a New Age* album was originally intended from my side as interludes for the next Dødheimsgard album. I don't think it was really very well received by the rest of the band, and they were like "This is bullshit." Anyway, they didn't like it. That's at least how I understood it at that time. So I just thought, "Well okay, now I have this, and I have this computer that I bought in 1998, and I've been using the same setup for all these years." After a while, in 2005–2006, I thought, "Well, if I don't take everything that I have on my hard drive and just make an album out of it, the hard drive is going to crash; all the material's going to be lost." I tried to put it together as sort of abstract black metal: taking away all the drums and the guitars—not all of it, but a lot of it, at least. Then just trying to extract from it the specific feeling that everybody keeps talking about. It's very analogous to abstract painting; you look at the landscape, and you take away the landscape and just try to keep the feeling.

I guess this kind of thinking is very inspired by the computer science artificial intelligence studies I was doing at the time; like if you have the same novel in ten languages, and you try to represent the information of the text in some kind of language, some nonspecific form. As I was saying earlier, with this box, the form is black metal. You have the spikes and the screaming and distorted guitars and the heavy drumming, but it's just the form. If you look inside, there's nothing in there. So I was trying to take away the box and keep all the stuff inside.

I wanted it to be presented in some kind of striking way that you were like, "What the fuck is this?" At this time, Myspace was becoming a thing, and you would see all these avatars, and they would be some unintelligible logo in white or black. So the first thing I did was, "Okay, I'm making an unintelligible logo, and I'll have it pink." Pinkness is not really a message per se. It's not really a pseudo queer statement; it could have been neon green or bright yellow. We have this other Fleurety album which is a very bright yellow cover. But seeing that this specific pink type of color would be considered the most *obscene* by its target audience, I went for that first, and then I thought, "Well, I can make a green or yellow record later or some other very bright color," but the pink just seemed to be a logical place to start. I guess you can't really do that without also in some way becoming satirical or parodic or being perceived as a parody, just because of this process of removing the box and keeping only the contents, or at least I didn't see any other way of achieving that. If there's no other way of doing this other than becoming a satirist, then, well, okay, let's go with that.

STAYING HOME AND LISTENING TO 1980S POP

I don't think Zweizz is over, but I'm doing other things. How can you keep making music in a way that just doesn't become the same or exploit the same ideas, stepping around in the same bucket? Most of the available time I have for music is with Strid, in which I play the drums, and then I have some time for other projects, such as making songs at home with my girlfriend—it's not like we've come very far with this, but we're making music, and we have all these ideas. Then a year or two goes by, and you put it together in some way and see if there's a common denominator or a way to stitch it all together.

With Strid the main focus is getting a live band together; that's kind of the commodity that we're working on on a daily basis. When you have this stable entity, you can try to capture that and make a record.

With Stagnant Waters I don't really know what's gonna happen. I went to France precisely one year ago and recorded some vocals for a second album. There are the other two guys, who very strongly disagree on the direction of the band, so I'm not really sure if it's still a band or not. I've been playing the ukulele and making riffs for the ukulele and then sending that in a zip file with twenty ukulele tracks, and then suddenly seven years later the song is finished, but then half a year after that the song's not finished after all. It's rather chaotic, I would say, so I'm not really sure how that's gonna end, but I don't think not releasing anything is going to be acceptable for any of us. I don't know, I just decided that they should make two separate but identical albums. That might be the way to solve it.

Regarding Fleurety, Alexander has been living in Romania, in London, in California, in Canada, all over the place. Would it feel wrong if we weren't in the same room making music together? We're trying to avoid this turning into an internet project. But that might be the only feasible way of doing it in the future. But I know he's coming back to Norway to visit some of us old folks living back home, so we have a plan to make some music in the very near future.

I've been hanging out at home listening to a lot of 1980s pop music: Duran Duran, Hall & Oates. There's this Norwegian singer called Brita Wallevik. We've been listening a lot to her. She has a very tragic story. And Stein Torleif Bjella, who is kind of a singer-songwriter, with rural themes in his lyrics. But, broadly speaking, it's a lot of 1980s pop music, on the bright side of pop music. We like the classics: What's the name of the band that came after Joy Division? New Order, stuff like that. [Kristoffer Rygg of Ulver] has these very George Michael-ish phrasings. Last time I met up with Tore [Ylwizaker] of Ulver, we watched this whole concert of George Michael playing live. A gig, from before the album *Older*, not very long before he recorded that album. Last summer, we were listening a lot to Prince and George Michael, that kind of soul-influenced music. A lot of people consider Prince very mainstream, but when I listen to it I hear a lot of weirdness.

It seems very much more pluralistic now. I guess that's because there's more space. So you can have your very conservative or formulaic record labels for the people who like that. Then you can have record labels with people who make something more like you, who aren't interested in that at all. Then you can have festivals and social get-togethers and everything. I guess that thing is peaking now. If airplane tickets get substantially more expensive and gas prices rise, you have to wait. That's the way it's heading in Europe, it seems. So I don't know how this is going to turn out in the next ten years or so.

Figure 1. Svein Egil Hatlevik, photo by ©Monica Fosser, November 2019.

Notes

[1]"Music: Interview: Zweizz. Black Metal– Black Noise," MStation.org, September 24, 2008, accessed May 20, 2021, http://mstation.org/zweizz.php.

[P]hilosophy takes *risks:* thinking is always a decision which supports independent points of view. The desire of philosophy thus has four dimensions: revolt, logic, universality, and risk.

— Alain Badiou, "Philosophy and Desire"[1]

Andrew Zealley
iNfect (II and IV of a series of V), 2018
digital infection of Apple Inc. iPhone (Product)RED advertisement, 15.24 x 15.24cm each
courtesy of the artist

(ARTIST STATEMENT)
ANDREW ZEALLEY

The history-present-future of HIV/AIDS is vexed by absence: uncertain forms of sociality—loss and disappearance—and the absence of cure. Artists and activists work overtime, for decades, to imagine an end to the crisis, but the lure of disease management eclipses cure. In its place, commodification and branding becomes the AIDS-industrial complex. Today's *New York Times* headline: "HIV Is Reported Cured in Second Patient, a Milestone in the AIDS Epidemic."[2] Fact check: the AIDS crisis is not an epidemic; it is pandemic. There is no outside to AIDS. Fact check: headlines of potential cures surface intermittently, restoring hope in utopian desires to cure, but the practical need to manage sweeps cure under carpets. Fact check: commodified histories of AIDS are not enough; my AIDS won't fit in your museum (Shan Kelley). HIV/AIDS is not a brand.

Risk: it's what we have left in struggles against worlds (and futures) where descriptive statements support, reinforce, and overrepresent HIV-positive people in pathological frameworks, through systemic stigmatizations and processes of social—and slow—death. Risk: an opposition to authority. Risk: an important—even necessary—tool toward erotic subjectivity and the creation of intimate (and controversial) spaces of autonomy, freedom, pleasure, and productive discovery. Risking the possibilities of sidestepping moral ethics, of sleeping around with ideas of risk that are creative, sexual, hallucinatory, and ludic. How can intervals of risk be put to work to expand and deepen harmonies of pleasure in scales (and tunings) of self-care?

iNfect is a series of five faux advertisements (for the Apple iPhone 8 Red Special Edition) that respond to these commodified histories, cynical branding exercises, exclusionary museum practices, red ribbons and parades, and queercore(porate) shame. Let's get infected with the shopping bug.

Your call is very important to us. Please hold.

March 5, 2019

Notes

[1] Alain Badiou, "Philosophy and Desire," in *Infinite Thought: Truth and the Return to Philosophy*, ed. and trans. Oliver Feltham and Justin Clemens (London: Bloomsbury Academic, 2005), 29.

[2] Apoorva Mandavilli, "H.I.V. Is Reported Cured in a Second Patient, a Milestone in the Global AIDS Epidemic," *New York Times*, March 4, 2019, accessed May 20, 2021, https://www.nytimes.com/2019/03/04/health/aids-cure-london-patient.html.

A Biatch in the Northern Sky

PATRIZIA PELGRIFT

Prior to 2002, Norway was the equivalent to that "observation = perception" thought experiment that raises the question: If I stop looking at a map of Europe, does Norway still exist?

I don't remember any memorable stories in the news. I never had any Norwegian friends. I never watched any Norwegian television shows or ate Norwegian food. When it came to music, I was more into Marilyn Manson than Mayhem. It was as if, on an international level, the country only became relevant when someone opened an atlas—a bit like Alaska. I remember looking at Scandinavia on the map and thinking, "I'd rather jump off a bridge in the Amazon rainforest." It was only when I moved to Oslo that I wished I had (gone to the Amazon rainforest, instead). Norway was as exciting as a New Year's Eve party at a retirement home (perfect if you have a family member who lives there, not so great if you're under thirty-five and single).

Sure enough, however, that country was not always such a *quiet* realm. Around 800 CE, the Vikings kept themselves busy for a couple of centuries by jumping on their ships and going on several rampages around the world. A quick detour—some people think the Vikings were hot, while others think they were a bunch of savages. I will mainly remember them for their funny nicknames

(Harald Bluetooth being my *favoUrite!*). During a live transmission of radio show *Tinitus* on NRK P3 (that I produced from 2005 till 2009), host Kirsti Thisland and I laughed so hard while reading out some of those Viking nicknames that I found myself having to cue and mix a song using one hand while holding my stomach with the other under the console board.

But back to Norway's *coloUrful* history. After a dark period during which the country was treated like a problem foster child by Denmark and Sweden respectively (mainly due to the Black Plague that decimated two-thirds of the population in 1349), Norway managed to blossom and produce artists such as Ibsen, Grieg, and Munch (among others). Still no match for the grandiose, internationally celebrated masters such as Da Vinci, Dante, or even Donatello, right? Hear me out—I was brought up in the most artistically and historically voluptuous universe of them all, Italy. I have never been much of a patriot in the traditional sense (guns and war, pizza and Tiramisù), however, once I moved out of my hometown, Milan, I began appreciating the fact that, artistically speaking, the sun truly shone out of my country's arse. Once I moved to London (toward the end of the 1980s), however, Norway barely made an appearance in specialist music magazines that linked the "black metal" subculture to murders and grave robbings. No great reasons to pick it as a holiday destination. Again, I am not much of a conservationist when it comes to bodies after death, but why would anyone want to dig up a grave? Silly boys and their dead toys.

At some point, however, Norway went from being this *acquired taste* (for trees and bubbling brooks) to this bastion of equal rights and upward mobility where I was offered several astonishing professional opportunities, which is why I lived there so long. My *business trip* to Oslo in December 2002 was the pivotal moment. In the summer of 2002, after severing family ties in England (broke up with a boyfriend), I was ready for a new adventure. Suddenly, there I was on Viking and grave robbers' land, with one clear goal in mind: go out for a drink (the dirty Brits had trained me well). My London-based partner in (all things metal) crime, Nelly (Liger) suggested that I visit Elm Street, the mythical watering hole where black metal *royalty* and hangers-on used to convene after their bizarre criminal activities back in the 1990s. While I vaguely remembered

the stories linked to that musical subculture, I was *way too old* for that shit.
I just wanted to have a drink without having to declare bankruptcy, and to meet
like-minded people.

Ironically enough, however, the first person I bumped into at Elm Street was
a drummer without a drum kit and someone who gave even less of a shit
about Norway's 1990s' nefarious nonsense: Darkthrone's Gylve "Fenriz" Nagell.
Unbeknown to me at that time, a month after the *grim* encounter, I would move to
the Norwegian capital. It is important to stress that the two things are absolutely
not connected. I did not move to Oslo for Fenriz (!), though I would go on to
work with him and his curmudgeon-like comrade Nocturno Culto when Moonfog
Productions hired me to run the label's press and promo department a few months
later. Chatting with Fenriz was intriguing and always quite challenging, in a way.
Like with everything else he did, his communication style ran on its own original
and quirky track. Fenriz used to appear disinterested in anything I had to say,
though after a long, awkward pause, he'd have a perfectly packaged quip about
the previous topic of conversation. Chatting with him felt akin to dancing to any
Tool record—never a straight 4/4. As time went by, I learned to enjoy this *genuine
soul's* verbal dissemination style. His idiosyncratic sense of humoUr was a regular
spray of Febreze—unexpectedly fresh.

A couple of years after I left Oslo, while recording a special segment for a radio
show that I was producing in New York (cleverly titled *That Metal Show*), I called
his cell. It was for an item branded "What Are They Doing Right Now?" I'd already
cold-called Ben Weinman from The Dillinger Escape Plan, Bill Kelliher from
Mastodon, and a couple of others whom I knew personally—and hoped would not
slam the phone down on me. Calling Fenriz, however, was like playing the lottery—
you never knew whether he'd even pick up. Oddly enough, he did, but he alerted
me that he was painting his house (that was his way to say to make it quick). Yet
the conversation flowed and even morphed into an appreciation of *Little Britain*,
with Fenriz emulating Vicky Pollard. The other half of the misanthropic duo, Ted
"Nocturno Culto" Kjell, was a lovely gentleman with a very well-developed dark
side that only tended to come out when he felt uncomfortable (his tolerance level
was higher than Fenriz's). Naturally handsome, Ted swung between acting like a
cuddly teddy bear, chatting about the most regular topics, and announcing that it
was time for him to leave "to get away from that circus." There was a good cop/
bad cop dynamic within Darkthrone that I had experienced when allocating media
interviews to each of them during my time at Moonfog (I worked *Hate Them* and
Sardonic Wrath). I used to think that Ted was "good cop"—he'd say yes to most
promo work; Fenriz, however, was "bad cop"—he would be a little more fastidious

about doing interviews and with whom (the only beating that Fenriz ever did was around the bush).

When Darkthrone's single "Too Old, Too Cold" shot to number one in the Norwegian charts in January 2006, the earth moved as fans and industry insiders alike fell to the ground and caused it to crack. The shock was real, and that included Gylve and Ted's. I had left Moonfog seven months prior to the *bloodcurdling event*, and I was invited on VG Lista to comment on this astonishing incident.[1] Much like the rest of the metal community (aside from Sigurd who'd have concocted something highly philosophical about Darkthrone *conquesting the mainstream* or thereabout), I felt speechless. The one thing that made sense to me was that the band had never put out a single before, and their fans were so loyal that they would buy a release from their anal cavity if anybody had the guts to put it out. The show's producer asked me whether one of the band members would agree to be a guest in the studio. Asking Fenriz would be a waste of time 'cos even though he lived in Oslo, he would *not* do it under any kind of duress (which would include the threat of burning his Ratt albums). I did text him and did, indeed, waste my time. Ted, who lived three hours away from Oslo, agreed to do it—over the phone. Not ideal for television, yet the show's producer accepted. A Darkthrone in the hand is worth two in the bush, after all. The show went out live and Ted chatted about his band's first number one chart *position* while the video for the single played in the background. Ted's comment: "It was the first time we have ever released a single, and we have no relationship to charts or things like that."

That was not the only instance of chart-topping success for black metal bands after Darkthrone paved the way. Six months later, Dimmu Borgir would follow with their seventh album *In Sorte Diaboli*, and Satyricon would eventually conquer the top spot with their eighth album *Satyricon*, in 2013. When Dimmu's Shagrath and Silenoz appeared on Norwegian TV talk show *Skavlan* and were asked about the secret of their chart ascension, their response was quick—they had no clue. One thing was certain, in the early 2000s, the mainstream charts were welcoming to those bands whose genre had frightened the Norwegian population a decade earlier, but, by then, not many of them were flipping the finger to the establishment like it was 1991.

Bands like Satyricon had aggressively pursued mainstream chart success since 2001—and achieved it, aided by the exceptionally slick music videos that accompanied their singles. When Mayhem's fourth album *Ordo Ad Chao* reached number twelve in the Norwegian charts, nobody in the band was setting churches ablaze. Things had changed for some, not for Darkthrone, though. They alone possessed the archetypal necro attitude of pure reluctant chart toppers.

All things considered, in hindsight, I realize that my life in humdrum Norway would never actually prove to be so *humdrum*.

During my first couple of years there, much of the excitement was brought on by the volatile relationship between me and my then-boss Sigurd Wongraven. An incredibly intelligent and witty individual, he had a knack for infuriating me. He made me laugh hard by telling me stories about people in the scene to get me in the right mood for the ridiculous demands pertaining to work for Moonfog that followed. While I thoroughly enjoy hanging out with Sigurd these days, I left Moonfog with a massive "fuck you" sign on my forehead, in June 2005. In fact, when System of a Down headlined Norwegian Wood in Oslo that same month, I did not ask for any favors to get into the show, even though I had been a huge fan of that band for years, after seeing their insanely epic first UK show when they opened for Slayer at the London Astoria in 1998. Satyricon had got a licensing deal to release *Volcano* in the US through Daron Malakian's label, EatUrMusic, and I did some peripheral work in preparation for its release. Luckily, the lovely guy who helped Daron run the label, Hamps, invited me to the show (he knew I was a huge SOAD fan).

But back to Moonfog and my relationship with Satyr. The only mitigating factor during the two years I was there was the co-owner of the label, Tormod Opedal. He was way more generou$ than Sigurd and did understand a lot of the concerns that I had regarding wages, overtime, and holidays/sick days. I have not seen Tormod since I left Norway in 2009, but I bet he is doing fine and is much happier now that he does "not have to deal with any of that black metal crap."

Post-Moonfog, my super-fun job as a producer/roving reporter for metal show *Tinitus* on NRK P3 made my life in Norway more bearable. In that role, I had the professional freedom that I craved. I negotiated national and world exclusives, both for playlists and interviews, attended award shows, festivals, gigs, interviewed several bands, and put 98 percent of them on the spot. I avoided sucking up to bands to get the most exciting content. Only one person put *me* on the spot and left *me* speechless, Seth Putnam from Anal Cunt. "You have brown hair and brown eyes of a Jew," and "If you listen to The Dillinger Escape Plan you are a *f-word*." While at the time, I thought he was cheeky (playful, but borderline rude), and I laughed my arse off, ten years of life in the US has taught me that politically incorrect communication gets you in trouble. It is just as well that I stopped smoking 'cos saying that I need to go for a *fag* would upset everyone in earshot. We ran Putnam's interview raw and totally unedited. We did take a perverse delight in feeling the burn of the cringe. A few months later, I interviewed Ben Weinman and Greg Puciato from Dillinger and got this reaction to Putnam's statement: "Yes, if you listen to DEP, you're totally gay."

✤ ✤ ✤

HERE ARE SOME OF THE MOST THRILLING MOMENTS OF MY TIME IN OSLO.

The time Darkthrone returned to the live stage in Oslo in 2003.

The Moonfog Jubilee featured Darkthrone's Nocturno Culto on stage in October 2003, after seven years of no live performances. Satyricon were the headliners, but the biggest draw was the return of Darkthrone live. The band had not played live since 1996, so how did someone manage to pull them back in? They got one of them, Nocturno Culto, to join Satyricon on stage to perform five Darkthrone songs, while Fenriz watched from the sidelines—with a beer in his hand and an upside-down smile on his face. Several bands from the label supported Satyricon, and even Snorre Ruch from Thorns came down from Trondheim for the event. Plus, there was a long list of people from the mainstream realm, including the Turbonegro boys. My day began at 10:00 a.m. and finished at 4:00 a.m. the following day, and the most bizarre thing I witnessed was a small altercation between Red Harvest's TurboNatas and Turbonegro's Hank von Helvete at the after-show—one called the other *tjukk* (*fat* in Norwegian)—just a night like any other when alcohol is in and egos come out.

That time Nocturno Culto performed live with Satyricon at the Wacken Festival in Germany in the summer of 2004.

Corpsepaint stayed on throughout, the soaring temperatures notwithstanding. The meet and greet was attended by an endless line of hardcore aficionados from as far away as Australia (they were all super excited to meet Ted, which isn't *necro* at all). The headline show was sold out, and the performance was outstanding.

That time the last Moonfog signing, Disiplin, split right before their second album and four members ended up hating the guitarist/founder.

———

In 2003, they were the big hope for Moonfog, but through a bizarre turn of events that involved the influence of Dissection's vocalist Jon Nödtveidt, who'd inspired the band's guitarist/founder to join the MLO (Misanthropic Luciferian Order), the Telemark ensemble went up shit's creek. The four members agreed to play Norwegian music convention, by:Larm, to promote their second release on one condition: that I ensured that the guitarist would not turn up on stage. Fun times on the phone. Not. The performance was great, and the guitarist was not missed.

———

That time the two Satyricon guitarists got arrested in Canada for alleged rape.

———

It was December 2004, and then-Slipknot drummer Joey Jordison was playing drums on that tour. I was in the Moonfog office when the media called to ask for a comment on that piece of news. I could not stop laughing. It sounded absurd. Then, Satyr texted me. "I know both Arnt and Steinar personally, and they would never do that!" I texted him back. His response startled me. "If the media calls you again, do not comment." *What!?* I got cold chills down my spine. As anyone in the legal environment knows, someone is innocent until proven guilty, but as I found out a few hours later, the news of the arrest was real. I hoped the investigation would clear them both. In the meantime, I wondered what kind of consequences this would have for drummer Joey Jordison, who, at the time, was a member of Slipknot, but was also donning his percussion services for Satyricon, since Frost could not get a visa to enter the US. I was the one who introduced Joey to Satyr at the Golden Gods Awards in London that year, and I felt somewhat responsible for getting him into *that mess*. I was dying to talk with Joey, though I chose to delay it until I saw him face to face in London the following year. The two Norwegian guitarists were released a few weeks later after the charges were dropped. Did I talk with Steinar and Arnt about this the next time I saw them? You bet I did. Did I talk with Joey about it? Yep. Awkward times peppered with giggling fits.

———

That time I was a judge on the Hard Rock panel at the Norwegian Grammies, passionately rooting for a band that did not win.

———

It was 2005, and I'd just started producing *Tinitus* on NRK P3. I do not know how I was considered for the thrilling opportunity to pick a Grammy winner, but the process was four months long. I was required to listen to over twenty albums for the initial short list (a process that was repeated three times in order to make the "short list" even...shorter). By the second "short list," I was over it. I had a really clear idea of who I wanted to see win: Extol. I loved their songwriting approach on *The Blueprint Dives* and I was intrigued by the fact they were a Christian metal band. By then, I was getting bored of Satan and his boutique Satan worshippers. Not a fan of Christianity as a whole, but even I felt I needed a change. Audrey Horne was a close second on my personal list of favorites, but they ended up *getting the gong*. Because of that, the whole Norwegian metal environment was highly pissed off that year. They felt that Audrey Horne weren't *metal* enough. Oh well, just imagine my frustration when I realized I could not air my dissent toward Satan publicly.

—

The time I bugged Destructhor from Myrkskog to audition for Morbid Angel.

—

In 2008, Thor Anders was against the idea. I texted him to let him know that he should audition. He sent me a curt response to illustrate why he could not do it: he was too busy with Myrkskog. *What?!* They barely played two gigs a year. So I bugged him (and begged him) to reconsider. The subtle form of harassment from my side went on for a few days. I knew he'd be perfect for it. My then-boyfriend, a good friend of Thor's, also began to harass him. Thor Anders ended up getting the gig, and I got to see him perform with Morbid Angel at B.B. King Blues Club & Grill in New York City a few years later. All's well that ends well, you might think? Well... after Thor Anders contacted me to let me know that he got the job, I e-mailed Dave Vincent directly and asked him whether we could break the news on *Tinitus*. I wanted an exclusive, since I felt I assisted in filling his band's vacant slot. He agreed, but on the day of our live broadcast, the news had already got out (Dave Vincent had mentioned it to *Metal Hammer*, and Blabbermouth.net had published a news article about it). I immediately hammered an e-mail out to David Vincent conveying my disappointment. His apology did nothing to mitigate my fury. Ask me how I feel about it now, and you'd be surprised at the numbers of shits I do not give about that turn of events. But back then, the wrath was real.

The time I booked Firebird to perform at the *Tinitus* launch party hoping to discuss a potential Carcass reunion.

—

It was September 2005, and I'd already booked a couple of good Norwegian bands to perform at the brand-new radio show's launch party. It was titled "Not Just Another Launch Party," and it was important for me that the list of bands performing on the night would include more than black metal. In addition, I wanted to inject an international feel to it. So, I booked Firebird. Odd choice? Not if you understood my strategy. Stay with me. I'd also invited Jeff Walker to copresent the evening (with me and host Kirsti Thisland). Hear me out. I'd designed the evening to reflect the contents of the show (songs and interviews would feature both on the air and at the launch party). In addition to the performance with Firebird, Bill Steer would do an on-stage interview. He accepted. I wanted him to discuss the potential of a Carcass reunion. Backstage, Jeff was vigorously into it, but Bill was cagey. Notwithstanding his reticence, he ended the interview with "I am not sure about a reunion, but one should never say never." The following day I sent out a press release that alleged that Bill Steer was open to a Carcass reunion. Bori from Blabbermouth.net ran it, and I felt like I'd hit gold even before the show had gone to air. I bet Bill thought I was an arsehole for it, but the band ended up reuniting a few months after that anyway. He probably still thinks I'm an arsehole.

The time I signed a band called Funeral whose guitarist passed away one month before their album release.

From These Wounds was love at first listen for me. It was a perfect concoction of tunes to slash your wrists to. The band had a history of members battling drug addiction and depression; some of them had attempted suicide, while others had successfully achieved it. When Chris (Christian Loos) passed away, however, I was faced with a new challenge—that of remaining professional while dealing with the record promotion cycle and the grieving in private for a friend's passing (a great loss for all of us who knew him). The album was a hit with the media, and its sales reflected the extensive coverage. Balancing professional and personal feelings was hard at that time.

The time I secured a world exclusive interview with the whole of Emperor to discuss their return to the live circuit.

It was the end of September 2005, and rumoUrs began circulating about an Emperor reunion. Out of all the black metal bands, I loved Emperor with a passion (for all the "wrong" reasons, since I was a huge fan of their proggie stuff). They were supposed to perform a three-song set at the Scream fifteen-year anniversary show at Rockefeller on October 1. I wasted no time in putting forward the idea of an exclusive for *Tinitus*, where the three members would discuss the event and any future live shows. Samoth agreed to it and, unlike David Vincent, he actually kept his word. On October 1, Ihsahn, Trym, Samoth, and I met up at a hotel in Oslo. While I'd met both Samoth and Trym on several occasions before, through

Zyklon, that evening would be the first time I'd speak with Ihsahn face to face. I'd had a short exchange with him on the phone a couple of years earlier when I worked at Moonfog. "Hi, is Sigurd there? I need to talk with him about..." He is not here. Would you like to leave a message? "This is Vegard." How do you spell that? "This is Ihsahn. Please ask him to call me." Ooooooh. I was dying to gush that "An Elegy of Icarus" was one of the best songs I'd ever heard in my life, but I opted to hold the hyperbolic statement inside and act professional that time. On the night of the 2005 interview, however, I gushed. While Ihsahn appeared pleasantly surprised at my fangirl hyperbole, he refused to disclose whether that song would make it onto the playlist at any future show. So when the Inferno Festival headline show rolled on, and my favorite song emanated from the speakers, I had live fireworks going off in my stomach.

The time I pissed off Emperor's original drummer Faust after he got out of prison was the day I wondered whether I'd live to tell the tale.

It was December 2002, and I was backstage at John Dee in Oslo after the Inferno Festival's kickoff show. While chatting with a bunch of unknown faces whose bodies lounged around on various couches, I began exchanging fun banter with an intriguing individual. My good friend Kristine Dufey was also there taking pictures (I had been commissioned by *Metal Hammer UK* to cover the live event, and she became my sidekick in charge of visuals). I was intrigued by his quick wit, so I introduced myself. Suddenly, I realized I was having trouble with his name. *Board?* Board? B-o-a-r-d? Why would anyone be called "*Board*," I wondered to myself. I asked him to spell it for me. "Faust. My name is Faust," he offered exasperated. Oh. That sounds familiar. Obviously, a stage name! Wait a minute... "Jesus Christ, are you the guy who burned churches and killed that homosexual back in the 1990s? And you went to prison for it?" My filter had taken the night off. The whole room erupted in laughter. "Yes, that's me," he grinned, half proud, half embarrassed. I sat right next to him and told him I had questions for him. We chatted for what felt like hours—it wasn't, I was just drunk. Before I left, we exchanged numbers, and he agreed to do an interview for *Metal Hammer UK*. I hadn't really cleared it with then editor Chris Ingham, but I knew that Ingham would jump at the chance of securing this exclusive—and he did. The interview took place at a quiet bar in the center of Oslo. At the end, Faust asked me to send him a copy of the transcript. I agreed to do it out of courtesy. What I did not expect was his response when he received the transcribed piece. I'd ended it with what I believed to be a strong, balanced, and eloquent response to the question "Do you regret any of the actions that landed you in jail?" I believed he came across as intelligent and brave, but I knew that it could be construed as controversial by some of the most conservative readers. Faust e-mailed me back right away explaining that he was uncomfortable seeing that statement in print, and, in fact, he asked me to take it out. While to him I did my best to be accommodating, inside I was unable to hold both my middle fingers in check. Worried about the possibility of my life ending prematurely, *Metal Hammer* editor Chris Ingham left it up to me to make the decision. I did what I always do when my integrity is on the line—I told Ingham to leave it as it was. "I will deal with the consequences," I stoically stated in my last e-mail to him. Then I communicated that decision to Faust. His response was curt but glacial, and, truth be told, I did spend a few days wondering whether I'd be around to see the magazine hit the shelves. Luckily, Faust turned out to be a lovely family man, and I am still here to tell the tale (he probably still thinks I am a bit of a cunt for that). The fear factor was real back then.

The time I left Tabu Recordings in order to produce a radio show with the Norwegian equivalent to Howard Stern, only to get fired after four months.

The radio station, which had headhunted outspoken and controversial Norwegian radio personality Mina Hadjian, made her several promises that they did not keep, from investing in proper equipment to salary and staff requirements. As we tried our best to keep up with the horrid working conditions they put us through day in and day out, we would regularly retaliate by communicating our discontent on the air. That approach might have worked for Howard Stern, but it was disastrous for us. After four months, we were out on our arses—without pay. Enslaved had been bounced around from A&R to A&R like an unwanted foster child after they signed to Tabu. By the time I appeared on the scene, *Ruun* had been out for a month, and they felt they'd lost ground on a great amount of solid promotional work, because the release had been dealt with by three different people, and they were sick of it. Right before they went into the studio to record *Vertebrae*, they requested a meeting with me to find out whether it'd be worth it for them to release the record through Tabu Recordings. They were an already established band so they could have left the label and got another deal elsewhere. But they were the biggest band on the label, and I wanted to keep them. Tabu Recordings was in the process of being bought by a big Scandinavian company, and I was in negotiations with Mina Hadjian to produce her new radio show. I was not sure that I'd get the radio job full time, so I held onto Enslaved and did not disclose my intentions. On their end, Enslaved wanted to work with one person from the beginning of the recording through the promotion cycle and beyond. They found out about my situation through a third party. Did the band end up thinking I was a cunt when I publicly announced that I was leaving? Yes, and quite rightly so. They ultimately extricated themselves from the Tabu deal and *Vertebrae* was released by Indie Recordings. I am sure they still think I'm a cunt.

This list is merely a teaser, for there were so many daft anecdotes. That first visit to Elm Street in December 2002 set in motion a series of events that created the *Biatch in the Northern Sky* effect. Truth is, one's path is never paved by oneself alone—others' kindness will assist your rise through the ranks by introducing you to the right people or by putting a good word in for you to those who will ultimately offer you opportunities. When I entered the bar, Elm Street was empty. It was a Sunday night. When Fenriz walked in, he was with three other people. One of them was the Norwegian national "Oracle of Metal" Gro Narvestad. Producer and host of metal show Ambolt on NRK P3, Gro had been a regular fixture on Norwegian radio and television for years. She was also one of the four original producers of the Inferno Festival. Through Gro's infinite kindness and absolute generosity, I got several breaks within the Norwegian media. It was Gro who told her bosses that I'd be the right person to take over the reins and produce the next metal show on P3.

I was intent on going back to media production, but I'd only been living in Oslo for around three years by the time *Tinitus* launched in 2005, and my Norwegian was not fluent enough to host a radio show. So I teamed up with rock journalist Kirsti Thisland, and we created a pilot that was recorded and mixed at Funeral's Kjetil Ottersen's home studio in Drammen (literally, it was done in his bedroom, and his eighteen-year-old cat usually hung out with us during the recording).

Once NRK P3 picked up our pilot, head of P3 Marius Lilellien and program director Håkon Moslet asked us to develop the concept further. There was only one small catch: we had to do it under the auspices of this very successful Norwegian radio production company. That collaboration went tits up pretty quickly, as I intercepted the contract between them and P3 (someone made a mistake by including me in the e-mail). I was incensed by the pay discrepancy. It was astronomical. They certainly had the "experience," but I had the contacts, the understanding, the historical knowledge of the metal scene, and I knew that without me (or Kirsti), there would be no show.

I negotiated with them politely, but things soon escalated. They responded harshly. I threatened to pull out entirely if Kirsti and I did not get paid a fair fee. They eventually relented and suggested that we produce the show by ourselves. That could have spelled disaster for us. Yet *Tinitus* achieved great ratings pretty quickly—thirty-six thousand listeners after its first three months, and sixty-four thousand after one year. My strategy of booking relevant guests, hitting them with offbeat questions, devising heterogeneous playlists, peppered with exclusives, and writing up captivating press releases that were regularly published by Bori Krgin at *Blabbermouth* paid off. The following year, P3 renewed our contract directly. No more go-betweens. *Tinitus* was a mishmash of fresh and eccentric ideas that perhaps the rigid black metal scene was not entirely on board with—judging by some of their e-mails, there were audience members who thought we were morons. Yet both Kirsti and I reveled in the notion that anything we did might have been considered "too mainstream" or "not grim enough" for them (it wasn't). My aim was to expand the show's ratings, not impress the *necro* brigade. For starters, I picked the riff from a non-Norwegian band for our opening titles—Mastodon's "Blood and Thunder" became the steeple to our sonic regime each Wednesday. There was something extremely special about those proggie grindcoresters after they released *Leviathan*. And look at them now—they won a Grammy in 2018.

In 2006, the Inferno Festival magazine editor Gro "a-finger-in-every-pie" Narvestad asked me to write a column for that year's magazine edition. I am going to spare you the overall contents. But this is how I ended it:

Has living in the black metal Mecca allowed me to experience the stretch of the imagination that I so craved? Sometimes. I mean, this is no Tibet. And even Tibet is not Tibet anymore. I certainly met heads with extravagant ideas and bumped into creatures with eccentric dispositions, but the only thing that, so far, has had a good stretch has been my wallet. When you live in a country where something as fundamental as a liter of milk costs you the equivalent to 1 GBP, then you know that love is not in the air. Then, again, I did not move here for love. I did it for *hate*. and that's still the most eminent reason for me to stay a little longer.

Hate? I never moved to Oslo for *hate*. I could barely recognize myself in that piece (I cringed as I read it recently). I have never had a bone of *hate* in my body. Frustration at situations I may have found myself in while dealing with some Norwegians (*coughs* Satyr calling me at ten in the evening to discuss the following day's tasks). Sure. Who does not feel frustration on occasion when dealing with their boss? Whatever negative emotions I felt back in Norway, they would pale in comparison to those that I have since experienced in New York City (especially after President Barack Obama left office). It is hard to ignore the current political situation in the United States. I was aware that life in this country was less fair and harsher toward its own citizens than in Europe, but I was not ready for the level of hysteria, viciousness, arrogance, and utter ignorance that I have experienced since Donald Trump announced that he was running for office. He and his administration are a far cry from the peaceful and equal society I was used to when I lived in Norway, the UK, or Italy. Even Italy, with its government corruption, is a fairer society than the United States. Having been exposed to a whole new level of inequality and a large chunk of society that believes in conspiracy theories and not in universal health care for all, I felt compelled to reassess my priorities. These days, I am more interested in repealing *Citizens United* than rating a new release, and I am more likely to attend a Bernie Sanders rally than a Blood Tsunami show. While I would not move back there in a heartbeat or anything—winters are way too cold and long for my aging bones—I am pleased to admit that I don't need to stare at a map of Europe to be aware of Norway's existence now. I am genuinely fond of the country, its people, and the friends I made there over the years. The more I live in New York City, the more I appreciate my European roots. I seem to have come full circle. But *that* is a whole other chapter for a very different book...

Notes

[1]Norway's top 40 TV show on state channel NRK1.

<Jonathan Mayhew
  *Blink. 2.0 (For Pelle Ohlin
  & Kiriko Takemura)*, 2019
  [continued from page 2]

le Corbeau
(THE CROW)

USUALLY, PEOPLE FIND A PRETTY PL
FOR THEIR FIRST DATE.

A FRENCH RESTAURANT...

désirez-vous autre chose?

A GOOD TEEN-MOVIE AT THE CINEMA..

BUT FOR THE FRIENDS : IT'S A SHOW.

HI!
HELLO!

A. FUCKING. BLACK METAL. SHOW.

Shyle Zalewski *Le Corbeau (The Crow)*, 2019

When Evil Comes A'Calling

EUGENE S. ROBINSON

There's an altar. It's festooned with some of the earmarks of a sort of theatrical doom: spider webs, upside-down crosses, bats maybe. Backstage, King Diamond and crew are facepainted and cranky. I've been there too, as a headliner. You get tired of waiting and want to get to getting off, but you also knew what the bill was when you booked it. So suck it up, buttercup.

The club owner was the kind of guy who sat way too close to his desk, his hands out of sight. He was telling me that the contract that I had signed had changed since I signed it. Oxbow, the band I sing for, would be playing only twenty minutes tonight. The contract said thirty. Our set was set to thirty. Which I said.

"Well, things change," he said, sliding his hips deeper under his desk.

"Ok. We'll leave then." I said it. I meant it. I've had it with jerk offs jerking themselves off at my expense.

"No. No. You do what you have to do." Which sounded grand. And backstage with the cranky King Diamond and crew and us watching them get...evil...it seemed to be what we were all about: doing what we had to do—which was *play*. And play we did. Right up until, at twenty minutes, they cut the power, and all hell broke loose.

We tore the PA stacks down, kicked the monitors into the audience, the audience that was now cursing us from the front, while King Diamond's people hollered at us from the rear, and the bouncers advanced up the side aisles toward the stage.

I unscrewed the mic stand from the base and started swinging it like a light saber toward the bouncers who, immediately, held their hands up. Like the five feet of steel in my hands was the problem. So I threw it into the audience and waved them in. To just my hands with only my hands. At this show of stupid bravado, the audience now cheered. Allegiances swinging wildly back in our favor.

The bouncers paused, stalled by the stage. King Diamond's crew disappeared, and it lasted until the cops came. Guns trump rage, just barely, but after fifteen minutes of mayhem, the point had been made: you should have let us play thirty minutes, since now we were five minutes over where we would have been if you just stopped the stupidity and let us play.

Much more significantly, King Diamond had to follow *that*. *That* specifically being very real nontheatrical darkness up against their very not real theatrical kind. Especially since the reality remains: very few people die at the movies. But lots of people die victims of very real jungle anger. And beyond that: rage, delight in cruelty, and, ultimately, in evil.

Having once seen it, like many who do, you might spend the larger part of your time post-viewing, hunting it down again. For a glimpse, again. A little taste. Blame dopamine or serotonin or just bad habits, but returning to the scene of the crime? Just about what we're all about.

We can't help it. This is one of the natures of evil.

Years earlier I tracked down Anton LaVey from the Church of Satan. He had to have seen it. He would know what I was talking about. He would tell me what he knew.

"Evil? Well, evil is what doesn't feel good," he told me. I understood what he was saying, but I was looking for more.

"Root canals don't feel good, but I don't think we'd call them evil," I said.

He looked at me, and we went back and forth before he capped it with, "Hey... I'm an atheist."

Before him, Charles Manson who, while he was curious about the "cryptic wingtip trip" he thought I was on, was nowhere near an answer despite being the closest one yet.

Hip-hop, or "pop thuggery" as the far-right Morrissey once dubbed it, sort of tried to own musical evil and failed as miserably as corpsepaint and upside-down crosses had. Hip-hop evil was all about commerce and crimes in the commission of commerce. Like the mafia. Even the big mafia mouthpiece I once interviewed, Bruce Cutler, John Gotti's defense attorney said, "Unless you're a degenerate piece of shit, there are only three reasons why you choose crime: poverty, despair, and culture."

So for him evil was transactional and, therefore, explainable.

So Satanic metal, death metal, black metal, mafia, hip-hop, Satanism, only casually and gradually sniffed around the essence of that which once viewed can never be unviewed. That is, specifically, the aggressive and gleeful drive to do damage in the face of an understanding that that is precisely what you should *not* be doing. If you could bottle that into your music and/or art, you'd have a wild new animal of a thing on your hands.

You'd have Nazi Germany.

Because while it's alleged that Aristotle (or Mary Wollstonecraft) once said that no person *consciously* does evil, in the case of the Third Reich this has been proven ultimately untrue. In some of the Hitlerian fireside chats, Hitler jokes about "resettlement" knowing what resettlement really meant. What they made it mean.

The boundless breaking of even the law of the jungle—aided and abetted by a machinery that focused savagery.

"I should prepare you for meeting my father." My friend was telling me his father would be picking me up from the hotel where I was staying and heading out to the wedding I was going to. You see, his father "had been" a Nazi.

"As long as he's just driving me to the wedding, I'll be fine," I laughed. At first.

But on the drive and during the evening's events, when he and his older friends gathered, whispering and looking in my direction, I caught a peek of what I had once felt. Of course, recognizing it in others starts with recognizing it in yourself, and I had, when during the course of some random street struggle, I felt the pull/ call beyond the human. The man who I had beaten lay broken beneath me and still there was a desire for more—much, much more. Starting with tearing him apart, and then tearing apart his soul. It was intoxicating. It was overpowering. It was all I ever wanted to feel again, forever: my boot on his face.

It was like love.

As these now old Nazis made periodic runs at me—"This is Germany, and because it's Germany we will speak German regardless of what our American 'friends' might like!" he said out loud during the opening remarks—I knew what they were still high on, and it was something that didn't die in 1945.

"It will be nice to do business with you." This was in a letter I got from Herbert Egoldt. He ran Rock-O-Rama records in Germany. He put out Skrewdriver and a klatch of other racist bands. He wanted to license the American band Stigmata, whose record I had just put out. Stigmata, as far as I knew, were not racists, and Egoldt may have not been either, but if I were to say I wasn't amused by him doing business with me in light of the fact that I am Black, well, I'd be lying.

But even bands that actually advocate real hurting and killing are missing the point. Which is to say, their "extrapolitical" solutions still fit fully into the realm of the logical. I mean, how many killings are truly senseless?

So, not sound logic, but not *evil* by any stretch.

They mostly vibed like boys that had been abandoned by their fathers.

So maybe what I saw on the Lower East Side when I had to use everything in my power and moral character to pull myself back from the dizzying and willful destruction of another human was just a momentary blip, or pop, on a screen of stupid.

Or so I would have continued to think had I not made the acquaintance of serial killer John Wayne Gacy. Sure, you could dismiss his crimes and the upward of thirty-some-odd murders as being fueled by something as simple as sexual sadism, but there was more to it than that, and it came through when he wrote me, and it raged like a river beneath the icy surface of all of the shit that we need to do to convince people that we shouldn't be where Gacy was before he was eventually put to death.

It was not in his letters, which were pretty anodyne, but in what was not said— maybe more in his denials of what we would call facts and he called "allegations." He would begin tearing us apart as soon as he got out if he could get out since, like Ted Bundy, a man he referenced more than once, said, "It's like a song that you can't get out of your head."

I never caught a direct glimpse of it again. More like something or someone that disappears around a corner right before you get there, but I had been there, so I am there, on occasion, to see the shadow and what it leaves behind. And in all of the music I like, it is there—and in all of the literature and art. It never leaves because it *can* never leave, as it has no place to go. It's ours and ours alone and forever.

Driving to an interview I once had with Ronnie James Dio, I got an urgent message from his publicist. "The interview is off. They're after him. He needs to be careful." I never heard from him again. Then he died. Gacy was put to death. Anton LaVey also died, as did Manson, and Rock-O-Rama was shut down in 1994, after a police raid.

So it goes—and how it ends. For us all. But not the river. Never that river.

While we craft deathless music, art, and culture, beyond commerce and, therefore, outside of any ideological usefulness, understand that though the music expresses a certain version of evil, we express it for the same way that people have since there were people: to protect us from it.

Does it work? Has it ever?

I suspect not. I suspect it cheerleads that which you want to be protected against, but protecting you from you has never sounded so good. So let it play and play on. And stay out of basements and crawlspaces.

END-END-END

Black Metal & Male Depression

NINA POWER

What is the distilled feeling of being truly, irreparably alone? The feeling that there is nothing outside your own sense of being barely alive? That every tie you might have had to life, to other people, to the world, has gone, or is meaningless? That no one needs you, nobody wants you, and that your existence is a stain upon the universe, a mistake, an error.

This is the slide from everyday sadness to melancholy to flat-out despair to absolute rock-bottom hopelessness. Male depression in particular is a massive and strange contemporary problem in this regard. Men are, simply put, more likely to be addicts and to harm or kill each other than women are, and they are also more likely to hurt or kill themselves. This may be because they use more violent means, but, as something like the opioid crisis in the United States reveals, men are routinely depressed and dying. Men's rights activists often describe what they perceive to be male expendability—that men are more likely to be killed in war or at work—while, at the same time, much mainstream discourse is today devoted to attacking "male privilege." The left in particular finds it difficult to feel sympathy for men's suffering, because of, among other things, historical asymmetries between the sexes and the ongoing damaging behavior of a few men. There is a miscommunication, or a misrecognition, happening between the sexes before our eyes; there is no doubt valid resentment on both sides, but male pain is strangely difficult to discuss on both the left (men are to blame; besides they have all the power anyway) or on the right (men should be tough; it's pathetic to be sad).

But there is a problem. Everyone should care about male sadness—no more or less than they should care about female sadness, of course, but our solidarity does not, or should not, stop because of someone's sex.

One way into this specific question of male sadness would be to examine the cultural forms that express these phenomena in the most extreme way: depressive suicidal black metal (DSBM) is uniquely tied, overwhelmingly so, to expressions of male anger, rage, and despair. I want to explore this genre in the broader context of male suffering and its potentially singular aspects—those kinds of experiences not available to most women, as we will see. The essay is written, therefore, in the spirit of a kind of disjointed sympathy and asks how is it possible to be sympathetic to male rage and pain, particularly when expressions thereof are often themselves so violent against the world? DSBM does not promote violence or rage but somehow channels it. Here we catch a glimpse of a possible understanding that bridges the gap between two different and incompatible kinds of resentment that vie for our attention today. DSBM is a key to understanding male pain, the better to grasp its ungraspable qualities, to prevent male resentment from becoming violent, to better prevent male violence against men themselves, against other men, and against women. What, we may begin by asking, is specific to the kind of male alienation expressed in this music?

We are used to understanding, from Marx and the Marxist tradition, at least four kinds of alienation: alienation from the product of one's labor; alienation from the production process as such; alienation from one's fellow man (particularly in the workplace); and alienation from the species, understood socially as such. But what about the kind of alienation that taps into something deeper than all this, deeper than labor and the social, something profoundly bleak and mind-bendingly meaningless? A relation to the void that no longer sees any distinction between you and the blackness that swirls outside and inside, that creates a plummeting feeling, a feeling of doom that transcends, or, rather, falls below, labor, because one is useless, not just for work or for others, but one is completely beyond the category of "use," as such. Such a feeling is at odds with the normal self-evaluation of oneself as a member of humanity. As Thomas Ligotti puts it: "But when it comes to existential judgments, human beings in general have an unfalteringly good opinion of themselves and their condition in this world and are steadfastly confident they are not a collection of self-conscious nothings."[1] To enter into the existential territory of being a "self-conscious nothing" places one at serious odds with one's fellow man. Not only is one incapable of "doing," but one's relation to "being" is also traduced. One is no longer "human" but has entered into cosmic, alien territory, where one is not only or just alienated, but rather has become the alien itself. In this state, one is undesirable, both to oneself and to the other, as a social or sexual being. One is of no use, has no purpose, no duty, and no future. One exists, but for nothing.

DSBM, the subgenre that mines these particular depths more than any other, is as melodic as it is mournful. Here we find Leviathan, Xasthur, Forgotten Tomb, Thy Light, and Wintercult, among many others, and the music includes classical strings, heavy guitars, piano, drone, sludge sounds, and screaming, howling, or shouting. It is somewhere between the black metal of Burzum and the plaintive complaints and deep bass of heavy grunge. DSBM tracks have names like "I Should Have Never Been Born" (My Useless Life), "Further into Nothingness" (Exiled from Light), "Losing the Sun" (Black Autumn), "Screaming at Forgotten Tears" (Xasthur), and "No Place for Joy" (Deadlife). But it is not solely an Anglophone affair; there are Scandinavian, French, German, Spanish, Turkish, and Latin American DSBM groups too. But it is also, perhaps above all, very male.

Listening to a range of DSBM bands, not all of whom would describe themselves in this way, but who nevertheless are placed in this subgenre, generates a paradoxical and quite specific emotional state. The fact that these songs exist at all is a testament to the minimal difference, or the line, between creating something and being unable to do anything at all: they exist, but barely. The music exists in a state that Wendy Brown describes as "depressive anxiety." "Depressive anxiety," she writes, "is a truly terrible state: you cannot move because of the bleakness but you cannot rest because of the anxiety; you can neither seize life nor escape it, neither live nor die."[2]

Depressive anxiety is, therefore, only productive in a state of minimal (and horrible) tension. Perhaps precisely for this reason, DSBM tracks are often exuberant in their misery: loud, emotional, excessive, trapped howls of suffering. Many of the tracks are outpourings of rage, despair, incoherence. There is also, and perhaps surprisingly, a sweetness to the melancholy, a recognition of a shared (in)human condition that exists on the edge of sanity, reality, and barely continued existence. The chords plug into a recognizably melodic framework: in a sense, the tracks, although extreme, do not engage in excessive experimentation for its own sake. The musicians recall Nietzsche's phrase in *Thus Spoke Zarathustra*: "I love all those who are like heavy drops falling individually from the dark cloud that hangs over humanity: they herald the coming of the lightning, and as heralds they perish."[3]

This is not noise music, or avant-garde particularly, although there is a uniquely hard edge quality to the sound that recapitulates certain emotional states, particularly those associated with feelings of regret, inwardness. Your solar plexus—or should it be lunar core—is drenched in waves of melancholy; your self is tugged. There is a sinking feeling, a feeling of doom over time. At the same moment, there is a comfort in these Saturnine arpeggios. I do not wish, however, to suggest that there is any easy redemption here, or that that is the point of the music. This is not music made to assuage, ameliorate, or elevate. It does not straightforwardly "help," or try to help, with depressed, tragic, empty or despairing states. It is, instead, music that reflects these states. If it paradoxically provides some comfort, it is against itself, because truly alienated moods struggle to recognize similarities. Nevertheless, there is comfort of a kind here, a kind of empathy in shared separation. DSBM is, above all, sincere. It lacks the irony and cynicism of the world as a whole. This, in many ways, is its greatest appeal and the basis for its minimal and paradoxical assurance.

Take Xasthur's *Subliminal Genocide* of 2006, a classic of the genre. The opening track "Disharmonic Convergence" is perfectly self-descriptive. A gloomy echo sound at the start, a detuned and horror-film piano plays three simple chords over and over, as a fractured and fragmented guitar traces the same chords with more color (or should we say darkness). "The Prison of Mirrors" follows, like stained glass windows filtering minimal light into an empty room. DSBM often oscillates between extreme eeriness and an almost excessive heaviness that jolts and shudders along like a piece of equipment in an earthquake, or like resonant frequency hitting a sheet of metal.

Many of our darkest moods do not want and, in any case, cannot find, acceptance or recognition in anything outside of themselves. They are alienated even from our usual categories of alienation. In them, we are, to paraphrase the claims Heidegger makes regarding boredom, not alienated from something, we are radically alienated, we are alienated as such. This alien state opens up some cosmic questions, not least regarding sexual difference. Why? Because in many of its dimensions the cosmos at its core is predicated on at least this binary. If you get down to the core of human things—life, nature, reality—you find a certain stubborn division. To dwell in this division alone is to confront the universe *as* a man, or *as* a woman. It is to be in relation to the last remaining thing—call it nature, call it being, call it nothingness. It has a quality because of this duality, and you are on one side of it or another. You might feel profoundly alienated from even this truth, but your alienation from sex is nevertheless lived *in a sexed way*. It is no surprise that today we are informed repeatedly by the media of the "problem" of "incels," that is to say, of this supposedly large number of young men who are "involuntarily celibate," who cannot find a girlfriend or someone to be physically intimate with, who apparently enter into states of anomie and despair, perhaps even rage, as this category has also been tied to some acts of extreme violence.

What more can we say about this relationship between being a man and being in the universe? The cult pseudonymous writer Zero HP Lovecraft (@0x49fa98) wrote in a tweet on October 30, 2018, that "The component of male lived experience that is wholly unaccessible to women, more than any other, is the colossal and abyssal apathy of the universe toward you."[4] Apathy is an interestingly ambiguous word. The Greek *apatheia* means *without suffering* or having suffered from *a*— *without*—and *pathos*—*emotion; feeling suffering*—and it originally had a more positive dimension. The later and current use of the term to indicate a feeling of *not being bothered* emerged in the middle of the eighteenth century. In what sense does Zero HP Lovecraft mean it here? The universe in a way cannot suffer on your behalf, although perhaps you can suffer on its behalf. But more than this: the universe does not care about you, about what you do. You are of no interest to it; it is indifferent to you. There is no measure; you do not have a place. You could be, and are, just anyone, or, seen another way, no one. We hear echoes of this claim in Jean Genet's narrator of *The Thief's Journal*: "I am alone in the world, and I am not sure that I am not the king."[5]

I am interested, above all, in this "unaccessible" component that "Lovecraft" identifies, in taking it seriously, even, or especially, from the standpoint of an experiential being that is excluded from it, at least on the terms set out by him. Zero HP Lovecraft qualifies his claim in the following way, shedding more light on what kind of apathy he means: "Women cannot relate to this, except perhaps women of exceptional ugliness, childless crones, and FtM transsexuals [sic]." By inference, then, we can understand that the apathy Zero HP Lovecraft means has a relation to sex in both senses. Women who are "exceptionally ugly" might be understood to have no relation to the sexual desire of the other, therefore, do not and never have "existed" on this plane of meaning; they are invisible women. "Childless crones" are women whose reproductive purpose, for whatever reason, has not been fulfilled (the deep social fear and pity toward post- or non-fertile women can be understood in the fictional depiction of witches, who, driven mad by their lack of childbearing, resort to entrapping and poisoning other people's children). Female to male transsexuals are, in Lovecraft's system, women who have presumably also exited the world of heterosexual male desire; they are no longer participants in a certain sexual game. All of these positions, the male confronted by the "apathy" of the universe, very ugly women, childless older women, and women who are no longer part of the female world, are positions that are absent of a certain meaning and a certain recognition. These are subjects who have no place, not being desirable, purposeful, useful, or visible. They are not "reproductive" subjects; they neither generate new humans nor contribute to the existing order of things (and order, we presume, is good).

There are always different ways one can relate to the apathy of the universe, of course. One can accept it. It could be understood to be a beautiful thing. Or one can embrace it, affirm one's contingency, and the absurdity of existence, as the Existentialists did. Or you can go all the way to the bottom and dwell in the imagination of one's nonexistence, in nihilism as such. Our usual social recognition depends in part on a sexual recognition. The idea that "nobody wants you" is multilayered: to not be desired socially overlaps significantly, though not entirely, with not being desired sexually. It is often understood as a marker of what it means to be valued and to be wanted more broadly; to be sexually undesirable is, from one angle, to see oneself as undesired by the world as a whole.

DSBM taps into this experience of sexless uselessness—a kind of post-sex state— and seeks to recognize it, to give it a name, to provide a sonic mirror. There is always, however, also what we might call "the allure of the alone," where one embraces one's total alienation, having become used to it, and, in turn, begins to seek it out, to give up on the other altogether, to start, however painfully, to embrace one's own irrelevance. One way of conceiving this would be to understand the move, widely noted in recent years, from the involuntary celibate to the "volcel" (voluntary celibate): the affirmation of one's own sexlessness. One does not, therefore, have to feel *only* lonely in aloneness; one can feel self-reliant or autonomous (giving oneself the law). These tensions—of the social, the sexual, the various possibilities of belonging, and the various drives to aloneness— are well-exemplified in Philip Larkin's 1950 poem "Wants":

Beyond all this, the wish to be alone:

However the sky grows dark with invitation-cards

However we follow the printed directions of sex

However the family is photographed under the flag-staff—

Beyond all this, the wish to be alone.

Beneath it all, the desire for oblivion runs:

Despite the artful tensions of the calendar,

The life insurance, the tabled fertility rites,

The costly aversion of the eyes away from death—

Beneath it all, the desire for oblivion runs.[6]

The antisocial sociability we all confront as beings in a society, or on the edges of it, the struggle between solitude and other people, between normativity and doing "what we want" (if desire even exists outside of our relations with others), the compulsion to conform (to attend things, to engage in sexual and reproductive behavior, to perform loyalty to one's country), and the inevitability of death, and even the desire for it—are perfectly balanced here, where "the wish to be alone" and "oblivion" are positioned in the same line in consecutive verses. Larkin posits the fine line between wanting others, of the allure of others, and the desire for a kind of "volcel" acceptance (and oblivion—a kind of desire for death).

So what about death? DSBM is preoccupied with it and with self-destruction of all kinds, from self-harm to addiction (think of Xasthur's "Beauty Is Only Razor Deep" as a critique of human aesthetics from a self-harm perspective or "Alcoholism" by Psychonaut 4, from the album *Dypsomania*). What exactly is the relation between the absence of Eros and the appearance of Thanatos? Suicide is the most common cause of death among men aged twenty to forty-nine in the UK, and men accounted for three-quarters of suicides as a whole in 2018. There is undoubtedly a serious problem for men concerning depression, self-harm, and suicide.

By exploring introspective, depressed, and a certain melodic suicidality, does DSBM provide something of a comfort or more of a reminder? I would like to suggest that DSBM walks a very fine line between confirmation of depressive feelings, of the recognition of suicidal ideation and self-harm, and the distancing of them. In this sense, I want to say, not that DSBM "cures" these ills, but that, by reflecting them, it permits a minimal distancing between thoughts and acts, that it slips in between feelings. In this sense, it could provide a very small but meaningful contribution to the prevention of harm by reflecting back from deeply horrible places the very small idea that one is not *completely* alone. Of course, this recognition is not always going to be enough.

There is a strange case, relevant to the preoccupations of DSBM. This is the case of Mitchell Heisman, who committed suicide with a .38-caliber pistol in Harvard Yard on Yom Kippur, September 18, 2010, at the age of thirty-five.[7] Like Otto Weininger, who shot himself in 1903, at the age of twenty-three, in the house where Beethoven died, Heisman has come to be something of a minor antihero among a small number of nihilistic literary men. Like Weininger, who had published *Geschlecht und Charakter* (*Sex and Character*) shortly before he died, Heisman had spent five years writing a 1905-page suicide note, "a dense, scholarly work with 1,433 footnotes, a twenty-page bibliography, and more than 1,700 references to God and 200 references to the German philosopher Friedrich Nietzsche."[8] His death, according to Heisman's text, was "an experiment in nihilism." The note, available online, states that the "prejudice" against death is "a kind of xenophobia" and describes how fear of death is used to control people's minds:

For most people, fear of death is the unquestionable master that establishes *all* other hierarchies—both social hierarchies, and the hierarchies within one's own mind. Most are humbly grateful for the very privilege of obedience *and do not want to be free*.[9]

Criticizing "viviocentrism," or life-centeredness, Heisman, whose text begins with a quote from Plato's *Phaedo*, wonders whether it is possible to "live" a philosophy of the nihilistic, to live in the modality of meaninglessness. He asks whether suicide could represent "the pinnacle of the rational life realized?" If Heisman somehow reasoned himself into suicide, does an exploration of death and nihilism necessarily lead to the conclusion that suicide is the best, or only, response?

DSBM does not conclude, or lead one to conclude, that Heisman's solution is necessarily the case, though it comes close to many of his arguments. There would, after all, be no more music after death (one imagines). The minimal difference between staying alive, but for nothing or for very little, and dying is imagined and rehearsed in the music; it is sad, of course, melancholic, but there is, after all, *something* here. As a genre, it thankfully lacks the certainty of Heisman's act, of Weininger's gesture, of these finished texts whose suicide provides the conclusion. We might ask: Does music do something that words alone cannot? The claim by Lovecraft that male lived experience is more open to the apathy of the universe may be true; it is unverifiable in certain respects, and, of course, it is foolish to say that women do not also suffer from meaninglessness. There are kinds of meaninglessness that accompany all lives, regardless of whether one is sexually desirable or has children or other markers of "inclusion" in the universe.

Men, as noted, commit suicide more often than women. The reasons for this have been widely discussed. Men tend to use more violent means, more violently. Men are not as good at describing feelings of unhappiness, shame, or loss of status. If they do not reproduce, it is not as unusual as women who do not. The male separatist movement, Men Going their Own Way, frequently cite a statistic that claims that 60 percent of men historically did not have children, as a result of dying in war or because of the injustice of sexual selection. From this point of view, women are "worth" more to the universe and, consequently, to "society," insofar as such a thing exists.

The apathy of the universe is, from this perspective, as real as sexual difference. One can accept it as a man or as a woman. One is positioned, beyond one's choice, in one of these two relations. Nihilism does not necessarily entail self-destructive or suicidal thoughts or actions, however. It could just as easily inspire acceptance of one's fate, a quiet kind of contemplation. One is alive, but for nothing. But how one understands this nothing is an open question. DSBM provides one kind of answer, and it is cold and dark, an asignifying howl before one is swallowed up forever. But it is not yet quite silence, and in the snow and the winter one sees, from faraway, a man who looks a little bit like you...and all is not yet quite lost. *Maybe.*

Notes

[1] Thomas Ligotti, *The Conspiracy against the Human Race: A Contrivance of Horror* (New York: Hippocampus Press, 2010), 20.

[2] Wendy Brown, "Untimeliness and Punctuality: Critical Theory in Dark Times," in *Edgework: Critical Essays on Knowledge and Politics* (Princeton, NJ: Princeton University Press, 2005), 11.

[3] Friedrich Nietzsche, *Thus Spoke Zarathustra: A Book for All and None,* trans. Adrian Del Caro (Cambridge: Cambridge University Press, 2006 [1883–1885]), 9.

[4] Zero HP Lovecract@0x49a98, accessed May 21, 2021, https://twitter.com/0x49fa98/status/1057382140281679873?s=20.

[5] Jean Genet, *The Thief's Journal*, trans. Bernard Frechtman (New York: Bantam Books, 1965), 36.

[6] Philip Larkin, "Wants," in *Collected Poems*, ed. Anthony Thwaite (London: Marvel Press/Faber and Faber, 1988), 42.

[7] David Abel, "What He Left Behind: A 1,905-page Suicide Note," Boston.com, September 27, 2010, tinyurl.com/2whbf6nr.

[8] Ibid.

[9] Mitchell Heisman, *Suicide Note*, Internet Archive, September 25, 2010, 23, accessed May 21, 2021, https://archive.org/details/MitchellHeismanSuicideNote/mode/2up.

Vincent Como
Black Metal, 2007
creased black paper, 62.9 x 46.4 cm
courtesy of the artist and Minus Space Gallery, Brooklyn, New York

Riton La Mort
Fuck Me Jesus, 2019
acrylic and ink on paper, 21 x 29.7 cm
courtesy of the artist

Marnie Weber
Spirit Girls, 2016
production still from *The Day
of Forevermore*, 2016
photo by ©LeeAnn Nickel
courtesy of the artist and
Gavlak Gallery, Los Angeles

Marnie Weber
Witches and the Devil, 2016
production still from *The Day of Forevermore*, 2016
photo by ©LeeAnn Nickel
courtesy of the artist and
Gavlak Gallery, Los Angeles

FICTIONALIZING
BLACK METAL
CATHERINE FEARNS

We herald the dawn of a new Dark Age...as we
metamorphose into inhumanity...I am Sound...
Sound becomes me.

—Vox Inferi

Vox Inferi are a black metal band with mythical status. Hailing
from everywhere and nowhere, they are rumoured to live off-grid
somewhere in the north of England, banned from most countries
due to their criminal records. Anarchist-misanthrope-conspiracy
theorists, they live in soundproofed containers to protect
themselves from the frequency warfare that they claim has been
waged on humanity since the Nazis adopted standard tuning in
1939. Their lead singer, known as The Messiah, is almost seven feet
tall and has no eyes—the unsubstantiated rumour being that he
gouged them out live on stage to heighten his musical sensitivity.
His wife, the band's female keyboardist, suffers from misophonia—
allergy to sound—and wears ear protectors at all times. Vox Inferi's
music, impossibly heavy and employing a wide range of instruments
from ten-string guitars to a child's xylophone, is accompanied by
offensively violent, disgusting lyrics. But they have never recorded
any of it, believing that sound is ephemeral and should only be
experienced in the moment, that to record anything is crass and
against artistic truth. Their live shows are rituals designed to
induce fear and disorientation, culminating in the moment when
their sound hits the "devil's frequency" and Satan is summoned, his
image appearing on a screen as a coloured spectrogram. These live
shows are never publicized outside of the dark web, open only to
members of the Church of Satan.

If you are a black metal fan, there is no need to panic that you have not heard of Vox Inferi. You will not find them listed on *Encyclopaedia Metallum* either. They do not exist. I created a fictional black metal band to feature in my latest crime novel *Sound*. Vox Inferi are murder suspects, but they also function to highlight themes in the book, to drive the narrative forward, and to illuminate aspects of other characters.

Fictionalizing black metal in a serious way presents unique challenges. How do you avoid writing unintentional comedy about a subgenre that is already almost a parody of itself, and, therefore, risk trivializing something that is in fact very serious? How do you avoid the clichés? As a metal journalist, musician, and fan, I am fully versed in the aesthetic signifiers of black metal. To me, the clichés and stereotypes I describe in the book act as a comfort, a scaffolding beyond which I can arrive at a higher discourse. Since I have internalized them as part of my culture, I am able to access meta levels of meaning. Paradoxically, this internalization can also have the effect of stifling analysis, of desensitizing me to potentially negative or dangerous aspects of these tropes. Writing about black metal from an outsider's perspective (the narrator) and for outsiders (readers who are not metal fans) allowed me to reconsider the clichés and stereotypes. For outsiders, they do not provide comfort; they are alien, and sometimes terrifying. In this chapter, I consider the fictionalization of black metal in light of literary and sociological theories of cliché. Clichéd discourse creates a connective pathos, and stereotypes function as an ordering process for the reader, but clichés and stereotypes have a very different function depending on whether you are an outsider or an insider. Clichés can both provide and stifle meaning, and recognizing this paradox can provide us with opportunities to reconsider and reframe a subculture.

Applying this to black metal in general, we can consider how a subculture with problematic aspects can embrace some of its fundamental clichés, while rejecting others, to redefine itself as a more positive force. With my fictional band Vox Inferi, I applied the familiar tropes of black metal, and then transcended them to resituate a band for whom nihilism becomes openness and acceptance and whose cacophony becomes beauty.

It is easy to identify a black metal band, and, therefore, it is easy to invent one. Quite apart from its sonic signifiers, black metal is defined by a specific array of aesthetic signifiers that have been fetishized as rules. Corpsepaint, black clothing, inverted crosses and other Satanic symbols, spindly, illegible lettering—these are all clichés of black metal. The word "cliché" tends to carry a negative connotation, denoting a phrase or idea that has been so overused as to have lost its meaning. But while they may not be sophisticated, literary clichés are the building blocks of language; indeed, the word *cliché* is derived from the French word *clicher*, referring to the clicking noise made by stereotype plates in printing presses, and, therefore, something that can be repeated indefinitely. Just as clichéd phrases are the building blocks of language, repeated until they enter the psyche, clichéd dress, behaviors, and images are the building blocks of a subculture.

Black metal has an inherent theatricality, while at the same time taking itself extremely seriously. It also has an undeniably dark and dangerous side. This paradox, this fine line between profundity and absurdity, means that black metal lends itself well to parody. When this underground subgenre of music makes its occasional forays into the mainstream—for example, the use of black metal fonts by fashion labels and pop stars, the Hollywood movie version of *Lords of Chaos*, YouTube joke videos, memes—the result is often humor. The fine line between seriousness and ridiculousness is necessarily crossed, because the alternative is to confront black metal's real-life dark side.

Black metal has rarely been fictionalized in a serious way, the 2018 novel *Corpsepaint* by David Peak being a notable exception.[1] Real-life black metal bands fictionalize themselves anyway, from the cartoon groups like Dethklok and Belzebubs, to the musicians who give themselves alter egos and/or surround themselves with myths about whether they are real Satanists or not. As an author, there was no way around the clichés, and so my challenge and opportunity were to transcend them, to employ them in such a way as to reveal lacunae, to reframe black metal in a new way.

The reader of *Sound* will initially view Vox Inferi differently, depending on whether they are an insider (a black metal fan) or an outsider.[2] For insiders, the tropes with which I created Vox Inferi act as signifiers; they establish a complicity with the author. As C. Namwali Serpell stated in her text "A Heap of Cliché": "it becomes art to the knowing viewer."[3] Those who know black metal will nod at the corpsepaint, the clothing, the lyrics, the gatekeeping. They may pick up explicit references to individual bands, which I borrowed to build Vox Inferi—for example, Sunn O)))'s extremely disorienting sonic performances, Behemoth's Satanic lyrics, Watain's staging, Batushka's ritualism. They will perhaps not find it so absurd that The Messiah removed his own eyeballs on stage in a musical genre that was derived from Black Sabbath (the most famous Ozzy Osbourne myth is that he bit the head of a bat on stage), and in which band members have been known to murder each other. These signifiers may seem ridiculous, but they are necessary, because they are the scaffolding of black metal. Clichés can be italicized, and, therefore, contextualized for the knowing reader by way of humor. For example, in *Sound*, Vox Inferi's keyboardist provides Helen and Mikko with a highly intellectual explanation that The Messiah is a parageologist who channels the Akashic records (the ethereal compendium of all human events) through a particular song. When they ask what the song is called, she replies "Regurgitation of Semi-Digested Eyeballs." The preposterous irrelevance of the title is a form of intertextuality that makes the metal reader aware of the author and complicit with the author.

But a large proportion of my readership are not metalheads but crime fiction fans, and, therefore, black metal outsiders. For outsiders, cliché and stereotype have a different purpose and a different effect. My protagonist, Detective Inspector Darren Swift, is a gay police officer who has suffered from homophobia in the police force and is now grieving the murder of his fiancé. He has already found comfort and acceptance with his new friends from melodic death metal band Total Depravity (another artificial construct). As part of a murder investigation, he now finds himself in the alien environment of a secret underground black metal concert, and this allows the reader to experience it through his eyes, rather than the knowing eyes of the author, who is well-versed in the subculture and, therefore, might make assumptions. His friend Helen has to explain the tenets of black metal to him, including the aspects that may potentially make Darren feel unwelcome, and this allows the author to explain them to the reader. As Namwali Serpell points out: "Learning about clichés from another place or era is fascinating, but for opposed reasons; we discover the wonders of either universality or idiosyncrasy."[4]

Metal fans are then able to reexamine black metal from the outside too, and perhaps reconsider it, as they see the band through the eyes of Helen and Darren. Readers may find the description of the black metal concert over the top—with its exaggerated seriousness and elaborate rituals—but is it any more absurd than real-life religious ceremonies, such as the Eucharist? This is of course one of the points that black metal is trying to make.

Clichés also condition behavior. Sociologist Anton C. Zijderveld likened the function of clichés to brainwashing—they are not heuristically convincing (this would demand reflection) but are magically compelling (they enchant through repetition). If clichés can condition behavior, can mold expectations, then they can be very useful for crime fiction. I can lead readers down a path of expectation, where they expect Vox Inferi to be evil and, therefore, involved in a murder. I throw in red herrings like the former murder conviction of their drummer and their claim to summon Satan, and this conditions the reader's assumptions. This is not unique to my novel, of course; stereotypes and stock characters are staples of crime fiction, designed to manipulate the reader.

This aspect gives us a clue as to how clichés can be dangerous. George Orwell railed against the use of cliché, because he associated literary laziness with moral laziness. Clichés allow people not to think about meaning—both writer and reader—and thoughtless phrases in literature—"tacked together like the sections of a prefabricated henhouse"[5]—are analogous with the political jargon of authoritarianism. In his 1961 book *Thought Reform and the Psychology of Totalism: A Study of Brainwashing in China*,[6] psychiatrist Robert Jay Lifton wrote about the "thought-terminating cliché." Controlling regimes use reductive, easily remembered phrases and truisms that discourage debate, becoming the start and finish of any argument. People repeat them, either out of habit or as a defense mechanism to reaffirm a confirmation bias, until they become "true." In her famous 1964 book on the trial of Albert Eichmann, *Eichmann in Jerusalem: A Report on the Banality of Evil*, political theorist Hannah Arendt claimed that he spoke in a series of "stock phrases and self-invented clichés."[7] His reliance on "officialese," on the euphemistic *Sprachregelung* (convention of speech) of Hitler's policies, showed both his inability to think for himself and suggested he had no genuine connection to remorse.

A link can be made here with black metal. Uncritical metal fans can be accused of moral laziness for accepting the unpleasant aspects of the culture as an intrinsic part of the whole. There are, of course, people who hold genuine fascist views, who are then drawn to black metal, because it provides a cover for views they find difficult to admit publicly. Here, we are not considering them so much as the black metal apologists who may not personally hold unpalatable views themselves. "But the riffs"—an accusation often made by critics of black metal apologists is a phrase that is becoming a cliché in itself, as metal fans allow the unpleasant aspects of their paramusical culture to slip through. As part and parcel of the whole, we accept them. We see the obvious signifiers (and the less obvious dog whistling) and listen to the music, happily turning a blind eye to the rest. Many black metal fans choose to ignore the negative aspects of the subculture, and this tacit acceptance amounts to complicity. In my own personal experiences with black metal, I have come up against this time and time again. Black metal bands who perform at festivals that include known NSBM (National Socialist black metal) bands in the lineup: they do not like it but see it as a necessary evil in order to be able to perform. A black metal store on a Scandinavian high street: from the outside it has an inverted cross and a fun, spooky window display; inside, among the more "mainstream" vinyl, CDs, and T-shirts, there are also Nazi insignia dotted here and there and one of Hitler's speeches in a frame behind the counter.

So clichés can be dangerous, since they can lead to moral laziness. But this presents us with opportunities. Zijderveld reminds us of the building block nature of the cliché: "Because of their reified nature, clichés can be collected like stamps...or jokes."[8]

If clichés can be collected, they can also be rejected, filtered. With a critical awareness, we can make moral judgements about those we wish to keep and those we wish to actively reject. This is what I did with *Sound*.

There is no doubt that an unthinking employment of cliché in literature is lazy. But when clichés are used knowingly, they have a different purpose. By using humor, I insert my authorial voice to show that Vox Inferi is an artificial construct—to imply their fundamental harmlessness. Vox Inferi is not only a made-up name; I obtained it through a reader competition to invent a Satanic metal band name— thus distancing the author even more from the construct. The Messiah character has an obviously trite name, and he speaks in a series of clichés and borrowings. Metal fans are able to reexamine black metal from the outside too, as they see the band through the eyes of Helen and Darren.

The artificial construction of a black metal band allows us to consider the purposes and dangers of cliché and how they can be used to change a culture with problematic aspects.

By considering them from the outside, we can select some, while rejecting others. For example, I selected corpsepaint, nihilism, ritualistic stage performances, spiky lettering...and explicitly rejected fascism, homophobia, and sexism. Vox Inferi are explicitly not fascist—they are the opposite—so much so that one of them was jailed for killing a fascist. This anti-fascism is stated through the voices of Helen and Darren, in case any assumptions were made by readers. Thus, while retaining their theatrical darkness, Vox Inferi are transformed into a somewhat positive force. They include female musicians as equals, accept a gay man as a friend, even help solve a murder—at the same time as they retain their ability to summon Satan.

All of this has parallels with real-life black metal in particular, with the so-called new wave of anti-fascist black metal. Since, as Zijderveld states, clichés gain their power to influence by repetition—black metal bands that reject racism, homophobia, and misogyny must continually state that fact.

We become inured to the meanings—new black metal bands have to keep repeating this "anti-fascist mantra" until it becomes part of the new black metal. It must be explicit, even if the word "anti-fascist" itself may be seen by some as trite—with the implication that anything not anti-fascist must be fascist. But in my naïve explorations of black metal, my repeated run-ins with unpleasantness have convinced me that nowadays black metal bands must explicitly reject the negative aspects. This is what is happening, and what must happen, in black metal at the moment, in order to change a culture. Some have been irritated by the explicit references to anti-fascism—as if this should be a given—but in the context of black metal, it is a necessary mundanity, to ensure the healthy incremental change of a culture. Anti-fascism needs to be overstated, to become a necessary cliché, for it to eventually become a given.

The new wave of anti-fascist black metal includes bands like Dawn Ray'd, Ragana, Ancst, and Thou, whose lyrics and statements are aggressively and unequivocally anti-fascist/anti-racist/feminist. They actively boycott and call out festivals and venues that accept morally questionable bands.

There are, of course, black metal bands that reject the gloriously kitsch aspects of the subculture too, opting out of corpsepaint and theater in order to focus on the music. If enough of the sonic signifiers are there, a band can label themselves (or be labelled) as black metal without the aesthetic signifiers. Indeed, the aesthetic signifiers can be actively selected, and so can the moral signifiers.

At the end of his work, Zijderveld suggests several ways in which an unquestioned acceptance of cliché can be challenged. He argues, for instance, that Brecht and the dadaists used clichés "cynically in order to shatter them."[9] A critically perceived cliché can have an intertextual effect—an intentionally obvious cliché reminds the reader of the preexistent discourse from which it was taken, and, therefore, allows the reader to reconsider this discourse. The paradox of the cliché is that it both prevents and calls for literary analysis, demanding an attitude and/or interpretation. It is with this paradox that we arrive at a solution. Ruth Amossy, author of a number of works on stereotype and cliché, points out that a single cliché, by definition, can give rise to two contrary attitudes, and the reversibility of these attitudes is the key.[10] On the one hand, there is passive absorption and immediate appropriation and, on the other, critical awareness or evaluation. This double reception of cliché is crucial. Cliché can both establish complicity and provoke criticism, and we need to move from one to the other.

To remove black metal's darkness would be to lose a fundamental aspect of its power, but there is enough darkness in the world without resorting to truly abhorrent views and practices for the sake of art. The theatricality of Satanism can easily be retained since it can be detached from any fascistic, misogynist, or homophobic elements. For a culture to change more quickly, it must be artificially influenced. For example, positive discrimination, while maligned by some, can improve the position of women in the boardroom or disadvantaged students in universities. This period of rebalancing is necessary to undo centuries of discrimination.

The use of clichés in literary texts make the addressee reconfirm, question, or modify his view of the world. Thus, Vox Inferi becomes black metal as a positive force. They channel Satan—from the depths of Hell onto a multicoloured screen— and end up saving lives in the process.

Notes

[1] David Peak, *Corpsepaint* (Petaluma, CA: Word Horde, 2018).

[2] Catherine Fearns, *Sound* (London: darkstroke Books, 2019).

[3] C. Namwali Serpell, "A Heap of Cliché," in *Critique and Post-Critique*, eds. Elizabeth S. Anker and Rita Felski (Durham, NC: Duke University Press, 2017), 164.

[4] Ibid., 161.

[5] George Orwell, *Politics and the English Language* (London: Horizon, 1946), 255.

[6] Robert Jay Lifton, *Thought Reform and the Psychology of Totalism: A Study of Brainwashing in China* (Chapel Hill, NC: University of North Carolina Press, 1961), 429.

[7] Hannah Arendt, *Eichmann in Jerusalem: A Report on the Banality of Evil* (New York: Viking Press, 1963), 49.

[8] Anton C. Zijderveld, *On Clichés: The Supersedure of Meaning by Function in Modernity* (London: Routledge and Kegan Paul, 1979), 16.

[9] Ibid., cited in Christopher Douglas, *Reciting America: Culture and Cliché in Contemporary US Fiction* (Chicago: University of Illinois Press, 2000), 39.

[10] Ruth Amossy, "The Cliché in the Reading Process," *SubStance: A Review of Theory and Literary Criticism* 11, no. 2 (1982): 34–45.

Sound[1]

CATHERINE FEARNS

The tent began to fill with white smoke, insidiously at first. It swirled around their feet until it became as thick as snow, then it rose up around their torsos and they could no longer see their own hands.

They were disembodied, unnerved. Mikko, standing now in between Darren and Helen, reached for both their hands and looked to Helen, but they could no longer see each other's faces.

As the artificial fog finally began to dissipate, they realized that the stage was no longer empty. A drummer was now seated behind the drum riser, his sticks raised in the air, poised to begin. He was shirtless but wore a black mask that covered his whole head, with holes only for his eyes and a zipper over the mouth. To the left and right of the stage stood a bassist and guitarist, both clothed in black robes and similar leather masks, their heads bowed. A female keyboard player wearing an elaborate headdress stood on a platform to one side. And in the centre, behind a microphone stand decorated with antlers, stood a minotaur. Even accounting for the mask he was wearing, he must have been seven feet tall, and looked almost as wide. He wore a bronze headdress that completely covered his eyes and had been wrought into a crown decorated with a pentagram, horns, and wings. His unkempt beard, a mixture of black and grey, reached down almost to his waist, and the blood that dripped from his mouth mingled with the bristly hair. He wore a guitar that looked comically small for him, as if it were a toy.

A hush had naturally fallen over the crowd, and The Messiah spoke, slowly and with a microphone delay effect, in a voice so deep as to be almost inhuman. "I am the androgyne who is the hieroglyph of arcane perfection, the Union of Opposites, Father Mithras, the Horned King, Prince of Beasts..." He continued with his pronouncements to an audience that was now completely still and rapt. "I am the Goat of Mendes. I am Baphomet, the All-Devouring, The Bringer of Darkness. These are the words of the Thelema."

A white noise emanated from the speakers, and amplified itself into a screaming feedback that they somehow knew was deliberate. It was almost unbearable, and the group all reached to protect their ears despite the earplugs that they wore. And then the music began, in waves and assaults of blastbeats and droning riffs. Any suggestions of melody that emerged were rapidly taken away. Only the memory of silence gave them any relief.

Lyrics were mostly unintelligible, but Darren caught the gist from the snippets that he could decipher: "We herald the dawn of a new Dark Age...as we metamorphose into inhumanity...I am Sound... Sound becomes me."

The Messiah's invocations comprised a general litany of nihilistic visions, monolithic doom, a sort of geocosmic drone that took itself far too seriously. To Darren, this was not music at all but simply a barrage of sounds, designed to be as unpleasantly loud and discordant as possible. Tendrils of noise slunk into every orifice of his body. His flesh crept with it, sending shivers down his spine. At one point, Darren texted into his phone, "Not sure how much more of this I can take?" and showed it to Helen. It was the only way they could communicate. But Mikko saw it and texted back, "Hold on, the best bit is coming!"

Notes

[1]Catherine Fearns, *Sound* (London: darkstroke Books, 2019), 69-70; reproduced with permission from the publisher.

O.B. De Alessi
Swan Song, 2011
documentation of live performance, photo by ©Michael Salerno

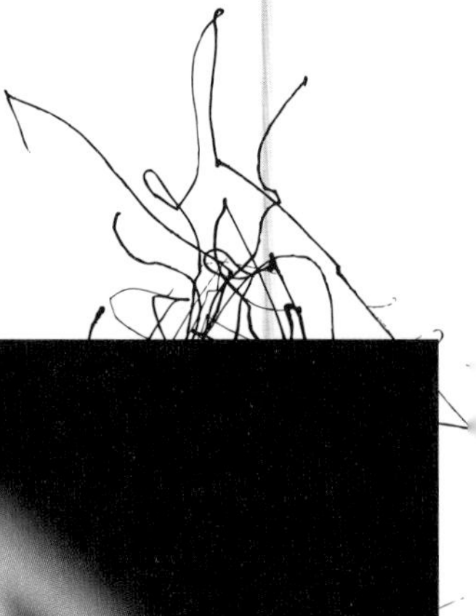

Black Ambiance:

WHERE DO AMBIENT AND BLACK METAL MEET?

ANGEL SIMITCHIEV

In 2013, during an interview with TV host Riz Khan, British composer and producer Brian Eno admitted that ambient music, the very genre he fathered in the late 1970s, has become something he no longer recognizes.

Indeed, during its forty years of existence, ambient music has gone places. Initially created with the purpose of not imposing itself on listeners but inhabiting their peripheral perceptions and interacting with the sonic environment, it did actually manage to penetrate way more musical genres than we (or its creator) can possibly imagine.

Brian Eno not recognizing his own creation anymore might feel like a bit of overstatement, as his own approach and sound have also evolved since the creation of the genre. One thing is certain; on that rainy day, when he came up with the idea of ambient music (while listening to harp music on low volume) he surely did not think that a time would come when black metal, one of the most extreme genres of music, would be so heavily scarred by the power of ambient music.

It is somewhere in the early 2000s, I am twelve years old and based in the small Bulgarian town of Sliven. I am not even in my teen years, but I am already baptized in the music of Mayhem, Dissection, Morbid Angel, Ancient, and Benediction. Having in mind that this happens to be the hometown of one of the editors of this book (Stanimir, wink, wink), it seems black metal did run in the veins of our not so distant generations. One day, after a good hustle and some trades with the local black metal kids, I come home with Ancient Wisdom's *For Snow Covered the Northland*. I open the case, pop the cassette in my deck and...wolves start howling and a grim piano tune unfolds under the attack of black metal shrieks. This cold and plain piano-based piece is the intro track, "A Hymn to the Northern Empire," which starts a revolution in my own understanding of black metal.

Ancient Wisdom is a solo project of Vargher, hailing from Umeå, Sweden, and while I will always highly praise *For Snow Covered the Northland*, the truth is that the album is far from being a genre landmark. However, so early in my history as a listener, it managed to show me that raw and primal black metal music could also hide a strong connection to nature, to the environment, and to the spiritual world and was able to evoke and convey a strong ethereal ambiance, achieving the signature atmosphere in a different manner.

The second thing I learned that day was that the very genre of music that my peers and the media would predominantly pinpoint as a conservative one can actually be as free and as multisided as, let us say, the electronic music we used to hate when we were worshiping and embracing the rebellious cult known as black metal. Among the reasons it felt that way was that it not only borrowed but seemingly welcomed experimentalism, a textural approach to sound, repetitiveness, minimalism, and nonconventional songwriting and structure.

Prior to writing this essay, I conducted seven interviews with people from the current generations of black metal listeners around me: Christo Gospodinov, Daniel Donchov, Nikola Shahpazov, Déhà, Jay Gambit, Todor Krasimirov, and Georgi Ivanov. With the exception of Georgi, all of them are older than me, meaning over thirty years old. Some are currently involved in writing, performing, or producing black metal; others are no longer actively playing black metal or have switched to ambient, drone, or hardcore punk music. Some, however, are still going for both ambient and black metal. What actually unites all of them is their somehow retained passion for black metal—be that the classics or all of the genre's current incarnations. Trying to trace how and confirm that ambient music has indeed managed to pierce black metal, and even transform it in its own ways, I was more than surprised to discover each and every one of the people I interviewed was more or less brought to ambient music via black metal. The interviews took place in early October 2018, via e-mail. Each interviewee had to answer the same set of questions. None of the answers received were followed up or additionally elaborated on. I was interested in getting their most impulsive, emotional, and unbiased opinions on the few things I asked them to consider while writing.

DEFINITIONS AND ATMOSPHERES

Be a total noob and ask Wikipedia what ambient music is, and the answer will be "a genre of music that puts an emphasis on tone and atmosphere over traditional musical structure or rhythm. Ambient music is said to evoke an 'atmospheric,' 'visual,' or 'unobtrusive' quality."[1] Other definitions say "a style of gentle, largely electronic instrumental music with no persistent beat, used to create or enhance a mood or atmosphere,"[2] or Dictionary.com's "[a]lso called ambient. A genre of instrumental music that focuses on sound patterns more than melodic form and is used to create a certain atmosphere or state of mind." The same source also refers to ambient as "background music."[3]

In an old digital copy of *The New Grove Dictionary of Music and Musicians* that I have, David Toop defines ambient music as "Brian Eno's own version of environmental music" and not much else.[4] In his entry for Brian Eno, David Buckley eventually gets closer to the essence of ambient by adding: "Although his ambient music has often been compared with such genres as muzak or new age meditative music, it is in fact more complex."[5] However, Grove sticks to Eno's own words from the manifesto accompanying his 1978 genre-defining *Ambient 1: Music for Airports*: "Ambient Music must be able to accommodate many levels of listening attention without enforcing one in particular; it must be as ignorable as it is interesting."[6]

It is puzzling why the aforementioned sources avoid the very definition given to ambient by its creator in the liner notes of *Ambient 1: Music for Airports* and have instead crafted their own interpretations of the genre. Indeed, Brian Eno's description of ambient does not contain any information regarding the sonic characteristics of the music, the instruments that are most likely to be found in use, or the certain moods that it might convey. In this sense all definitions are in one way or another correct. Bear in mind, ambient music is now forty years old, and, while the genre spent its first few decades as a predominantly beatless subgenre of electronic instrumental music that relies more on texture, atmosphere, and unconventional sound sources and avoids traditional song structures, it has now become a hard to pinpoint musical phenomenon. Ambient is not only interpreted in various ways, often quite different from each other, by thousands of composers, but its fluid nature has also allowed it to directly influence a number of other genres, including the one this book is dedicated to.

Knocking on the internet door of black metal, the first online definition one will spot is "an extreme subgenre of heavy metal music. Common traits include fast tempos, a shrieking vocal style, heavily distorted guitars played with tremolo picking, raw (lo-fi) recording, unconventional song structures, and an emphasis on atmosphere."[7] A rather spot-on Wikipedia-style definition, clearly a mixture of sources. It is mainly based on the definition given of the genre in *Black Metal: Evolution of the Cult*, a book by Dayal Patterson, where black metal is "characterized by screamed, high-pitched vocals, extremely rapid tempos, 'tremolo' riffs, a 'trebly' guitar sound, and simple production values."[8]

The Oxford Dictionary of English (3rd ed.) black metal entry was probably the work of a very Christian author, as according to it black metal is "a type of heavy metal music having lyrics which deal with the Devil and the supernatural."[9] Not completely wrong but surely very superficial, especially having in mind the political, social, personal, folklore, and fictional subjects often found in black metal lyrics.

In a short opinion piece about the (mis)uses of the term *black metal* for the webzine *No Clean Singing*, journalist Andy Synn aims at a more abstract take on what black metal music is about. He writes that the genre "is a refusal to be restricted or defined by the expectations of others. It's about freedom and the ability to 'do what thou wilt.'"[10] I think that's a convenient place for us to stop as, judging by the book you are currently reading, you are already convinced about what black metal is in your own terms and are starting to slightly suspect there is even more beyond that.

So where do ambient and black metal meet? By popular definition, one certain crossing point is their common affection for atmosphere—neither light nor dark, just atmosphere.

Probably each and every genre of music is dedicated to evoking a certain atmosphere. However, go and research thrash, death, or speed metal, and you will hardly spot a hint about the importance of atmosphere compared with definitions of black metal. Except for maybe doom metal, which most likely will be narrowed down to being melancholic, depressive, pessimistic, nihilistic, or whatnot. Yes, you could apply those adjectives to black metal as well, but the definitions were mostly neutral, so I would like to think nobody pinpointed it any further for a reason.

COINED AND EXPLORED IN SOLITUDE

Daniel Donchov, bass player in several black metal bands in Bulgaria during the 2000s, currently working within hardcore punk, drone, and singer-songwriter music, managed to put his reasons for embracing black metal in two sentences. "A sixteen-year old mind is easily impressed, especially with darkness and atmospheric music. The same amount of years later I still find beauty in questionable production and blast beats." He admits to have discovered ambient many years after black metal but believes that "ambient is the natural extension of black metal. [Both genres] meet at the point where the music is not only a band or person playing on some instruments [but something more]."[11]

This separation of art and artists is an aspect very much shared by underground metal projects and experimental electronic acts. An ambient artist or a one-man black metal "band" will never be a rock star in the ordinary sense. If there is something to be worshipped, that would probably be the music, the concepts, or the mystery enshrouding both. The freedom to create for the sake of creating, the freedom to explore music in full anonymity, or simply without the cult of the personality, makes the music the main focus—something that is precious about underground music in general.

Once black metal might have appeared to raise and carry the banner of paganism, atheism, and Satanism and to glorify everything that is "grim and frostbitten."

Still, one can hardly argue against there having always been, in the sound, aesthetics, and essence of black metal, a deep gaze into the human self. The worship of solitude that might come from both nihilism and the love of nature, plus everything in between, or both, is often the subject of black metal lyrics, track and album titles, and artwork in particular. Let us add to this the fact that black metal is probably one of the genres of extreme music that is most densely saturated with solo projects.

This creative self-sufficiency heavily resembles the similarly solitary process of producing electronic music, even if not (always and necessarily) because of unbearable hatred for humanity or obsession with nature. Unlike black metal, which originated around the usual "rock band" dynamics, Brian Eno's ambient was actually conceptualized in solitude. After a car accident, Eno had to take several weeks off at home to recover. One day his then girlfriend brought him an LP of harp music. In an interview for the *Telegraph*, he recalls:

After she had gone, and with considerable difficulty, I put on the record. After I had lain down, I realized that the amplifier was set at an extremely low level, and that one channel of the stereo had failed completely. Since I hadn't the energy to get up and improve matters, the record played on almost inaudibly. This presented what was for me a new way of hearing music—as part of the ambience of the environment just as the color of the light and sound of the rain were parts of the ambience.[12]

If within ambient (a type of music it would take me another five years to come across) the fragile, yet visual atmospheres were achieved by delicate synth melodies, spacious pads,[13] and repetitive melodies, in black metal, ambiance is often built by the complete opposite approach: lo-fi production and/or epic walls of sound.

MEANS OF PRODUCTION

Production is another key factor in black metal's bond with ambient. As Bulgarian music journalist Nikola Shahpazov, who has been covering extreme music for various media outlets for nearly two decades, puts it, "feral black metal like good ol' Ildjarn is so muddled and meditative that often sounds like noise ambient and industrial and not actual music consisting of riffs, drumming and shrieks."[14]

This textural perception of black metal heavily resembles the way ambient music is defined, structured, and listened to. Just like it is hard and rather pointless to sit and separate the musical elements in the guitar-driven but heavily processed ambient drone of *October Language* by Belong, I find it similarly inappropriate to dissect the abrasive worlds of Ulver's *Nattens Madrigal* or *Subliminal Genocide* by Xasthur. No longer can the elements that shape the immersive worlds of these works be separated; it is the sum of all parts, from music writing to production, that we owe their memorable atmosphere to. A main difference between ambient and black metal music is the lyrics. This additional layer allows artists to deepen the meanings and moods hidden within the music. Ambient being a mostly instrumental genre also features vocals (for example Juno Reactor's fifty-plus-minute dark ambient heavyweight *Luciana*), but often their function is to somehow preserve and present a human element, yet without all the meaning and message language is capable of transmitting. Lo-fi production and sonic aesthetics allow black metal to treat vocals in a very similar way. Through excessive reverberation, audio effects, or simply keeping them low in the mix, vocals in black metal become a layer almost completely detached from any meanings they are intended to convey.

Talking about Ulver, their dive into the realm of electronic music, which often led to them being labeled ambient black metal, started with the raw atmosphere of *Nattens Madrigal*. Releases like the predominantly electronic full-length *Themes from William Blake's The Marriage of Heaven and Hell* (1998) and the *Metamorphosis* EP (1999), whose direction would climax in the cinematic *Perdition City* (2000), see Ulver exploring the mostly minimalist and beatless soundscape-based side of their music. In the liner notes for *Metamorphosis*, the band pays its dues to the black metal scene but does its best to inform their listeners they have gone beyond and do not plan to return:

Ulver is obviously not a black metal band and does not wish to be stigmatized as such. We acknowledge the relation of part I & III of the *Trilogie (Bergtatt & Nattens Madrigal)* to this culture, but stress that these endeavours were written as stepping stones rather than conclusions. We are proud of our former instincts, but wish to liken our association with said genre to that of the snake with Eve. An incentive to further frolic only. If this discourages you in any way, please have the courtesy to refrain from voicing superficial remarks regarding our music and/or personae. We are as unknown to you as we always were.[15]

Ulver have further explored vast territories in music ranging from the compilation record *Teachings in Silence* (2002), which offers a more minimalist, ambient, and beatless side of the *Perdition City* recordings, through classical music with a strong atmospheric feel (*Messe I.X–VI.X*, commissioned in 2012 by Norway's Tromsø House of Culture as a peace mass for Lebanon) and, finally, to the synth wave–influenced *The Assassination of Julius Caesar* (2017). At the time this essay was undergoing its second revision, they released *Drone Activity* (2019), their most full-on ambient work to date consisting of four tracks each spanning over fifteen minutes with the longest exceeding the twenty-one-minute mark. While by no means deprived of percussion, *Drone Activity* sees Ulver delving into drifting layers of sustained notes assembled in repetitive minimalist pattern clusters over deep, vast drones, layers of heavily processed textures, and minimalist drumming. The result is an almost Terry Riley– and Steve Reich–style playfulness that somehow still manages to convey a darker, more intense, and menacing feel with a very limited set of sounds.

For Georgi Ivanov, self-taught illustrator, avid black metal fan, and the youngest person I interviewed before writing this essay, what has constantly drawn him back to black metal is "the stripped-down production, the abstract and flowing musical structures, the occult thematic elements, and the use of melody without sacrificing the 'edge' of the music."[16]

Another feature that unites ambient and black metal are the nonmusic sound elements we can for convenience refer to as noise. It was exactly noise that bridged the two realms for Belgian black metal artist, multi-instrumentalist, and producer Déhà. "Somewhere around the beginning of the 1990s with the Black Legions from France ('Les Légions Noires'), being nowadays called 'black ambient.' Many other bands were also working within the same 'style,' like Abruptum from Sweden. But here, we could also go with some older recordings which contain the essence of black metal, but personalized into something else (let's mention [harsh noise artist] Merzbow)."[17]

In black ambient both genres simply coexist. Music under this banner relies heavily on extreme use of distortion, which results in a sound quite similar to what one-man black metal projects like Utarm, Paysage d'Hiver, Xasthur, or even Sutekh Hexen sound like. While the atmosphere remains alike, the tools may vary.

So far, we have been mostly talking about ambient influencing black metal. However, it is necessary to make it clear electronic music in general affected black metal, but maybe it was the language of ambient (and maybe drone) that felt the closest. I doubt that Varg Vikernes wrote "Rundgang um die transzendentale Säule der Singularität" thinking about *Ambient 1: Music for Airports*, yet, along with the albums to follow, *Filosofem* is among the first examples of black metal and ambient actually crossing paths. Vikernes himself would be "rather puzzled by the fact that [his] electronic albums were placed in the 'Black Metal' shelves in the record shops";[18] as with Ulver, it was no longer about the genre tag. The band, with all of its possible stylistic deviations, almost became a subgenre tag of its own. Actually, in a 2004 prison interview,[19] Vikernes lists Jean-Michel Jarre, Vangelis, and Kraftwerk as his main electronic influences. He also mentions his preference for house and rave music. In a more recent source, namely, Vikernes's personal YouTube channel (often an outlet for his questionable political beliefs and his worldview), he shared a video named "Top Ten Non-Metal Albums that influenced Burzum." At number eight we find an entry called "electronic music in general" with Jarre's *Oxygen* as an example. Curious enough, at number one, Vikernes has listed "white label underground techno/ house music from the early 1990s," adding, "I used to listen to that until the morning hours, and then I went home and made music. Inspired."[20]

Rave music and Jarre are the closest Vikernes gets to ambient, and while it is clear that when in prison he could not live a life so tightly linked to rave culture, it is still confirmed that electronic music has always been ranked high in his modest list of influences, where one also finds bands like Das Ich, Dead Can Dance, the Cure, and Russian folk music.

For Todor Krasimirov (singer of Bulgarian black metal band Dimholt), it was precisely black metal's most hated (for reasons outside the music) Burzum that was the entry point into both black metal and ambient. He explains that "tracks like 'Tomhet' and 'Rundtgåing av den transcendentale egenhetens Støtte' and the albums *Dauði Baldrs* and *Hliðskjálf* make you immerse yourself in them and understand them. This is not music to play in the background. To this day, while listening to music like this, I always prefer to surrender to it entirely."[21]

While Georgi Ivanov also points to Burzum's two ambient albums as his first entry points into the world of ambient, he adds Darkthrone, for their "repetitive and hypnotic guitars, stripped-down compositions, obscure and textured sound brought by the lo-fi production" and Ildjarn's *Forest Poetry*, whose "pulsating, textured compositions sound extremely similar to each other but become more and more interesting with each subsequent listen because [of] all of the details that start to unravel." For Ivanov ambient and noise also meet in the music of Xasthur and more specifically his *To Violate the Oblivious*, which "truly crosses into ambient territory, especially if you imagine how it would sound with the whole rhythm section removed."[22]

And while the electronic (but not only) albums of Burzum or the (recently revived) dungeon synth world of Mortiis are clearly obvious entries to the subject, Jay Gambit, of prolific US black metal and noise project Crowhurst, reminds us of "synth-driven black metal of the early 1990s like Valor and Forgotten Pathways... These all have such a heavy emphasis on an evocative presence, relying much less on aggression than standard black metal—yet feel just as 'evil' or menacing."[23]

SPIRITS

In the first half of the 1990s, after already following the death metal scenes for several years, Christo Gospodinov, mostly known for his work with the dark ambient project Shrine (currently a Cyclic Law artist), recalls that he discovered black metal as "the next interesting form of music" and followed it "with passion." However, when the black metal scene became too popular, he moved away again, just as he moved away from death metal prior to that. "I witnessed the birth of both death and black metal in real time and experienced their growth, influence, and charisma before they collapsed into mundanity."

What is more interesting, however, is that it was precisely black metal that pointed Christo in a new direction, a transition that many other more (dark) ambient fans will probably feel at home with. Ulver's *Nattens Madrigal* played a key role in his new taste for atmosphere. The album features heavily atmospheric and raw soundscapes between the songs. I recall an interview that Christo Gospodinov gave to the now defunct Polish zine *Birds of Prey*, and I remind him that, as I recall, it was not just the tracks on the album that affected him but what is between them as well. "Those short interludes between the tracks are pure industrialized dark ambient at its best—highest quality. It's a real shame that we will never see a full Ulver album exploring this direction of theirs."

Just like black metal, ambient is far from being a homogenous musical form that all sounds alike and fits in the same mold. Having soaked influences from techno, dub, and trance, ambient is a varying experience that finds home in various musical contexts. In this puzzle of subgenres, dark ambient is what usually feels the closest to black metal. Brian "Lustmord" Williams and his late 1980s work outline the genre. His music was heavily based on recordings done within crypts, caverns, mines, and catacombs. Those were fused together with tectonic sub-bass frequencies, sounds of seismic nature, and basically everything deep and grim but still somehow subtle yet immersive. This is an approach that is not only heard on iconic records like *Heresy*; it is re-created in the live setting. Nowadays the tools might have evolved, but the specific dark ambient sound of not only Lustmord but Biosphere, Svartsinn, Raison d'être, or Asmorod (whose first album is actually pure black metal) more or less remains unchanged in terms of aesthetics, despite progressing in terms of production, recording tools, and possibilities for live performances.

"Discovering Raison d'être's 'The Awakening' was an awakening indeed," recalls Christo Gospodinov. "That single track forced me into an intensive period of research and discovery, which in the end profoundly changed my understanding of music in general. The internet was in its infancy back then, and it was painfully slow and rather empty, but still it helped me a bit. When I heard that track for the first time, it was a truly overwhelming experience and a revelation of some sort, as I suddenly realized that there is a 'bridge' between electronic music and what I used to like in metal when I was younger, not in sound, of course, but in 'spirit.'"

FREEDOM

Black metal and ambient are vast genres of contemporary music, but for this essay and by current music industry standards, I would still rather consider them underground. However, each of them has managed to build its own ecosystem and supporting subcultures. Both genres have also managed to outgrow their initial concept by spawning multiple subgenres, each more niche and specific than the next. We have depressive and suicidal black metal, and while we will skip the pro-Christian unblack metal, we will stop and take a look at Cascadian black metal. Despised by many writers and listeners, this subgenre was coined by journalists to describe the sound and environmental focus and politics of bands like Threnos, Wolves in the Throne Room, Addaura, or Alcest. These are often referred to as ecological black metal. But what do we do with the atmospheric black metal tag? Did we not already agree ideally all black metal is atmospheric?

As much as ambient and black metal appeared on the musical horizon for quite different reasons, the deeper we dig, the closer they seem nowadays. Numerous books have been written about black metal, from iconic reads like 1998's *Lords of*

Chaos by Michael Moynihan and Didrik Søderlind and *True Norwegian Black Metal: We Turn in the Night Consumed by Fire* by Peter Beste to more recent examples like *Black Metal: Evolution of the Cult* by Dayal Patterson, the very curious sixth volume of the Glossator series titled *Black Metal*, and *Helvete: A Journal of Black Metal Theory*, which deals with the most abstract aspects of the genre. Researchers, journalists, and fans have been attracted by different aspects of the genre. Some trace its musical origins, and some dissect its aesthetic choices, imagery, or relations to (radical) politics, while others are focused on the most notorious side of black metal, namely, the church arsons and crimes committed by leading figures in the 1990s scene, etc. However, as much as people want to build and sustain this profitable perception of the genre as an underground world of murderers, racists, mentally troubled people, and whatnot, black metal music has managed to really outshine its grim past.

Yes, there will always be people who are attracted to and obsessed by the perception of black metal as a threat and a cult to be followed, but that very genre of music has managed to reach beyond its core audience. I am not talking about Deafheaven playing Pitchfork Festival or Primavera. I am talking about thousands of bands across the world that constantly challenge their roots by rediscovering the freedom of black metal. Be that bands like Oranssi Pazuzu, whose more experimental approach often takes them to the ritual side of black metal; Botanist, whose environmentalist concepts are accompanied by an unorthodox choice of instruments, having replaced guitars with distorted hammered dulcimers; Skagos, who indulge in anarchist lyrics and long acoustic atmospheric passages; the female duo Ragana, with their DIY punk-influenced atmospheric black metal; Australia's one-man black metal project Nekrasov, whose records often feature pure long-form dark ambient pieces; or Zeal & Ardor who go as far as mixing black metal with blues, gospel, and trap.

I will leave the last words about the freedom of black metal and its interconnection with various music genres to Jay Gambit: "Black Metal is one of the most forgiving and expansive genres out there, despite what the purists would like to believe. You can be like ColdWorld and play music that's almost like shoegaze, you can go full keyboard like Mortiis, full aggression like 1349, or go in the opposite direction and play beautiful post-rock influenced black metal like Alcest. The tie that seems to bind all of these is more thematic than musical, allowing people who would want to explore these genres to do so within the context of a larger genre that they're comfortable with."[24]

We already mentioned Wolves in the Throne Room, but what we did not mention is the follow-up to their highly acclaimed 2011 *Celestial Lineage*. Released three years later, the completely ambient album *Celestite* sees their music completely abandon the sound they have been mostly known for, while somehow allowing them to reinvent their means. "Working on this album has revealed a whole new vein of creative energy for WITTR. Now that the long trip of creating this album is finished, our appetite is whetted for future projects, thus we feel it necessary to pre-empt the inevitable chatter that will accompany the release of this record. Wolves in the Throne Room has not permanently abandoned the guitar and drums! We sense that one day—perhaps sooner, perhaps later—we will be inspired to return to our stacks of amplifiers and cabinets to create new music."[25]

The album did not exactly receive praise from the media and was accepted as the necessary "strange" and future underrated album that each metal band is doomed to have in their discography, with *Metal Injection* coining "blackened new age" to describe it and *Pitchfork*, not particularly convinced of its importance, giving it a mere 4.7 rating.

However, with audiences tending to mature, I am pretty certain that listeners who loved or hated *Celestite* would still label it black metal, or at least atmospheric black metal, because that spirit is indeed there, even if it is sometimes colored by obvious psychedelia, Berlin school–style electronics, and early ambient influences. It is definitely an example of what I am going for in this chapter— ambient and black metal intertwined, no matter on whose musical territory.

Ambient also appeared as a niche genre and has carried a strong political manifesto ever since its creation. Its agenda has not been rebelling against organized religion, worshiping nature, or hoping for the eradication of the human race, but, still, ambient was a rebellion on its own terms. The genre had the important mission to become a more intelligent take on background music that was nothing like the sterile and soulless output of the extremely profitable muzak industry of the late 1970s. Through its subtlety, free form, and unobtrusive quality, ambient has walked a long way over its forty years of existence. Its evocative nature and ability to create worlds with minimum tools allowed the genre to penetrate pretty much all contemporary genres of music. It does not matter if ambient brought you to black metal, industrial brought you to ambient, or vice versa. What matters is that ambient and black metal meet in the contexts of both genres and in all the anticipated or unanticipated musical encounters that result from this.

Notes

[1] "Ambient Music," *Wikipedia*, accessed May 21, 2021, https://en.wikipedia.org/wiki/Ambient_music.

[2] "Ambient Music," *Lexico*, accessed May 21, 2021, https://en.oxforddictionaries.com/definition/us/ambient_music.

[3] "Ambient Music," *Dictionary.com*, accessed May 21, 2021, https://www.dictionary.com/browse/ambient-music.

[4] David Toop, "Environmental Music," Grove Music Online, accessed May 21, 2021, tinyurl.com/4rxvd6ej; originally published in *The New Grove Dictionary of Music and Musicians*, eds. Stanley Sadie and John Tyrell (Oxford: Oxford University Press, 2001).

[5] David Buckley, "Eno, Brian (Peter George St. John Le Baptiste de la Salle)," Grove Music Online, January 31, 2014, accessed May 21, 2021, tinyurl.com/anaahpx2.

[6] Brian Eno, *Ambient 1: Music for Airports* (CD booklet) (London: Polydor Records, 1978).

[7] "Black Metal," *Wikipedia*, accessed May 21, 2021, https://en.wikipedia.org/wiki/Black_metal.

[8] Dayal Patterson, *Black Metal: Evolution of the Cult* (Port Townsend, WA: Feral House, 2013).

[9] "Black Metal," *Oxford Dictionary of English* (3rd ed.), ed. Angus Stevenson (Oxford: Oxford University Press, 2010), 174.

[10] Andy Synn, "We Need to Talk About... Black Metal," No Clean Singing, November 21, 2016, accessed May 21, 2021, https://www.nocleansinging.com/2016/11/21/we-need-to-talk-about-black-metal.

[11] Daniel Donchov, e-mail correspondence with the author, January 2018.

[12] Ivan Hewett, "How Brian Eno Created a Quiet Revolution in Music," *Telegraph*, January 5, 2016, accessed May 21, 2021, https://www.telegraph.co.uk/music/artists/how-brian-eno-created-a-quiet-revolution-in-music.

[13] A synth pad is a synthesizer-generated tone or chord, usually with a timbre reminiscent to that of a string section. It's used to create or enhance a certain atmosphere or as a harmonic background.

[14] Nikola Shahpazov, e-mail correspondence with the author, January 2018.

[15] Ulver, *Metamorphosis* (CD booklet) (Oslo: Jester Records, 1999).

[16] Georgi Ivanov, e-mail correspondence with the author, March 2019.

[17] Déhà, e-mail correspondence with the author, February 2018.

[18] BG, "Interview with Varg Vikernes by BG (12.08.2004)," Burzum Website, August 12, 2004, last accessed May 21, 2021, http://www.burzum.org/eng/library/2004_interview_bg.shtml.

[19] Ibid.

[20] Thulean Perspective, "Top Ten Non-Metal Albums that Influenced Burzum," YouTube, January 24, 2017, accessed March 1, 2018, unavailable May 21, 2021, https://www.youtube.com/watch?v=yO-SQsie2eU.

[21] Todor Krasimirov, e-mail correspondence with the author, January 2018.

[22] Georgi Ivanov, e-mail correspondence with the author, March 2019.

[23] Jay Gambit, e-mail correspondence with the author, January 2018.

[24] Ibid.

[25] Kyle Ward, "Wolves in the Throne Room Detail New Album," Sputnik Music, January 30, 2014, accessed May 21, 2021, https://www.sputnikmusic.com/review/45550/Wolves-in-the-Throne-Room-Celestial-Lineage.

Pretty in Black:

THE TEMPTATION TO MELODY AND AMBIENCE IN BLACK METAL

STEVEN SHAKESPEARE

Black metal is steeped in a harsh, raw, dissonant sonic world. Its misanthropy and blasphemy are screamed into the void.

However, this is not the whole story. Black metal has always also been about songs and atmospheres, and many acts have taken it into a more melodic, harmonious, and/or dreamlike direction. I will argue that this should not be dismissed as an abandonment of black metal's "purity," much less a commercial sellout. Bands such as Blut Aus Nord, Wolves in the Throne Room, Deafheaven, Alcest, and Lustre have hardly scored mainstream commercial success, but their body of work brings both melody and meditative immersion into the heart of a recognizably black metal ambience.

This essay will argue that such experiments in sound offer a mutation of black metal, not its surrender; and that it is possible to encounter the radical, iconoclastic spirit of the genre in what could be called a *blackened naïveté*, which resists the attempts of even black metal purists to define and domesticate it.

I will try to show this by considering some of the abovementioned acts alongside what I take to be a more obviously recognizable exponent of the black metal aesthetic. By setting up a sequence of paired artists, I hope to show how the sense of black metal flashes between them, rather than just being located in one narrowly defined set of aesthetic parameters. The acts I will consider in pairs are: Lustre/Darkthrone; Blut Aus Nord/Emperor; Alcest/Inquisition.

In conjunction with this approach, I will also consider some aspects of the philosophy of music, especially as articulated by the idealist thinkers Hegel, Schelling, and Schopenhauer. My aim is not to try and fit the music into the philosophy or to presume that only philosophy can tell black metal what it "really" means. The interest of the three thinkers cited is that they recognize ways in which music outstrips thinking, or, rather, how music itself, as a form of thinking, intuition, and vision, mutates our experience of thought and our sense for the infinite and unconditional otherness of reality.

As Andrew Bowie puts it, writing of very different forms of music, "music need not be understood just in terms of what is described by theories of music, because it can itself help to constitute new kinds of thinking."[1]

Black metal—as theory, mysticism, ethereal atmosphere, defiance of the divine, immersion into nature—is already engaged in this mutation of thought. By paying attention to what these thinkers say especially about harmony and melody, I hope to explore the ways in which melodious and harmonious black metal offers an intense unfolding of this engagement rather than its reversal or betrayal. Beauty and the beast are two faces of the same monster.

Black metal's originary sound can be characterized as transcendentally dirty. Low production values, with a rattling, undeveloped drum sound, rasping high tremolo guitars, underpinning bass low to the point of absent in the mix and vocals that are largely unintelligible beyond their chaotic form as demented scream. These ingredients are allied to the visual and ideological aesthetic of the music to forge that elusive but vital term of reference for black metal: atmosphere.

Atmosphere is something presupposed by black metal music. What I mean by this is that atmosphere is the intangible but essential matrix out of which the music emerges. However, this can be misunderstood. I do not mean to suggest that there is some abstract set of concepts or structures that provide the rule according to which the music is made. That would subordinate music to idea. Black metal would be reliant on the expert (perhaps the philosopher) to tell it what it means—or else the idea of black metal would be a banal set of rules that would foreclose any possibility of creative invention.

Atmosphere, then, is something different from a set of concepts or rules governing an artistic practice. By describing it as transcendentally dirty, I am trying to suggest that while atmosphere does precede and exceed any particular expression of it, this does not make it a rarefied or transcendent reality. It exists only as expressed and distressed in and through the distorted amplifier of black metal. Yet no specific expression exhausts it. Atmosphere is the cloud out of which particular meteorological events coalesce, but in these expressions it always retains its unsystematic, probabilistic, chaotic aura.[2]

This means that the atmosphere of black metal is always contaminated. It is never a pure set of eternal ideas or abstract possibilities. To say it is transcendentally dirty attempts to capture just this: that the unconditional reality that is heard in and through black metal *is never pure*. It is antithetical to either a pure transcendence or an absolute immanence that would dissolve all particular determinations into a single essence.

For one thing, this means that black metal acts that embrace some sort of national or ethnic purism are caught in a performative contradiction. They are subordinating the music to an alien concept of *wholeness*, which seeks to reassure "us" that "we" are home, and "they" should be expelled. But the blackened self is alien through and through. It cannot exist without being indelibly stained, even as it screams its blasphemous protest against all the hallucinations of holistic whiteness.

Another consequence of this is that the quest to define black metal's own musical purity will be doomed to fail if it is defined only by the repetition of some "original" sound, look, production value, or whatever. That would be to subordinate the music to an alien concept of aesthetics in which the form and content of the art is defined according to preexisting criteria of taste.

Given this, there is no a priori reason why black metal music should not be melodic or harmonious or why it should not lead to rapture and bliss in the ecstasies of ambient sound rather than being wholly driven by the aesthetics of violent speed. The mystical love of black metal circulates around an indefinable core, a black vortex, to which neither rule nor concept are adequate.[3] It needs only the atmosphere: that chaotic, always half-born matrix that hovers between the possible and the actual, always on the verge of incarnation and decomposition.

In this light, the introduction of melody, harmony, and ambient washes can and should play a significant part in black metal (as they have done in actual fact). Given the atmosphere of transcendental dirtiness, the key thing is that such musical elements express their own disintegration even as they assert themselves. It is this paradox that structures and warps black metal sound, between the indelible, singular assertion of the individual and the divine inevitability of their decay and dissolution.

We are cursed, every wedding dress a withered shroud.

To articulate my reflections, I offer a triptych. Each of these three sections is further organized around three points: a band that represents the "traditional" sound of black metal; one that develops elements of melody or ambience more explicitly; and a classic philosophical theory of music. I choose this mode of presentation to avoid the impression that any one aesthetic form or theory should be the dominant partner in the conversation.

DARKTHRONE [HEGEL] LUSTRE: FALL AND ASCENSION

Darkthrone's *Under a Funeral Moon* is a classic black metal album.[4] On the cover, a grainy shot of a corpsepainted figure stands under a tree whose branches merge with the jagged logo of the band. Put the record on, and we are instantly in the middle of things. Without introduction, a riff careers off, fast and insistent; the voice croaks. The drums do not underpin the beat so much as ride on top of the tremolo. The song ends without any indication that it was going to do so.

It is a song of eternal sleep, the sleep of a Satanic witch. She has gone down into the grave, but it is her inversion of Christianity ("turn it upside down like you did") that makes possible a rising, a resurrection ("You live in me...your thoughts/and your pains are my wine"). The music is intoxicating, a dissolution of the form of reality in which we take into ourselves the sweetness of a wine that was never consecrated, a wine that needed no transcendent legitimation.

There are shifts of pace through the album—like the slow section in "Summer of the Diabolical Holocaust," which builds to the climax of "as I reach for hell/I am free." The sound approaches doom metal in "The Dance of the Eternal Shadows." All these variations return to the vortex of noise with which the album starts.

This mystical love in and of black metal fills space and overwhelms sense in an excess of meaning without order: "I'll shoot you full of signs." Lyrically, the constant themes are desecration, inversion, blasphemy. The singer is always being possessed, finding divinity in an identity consumed by an absolute parasite: "You watch me face the mirror/And see desecration"; "I am Lucifer...In other dimensions/My visions grow black wings."

This dynamic of descent and ascent becomes vertiginous in the musical journey that expresses it. It is no longer clear which direction we face in the whorl and whirl of buzzing guitar. The aural experience of being sucked in and ejected is replicated in the words:

Glance into my eyes
And see the darkest shadows dancing
Playing in the desert of my life
Burning
And my soul is descending...
Lover of all—face the apocalypse
You fade away under the black rain
And flowers remain
Flowers to step on, flowers to burn
Am I ready for the God below

Later, in "Under a Funeral Moon," the flowers return as "Flowers of doom/Rising in bloom/You will see/Our immortality!"

Flowers dying under a black rain...flowers rising to witness diabolical immortality...apotheosis and destruction... "Possess me as I burn." There is no contradiction in this mystical vertigo, *in which all directions can be taken at once* and all express the tainted atmosphere of an unconditional power stripping us of form and identity.

In this multidirectionality of the formless universe, a path of wonder and innocence can still be taken. Lustre have charted this route over ten years of making music, including six full lengths. The titles of the latter give a sense of the ambience: *A Glimpse of Glory*, *They Awoke to the Scent of Spring*, *Wonder*, *Blossom*, *Still Innocence*...

Darkthrone's dying and rising flowers haunt *Blossom*, a wordless composition in four parts.[5] Lustre's signature sound is to the fore; sweet synths play an almost absurdly naïve melody above a swirl, a cloud of ambient black metal and funeral/doom noise. The drums keep a basic walking rhythm. As each track progresses, it seems as if first one and then the other element of the music might be entirely overwhelmed, but the tension is maintained. All the work is done *between* the melody and the howling fog of distorted guitar and what may be inarticulate screams.

There is a strange coincidence of comfort and unease. As the explicit appeal to childlike wonder calls for a suspension of belief, so the melody is itself suspended...above a chaos. The saccharine splendour of Lustre shines above a horror that is barely intelligible: "Make way for the night/Lightless, yet so bright/Gracious, luring, dreaded still..."

There is something seductive about the path that is opened up, the demand for naïveté it entails and the exposure to the formless abyss over which it hangs, as if (to use Kierkegaard's phrase) suspended above seventy thousand fathoms. "Moonlit Meadow," the opening track of *Wonder*, captures the ambiguity of the way that is set out:

Through grasses brightly lit
Our walk begins in wonder
Here, where mighty trees lay split
And rocks are torn asunder[6]

Wonder walks in the light, but a light that flows only through the splitting of what was whole. The singing is snake-like—something hisses and writhes in the brightly lit grass.

To take this path is to reforge the division; one's wonder at the world is also its desecration and the desecration of the one who is united with that world. This is black metal mysticism, that experience of cosmic expansion and unity that is at one and the same time the death of all dreams of a lost purity.[7] So following "Green Worlds," an instrumental evocation of arboreal wonder (the notes evoke the motes of dappled light), we arrive at "Summer Night," in which (over a background at once soothing and mechanically repetitive) the protagonist cries out: "Burn our smouldering hearts/On a summer night/Burn them." We are again possessed by the black metal spirit: deified yet defiled, blackened by fire.

By its use of melody, Lustre might seem to be taking black metal toward the light demanded by Hegel's account of musical art. For Hegel, music expresses the inwardness of subjectivity, of immediate feeling, but in a structured way. Music helps the inward spirit hear itself, resound for itself. The healing path of music is, therefore, one from dissonance toward tranquillity. He, therefore, asks what it is "that make it possible and necessary for the notes not to be a purely natural *shriek* of feeling but the developed and artistic *expression* of it."[8]

Rhythm and harmony are essential aspects of structuring and grounding musical expression, but the culminating element is melody: "it is melody whereby, on these foundations of the rhythmically animated beat and the harmonic differences and movements, the realm of notes closes into one spiritually free expression."[9] For Hegel, the essence of music is not to mirror the static harmonic proportions of the cosmic but to give flight to the freedom of the spirit. Nature is here transcended and transformed:

The poetic element in music, the language of the soul, which pours out into the notes the inner joy and sorrow of the heart, and in this outpouring mitigates and rises above the natural force of feeling by turning the inner life's present transports into an apprehension of itself, into a free tarrying with itself, and by liberating the heart in this way from the pressure of joys and sorrows—this free sounding of the soul in the field of music—this is alone melody.[10]

This is a vital insight: melody is not merely imitation of the beauty of nature. In a sense, Nature is *riven* by melody. It is the sublime apprehension of oneself as undetermined by what is merely given. Music offers an alchemical transformation of shriek into expression.

Yet what resounds in music, and melody in particular, is not just an escape from nature (the dream of philosophy, to take a distance from all that is earth and embodiment and becoming) but a *suspension* over and within it. In black metal, this suspension is articulated by a constant reversal—of the artistic expression back in to the shriek from which it came.

Hegel pulls back from this, tries to get music to move toward a higher goal, in which it will give way, or at least know itself and its meaning as clarified in the philosophical concept: "melody is the infinite determinability and possibility of the advance of the notes, but it must be so regulated that what we apprehend is always an inherently total and perfect whole."[11] Hegel does not want continual suspension, the lightning flash across the gap, the simultaneous ascent and descent into and out of Nature/God. For him, suspension must give way to mediation, in which spirit always returns to itself—and so finds that "ideality and liberation which, being obedient to the necessity of harmonic laws, yet at the same time lift the soul to the apprehension of a higher sphere."[12]

Black metal, in both its ugly and pretty iterations, allows us to hear this lifting of the spirit, weighted down by harmonic necessity, yet raising up. But it also keeps us in suspense: where melody appears in Lustre, its naïveté resounds with a mystical innocence, a lack of worry about being anything or getting anywhere that is able to coexist with the impersonal horror and wonder of a universal darkness and decay.

EMPEROR [SCHOPENHAUER] BLUT AUS NORD: WILL AND ITS NEGATION

The use of synths in black metal is, of course, a long-standing tradition. We need only think of Burzum's early ambient experiments or Emperor's "symphonic" sound. The latter's classic album *In the Nightside Eclipse* opens with a keyboard-infused horrorscape that invites us "Into the Infinity of Thoughts."[13] There is a fusion of sound: drums, guitars, synths all carry the same urgency and atmosphere. There is little respite in Emperor's work. It is a kind of total music that overwhelms the senses and our capacity to distinguish the different elements.

Emperor's music is also self-referential. The figure of the "emperor," the Satanic archetype of will, strides through the lyrics, which are articulated in Ihsahn's distinctive goblin croak: "In the name of the mighty Emperor I will ride the Lands in pride." The land is polluted and blackened, the "childs [*sic*] of happiness" will be cast into fear. Yet this remains a work of *theory*; it is into *thought* we ride. This is a theory that is not locked into the mode of propositional knowledge and hypothesis, however: "black metal is theory in the sense of affective-intellectual experience that reveals by re-veiling everything in its own obscurity."[14]

I gaze into the moon which makes my mind pure as crystal lakes
My eyes cold as the darkest winter nights
But yet there is a flame inside
It guides me into the dark shadows beyond this world
Into the infinity of thoughts...
Thoughts of upcoming reality
May the infinity haunt me...
In Darkness

The album often focuses on moments of crossing: beyond the forest, the key that opens a cosmic gate, toward the pantheon, walking through woods, riding across lands. In tandem with this, the identity of the singer crosses and recrosses the border of the self, morphs from devotee to dark lord—a unity of worship and identification in which "I will realize I existed before myself" ("Cosmic Keys to My Creations and Times") and "I am the spirit of their existence/I am them" ("I Am the Black Wizards"). This is a twisted way, but one that matches the twisted nature of the cosmos: "Thy path is capricious but yet so wide" ("Inno A Satana").

Emperor's music is far from lacking harmony or melody, but all is subordinate to the "wall-of-sound production" of the album.[15] It acts as a battering ram to shock the listener out of their ego image, and to envelop them in an experience of the black universe.

In some ways, we find more overt use of dissonance in Blut Aus Nord's back catalogue. This is especially so on *Odinist: The Destruction of Reason by Illumination* (Candlelight, 2007). There is a continuity with Emperor's work here: an invitation into the excess of the real that is accessed by an intellectual illumination beyond reason, attained through the ruins of reason. Kierkegaard, writing as Johannes Climacus (and so invoking the mystical desire for ascent into illumination) puts it like this:

Neither rational comprehension nor clear intuition but the borderland of collision with the unknown is the goal and ruin of reason. Blut Aus Nord's illumination is expressed in and through this perversity of sound ("The Sounds of the Universe"), a coagulation of will and mind turned back upon themselves ("A Few Shreds of Thought") and so open to the heavy mystical core of being beyond light ("Mystic Absolu").

There is a more ancient echo of the dispute within Neoplatonism between Plotinus and his heirs here. Plotinus held that there was a purely intellectual aspect of the soul that never descended or fell away from contemplation of the purity of the divine. This was the only way in which we could attain knowledge of the divine— by awakening what was within us but veiled—since our ordinary reasoning could only comprehend things by comparison and differentiation, by the step-by-step methods appropriate to temporal thought. Plotinus, therefore, distinguishes between *dianoia*—our ordinary discursive reason—and *noesis*—that higher intellectual illumination that realizes our underlying unitive contemplation of the One.[17]

However, a number of Neoplatonic thinkers refused this idea of an undescended soul. How can it be that there is an aspect of our soul that is continuously conscious of the divine forms, yet we are unaware of this? For Iamblichus, rather than awakening a consciousness already within us, we needed to go beyond even intellect: to attune ourselves to the influence of the gods through ritual, sacrifice, and magic.

It is not thought that links the theurgists to the gods: Otherwise, what would prevent theoretical philosophers from enjoying theurgic union with them? In fact, the truth is quite otherwise: theurgic union is brought about only by the perfective operation of ineffable acts correctly performed, acts that are beyond all understanding, and by the power of the unutterable symbols that are intelligible only to the gods.[18]

For black metal, it is neither a matter of choosing between act and theory or intellect and will nor of achieving some kind of comprehensible harmony of those faculties. Black metal is an enactment of will ("belief is not a knowledge but an act of freedom, an expression of will")[19] and a discipline of magical transformation. However, in the Western esoteric tradition, magic has been closely associated with contemplation,[20] and the matching of the self with the absolute—even when the self is seen as void of essential nature or the universe as chaotic.[21]

Blut Aus Nord's own magical alchemical transformation of black metal builds on the symphonic sound of Emperor, especially through the bending of the riff away from its harmonic root.[22] This method lends itself to dissonance, as on the infamously twisted *Odinist*, but also to a smoothing into the seductive melodies of its succeeding album *Memoria Vetusta II: Dialogue with the Stars*.[23]

Of course, *Memoria* is by no means a total departure from its predecessor. There is plenty of recognizable influence from classic Norwegian black metal. But it is striking how often the synths or the high guitar tremolo pick out a hypnotic melody amid the haze and intensity. Hegel's subjective freedom returns as a lightness, an embrace of "non-matter," the "translucent body of air," the "antithesis of flesh." Rather than Satanism or Odinism, the references are to Buddhist meditation (Ānāpānasati Sutta—the mindfulness of breathing; and Vipassanā—insight into the nature of reality). In this tradition, through an intimate mindfulness of one's body, feelings, and thoughts, focused on the breath entering and leaving the body, we can gain insight into the pervasiveness of impermanence and overcome the illusion of having an abiding core of selfhood. For Hegel, the melodic needs regulation to return to itself and express something holistic and intelligible, but for Blut Aus Nord, the melody pierces flesh, the veil of matter's form, culminating in the repetitive beauty of "Elevation"; here, will and illumination are honed to expose their own emptiness, beyond any closure or concept.

There is an echo here of what James Harris, writing in the context of drone music, calls a "non-performable" state of non-differentiation between subject and object, knower and known: "One may not 'perform' actions leading to this state, but may only experience it passively after performing modulations on the surface self that allow the Outside to 'leak in.'"[24] In a different mode, Blut Aus Nord's transition via melody to blissful ambience negates the differentiating impetus of will and knowing. Will's apotheosis—like that of reason—is found in its downfall.

The intimacy between will and music inevitably invokes Schopenhauer, for whom music is not to be subordinated to linguistic expression in the hierarchy of the arts. For Schopenhauer, reality in-itself is not located in an inaccessible beyond but is immediately accessed through the will. It is the blind, striving will that gives rise to the world of appearances, including the divisions we make between subjects and objects, but the will itself is beyond all representation and division.

However, music is not subject to this limit, since it is nonrepresentational in its essence. Schopenhauer writes that "music differs from all the other arts by the fact that it is not a copy of the phenomenon"—it is an expression of will itself, one which reason alone cannot grasp.[25] Indeed, "we could just as well call the world embodied music as embodied will."[26] Music "gives the innermost kernel preceding all form, or the heart of things" and, strikingly for our purposes, this is best expressed in melody: "in the melody...the uninterrupted significant connexion of *one* thought from beginning to end, and expressing a whole, I recognize the highest grade of will's objectification, the intellectual life and endeavour of man."[27]

This seems to parallel Hegel's insistence on the continuity of melody, but there is an important difference: "Here, as everywhere in art, the concept is unproductive."[28] It is vital that music is not dominated by a libretto, for instance. Melody expresses the will's renewed striving through its digression from and return to the keynote, but by doing so it expresses reality in itself as nonconceptual craving. The will is not objectifiable but constantly wills itself into form and expression; music gives voice to this, especially through melody, and by doing so becomes a coincidence of opposites. On the one hand, the inexpressible is always being expressed; on the other, the inner core of the articulated expression—what it is that is being expressed—is itself the constant dissolution into impermanent flux.

If Lustre turn to melody as a suspension over the flux, Blut Aus Nord use it as a voice to give twisted form to the flux itself. Doing so underlines the accessibility of the real as resounding within us, while insisting on its inaccessibility to any thought or conceptual grasp. For Schopenhauer, music remains a staging post, a temporary salve that must give way to the negation of will. For Blut Aus Nord, that negation is not something separate from and after musical expression but is always finding voice in the music's own embrace and negation of tonality and melody.

INQUISITION [SCHELLING] ALCEST: TRANSCENDENTAL CHAOS AND CLOUD

Hear a Haunting Chant
Lying in the Northern wind
As the Sky turns Black
Clouds of Melancholy

—Darkthrone, "A Blaze in the Northern Sky,"
  A Blaze in the Northern Sky (Peaceville, 1992)

Amidst the embers, a spark of times of old
Where rivers run, phantoms drift, veiled in mist

—Lustre, "A Spark of Times of Old," *A Spark of Old Times*
  (De Tenebrarum Principio, 2013)

Lightning cracks the sky and thunders roll
Through the night a chaos of storms arise

—Emperor, "The Burning Shadows of Silence,"
  In the Nightside Eclipse (Candlelight, 1994)

Ma prière résonne au loin puis disparait derrière des nuages
de mélancolie.
Jusqu'à ce que les autres mondes s'ouvrent à moi je serais seul.
[My prayer echoes in the distance and then disappears behind clouds
of melancholy.
Until the other worlds open to me I'll be alone.]

—Blut Aus Nord, "My Prayer Beyond Ginnungagap,"
  Ultima Thulée (Impure Creations, 1995)

Lonesome realm where the spirits are dust
Poison clouds are the breath of life
Tunnels of death are invisible wings
Mystique moons are floating tombs

—Inquisition, "Astral Path to Supreme Majesties,"
  Ominous Doctrines of the Perpetual Mystical Macrocosm (Icarus, 2010)

J'aime alors contempler le ciel
Avoir l'impression de m'envoler
Vers les nuages qui passent puis s'effacent
Dans le bleu d'une mer sans fin
[I like to contemplate the sky
To feel like flying away
Toward the clouds that pass and then disappear
In the blue of an endless sea]

—Alcest, "Ciel errant," *Souvenirs d'un Autre Monde* (Prophecy, 2007)

I began by saying that black metal is transcendentally dirty, that it presupposes an original impurity in the fabric of being. The absoluteness of the music is not separate from its decay and impermanence. It is an incoherent whole, deliberately so.

I associated this transcendental dirtiness with the centrality of atmosphere in black metal: the chaotic cloud of possibilities which gives rise to and undermines every form. Emerging out of this atmosphere—clouds of feedback, of chaos, of melancholy, of poison, of longing and remembrance, of impermanence—black metal must unhinge even its own orthodoxies. It evokes the clouds of separation and unknowing that attend the mystical stripping of the self, ready for divine union.[29]

As we have seen over the course of its development, black metal has especially lent itself to ambience and to the stretching of the song form. American acts, often Cascadian, have been at the forefront here, from Weakling to Wolves in the Throne Room. The latter, because their music evokes a positive communion with nature, even deny that they play black metal, which is associated with hate and negation.[30] Many who heard the ephemeral sparkling beauty of their album *Celestial Lineage* might agree. Have we gone beyond the intelligible limits of the genre here?[31]

This disavowal of black metal is, however, hard to dissociate from the genre's own self-negating and self-overcoming core. It spills into and out of the atmosphere that liquefies its boundaries, such that different instrumentations, melodies, and harmonies become possible. If it is hard to deny that the suicidal ambience of Nortt is black metal, can we withhold the title from the shoegaze-influenced dreaminess of Alcest? However different in feel and direction they may seem, they commune through the atmosphere of chaos, the shifting intensities of an impermanent field of possibilities.

Alcest's 2016 release *Kodama* (Prophecy, 2016) certainly offers more recognizably black metal soundscapes and lyrical negativity. However, this is no reason to marginalize the more obviously shoegaze-inspired offerings that preceded it. From *Souvenirs d'un autre monde* to *Shelter*, Alcest's work conjures a kind of ecstatic nostalgia, an atmosphere of floating away from the constraints of this world: "Since the age of five, Neige has longed for a place far removed from our Earthly plain, experiencing vivid memories of a joyful, otherworldly place."[32] The sea returns again and again as an image and realization of oceanic bliss. And through this weaves an occult drama of simultaneous ascension and descent:

Old souls fallen from the sky
Stream down in a starry flood
To occupy living temples
Filled with secret glimmer

Listen to "L'eveil des muses": the extended melodic vocals above the insistent tremolos, it dissipates into a black metal classic. Invoking "nonhuman souls," it resolves into isolated chords echoing in the void. Old souls descend like the overflow of oceans from the stars to take their place in living temples. On Alcest's trajectory, "The night walks by my side...Part of us has flown away...Toward the ocean" ("La nuit marche avec moi").

By another shore, by the "black cosmic sea," Inquisition invite us to take a different astral path into the night sky. That path to the heights is also one to the grave, to the mystical death that is union with all: "Infinite universe as/silent as death/In this coffin I lay to rest."[33] The musical vortex of this song offers an aural assault worlds away from Alcest. But here worlds collide: in Inquisition's "floating tomb," the indifference of death and ascension is crystallized, and the ethereal dissipation of Alcest's starry, oceanic voids resounds.[34] We become the weightless yet infinitely heavy black hole toward which the old souls and even the divine will must gravitate: the self obliterated and elevated beyond its humanity.

Indifference—the ultimate identity of the infinite and the finite—is at the core of Schelling's early nineteenth-century thought. What is striking is how Schelling argues that this indifference takes shape in the work of art, especially in music: *"The indifference of the informing of the infinite into the finite, taken purely as indifference, is sonority."*[35] Schelling understands sonority as a resonance possessed of "continuity," "uninterrupted flow."[36] It tends to coherence and harmony. However, left to itself, harmony tends to dissolve the finite into the infinite. Melody, uniting both harmony and rhythm, makes the finite into something real, a real manifestation of the infinite.[37]

All of this looks like another idealist balancing act, in which the infinite and the finite are resolved into a higher unity. However, this does not do justice to the absoluteness of chaos in Schelling's work. Every finite reality is an expression of the indifferent infinite, every idea is a god. Every note resounds with the atmosphere of the absolute, always already expressing and dissolving itself. Schelling celebrates music as a "pure movement as such, separated from the object," divested of the gross body, flying on "spiritual wings."[38]

This is not just a repetition of the age-old philosophical suspicion of the body and matter. For Schelling, every body is the infinite in condensed form. Music is itself a physical phenomenon, but it has the capacity to dissolve the false, self-imposed limits of the body ego, its refusal to accept its own infinity.

There is an echo here of black metal's mystical affirmation of decay. For Schelling, nature itself tends toward liquefaction, to ceaseless flow: "The most original product of Nature is, therefore, the formless or the fluid."[39] However, this inexhaustibility of the unconditional does not exist in any pure state: "the absolutely fluid can reveal its existence in no other way than through decomposition."[40] The force of decomposition is the unity of negation and affirmation, in which "nature will possess the means to generate everything from everything."[41] For Schelling, then, the unconditional force of decomposition flows in nature and in music as an endlessly generative and destructive matrix.

The problem Schelling faces is how to display the indifference of unity and decomposition in a philosophical text. The text is constrained; it has to make sense and attain clarity and coherence, which forces even Schelling into a one-sided idealism, where decomposition is overcome in rational clarity.

In this sense, black metal offers a higher theoretical realization than philosophy. If black metal is that "affective-intellectual experience that reveals by re-veiling everything in its own obscurity," it is because it is able to let the real resound in and through our bodies, a process in which our material decay and the decay of sound itself are entangled.[42] With the acts we have been considering, melody and ambience perform the suspension of form and intelligibility over the flux in a way that has to be known in the hearing of it.

The philosophical reference points in this essay have themselves performed a straining of the conceptual net within which music in general, and black metal in particular, might be caught and known. In Hegel's account of melody, it erupts as the dislocating voice of spirit, leaving nature out of joint. Schopenhauer pushes the nonrepresentational meaning of music further; in melody we encounter the ultimate objectification of the irrational striving will. But, here, "the concept is unproductive"; there is no philosophical resolution of the agony of existence. While, for Schelling, music decomposes us and our false distinctions, letting an infinite chaos be heard.

Black metal is the sonorous and mystical realization of this entanglement of expression and decomposition:

This is the essential reality of black metal as mysticism, its being a musical materialization of the mystical relation in which the transcendent subject and object, self and God, are equally dislocated and secreted in an immanent and blackened inter-becoming of metal with everything, an amorous pestilential alchemy that nigredically melts being into an ancient cosmic essence that cannot be, taking flight through clouds of chaos where stars die, into the darkest divine body.[43]

No single form exhausts this potency, this dynamic, this love: Lustre's melodic lines of innocent naïveté suspended above the haze of chaos; Blut Aus Nord's twisting of melody toward the overcoming of form; Alcest's dreaming dissipation of black metal sonics into the ambient cloud—all are birthed from the impossible atmospherics of the cloud, in which the thickest darkness is coincident with a floating fragility.

Notes

[1]Andrew Bowie, *Music, Philosophy and Modernity* (Cambridge: Cambridge University Press, 2007), 77.

[2]"In the words of Masciandaro, 'black metal vibrationally unhinges the order of things,' and 'annihilates every binding of the chain of being.' Black metal is an amusic, says Scott Wilson, an organization of sound that places 'oneself at the very limit of oneself where one is dissolved to NOTHING.'...In black metal, sorrow is a labouring that seeks beyond the given. Xenharmonics points to the essence via the definition of sorrow that Masciandaro desires, the one found 'not in a void, but in a cloud. Nor is a cloud not a void of its own. Or that is exactly what a cloud is, a void of one's own'"; Brooker Buckingham, "Xenharmonic Black Metal: Radical Intervallics as Apophatic Ontotheology," in *Mors Mystica: Black Metal Theory Symposium*, eds. Edia Connole and Nicola Masciandaro (London: Schism Press, 2015), 275.

[3]Nicola Masciandaro, "On the Mystical Love of Black Metal," in *Floating Tomb: Black Metal Theory*, eds. Nicola Masciandaro and Edia Connole (Milan: Mimesis International, 2015), 104.

[4]Darkthrone, *Under a Funeral Moon* (Peaceville, 1992).

[5]Lustre, *Blossom* (Arvidsjaur, SE: Nordvis, 2015).

[6]Ibid.

[7]See Nicola Masciandaro and Edia Connole, "Introduction: Mystical Black Metal Theory," in Masciandaro and Connole, *Floating Tomb*, 7-31.

[8]G.W.F. Hegel, *Hegel's Aesthetics: Lectures on Fine Art*, vol. I2, trans. T.M. Knox (Oxford: Clarendon Press, 1975), 910.

[9]Ibid., 912.

[10]Ibid., 929-30.

[11]Ibid., 933.

[12]Ibid.

[13]Emperor, *In the Nightside Eclipse* (Candlelight, 1994).

[14]Masciandaro and Connole, "Introduction," in *Floating Tomb*, 13.

[15]Dayal Patterson, *Black Metal: Evolution of the Cult* (Port Townsend, WA: Feral House, 2013), 225.

[16]Søren Kierkegaard, *Philosophical Fragments/Johannes Climacus*, trans. Howard Hong and Edna Hong (Princeton, NJ: Princeton University Press, 1985 [1844]), 37.

[17]Plotinus, *The Enneads: Abridged Edition*, trans. Stephen MacKenna (Harmondsworth, UK: Penguin, 1991), 26-27, 341-42.

[18]Iamblichus, *De Mysteriis Aegyptiorum*, quoted in John Dillon, "Iamblichus' Defence of Theurgy: Some Reflections," *International Journal of the Platonic Tradition* 1, no. 1 (2007): 37, accessed May 22, 2021, https://www.researchgate.net/publication/233525702_Iamblichus'_Defence_of_Theurgy_Some_Reflections.

[19]Kierkegaard, *Philosophical Fragments*, 83.

[20]Pico della Mirandola contrasts two forms of magic: one that is demonic and deceitful, the other "a higher and holier philosophy" that "embraces the most profound contemplation of the deepest secrets of things and finally the knowledge of the whole of nature"; see Giovanni Pico della Mirandola, *Oration on the Dignity of Man*, trans. A. Robert Caponigri (Chicago: Gateway, 1956 [1486]), 54-57.

[21]"Man is capable of being and using anything which he perceives, for everything that he perceives is in a certain sense part of his being. He may thus subjugate the whole Universe of which he is conscious to his individual will"; Aleister Crowley, *Magick in Theory and Practice* (London: Routledge, 1973 [1929]), xvii; cf. Pico, *Oration*, 7: "We have given you, Oh Adam, no visage proper to yourself, nor any endowment properly your own...The nature of all other creatures is defined and restricted within laws which We have laid down; you, by contrast, impeded by no such restrictions, may, by your own free will, to whose custody We have assigned you, trace for yourself the lineaments of your nature. I have placed you at the very centre of the world...We have made you a creature neither of heaven nor earth, neither mortal nor immortal, in order that you may, as the free and proud shaper of your own being, fashion yourself in the form you may prefer"; also see Peter Carroll: "The magician can only change something if he can 'match' the Chaos which is upholding the normal event. This is the same as becoming one with the source of the event. His will becomes the will of the universe in some particular aspect"; Peter Carroll, *Liber Null and Psychonaut* (San Francisco: Weiser, 1987), 55.

[22]Brooker Buckingham identifies the material basis of this in the use of fretless guitars, enabling a "microtonal" abandonment of the Western twelve-tone scale; see Buckingham, "Xenharmonic Black Metal," 269.

[23]Blut Aus Nord, *Memoria Vetusta II: Dialogue with the Stars* (Candlelight Records, 2009).

24James Harris, "Pleromaticatalyst: Ritual Intoxication toward the Universal Field," in *Sustain//Decay: A Philosophical Investigation of Drone Music and Mysticism*, eds. Owen Coggins and James Harris (London: Void Front Press, 2017), 111.

25Artur Schopenhauer, *The World as Will and Representation*, vol. 1, trans. E.F.J. Payne (New York: Dover Publications, 1966 [1818]), 262.

26Ibid., 262-63.

27Ibid., 259.

28Ibid., 260.

29Best evoked by the anonymous English medieval mystical text, *The Cloud of Unknowing*, accessed May 22, 2021, https://www.catholicspiritualdirection.org/cloudunknowing.pdf.

30Brad Sanders, "Beyond the Darkness: An Interview with Wolves in the Throne Room," Quietus, September 28, 2011, accessed May 22, 2021, http://thequietus.com/articles/07073-wolves-in-the-throne-room-interview.

31Wolves in the Throne Room, *Celestial Lineage* (Southern Lord, 2011).

32Tom O'Boyle, "How Terror Attacks and Spiritualism Inspired the New Alcest Album," *Metal Hammer*, August 22, 2016, accessed May 22, 2021, http://teamrock.com/feature/2016-08-22/how-terror-attacks-and-spiritualism-helped-create-the-new-alcest-album.

33Inquisition, "Astral Path to Supreme Majesties," *Ominous Doctrines of the Perpetual Mystical Macrocosm* (Season of Mist, 2015).

34The "floating tomb" is, of course, the key image for Masciandaro and Connole, *Floating Tomb*, esp. 13ff.

35F.W.J. Schelling, *The Philosophy of Art*, trans. Douglas W. Stott (Minneapolis: University of Minnesota Press, 1989 [1859]), 107.

36Ibid., 108.

37Ibid., 114-15.

38Ibid., 116.

39F.W.J. Schelling, *First Outline of a System of the Philosophy of Nature*, trans. Keith R. Peterson (New York: State University of New York Press, 2004 [1799]), 27.

40Ibid., 29.

41Ibid., 32.

42This is explored brilliantly in relation to doom metal in Aliza Shvarts, "Troubled Air: The Drone and Doom of Reproduction in Sunn O)))'s Metal Maieutic," *Women and Performance: A Journal of Feminist Theory* 24, nos. 2-3 (September 2014): 203-19.

43Masciandaro, "On the Mystical Love of Black Metal," 104; also see Brenda Walters, "Through the Looking Glass Darkly: Medievalism, Satanism, and the Dark Illumination of the Self in the Aesthetics of Black Metal," *Helvete: A Journal of Black Metal Theory* 2 (Winter 2015): 22, accessed May 22, 2021, https://blackmetaltheory.files.wordpress.com/2011/02/2_02_glass_darkly_gardenour_walter.pdf.

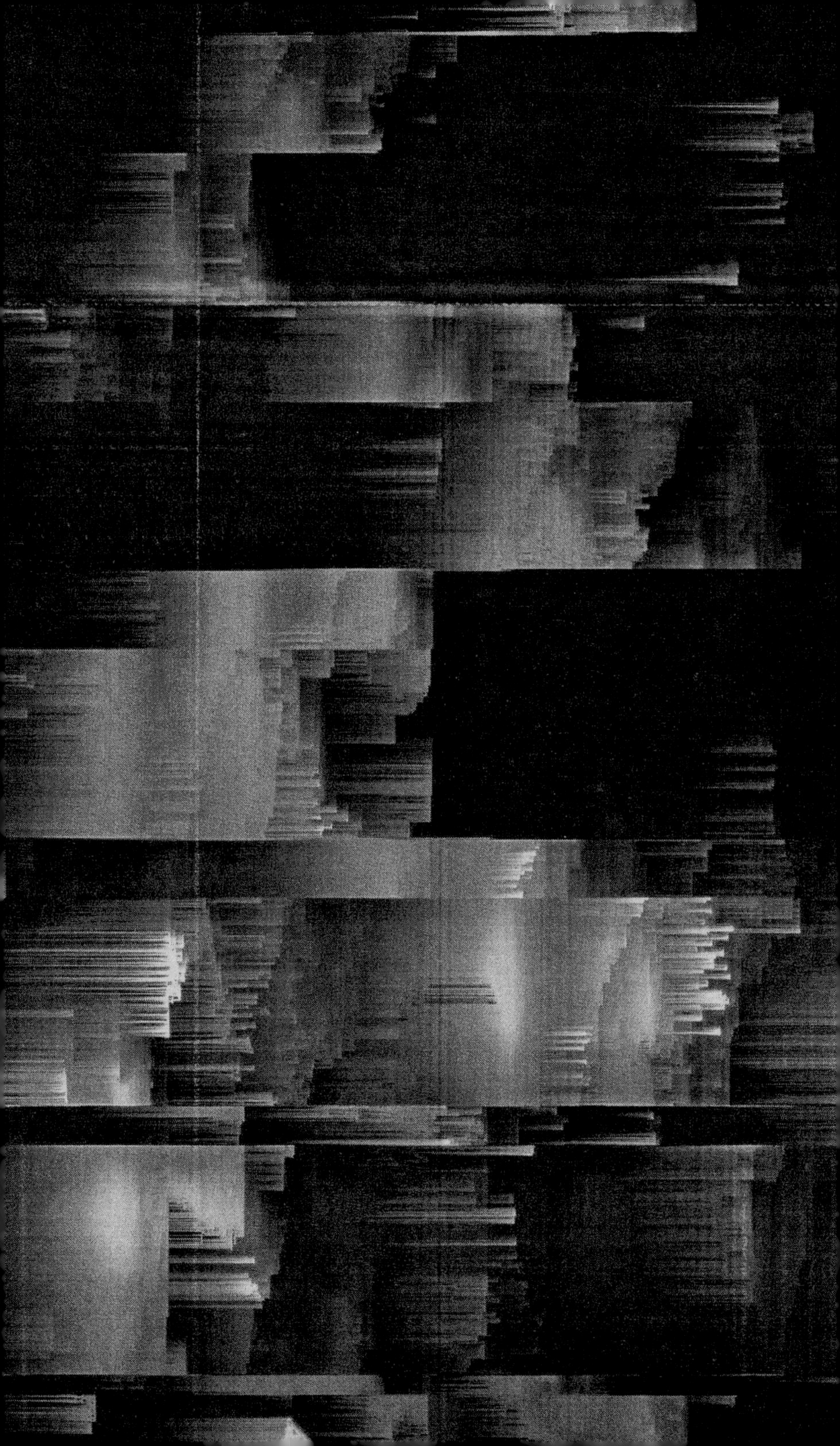

Black Metal Is Feminine

AVI PITCHON

In recent years, a mysterious yet not unlikely channel of communication has opened between some dark outer limits of indie and black metal. It is a good and important thing to be taking place, and it is interesting to point out just how inconceivable it seemed a decade or two ago.

But beyond the fact that musical cross-pollination is often rewarding, something more specific, deeper, and more substantial happened when, for example, Chelsea Wolfe's brand of singer-songwriter-from-the-depths-of-purgatorial-annulment encountered the hardened, apocalyptic aesthetic and emotional palette of black metal, the genre that welcomes the inevitable demise of the human race, that puny slave race with its pathetic, righteous beliefs. More recently, it was Lingua Ignota who channelled titans like Diamanda Galas, Blixa Bargeld, and Attila Csihar into feral, vengeful aural exorcisms she tagged "survivor anthems."

What happened is that earthy, animistic, pagan, feral, justifiably murderous femininity—the kind of femininity that rose and pounded our skulls open through Lars von Trier's *Antichrist*, a title unsurprisingly in correspondence with that cold, dark, lethal genre of Scandinavian metal—announced and informed us of the pending demise of male, white, Judeo-Christian order.

Scandinavian black metal was born as Satanist negation of that Christian order. Its adherents burned churches to the ground and played music that was intentionally primitive. Indeed, part of that Satanic resurgence was also a punk gesture of sticking two fingers up the face of the once subversive but by the late 1980s increasingly commercialized and professionalized death metal. At that point, black metal found it natural to champion virility and a will-to-power as opposition to both the weakness and dilution of death metal in particular and Christian values in general. In that sense, it was still serving as yet another continuation (vis-à-vis radicalization) of the rock 'n' roll ethos in its "censored" form: rising from the swampy voodoo deltas of the Mississippi as a primal, sexual, ungovernable force, but a force appropriated and monopolized by white men to wield exclusively. Potent, dangerous, anti-Christian, yet never going all the way to attack the paradigm that lies at the foundation of Christianity: patriarchy. Rock 'n' roll was, therefore, an absurd balance of opposites; scaring the wits out of decent American society but safeguarding and perpetuating gender hegemony. It goes without saying that exploding young female sexuality, responding uncontrollably to male pelvis moves and the sacrilegious rhythm accompanying it, thus bypassing all prior programming, was a concrete threat to decent society.

At the same time, men were still calling the shots. Male sexuality was liberated from Victorian puritanism, leaving women with the sometimes uncontrollable yet nevertheless defined role of followers, later on groupies: passive receivers or victims, virgins to be sacrificed on Satan's altar. With the risk of historical inaccuracy, one might say that it was not until a force of nature harnessed by the body and mind of Tina Turner was unleashed that women were able to claim a space to be operators and cabals, not just receivers, of that primal force.

black metal was, and will sadly remain, largely male in both participation and essence. However, a portal opened within it following that initial Satanic phase. Black metal took a step into the unknown and the subconscious, toward the primordial archetype. It did that first through sound; the emphasis on taking blastbeats to an absurd logical conclusion meant that rhythm lost all touch with human scale—too fast to dance to, too fast to be experienced sexually, through hips and pelvises. When rhythm escapes dancing it becomes abstract. The emphasis shifts from rocking and rolling to accentuating the atmosphere. This shift negated rock 'n' roll, just like shoegaze did at more or less the same time (therefore, it is of little wonder that the genres eventually resonated and became mutually integrated). Now, there is an apparent sonic inversion here that needs to be examined. In a sense, it is as if black metal disarmed itself of its grounded virility and bond with male physicality; it is as if it forfeited to Christianity and joined its legacy of disembodied sublimation. Even worse, it seemingly nullified its own hegemony in an act of almost Jewish self-circumcision through devotion to the abstract at the expense of the earthy, the pagan. But what transpires here is that this inversion cuts so much deeper than that of the inverted cross; by capitulating to the abstract, black metal was subconsciously answering a call from under and beyond the depths of Christian oppression. It inadvertently communed and colluded with the lingering echo of the witches burned at the stake, femicide in the name of the Holy Ghost that negates the earth itself in favour of the binary of good and evil, crime and punishment, leading us sheep in an orderly manner to the afterlife. In other words, black metal inadvertently led itself through the evolution of sound to a place capable of hearing the call. Once one hears it, it cannot but heed it. Negating rock 'n' roll, then, was not an act of forfeiting the earth; on the contrary, it was a letting go of a distorted, controlled mutation of the pagan, a retreat that allowed the feminine reentry into the collective psyche. Atmosphere, it must also be stressed, is not only or necessarily monotheistic, since abstract deity comes with concrete doctrine. Separated from commandment, atmosphere lends itself to the formless and fluid, resisting humanly structured striving for order and logic, good and evil; the black metal warrior is grotesque and ghostly, out of this world, thus, mirroring the self-mutilating, fierce uprising of female anorexia. In this, black metal's misanthropy resonates with the contemporary archetype of the non-fertile woman; thus, male and female unite in negation of the very desire for human continuity.

Certainly, not everyone in black metal did that; the notion of "trve" black metal arose as result of men fearing the tipping of the balance, pathetically holding on to the "golden age." More radically, Burzum's phase of shifting from epic guitar-based harshness to what contributed to inspiring the dungeon synth subgenre was probably caused by Varg Vikernes's limited access to instruments in prison, yet it was framed as rejection of that same voodoo "Negro music." It is morbidly hilarious to witness Vikernes's solidarity with the pre-Christian as secondary to his solidarity with the white race. His negation coupled with his traditionalism renders his music equally anti-rock and anti-female. There are numerous inconsistencies in Vikernes's work and ideas, fortified by his seemingly pragmatic post-incarceration return to the very Negro sounds he condemned. Ultimately, the last laugh is reserved to anima, as regardless of Vikernes's statements, it is the sound that invokes and liberates the feminine spirit despite male attempts to shackle it into theory or ideology.

To summarize, it is black metal that tipped the balance and unleashed the medieval witch's cry for vengeance against the Christian establishment, a cry hovering as a specter in the back of the Western mind. The aforementioned shift from rock 'n' roll—a form hijacked to celebrate male hegemony and, in all too many, many instances, rape culture—to abstract, atmospheric soundscapes only seemed monotheistic but in actuality cleared the path for feminine darkness. In such Zeitgeist, it is no wonder that someone like Gaahl found it bearable to come out as gay, and it is no stretch to expect more to follow his commanding lead. It is no wonder that the bleakly fucked-up, death-wishing, mournful edge of female-led indie music is the one that ventured to meet black metal halfway. In its footsteps comes the celebratory, folk-tinged black metal leadership of Myrkur, her majestic dominance emphasizing the murky netherworlds from the depths of which roared earlier pioneers like Runhild Gammelsæter, Murkrat, and, with a different slant, Aghast.

When gazing toward black metal from indie's vantage point, an important band has undergone a long journey to that halfway meeting point yet is rarely acknowledged for doing so, partly because it speaks a different aesthetic language, more contemporary, less indebted to folk, the arcane, the fantastic, or the mythical. Yet before delving into its sound and vision, even by moniker alone, HTRK (Hate Rock) resonates firmly with black metal. The band's brand of wounding indie-industrial minimalism combines with its moniker to present a total, ultimate inversion of the 1960s Summer of Love rock 'n' roll, which instead of a sexual revolution mainly provided men with a looser paradigm within which to get laid or, worse, exploit women outright. HTRK—an Australian outfit formed as a cult of sorts in worship of the anticrucified Nick Cave and his death/hate rock pioneers The Birthday Party—consisted of two men to begin with, bassist Sean Stewart and guitarist Nigel Yang; however, their work became meaningful once they recruited dead on the inside front woman Jonnine Standish. In 2004, they released *Nostalgia*, which reverberated in a humanity-free industrial vacuum. Ever since, they have carried on perfecting their feminine deathwish formula, one that posited anorexia as a sickly, lethal form of uprising against male rock 'n' roll. If men desire an objectified body, women will forfeit the body altogether. If male subconscious, liberated by capitalism, exchanged the puritanism of the nuclear family for gang rape as the ultimate, most sinister logical conclusion of rock 'n' roll mentality, women respond by shedding the body itself and becoming devoted to the abstract, monotheistic spirit, an act of macabre parody of Christian self-righteousness and witch hunts. The heroin chic of supermodel catwalks of the 1980s and 1990s answered male objectification with a death wish. That death wish echoes on HTRK's albums, becoming ever more pure, weightless, and indifferent to human emotion with each release.

This is the right moment to mention that Sean Stewart committed suicide in 2010 at the age of twenty-nine. The male cul-de-sac, expressed so coldly, sharply, and exaltedly in HTRK's music was apparently wholly authentic. Because it was wholly authentic, it did not halt the band's activity. After fulfilling a dream and recording 2009's *Marry Me Tonight* with The Birthday Party guitarist Roland S. Howard, they released their magnum opus *Work (Work, Work)* following Stewart's death. That album distilled their sound, hooking it up with the minimal synth underground that worships the kind of 1980s alienation that never made it to the charts and remained esoteric until the posthumanism it emanated suddenly touched the frozen hearts of indie kids, those who internalized civilization's exhaustion and welcomed it in a stoicism beyond good and evil and outside human slave morality.

2014's *Psychic 9–5 Club* takes a further step toward the abyss of the *muselfrau*, a woman in physical and mental decay, marching on the catwalk toward her imminent death. *Psychic 9–5 Club* sounds like de Sade in the midst of a harrowing comedown from an impossible cocktail of heroin and ketamine, accompanied by, instead of the warmth of soul music full of human flesh and blood, electronic, sterile, dead minimalism. Again, in macabre form, the seemingly most repeated theme—and word—on the album is love. On the opener "Give it Up," a final dissociation from human desire with the sterile, Standish recites the no second chances promise that "this time I'm gonna love you much better." The third track, an instrumental titled "Feels Like Love," feels like a camera panning in slow-motion across a pile of junkies strewn in overdose-bordering coma in a crack den that flickers in and out of a parallel dimension at the eighth gate out of nine on the path leading to surrendering one's soul to Satan. And that is what separates hate rock from rock: the Rolling Stones sold their soul to the devil; HTRK give it away for free, expecting nothing in return.

Track five, "Wet Dream," revolves around a vocal loop, Standish's robotic zombie mantra about being in love with herself. In other words, we have shifted from the ideal of romantic partnership toward a female body that simultaneously worships and devours itself. Anorexia as the self-exterminating extreme logical conclusion of the aforementioned resistance to male objectification. The body that nullifies itself to nullify the notion and option of female fertility. A body in love with its own voluntary disintegration, its freefall toward the chaos/entropy of natural decay within which nature is devoid of will, and, therefore, all human faith in progress and striving for good is nothing but puny, ludicrous, and absurd. Next follows "Love is Distraction." Distraction from what? From the only tangible aspect of human existence, death. The album's closer is titled "The Body You Deserve." Standish sings about how women have been lied to all these years, but now that they know the truth, they are rewarded with the body they dreamed of. The *muselfrau* fades away, exchanged for a nonphysical, glowing astral body, celebrating in indifferent vengefulness the extinction of mankind presided over by men. The hubris of championing free love ushered in the victory of the urge to rape over the urge to obey DNA. Black metal, therefore, is the fiercest form of male resistance to patriarchy's pretence of order. As pagan celebration of DNA's mysterious will-to-power was exchanged by patriarchy's murderous, phallic duality, black metal boldly channelled the witch and joined the anorexic in a suicidal mission to save life by ridding it of humanity. And, while feminism strives for positive, revolutionary change, feminine black metal maintains the genre's stance of absolute, self-annihilating negation.

Is Fucking Dead

EDWARD BLAIR

I first met Patrick Loy working at the warehouse
for an online bookstore in Skokie, in either 2006
or 2007. I had just moved to Chicago, lost a job
at a circus school, and was scrambling to figure
out adult life.

I had been working there for about a month, with a couple of other
early twenty-somethings. We were not allowed to listen to music on
headphones, so we had a shared workstation where we could trade
off Pandora stations. When Patrick started working with us, we
asked what kind of music he liked. "Folk music?" he replied.

It became quickly apparent that Patrick's musical interests
were far-ranging and tended toward the more esoteric side
of things than his original assessment implied. While at the
warehouse, we bonded over many shared interests, swapping book
recommendations, placing shared Aquarius Records orders, and
trying our best to live on a thirty-two-hour-a-week minimum wage
job. We would troop over to Wendy's on especially rough days to
enjoy the luxury of one-dollar chicken nuggets and Frosties.

We stayed friends even after we left that awful job, and one day in
2011, spurred on by an awful and pretentious *New Yorker* article,[1]

we decided to start a zine. We were both tired of the Eurocentric narrative of black metal, how often people rehashed the Norwegian second wave, and so we wanted to focus on the scene we saw expanding daily, North and South American black metal. We saw a gap in coverage and figured, fuck it. At the time, *Decibel*'s coverage of the non-European black metal scene was limited to short profiles of the bands already on everyone's radar. The only other folks writing about this stuff that we were aware of had abandoned their projects, like Brandon Stousy's oral history or zines like *Oakenthrone* or *Convivial Hermit*. In our hubris, we thought we could step into their shoes. I have never been good at naming things, so we decided to call it exactly what it was: *Black Metal of the Americas*, a zine about North and South American black metal bands. Simple.

We put our first issue out on March 4, 2012. We got to interview Horseback about the influence of Joseph Campbell on his music, which was a real thrill for me, a big mythology nerd. We sold copies at Quimby's, an alternative bookstore in Chicago, and on a Big Cartel site, and then, two months later, put out a second issue. We gave them away at the first Gilead Fest. I remember watching people take copies and use them as rain shields as they dashed from the venue to their car. I have no idea if any of those people ever read it.

The first two issues were fairly short, under forty pages, but our ambitions expanded with the third issue. This was also when we started to pick up a small amount of steam; we were mentioned in brief in the "Gossip Wolf" column in the local alt-weekly, the *Chicago Reader*. "The zine features metal-mag staples such as concert 'reports,' album reviews, stark black-and-white nature photos, and informed interviews with serious vermin," read the brief but flattering article. A coworker of mine gave me a stuffed rat to commemorate the occasion. It was a bit of validation for us to be mentioned in an actual printed newspaper, especially since we had little way of getting the word out about the zine, aside from our meager number of Twitter followers. We honestly did not expect anyone to pay any attention to us.

We kept working, and the zines kept getting bigger, until finally we released the eighty-page behemoth that was *Black Metal of the Americas* vol. 4. This was not only an expansion in size but also in scope. We added academics, theorists (the rise of black metal symposia like Hideous Gnosis were a big influence on us),[2] photographers, and journalists to our interview subjects, allowing a more comprehensive look at the scene. This issue also marked a shift in our approach. While we had definitely tackled some thorny ethical/political questions in earlier issues (asking Wrnlrd why he called his makeup for the *Death Drive* EP "blackface," in vol. 2, for instance), this was the first issue with an editorial, which was my attempt to grapple with some of the moral blind spots of the US black metal scene.

I wrote a long essay detailing my concerns with the record label Profound Lore, sparked by the release of *Death Mask* by Lord Mantis. The cover of *Death Mask* was a brutal depiction of a tortured trans woman, another example of cheap edgy shock value by a group of cis men. The artwork was by Jef Whitehead, also known as Wrest, the lead singer for Leviathan, a controversial figure in black metal, and another Profound Lore roster member. In 2011, Whitehead was arrested on six charges of sexual assault and battery and, in 2012, found guilty of one charge of aggravated domestic battery. He would write and release *True Traitor True Whore* on Profound Lore before the conviction, a vitriolic album directed at the person he was accused of abusing.

Profound Lore relished in these offenses, tweeting about how dark and dangerous this music was. I did not think abuse should be a marketing bullet point, and went on for about 1,500 words on why not. We also interviewed Adam Schrigin, a journalist from Texas who had done extensive research on white supremacy in black metal. I was unable to ignore these aspects of this music I loved, and it was because of that investment that I wanted to bring these conversations to the forefront of our zine. It also seemed like a way to push back against these pervasive societal attitudes with a small-scale approach that might have tangible benefits. I firmly believe that any kind of activism needs to be incrementally built from the ground up. Even a small amount of pushback could make a difference in a small scene.

Being concerned about the normalization of abusers and Nazis seemed like a low bar, but looking back, even this line in the sand was a harder stand than most people were willing to take in 2014. Thankfully, being an offline publication shielded us from the kind of abuse that other journalists faced, which means instead of getting daily Twitter abuse or doxed, we got called soy latte-loving PC leftists on the Nuclear War Now! forums and got a bad review on a metal blog or two. We certainly did not run into any issues tabling at the second Gilead Fest, though we did get a bunch of folks who asked us why we did not run a blog instead. I was surprised by the limited blowback but chalked it up to provoking the fans on the margins, naïvely assuming that larger publications that continued to cover racists and abusers were operating out of ignorance.

2014 was a big year for the mainstreaming of hatred in niche communities though, and my eyes were swiftly opened. In August, the harassment campaign colloquially known as #GamerGate kicked off.[3] It was quickly infiltrated by white supremacists (misogyny and racism have always been close bedfellows) in a way that I found particularly distressing, as white nationalists had attempted to use black metal as a recruiting tactic in the past. We had just released our seventh volume in July and, appropriately enough, had run an article by Jonsan van Johnson (previously published on his blog, *shamelessnavelgazing*). Van Johnson had interviewed a former white supremacist who alleged that the black metal band Inquisition had enthused about his Nazi tattoos. Van Johnson linked that testimony to other concerning moments in Inquisition's career. This was the first time we would cover a pressing issue that would make it to the pages of *Decibel*, and watching their coverage made me even more convinced that we needed alternatives to metal magazines/metal blogs/mainstream music blogs. They gave Dagon the first chance to respond, did not press him on any of the obvious falsehoods or dog whistles (almost every other artist he mentions has very serious ties to white supremacy), and published an interview with the former white supremacist Daniel Gallant days later. Gallant was pressed on almost every claim he made.

Even without Gallant's testimony, there was more than enough evidence of Inquisition's right-wing flirtations to concern anyone. Dagon's side project 88MM, for instance, contributed a song called "14 Showerheads, 1 Gas Tight Door" to a compilation titled *Satanic Skinhead: Declaration of Anti-Semetic Terror*. Somehow, this connection was overlooked by *Decibel*. This was four years after the racist murderer Varg Vikernes was featured on a *Decibel* cover, but it appeared any hope I had for growth having occurred in that time was misplaced. In the scrum of #GamerGate, it felt even more important for visible voices to be more discerning. Watching a major publication fail only increased my certainty that *someone* needed to highlight these concerns.

It was a sentiment we often heard at the zine fests we would table at as well, as we often had to assure potential customers that we vetted the artists we covered (something we made a priority in the later issues; looking back, there are artists we covered that we would have approached differently or not covered). Extreme Noise, the long running collective-owned punk store in Minneapolis, initially refused to stock our zine until I clarified that we absolutely did not cover any Nazis.

I felt like providing this lens on black metal could be our calling, but that conviction took a toll on both my relationship with Patrick and with the rest of the world. I wanted to keep pushing ahead and continue expanding our coverage, feeling like we had a chance to both grow our operation and hopefully have some kind of small impact on the way people participated in the black metal scene. I found myself getting into Twitter fights, constantly explaining the minutiae of black metal scene drama to my very patient therapist, and complaining about how much I disliked trying to cover a scene that actively welcomed so much cruelty. The drummer of Emperor murdered Magne Andreassen for being gay in 1992 and was welcomed back into the band with open arms for their 2014 reunion shows, and I do not remember seeing anyone mention it. Emperor's *In the Nightside Eclipse* is still considered a classic of the genre. How do you cope with that level of constant viciousness and apathy? Patrick stuck around for one more issue, and, after that, what had already felt like a fairly lonely fight felt pointless. I put out a final issue, more to showcase frequent contributor SJC's essay about coming to grips with the death of a friend through inheriting his black metal record collection than anything else, and the zine quietly died in 2018.

I was very burned out by the end of the whole thing. We had produced over four hundred pages of work in six years, and for nearly half of that I felt estranged from the community we were writing about. Trying to carve out a space in a hostile environment with what felt like no real reward is exhausting work. It was a demoralizing thing to have something I took a lot of joy in turn into a millstone around my neck. I am partly to blame for that. I took a collaboration with a friend and pushed it into a solitary crusade, and that isolation led to a lot of frustration.

Things are slowly changing in the metal community, though, and that has felt really heartening. I was offered the chance to table at Black Flags over Brooklyn in January 2019, an explicitly anti-fascist metal festival organized by Kim Kelly. It felt like a fitting time to really say goodbye to the zine, and so I printed limited sets of the complete run of *Black Metal of the Americas*. All profit from those sets went to Black & Pink, a prison abolition nonprofit focused on supporting LGBTIQ+ and HIV-positive prisoners. While I was tabling, I got to talking with a reporter for the *New Yorker* who was covering the event, and we chatted for some time about the importance of inclusive spaces in a traditionally thoughtless scene, a far cry from both the insipid pretension that we found in Frere-Jones's 2011 article and the "apolitical" posturing still on display at *Decibel*.

Near the end of 2014, Phil McSorley from Cobalt and Mike Meacham from Loss went on tandem Facebook rants aimed at recently outspoken feminist members of the metal community, namely, Kim Kelly and, less namely, Andrew Curtis-Brignell from Caïna. McSorley, in between homophobic slurs, aimed his ire specifically at what he called the "USBM Friendship Circle," a designation that I quickly decided was too rad to not claim. We swiftly printed patches for the USBM Friendship Circle, and gave them to trusted friends and long-time fans of the zine. McSorley got kicked out of Cobalt rather quickly after that.

While the patches were partly a joke, they were partly a manifestation of desire too. It's a discomforting feeling to walk into a metal show and see folks wearing patches for bigoted bands. I wanted to make something that engendered the opposite feeling. Celebrating the end of it all at a gathering like Black Flags over Brooklyn felt perfect, a recommitment to a scene I had left due to frustration and perceived abandonment. There is still a lot of work to be done, but the isolation I felt at the end of *Black Metal of the Americas* has lessened drastically, and that is such a relief. Long live the USBM Friendship Circle.

Notes

[1] Sasha Frere-Jones, "The Dark Arts," *New Yorker*, October 3, 2011, accessed May 21, 2021, https://www.newyorker.com/magazine/2011/10/10/the-dark-arts?verso=true.

[2] Hideous Gnosis was a symposium on black metal theory that took place on December 12, 2009, in Brooklyn, New York. It was organized by Nicola Masciandaro. A collection of the papers presented was published a month later; see Nicola Masciandaro, ed., *Hideous Gnosis: Black Metal Theory Symposium I*, (Charleston, SC: Create Space, 2010), accessed May 21, 2021.

[3] #GamerGate refers to a harassment movement that originated in August 2014. Deadspin provided an excellent summary of the early days; see Kyle Wagner, "The Future of the Culture Wars Is Here, and It's Gamergate," *Deadspin*, October 14, 2014, accessed May 22, 2021, https://deadspin.com/the-future-of-the-culture-wars-is-here-and-its-gamerga-1646145844.

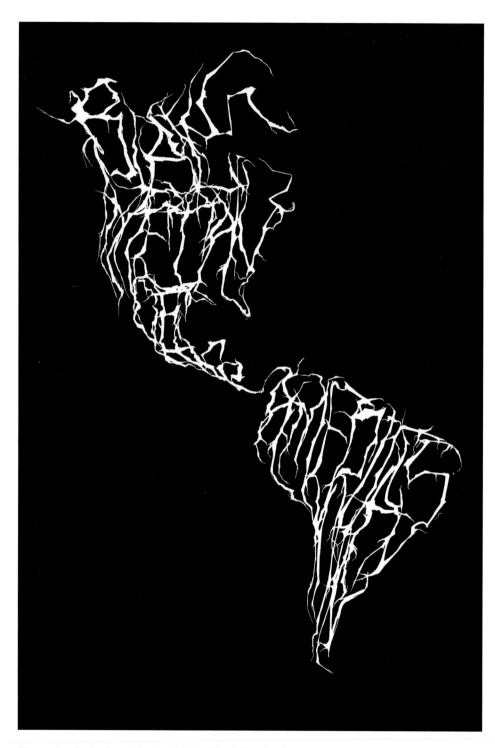

Figure 1. ©Dante Augustis Scarlatti, *Black Metal of the Americas Logo*, 2012.

Black Metal of the Americas was Edward Blair and Patrick Loy.

Black Metal of the Americas contributors: SJC, Jonsan van Johnson, Scott Wygmans, Christian Degn, JB Roe, M. Foody, Buttcoffin.

Black Metal of the Americas vol. 1 (2012)
INTERVIEWS: Horseback and Scroll
FEATURES: Velvet Cacoon and Mamaleek

Black Metal of the Americas vol. 2 (2012)
INTERVIEWS: Lonesummer, Owlscry, Wrnlrd, and Vattnet Viskar
FEATURES: Cobalt

Black Metal of the Americas vol. 3 (2013)
INTERVIEWS: Botanist, Skagos, Bound by Entrails, Jute Gyte, and Merkaba
FEATURES: Cobalt

Black Metal of the Americas vol. 4 (2013)
INTERVIEWS: Book of Sand, Cara Neir, Æsahættr, Queen of Heathens, and Bastard Sapling
FEATURES: Servile Sect

Black Metal of the Americas vol. 5 (2013)
INTERVIEWS: Deafheaven, Dressed in Streams, Aksumite, Chrome Waves, and Yellow Eyes
FEATURES: Emotional Punk's Influence on Black Metal

Black Metal of the Americas vol. 6 (2014)
INTERVIEWS: Zareen Price, Sarah Kitteringhman, Clouds Collide, Hexer, Ashencult, Adam Schragin, Woe, and Jason Wallin
ESSAY: Profound Lore's Use of Abuse as Advertisement

Black Metal of the Americas vol. 7 (2014)
INTERVIEWS: Barbelith, Black Palace, Epistasis, Jeffrey Podoshen, Vivek Venkatesh, So Hideous, and Mutilation Rites
FEATURES: Fascism in Black Metal and High Art/Black Metal

Black Metal of the Americas vol. 8 (2015)
INTERVIEWS: Vile Creature, Immortal Bird, Grue, Woman Is the Earth, Chuck BB, David T. Posey, Vattnet Viskar, and Petrychor

Black Metal of the Americas vol. 9 (2018)
INTERVIEWS: Mark McCoy, Ipos Music/Void Ritual, GIDIM
ESSAY: Remembrance, Death, and Black Metal

< Frederic-Vivianne Auln
My Inner Circle, 2020
ink drawing with
digital painting
courtesy of the artist

Charles Forsman
Witchzard, 2012
ink on Bristol and colors
on photoshop, 15.2 x 23 cm
courtesy of the artist

Julien Dallaire-Charest
Witch, 2020
black ink on paper,
10.16 x 15.24 cm
courtesy of the artist

Julien Dallaire-Charest
Wizard, 2020
black ink on paper,
10.16 x 15.24 cm
courtesy of the artist

Interview with Christine Kelly

DANIEL LUKES

Envision constructing a platform of analog cassettes and Norelco cases, one that refuses to crack under the weight of the marginalized but instead boosts them up—this is the drive that brings each Tridroid Records release from proposal to "pre-order now!"

Through the voices imprinted on each spool of reel, Tridroid sets fire to the flags that forced its artists out, ripping through the threads of misogyny, homophobia, racism, and xenophobia with hollowed-out blast beats and thunderous chords. Since taking the helm in 2016, Christine Kelly has piloted Tridroid through the storm that has erupted in a metal scene that was once home for the outliers and outcasts, where people proclaiming stances built on oppression still become immortalized on Gilead fabric. Yet the voices calling out against this hate are many and permeate the genres of black metal, doom, blackgaze, thrash, and other heavy sounds. Tridroid preserves these voices in physical media, allowing freedom of expression, creativity, and self to be held and handed off from one to another. Christine and her label proclaim the cassette as an anchor amid the waves that say there is no room for women in metal, no room for gays in metal, no room for progressives, the transgender, or the socially conscious. Tridroid stands as a testament that there is a place of power for the marginalized in the extreme metal community but no longer any place for Burzum T-shirts.

DANIEL LUKES: Could you give a brief history of how Tridroid Records came to be: the why/how/when, etc.? What were your goals and intents when setting up the label? What were your first releases, and how did they come about?

Figure 1. ©Nate Burns, Tridroid Logo, 2016.

CHRISTINE KELLY: Sure! Tridroid was founded by Andrew Rehberger back in 2012—he lived in St. Paul, Minnesota, and was focused on releasing music (mostly on cassette) from the local St. Paul/Minneapolis scene (with some notable out-of-town exceptions). Tapes are more "en vogue" now, but back in 2012 it wasn't as big a thing. In 2016, he decided he wanted to pass the label on to someone else. I'd actually been buying tapes from Tridroid for years anyway and had a bit of label-running experience. I showed my wife the post about finding someone new, and she said, "Well, you *have* to do that." I submitted a plan to Jason Oberuc [of Suffering Hour, who co-ran the label with Andrew at the time], and he liked it so much I landed the label. Soon after I took over, Andrew was tragically killed. Since then, I've tried to run the label partially as a tribute to his legacy, and so I work with a lot of Minneapolis/St. Paul bands and musicians, in addition to keeping the tape cult alive. I don't have a lot of information about the early releases due to Andrew's passing, unfortunately.

As far as releases I did when I first took over, there were four in 2016 (all cassettes): 1. Final Sign, *Hold High the Flame* (which Andrew had been working on before he passed the label on to me—such amazing and underrated US power metal [USPM]); 2. Re-press of Mantar, *Death by Burning* (which was licensed from Svart Records, their label at the time); 3. Un, *The Tomb of All Things* (a total fluke since their tape label at the time wasn't able to release the album, and I stepped in at the last minute!); and 4. Violet Cold, *Magic Night*. Emin of Violet Cold reached out over the Facebook page's Messenger, and I nearly lost it when I saw that he wanted to work with me! Totally one of those out of the blue things that I'm so glad happened, since he's definitely someone I love working with. Honestly, it was an excellent start for me taking over the label, looking back!

DANIEL LUKES: Is Tridroid Records the *first label* you have been involved in, or have you released records and worked in the music industry before? Please describe your path to owning a label and your career in music. What first got you into heavy music and metal as a young person, and what was the evolution of your musical interests?

CHRISTINE KELLY: Before running Tridroid, I'd briefly co-run a label with a business partner—that partnership didn't work out, but I did learn the ropes a bit and had wanted to start my own label but not add to the glut of labels that popped up and fizzled out so frequently. I'd previously written reviews for a webzine under the tutelage of Marty Rytkonen of Bindrune Recordings fame, and before that I'd been the metal director at my college radio station. I'd been in contact with lots of PR people and labels for that, so working on the business side of the music industry was something I was at least a bit familiar with. Around the same time, I was also a goth/industrial DJ at a local club. I ran with the goth/punk/metal crowd back then, and my college radio station friends first introduced me to metal.

My first metal show was Gwar back in early 2002. Not long after that, I got into a lot of black and death metal. I was nineteen or twenty at the time, so not *that* young a person, if I'm honest. Back then I would only listen to the most "extreme" metal, and I thought trad/power, etc. was for old softies. I guess I turned into an old softie, though, because I definitely like all that stuff now!

DANIEL LUKES: What would you say are some of the releases you are most proud of and why? For listeners new to Tridroid Records, which records would you suggest they check out first? What are your best sellers and/or highest profile releases?

CHRISTINE KELLY: Picking favorites is way too hard, since basically I'm just a big fan who gets to release some of my favorite music. As far as top sellers, definitely Violet Cold's *Anomie* (DLP and tape), Bull of Apis Bull of Bronze, Enslaved, and Wardruna.

DANIEL LUKES: How does Tridroid's output dovetail with your own personal musical taste and your sense of where the creativity is? What are the heavy genres and styles you are most drawn to, and how do you evaluate what could be a Tridroid release? The label seems to balance well the traditionalist side of metal with more experimental and progressive sounds, including, among others, death and thrash metal, old school, cosmic, and post-black metal, funeral doom, dark ambient, and melancholic pop. What do you look for when considering music to put out? Is there any kind of thread tying together Tridroid releases? I assume being a "heavy music" label is different from being a "metal" label: Could you perhaps spell out that difference?

CHRISTINE KELLY: I switched it up to a "heavy music label" back when I released an album for The Blight, which is straight up noise/ambient weirdness. I think heavy music can take on a lot of forms, so I decided I wouldn't limit the label. I also let Tridroid run the metal gamut as far as subgenres go, partly because that's what Andrew did, and I want to honor his legacy of not being so specific in sound. He released what he liked and what he thought was good—and the same goes with me. A lot of labels have a definitive "sound," and I toyed with that idea back when I took over, but keeping with that wouldn't reflect me nowadays as a heavy music fan. I used to be drawn pretty much solely to black metal, but that's definitely not the case anymore, for a whole multitude of reasons.

The way I evaluate what could be a Tridroid release is difficult to qualify, but I'll try. It definitely helps if I know the musician or we're connected in some way, because before I even listen to tunes, I try to evaluate whether this voice is one that I would like to center and promote. By that, I mean I'm pretty open with who I am as a queer lady and what I support and what I don't. If you're a white supremacist, misogynist, homophobe, or transphobe—or even if you don't think those things are gigantic problems that need to be dealt with—you're not a good fit for what I'm doing. There are plenty of other labels out there that don't give two shits about anything, and anyone who doesn't appreciate my views is welcome to submit music to them instead. Once I feel comfortable on that front, I give a listen to the tunes. If I like it, I work with it. If it's not my thing, I won't—even if I know it'd be commercially viable. I'd rather work with music I'm 100 percent behind. There are bands I've passed on that have gone on to do great things and get (relatively) big, and I'm so stoked for them! Basically, I guess I run my label as a way to get my fave tunes on cassette, by making them myself.

DANIEL LUKES: To what extent are you a cassette label, and how many of your releases are on tape? What does the cassette revival mean to you and to physical media in general? I grew up in the 1990s, and, for me, having a CD of an album feels like I own it in a different way. Can you explain what significance physical media, including merch, have for you? Are there any specific limited edition Tridroid items you'd like to tell us about?

CHRISTINE KELLY: Tridroid started as a cassette label that then released some CDs and a couple of records; I honestly love cassettes as a format, so that model works great for me. The overhead on tape releases is low, which is excellent, because when I took over the label I had no capital built up. I also lived in New York City at the time, and cassettes took up way less room and were way more sturdy than records and CDs. I commuted on the train every day with a Walkman in my jacket pocket. As far as I'm concerned, tapes rule!

I'm super stoked by the current cassette revival, because it means other people see what I see! The difficult part is that because everyone from DIY musicians to major label artists are making tapes now, materials have become scarce and tape manufacturers get overwhelmed. They're also having to basically reinvent the manufacture of tape reel from raw materials, so that switchover has been rocky. Sony stopped manufacturing the Walkman cassette player back in 2012 too, so that means it can be difficult to get your hands on a good working player.

I honestly love physical media. I started buying CDs and tapes back in the early 1990s, and being able to flip through liner notes and read lyrics was (and is!) really important to me. I like creating things that people enjoy looking at *and* listening to, so I've always put a lot of effort into design and aesthetics for my releases, while still keeping them the right size to fit onto a standard shelf (I have a lot of feelings about this, hah!).

DANIEL LUKES: You have released cassettes by big names, such as Voivod, Unleashed, and Enslaved: How did those come about?

CHRISTINE KELLY: The Voivod and Unleashed albums were licensed from Century Media by Andrew. The Enslaved and Wardruna releases came about because I was connected with the label that works with both bands through an associate. I showed one of the label heads a copy of the Uprising tape I put out (with a hand-stitched booklet and a screen-printed pouch), and he said, "This is exactly what I want for Enslaved. Would you like to put out *Vikingligr Veldi*?" I nearly fainted. Those releases took a lot of time and work to accomplish, and I'm extremely proud of them.

DANIEL LUKES: I feel that in the last five years or so, underground metal has entered a new phase in terms of its politics coming to the forefront or at least becoming clearer, both on the right and the left. To what degree would you say that there is a political consciousness to the music you work with? The statement on Bull of Apis Bull of Bronze's album page says: "We aim to use the frustration, anger, and horror of our time to pursue meaningful change. Black metal is about power. That fire in your belly can be harnessed. It can be pointed in a direction that moves us forward. That is what we hope to accomplish." These are encouraging words. And in a sense, as far back as Black Sabbath, behind the wizards and dragons, there was always a political conscience to metal, which involved fighting tyranny, authority, and power. It sometimes got lost along the way, but I feel it's back in full force today in the underground metal scene. Do you have any thoughts about this or about fantasy vs. politics in metal?

CHRISTINE KELLY: As a person whose identity is used as a political football, it's impossible for me to avoid being "political," no matter how I feel about that fact. It seems like massive privilege to me to be able to stay "apolitical"—it's just not something that's available to me, and that's fine; I can work with that. If my very existence is political, then everything I do is political, so I embrace that and do what I want to do. I center marginalized voices as much as I can and speak out against Nazis in the scene, both through my voice and the voices of the artists I release. Working with Bull of Apis Bull of Bronze was a huge honor and privilege, because their message is what I want to put out there: extreme metal isn't for violence, misogyny, white supremacy, homophobia, or transphobia; it's about the rage of existing in a society that hates people like me. I take comfort in that primitive anger, and I'm so glad to see that others crave the same sounds for similar reasons.

DANIEL LUKES: What kind of response has being an openly "queer lady-owned heavy music label" received, positive but also negative? I have noticed hostility and trolls harassing you online, but I also see an emerging and vocal online community actively in support of metal and heavy music that is made by people who are queer, LGBTIQ+, and of color and people hungry for metal that is explicitly left-wing, socialist, anarchist, communist, anti-fascist. To what degree do you feel part of a movement that counts among its goals centering non-white non-male voices and reclaiming metal from Nazis? What would you say are the rewards, challenges, and emotional and psychological costs of this struggle? To what extent can metal be a channel for political struggle, a message of hopefulness and a means for building community and solidarity on the left?

CHRISTINE KELLY: I have a heavy hand with the "block" button, I'll say that! I definitely get some hate, even some doxing and threats at times, but, honestly, way more support than negativity. It was a very intentional thing for me to put the "queer lady-owned music label" wording out there. Back when I took over Tridroid, it didn't even occur to me that not many women did what I was doing, and even fewer queer women. Even after I realized it, I took a bit of time before putting that information out there, because I didn't want to use my identity as a selling point or a prop. But after some time passed I thought about the fact that back when I was coming up in the metal scene (almost twenty years ago now, yikes!), I didn't know of any queer women involved in extreme metal, either on stage or behind the scenes. I think that for younger me, it would have been really great to see someone like me running a label unapologetically.

I definitely see myself as part of a movement to push Nazis out of metal and pull queers, anti-fascists, and POC in; we've always been here, and I want to spotlight that fact. We've been pushed to the sidelines, and my goal is to use all the resources at my disposal to bring our voices to the forefront. If you're not using your platform for good, what are you doing?

The challenges, I suppose, would be the amount of vetting I do for every artist and musician I work with, and the scrutiny I incur for being open about who I am and what I do. I'm a very private, introverted person who always wanted to be the one behind the curtain, but I also recognize that it's important that I'm visible, so I try to balance those two things. I mostly just want to do my best, and my biggest fear is that it will never be enough. As far as rewards, I guess running Tridroid makes me feel as if I'm doing something positive when so many horrible things are happening all over the world and in this country. It never feels like enough, though.

DANIEL LUKES: You have recently released cassette versions of Violet Cold albums, which are fantastic: are there any dream artists you would love to work with? What can we expect from Tridroid in the near future?

CHRISTINE KELLY: I'm so honored that I get to work with Violet Cold. Emin and I have been friends since I put out *Magic Night* on cassette in 2016. He's very much on the same page as I am as far as viewpoints and "the scene" go, so he's an absolutely perfect fit for Tridroid, not to mention a truly brilliant musician (he's entirely self-taught!) and just an excellent person in general. I've gotten to work with so many of my favorite artists, but my absolute dream would be to work with Obsequiae someday. It's my favorite project by my favorite people.

Figure 2. ©Nate Burns, Tridroid Logo, 2016.

Liz Hoge / Carrion Creations   ceramics, various dimensions
Corpse Paint Teacups, 2013-2020   courtesy of the artist

< Élodie Lesourd
  Lifecrush, 2017
  acrylic, gaffer on
  paper, 15 x 21 cm
  courtesy of the artist

Bernd Preiml
From the series *The Kid*, 2017
photograph
courtesy of the artist

Marnie Weber
Young Witch as Devil, 2016
production still from *The Day of Forevermore*, 2016
photo by © LeeAnn Nickel
courtesy of the artist and Gavlak Gallery, Los Angeles

Sludgework Meg
Black Metal Mickey Mouse, 2018
pen and ink on Bristol board, 14.8 x 21 cm
courtesy of the artist

The Dialectical Satan

LANGDON HICKMAN

NULL. ABSTRACT AND FOREWORD

This is a personal thing for me.

I should state immediately that I am a cis het white man from the United States of America. I cannot speak to the fullness and potentiality of black metal for people beyond that pedestal of privilege built on the backs of oppressive violence. But as an occultist, a matter I typically keep terribly private, considering the way it seemingly clashes with my otherwise materialist dialectical leftist bent toward the world, I can speak to the way Satan is used by some within black metal. Because I see not just a right-wing interpretation tabled by some groups, be it outright fascism via racism by some or a generalized angst toward anti-fascist action by others, but also a seemingly blanket acceptance that those groups are right-wing somehow, theologically if not politically or morally or ethically. Black metal is a vast and incredible whole, containing the works of Darkthrone and Deafheaven, Emperor and Cloak of Altering, Limbonic Art and Locrian; it manifests as throat-ripping thrashers and ornate progressive epics and post-punk mechanized nightmares and more. Like any art space, it is frustratingly blank, able to contain works by explicit fascists like Grand Belial's Key right next to explicit left-wing groups like Light Bearer. Black metal, however, seems frustratingly singular in the way that fascists and fascist sympathizers in the genre can seize a mic and align Satan with their politics, and no one seems to bat an eye, even those that perhaps should know better.

What follows is an inroad for an outsider to a set of ideas and approaches to Lucifer worship, to how we conceive of it culturally and socially and what the effects of both the improper and a proper conception might be. The similarity to the bog-standard black metal manifesto, all fire and thunder and drama, is deliberate. This is, in brief, an attempt to fight fire with fire.

The image of Satan, one that is integral to black metal whether we want it to be or not, has been allowed to be seized by fascist interpretations. Those interpretations have been left largely unchallenged, with any given fascist fucking dork black metal front man whinging in gothic font to zines named after Buddhist theological terms being allowed to define the theology and implications of a symbol that they frankly know nothing about. There is a joke that Satanism, especially the post-LaVeyan sort, is a child's temper tantrum dressed up in spooky robes, and this is not an unfair criticism of that, again to be blunt, Halloween Ayn Rand cosplay nonsense.

But we absolutely do not have to accept these interpretations of Lucifer worship and the symbol of Satan, because it's not just their politics that are wrong, ruining the world broadly and black metal specifically, but their theology too. The temptation to fall down this rabbit hole completely and produce a more totalizing work regarding liberatory Lucifer worship and occult praxis as a means to heal both black metal and the world is a tempting one. What is intended here is enough rigor that a passerby would know these thoughts and rejections of fascist interpretations of Satan are not flippant and groundless but are based in theological analysis but, ideally, not so much rigor that an outsider would find them completely unintelligible. This is a somewhat risky and atypical but deeply sincere piece for me, and so trying to convey the amount of research and thought without it being either pretentious or unapproachable has been tricky. This is probably going to be a long-term project. I think I bit off quite a lot, but it's been invigorating to work on.

The central thought, the contributing hue to the overall rainbow of thoughts and forms regarding black metal this shares space with, is that we don't need to only reject fascist Satanic images of black metal purely on their politics but also on the grounds that their supporting theology is resolutely false. If black metal is to be the music of Satan, then right-wing black metal must be expunged from its ranks.

Lastly, and most vainly, I hope this inspires people to make black metal that has as much left-wing ideology as it does Satan.

I. INTRODUCTION

It is tempting with black metal to be reductive. (This temptation extends beyond black metal, but let us now limit our scope.) While this urge to reductivity, an understandable urge to blunt the edges of a complex and messy idea-form, to make it easier to parse and simpler to classify, extends in many directions, one of the more immediate directions is of the role of Satan within the music. Satan is, of course, a key semiotic figure within heavy metal in general and one that a vast amount of black metal in specific refers back to. So it is easy at times to reduce the genre down to one of purely "Satanic heavy metal" and to castigate those who do not conform to this ideological impulse behind their music as somehow "not black metal." This impulse is wrong; we have a number of black metal bands who elaborate on the aesthetic elements of black metal in manners that do not include Satan whatsoever, and in art and art theory aesthetics is God, the theos to which we gesture, given that art is the circuitry of dead aesthetic animated by the will and pathos of an observer in an art experience.

I mention this so as to bound the limits of this essay. Reductiveness does us no good, and there is no shortage of bad writing on heavy metal in general, let alone black metal in specific. I seek not to address all of black metal in all of its contortions and forms but specifically those of Satanic impulse or who drape themselves in Satanic imagery. The notion of what constitutes the Satanic impulse in heavy metal has its own elaborate contortions and tendrils, of course, but those will come later.

We are presented often, even by the more Satanically inclined bands, with a narrow conception of Satan. The image of Satan has often been used to promote notions of cruelty, of baseless violence, of sexualized abuse, racism, and superiority, a superiority that is then further bound to be essentialist supremacy rather than a modal superiority. This is beyond a simply bad reading of Satan as semiotic image but a misleadingly inaccurate one driven more by puerile dreams of power than any serious studied heft, something that arises from predominantly straight white male temper tantrums than a learned and appreciative approach to the image of Satan.

II. PATROS

The first notion we must begin with regarding Satan is, of course, Jehovah, Allah, El, Yahweh. It is with this theological aspect, the Patros, that Satan finds itself in conflict, and so to separate Satan too quickly from this dialectical relationship weakens the image of Satan and disorders its internal logic to nonsense. A proper reckoning of the Patros in non-Christian terms is of the energizing force between the atoms, not the forces of the machine itself but the figure beyond its walls that assembles it. A helpful story in this space is that of the Temple, the place in Jerusalem where the Patros was able to live. This was not an abstract story meant to delight; in theologically simplified terms, the realm of Earth's separation from Heaven following the Fall also rendered the Patros unable to enter the world save for through the intermediary of angels or in brief glimmers. The construction of a temple was to allow the entrance of the Patros fully into the world through the space of the tabernacle, in which the Patros could remain and be communed with by sanctified priests able to withstand the pure presence of the Godhead. The tabernacle of the Patros's presence had been constructed by Moses during the pilgrimage in the desert, its full Hebrew name meaning literally "tent of meeting," and its interiors were transferred to the Temple of Jerusalem following its construction by Solomon. Following the destruction of the temple, the tabernacle was lost and with it direct communication with the Patros was severed; from that point forward, theologically speaking, all communion was to be done via angels or via faith, with little direct communication and no earthly home for the divine Godhead.

From that point, the branches of the Abrahamic faith through which the initial image of Satan used by black metal is formed differ. In contemporary Judaism, there are of course theological conflicts, but the general thought is that a third Temple must at some point be constructed in Jerusalem replete with another tabernacle to bring at last the full and final days of the Lord. Christianity posits that the Christos, a theological image to be described later, interceded on behalf of humanity and opened a tabernacle of the heart, a sentiment that is not metaphorical but literal, a metaphysical space in the heart for the Patros to reside in and thus have direct entrance to earth again. Islam largely agrees with this sentiment, differing mostly on specifics on how precisely the Christos was formed and whether it was literally Jesus's person or whether he was more of a sainted vessel for this necessary spirit.

The Patros' separation from earth, only bridged temporarily and often by an intermediating force, is the necessary component for understanding Satan. Satan's initial name, Lucifer, is a title more than a name: "Lightbringer," the one who carried the torch into the darkness of the womb of the prenatural world. When the Godhead uttered the *fiat lux* (let there be light), it was Satan, itself more a title than a name, under the older name of Lucifer, who carried that light into being. Even in this pre-world state, there was some operating veil of separation between the purity of the Godhead and the world itself. This is where the Gnostic understanding comes from that the Fall may itself be a nonliteral translation of this initial creation of the earth, itself a space separate from the purity of the Godhead. Regardless of the precise placement of the Fall within the theological framework of the creation of the universe as an object separate from the Godhead, this separation still exists, and it was only once the gates of Eden were closed that the limits on the Godhead's entry into the realm of the Actual were fully erected, introducing a fallen world of murder, disease, childbirth, and death.

This separation can be seen as the initial trauma of the Godhead. The creative act was misunderstood in the perfect lonely deathlike purity of the Godhead alone as mere multiplication, but there is no generation that is free, and so creation looked more like subtraction, like removing a tumor from the Real that is the metaphysical flesh of the undifferentiated nirvanic Godhead and forming almost a cell membrane around it, making the universe. But the jealousy of the Patros is well-noted, and nothing can be removed that is not then desired to be returned. So the proper modality of the Patros is not creation, which is more in line with the unified Godhead rather than this facet or enunciation of it, but of control and power. It is, after all, only the Patros that demands worship, demands sacrifice, punishes evildoers. There is a complexity to this desire, however, which is that the desire for control and power emerge in the form of the Patros being the archon of Law.

Law in this sense is the metaphysical calcification of desires for order, control, and power. These desires are not wholly inexplicable or unjustifiable; in a resolutely real sense, social and personal chaos are disorienting and often quite troubling, and enacting borders and methods of navigation in those states helps us to achieve ourselves or maintain a sense of harmony. However, any decent reader of Foucault will also note the intoxicating nature of the methodologies of order, how possession of those capabilities can quickly become corruptive forces that view order itself as more important to maintain than the health, well-being, or Becoming of those ensnared in our order. This is the ultimate limit of pure Law and why often in theological spaces we see the Lawbringer dialectically opposed by the Advocate, which in some Abrahamic interpretations is the Christos, the spirit that values the lives of those ensnared by Law as having occasional precedence in value over Law itself.

III. SATAN I: VIA GOD

In theological terms, the Christos is not the first example of an interlocutor who opposes the function of the Patros as archon of Law. The initial figure is Satan, a title that means "opposer." Most thorough biblical reads place the term Satan as rarely referring to a coherent and singular figure but instead referring to any who oppose the will of the Lord; however, despite the lack of a centralizing figure to pin this Opposer-nature to, we have, nonetheless, culturally developed a figure of the concentrated Satan, and in a Campbellian mythic sense this takes precedence over a textual Satan. The first notion of the dialectical Satan is this juxtaposition, that the Lightbringer would then become the first opposer to the Patros, the archon of Law. It is not an uncommon comparison to cite this as a Promethean moment, that the light brought into darkness here represents not just a literal light but also a fundamental opposing force to the darkness of the world of unity with the Godhead, as seen in the monastic mystical text *The Cloud of Unknowing*. The Patros does not create a world of light but a world of darkness, a creation that is bound up in darkness, because it emerges from the darkness of the Platonic Real into the physical darkness of the Platonic Actual, a darkness that must be lit from within, because there is not even a notion of light beyond. There could not be this notion, in fact; in perfect unity, the function light serves as illumination is moot, as all is tied up in all, rendering notions such as vision or clarity absurd on their face. In this sense, Satan's Opposer-nature becomes bound up and elaborated on by his position as Lightbringer, not countered by it; it is a command to differenciate, in a Deleuzian sense, the nature of the world from the pure Godhead beyond.

When we add in the story of the Fall, with the serpent, acting as vehicle for Satan-nature, tempting Adam and Eve to partake of the fruit of the Tree of Knowledge of Good and Evil, a literalized epiphanic moment of wisdom, we see a nobility in Satan begin to arise. It would be banal to say that this more accurately mirrors the Promethean tale of the gift of fire representing primal wisdom and the punishment of the Titan by an angered and defied Zeus, himself a sky deity, just as El once was merely the god of skies in pre-Judaic Semitic polytheism. But this juxtaposition unfortunately sets up the same poor reading of the Satanic spirit that pervades right-wing enunciations of the Luciferian ideal, presenting Satan as an aimless agitator "waking people up" to base and petty rebellion with no real motive. In this instance, Satan is best read not as mere petty rebel but instead as a Hegelian archon of antithesis, the rejoinder or correction offered to Yahweh as the Hegelian archon of thesis-via-Law. As we know from Hegel, it is a shoddy read to view the thesis as the Yes and the antithesis as the No with the synthesis being a mere reconciliation of two totally opposed viewpoints. The relationship is more dynamic than that, with the thesis (or, in this instance, Law) being the current position of structural order and the antithesis (here as Chaos or Satan) being a set of nuanced critiques, some with stronger basis than others. What matters is not blind adherence to either figure, at least in this instance, but more respect to the nature of this dynamic, which, by its nature, produces syntheses via reformations of divine law.

This process is represented in talmudic and qabbalic traditions in Judaism, tafsiric and ta'wilic traditions in Islam, and various efforts across the history of Christianity. It is a process at once decried, treating the *fas* of the divine word as a text on which to engage in hermeneutic exegetic exercises, while simultaneously being celebrated. Historically, we tend to see accepted interpretations or critical pieces being absorbed into a broader canon, be it the Catholic catechism or the Talmud of Judaism, while unaccepted exegeses are decried as heretical, eventually falling out of favor or into the murkier realms of lived preservation via mystical/esoteric traditions. It is precisely in these esoteric traditions that we see a preservation of the notion of Satan as a necessary figure who is critical of Yahweh, freed from the bounds of being an infantile and aimless tempter and instead taking on the affect almost more akin to the security-testing hacker hired by a firm to test the bounds of a proposed system. The purpose of meditative exercises in this mold is not to select one figure or another but to put oneself through the dialectical exercise of hearing a divine edict and challenging it in various ways, rolling it over in prayer or meditation, not to necessarily reconcile ourselves to it as is but to have a robust engagement that may resolve itself to be a modified form or even potentially a total rejection. Bounding the options of

Satan and, thus, our own options in this mental model as either pure and total acceptance or pure and total rejection weakens, not strengthens, the power of Satan, and weakening the necessary jester-like critical figure in turn weakens both the Law itself and the archon of Law through relation.

IV. SOPHIA ET CHRISTOS

But the Patros and Satan are not the only two theological forces broadly acknowledged in this relation, either in the cultures that birthed them or in black metal, which will inevitably become the focus of this chapter. There are yet two remaining forces: the Sophia and the Christos.

While it is tempting to jump the gun and engage with the Christos first, given its more obvious dialectical relationship with Satan, it is a force only empowered and made sensible by the ground of the Sophia. In the context I am referring to, the Sophia is a general term for the Holy Spirit, the spirit of the divine Godhead that permeates the Actual, the physical world, as opposed to surrounds and infuses the space between and behind in the Real or the nonphysical world. Conceptions of the Holy Spirit differ quite wildly in the Abrahamic traditions from which our common black metal conception of Satan is drawn; the most widely understood is the Christian notion that it is the element of the Godhead that is present on earth and is separate from the Patros by means of being beyond the divine veil between the Real and the Actual, while in Judaism it largely correlates specifically to divine wisdom and revelation and in Islam most directly to the creative force of Allah. These notions circle the same center, however; the Sophia represents not law, power, or punishment in archonic form but instead creation, wisdom, and love.

This presents another dialectical opposition to the Patros separate from the relation of the Patros and Satan. In that latter relation, we often see a theological override not unlike a parent telling an inquisitive child to be quiet even when they are right, while the relation of the Patros and Sophia is more akin to spouses arguing or self at war with self. In most binary gendered Gnostic traditions, we see a correlation of the Patros to a divine masculine and the Sophia to the divine feminine, mapping in theological space the oppressive and abusive patriarchal relationship we see both in most cases of the Abrahamic faiths and in broader Western society as a whole (deliberately sidestepping non-Western theologies or cultures, as they are not the purview of this essay). The Actual, the world of bodies and lives, is considered a secondary element to the Real, the world of Heaven and the undifferenciated Godhead; the female is a derivative of the male, a cosmic Eve to a greater cosmic Adam, the *fiat lux* just another kind of plucking of a rib. While this offers a pat corollary between theological moments large and small, it also unfairly places the feminine at a disadvantage to the masculine going back to the first instant of Being, offering a permanent ground to unlimited misogynistic action. This becomes even more troubling when we begin to view the archonic aspects of the two forces as determined by theology, with law and power ruling over love, wisdom, and creation. The interpersonal wisdom of the Sophia, that of the world knowing itself and coming to know things beyond itself as equal to the self, is sublimated into the notion of simple obedience. The nuance of the self-dialectic, the notion of culture explicating itself into the complex bylaws of adequate, fair, loving, and wise relation of objects, is crushed beneath an unbending near-Kantian sense of ethical imperative derived from *fas*, not relation.

It is from the fruit of this unbalanced dialectical exchange that spring most of the tales of the Torah and the Old Testament, stories in which the flesh and blood of the earth resists and revolts as it must against the unbending sky of the Lord and finds itself tortured and punished for doing so, that we eventually see the necessity of the Christos. The Christos arises as a dialectical synthesis of the Patros and the Sophia, the child of the divine masculine and divine feminine of the Abrahamic Godhead, acting as a link between the flesh of the earth and the wiles of the spirit. The Christos was granted as a form of concession to the Sophia, the Patros conceding that perhaps direct experience would aid in understanding the nature of the world so as to better form laws to conform the world to. The embodiment of Jesus as carrier of the Christos is acknowledged in Christianity, Islam, and the faiths that followed, viewing him either as the direct son of God or else as a particularly important sainted figure, largely depending on whether a particular faith allows for plurality of the Godhead or singularity, while Judaism has parallel structures developed as the undelivered King of Jerusalem who will come to build the Third Temple and unify the world before Yahweh.

The Christos in this fashion reads much like a second draft of the figure of Satan, a refinement only in specific details rather than mode or function. The role of carrying light into darkness is repeated, except this time it is the light of the world carried back into the darkness of God and the void of perfect unity in the undifferenciated Godhead. There are material contradictions, the Christos unable to overthrow old laws but simply to reform them, modify them, seeking to find accordance between the Patros and Sophia. This can be viewed as a rigid Kantian structuralist ethical framework encountering a Deleuzian or Wittgensteinian organic/rhizomatic ethical framework, finding accordance with one another via a Hegelian dialectical action. The role of the Christos then is not to deliver a certain end but to perform a certain action, to pit the Patros and Sophia against one another in dialectical action again and again to gradually reform the *fas* into something that meets the challenge of responding to the organicism of the world. As we so often see, this is not enough.

V. SATAN II: VIA NIETZSCHE

In most trinitarian theologies, this set of three comprising the thesis, antithesis, and synthesis as portrayed in the Patros, Sophia, and Christos is considered a complete set capable inevitably of overcoming any great theological or philosophical challenge no matter its shape. Still, we witness the abuses of the world and the institutions that carry this relation, whether they be so crass a comparison as churches to more sophisticated mappings such as nation-states, the oppressive actions of social structures that wield specific weaponized forms of gender, race, and class to the detriment of its people, or even the abstract underpinnings that make us yearn for these discrete and recognizable forms of structure, even when they wound us. It is thus that the Hegelian model of theology as exemplified by this triune system shows its weaknesses, exhibiting the reformist nature of its mode that is ultimately incapable of responding to the depths of the suffering of the world. The Patros never relinquishes control; the meta-physis that this metaphysics describes ultimately places the unembodied Platonic Real of the heavenly world and the force of the Patros above the embodied Platonic Actual of the Sophia and the mediating synthetic Christos. Everything is reform of law, and law rules above body and being.

Hence, the necessity for the Nietzschean anti-Hegelian Satan. It is important at this point to make sure our definitions are in order; while in all likelihood whoever is reading this has at least a decent grasp of Nietzsche outside of his social image as the preeminent philosophical tryhand edgelord, it's still important to dispel these notions. Just as Hegel responded to Kant, Nietzsche in turn responded to Hegel, rejecting the notion of a purely logical reformist system of the world. Granted, it is a limpid interpretation of Hegel to believe that he argued for a general progressive arc to history, each generation discretely bettering the last. While the common projected leftist reading of Hegel via Marx presupposes this general arc to history, more robust leftist and even general philosophical interrogations of Hegel's dialectical theory dispel the idea of a linear progression to the arc of humanity. However, though the dialectic is powerful enough to generally account for the world as a preexisting system modified by events and beings, with the most powerful read of the dialectic being that any given object, concept, or act can function as a nuanced antithesis to the thesis-object of the existing world, it struggles to account at times for radical or cataclysmic action. This is not so much an issue with the dialectic itself as with its practitioners; hardline Marxist-Leninists, for example, tend to prefer a controlled centralized state as a means of limiting the vast and swarming number of variables that can enter a dialectical system than, say, a more anarchistic arrangement of connected communes and communities. In turn, this means that certain events, be they the looming climate apocalypse or historical events like the Holocaust, the African diaspora, or the development of nuclear weaponry, can sometimes thwart our more immediate and well-grounded understandings of the systems of the world.

This is where Nietzsche arrives conceptually. He doesn't so much overthrow the dialectic, as much as he would have wished to, as he amends it, appending first the psychological impulses of culture and ego through the Schopenhauerian will-to-death and his own will-to-power, and then interpolating them through a complex system of hermeneutics and phenomenology. To Nietzsche, the phenomenon was not an unimportant spectral figure haunting the critical noumenon but instead the supreme figure, for it was not necessarily by the noumenon of Being but instead by the phenomenon of Will that actions occurred, and through actions vaster changes to the world. To Nietzsche, the radical reduction of the world to purely logical synthetic relations abstracted out the presence of Will, and by doing so left us unable to grapple with events that seem alien, cancerous, or deeply incompatible with the systems of the world as we know them. The Holocaust, for instance, is a particularly challenging event to synthesize into a purely Hegelian dialectical view of history, having clear logical predicates or causes but having a critical ethical gap that can only partially be cleared in a manner that seems impossible even when added together. In general, the pre-Nietzschean concept of a dialectic, lacking the impulses of psyche, phenomena, and will as forces of power, was strongly capable of grappling with normative history and averaged figures and events but struggled in moments of extremity, be they saintly compassion or despicable evil. It is not unlike the battle in physics between general relativity and quantum mechanics, each seemingly an accurate model to describe their own fields but deeply incompatible with each other in other instances.

We tend most often to see misapplied readings of Nietzsche in this manner, attempting to place his meta-ethical model for life within the extremity of these structures at its center. The figure of the *Übermensch* to Nietzsche, the figure that through will alone overthrows the dialectical arc of history and instead bends it to their will, is described by Nietzsche as one that by its nature cannot occur terribly often and, ironically, can be forced into being far less often than fate thrusts that role onto a figure. The primary motive of the *Übermensch* to Nietzsche are not the affects of the tryhard edgelord who spits at the rules of society and does whatever they wish like a petulant child but, instead, the figure that by will alone recurs. In this mode, the founding of new genres of art is a movement of an *Übermensch*, as are the creation of pivotal works within a genre. Indeed, while recurrent figures are tremendously rare (a fact assumed by Nietzsche, given the tremendousness of social pressures to remain within its bounds, be they ethical or formal), that percentage chance still occurs more often than we might think, just not always in such clear figures as Christ or Hitler or Marx or the Buddha.

What matters most is the meta-ethical imposition. It is wrong to view Nietzsche as a moral nihilist alone; instead, that nihilism is like opening a door, the first utterings that the way things are does not need to be the way they remain, and that we don't need to reform a broken system when we can destroy it and make something new. Thus, the meta-ethical urge of Nietzsche is not to discard all morality forever but, instead, to discard moral systems handed down that make no sense to us and no longer conform to our will or to the world. Instead, the *Übermensch* is one who destroys the system presented to them, not being a mere antithesis in the dialectical process but, instead, its null state, resolving all to zero, and then from this position of formlessness seizing the infinite creative potential of void states to create a new and better moral or formal framework *ab nihilo*. The *Übermensch* is viewed as a destroyer only by those who cleave to the system as it is, feel protected by its lofty walls and soaring towers; to those oppressed or maligned by these structures, the *Übermensch* is a creator at last enacting a salvation that mere reformist policy denies. Thus, a new dialectic can emerge from this new system, until, in time, it too is overthrown, another in a series of infinite overthrowings.

Thus, the connection to Satan's figure in relation to the trinitarian conception of the Godhead becomes apparent. This relation persists even in faith structures within Abrahamic conceptions of the Godhead that resist pluralist structures; the self-reformer of the Jewish Yahweh and the dense monadic singularity of the Islamic Allah contain these elements equally distributed internally rather than segmented and demarcated. Satan is spurned in these systems, because the various aspects or figures within the Godhead reform the Godhead and its works and systems but ultimately refuse to overthrow them. Thus, the patriarchal oppression under the Abrahamic faith is only ever amended, never overthrown, and the contradictions of capital versus communal ownership are never sought to be resolved except in the dissolution of the self into the Godhead. While this is a beautiful metaphysical dream, Satan reminds us that the self persists in the body as an atom even in the wave state of culture and community, and that often these calls for pure selflessness are carried out by the priest, politician, and capital class as means of urging oppressed classes never to communally rise against their oppressors. In this mode, Satan becomes a figure of inspiration, offering a burning spear to impale the cross-hung figure of the self-martyring oppressive structures of the world, bemoaning their sacrifices even as they are lifted eternally to heaven, while those they hate unduly are ground to dust in silence. The ethnic genocides carried out in the name of the Lord become pardonable offenses, while challenging the eternal domain of the God that commands them becomes a mortal sin; to this, Satan says no. To Satan, it is better to reject the poisoned fruit of the systems of the world wrought by the oppressor class utterly, to tear the tree out by the roots and attempt, perhaps vainly, to grow something new rather than to be party to the evil and suffering it has caused. This is a resolute radical response to the failures of a reformist system, one that is easily castigated by figures within that reformist mode as infantile rebellion but only through their own privilege-born blindness. To the middling "tomorrow" of God, Satan is a resolute "today."

VI. SATAN III: VIA BLACK METAL

This leads to the profound metaphysical misreading that underlies the right-wing image of Satan that is wielded by many black metal bands. To them, Satan is a figure of strength, of rejecting weakness, of nihilism, of death, of erasure. This is certainly true, but their understanding of what these words mean or their directionality is either completely backward or nonexistent. Luciferian strength, for instance, is not in merely saying no to the world in every instance, not in rejecting all of its morals for the mere sake of rejecting morals. It's the toddler that shouts "no" at the table, while the radical adult says, "No, but instead." This ties back to the Nietzschean meta-ethical framework of the *Übermensch*, not a call to do away with morals but a call to seize upon the terrifying Sartrean responsibility of forging our own morality without the comforting metaphysical basis of a God to back it. Indeed, even many leftists fail at this juncture, replacing the image of God with the similarly sainted image of historical materialist dialectic, passing off responsibility for a moral and ethical framework onto the ghost of an illusory history we have no direct access to rather than seizing it up for themselves.

What this underscores is that the paltry and infantile image of Satan touted by the more right-wing black metal groups, a Satan that represents death and cruelty and nothing else is a shallow and flattened image. Despite their words, it requires no strength to say "no," no strength to throw a tantrum like a child. It is true that Satan is only for the strong, but, ironically, they fail the primary test of strength: to reduce all structures to zero within yourself, burn them to the ground, and then replace them with something of your own making. The obsession that the image of the void of death is only erasure and, not ironically, a great fundament of creative power is a failure of imagination, a showing of existential weakness in the face of the death urge. It is easier to retreat from the guiding structures of the world, no doubt rotten, and sit in bitterness than to make effort to resolve, replace, and radically transform them.

But we also see a parallel cowardice even in those who embrace the radicalist urge not to reform the world but to remake it. There are many who view this revolutionary praxis as a single event, one momentous dialectically driven revolutionary act before the dawning of the new world. This is not so; for every Deleuzian hardness of the meta-physis of the world that Satan radically overthrows, the replaced figure will in turn harden, become oppressive or blind in some manner. See how base feminism became inevitably blind to trans issues or how a generalized queer politics eventually lost track of individual queer communities and instead foregrounded middle-class normative queerness over more radical forms. We falter in the face of the fact that we may overthrow the orders of the world and not be sainted, not be viewed as heroic, but in turn be deposed. This is the test of Satanic strength, to always be willing to overthrow the dialectic, to create something new in the void of Being, to never rest or reward ourselves. How can we claim an enabled Satanism and Luciferianism if we rise from hell only to seek a seat in heaven? No, hell must always be the great mouth of radical transformation, a gate that is never closed, and we must allow ourselves to be consumed by it when it is time for those who can better what we have made arise. One does not act in the spirit of Satan to become Jehovah.

VII. WHY?

The right-wing and fascist-enabling (and sometimes explicitly fascist) interpretation of Satanism and Lucifer worship has been allowed to assert itself unchecked in black metal. We can and should challenge this image with groups that sit outside of political aims altogether, as well as groups that challenge it politically head-on with leftist logics and motivations. But if we think this is enough, we are fooling ourselves, to be painfully blunt. Black metal, no matter its history, is tied to that image of Satanism; the burning of churches and the murders in Norway made sure of that—forever. This compounds with the generalized association of Satan worship with extreme metal, with heavy metal, with rock music, with blues and blues-derived music, with folk, with music-making, with the act of making art generally, back and back and back. When we abandon checking and crossing out even the theological underpinnings of the arguments for fascism, deeming them less important than other aspects, we do not save the world; we leave those spaces to fester.

We don't save black metal by simply telling bands to sing about other things and use other symbols, because we have never broken the bond those symbols have to right-wing thought. Having a deeper understanding of some of the theological underpinnings, thoughts, and motivations within proper Lucifer worship does not explicitly save black metal either, granted, but it does give us another set of tools to tell the fascists in the genre to fuck off, as well as to enjoy the works of groups like Light Bearer who have a fuller grasp of the symbols they work with. You would not be reading this collection if you did not love black metal and find it valuable, and I would not be writing this if I didn't feel the same. It is hard to enunciate to someone outside of, well, all of this how terminally frustrating it is to see some knob speak to a report and in the same sentence proclaim Satan his (always a "he") inspiration and then cite fascist sympathies or even a generalized resistance to anti-fascist action.

There are other voices, ones less pseudo-formal than my own, ones less white, ones less male, ones less cis, ones less straight, ones less Western. Their voices are important and imperative to hear, especially in grasping the fullness of what black metal is and what it can be. But those are not my voice, and I cannot say what they would say. I can communicate the theology of Lucifer as I understand it. I can tell you that this is incompatible with the image of Satan as presented by right-wing black metal bands, even the ones that disguise their Satanic motif as generalized anti-Christian paganism. We hear enough about black metal's issues more generally, but Satan doesn't need to be one of them. Lucifer can and has been a good proper motivating force in black metal; the group Light Bearer, for instance, wields a particularly astute leftist dialectical interpretation of Lucifer toward music as incredible as it is thoughtful. There are enough fiery and dramatic inspiring manifestos in black metal pointed toward fascist ends. Here's one for the other side.

Notes

[1]Like many Latin terms, *fas* is a theological term meant to elevate the banal and literal translation of *divine law* into a set of spiritual mandates, under which many things fall: spiritual texts, especially of celestial authorship; spiritual rites; the building of temples; prayer; obeying laws set forth within the divine texts; etc.

Artetak

CAITY
HALL

< Artetak
Sparkle Satanas, 2019
digital illustration,
11 x 17 cm
courtesy of the artist

Caity Hall
A Unicorn at the Rock Show, 2019
digital media
courtesy of the artist

Rape Culture and Metal

GEORGE PARR

In July 2019, Nuclear Blast, a label with considerable pull in the metal scene, announced it would be releasing the brand-new album from As I Lay Dying, the band's first since front man Tim Lambesis was sentenced to six years in prison for hiring a hitman to kill his wife.

While many no doubt anticipated the vocalist's attempted return to music, the most shocking part of the news was that a well-established name in the scene was legitimizing his comeback, presumably only in an attempt to bolster its profits. Yet it was hard to be truly surprised, because while the development was appalling, it's very much in line with the metal scene's continued normalization of rape culture and violence against women.

From victim blaming and casual jokes in conversation to pop stars like Robin Thicke singing lines like "I know you want it" or a man who has bragged about sexual assault being sworn in as the President of the United States, rape culture—the societal attitudes that normalize and trivialize rape and sexual assault—is regrettably prevalent in modern society as a whole. So much so, in fact, that efforts to fight against it seem to be getting nowhere.

So institutionalized is this problem that the Rape, Abuse, and Incest National Network (RAINN) reports that only 3 percent of rapists ever serve a day in jail, and despite the genre's continued insistence that it is rebellious music that stands for the marginalized and oppressed, this terrifying facet of our culture is easily perceptible in metal, which, as a musical genre and subculture, has long had issues with misogyny.

Recent examples of violence against women include cases involving the likes of Lambesis, as well as Jef Whitehead of Leviathan and Lurker of Chalice, who was charged with aggravated domestic battery after being tried on four counts of aggravated criminal sexual assault, one count of unlawful restraint, and one count of aggravated domestic battery—or Vektor's David DiSanto, whose wife Katy DiSanto shared footage of him assaulting her online. But rape culture doesn't come solely in the form of outright rapists and abusers—it can be seen more implicitly across the cultural landscape. It's present in casual jokes, victim blaming, toxic masculinity, and the mental gymnastics used by fans to continue to listen to artists who've been accused of horrid acts.

Metal's issues with rape culture are perhaps best exemplified by the extremist lyrics found in subgenres like death metal, goregrind, and pornogrind. This is where the issue is at its most blatant, with lyrics often coming across as little more than an attempt to see who can be the most shocking. Cannibal Corpse have sung in graphic detail about necrophilia, while Torsofuck released the ever-so-funny "Raped by Elephants" and Cradle of Filth wrote "Lord Abortion" about an unwanted baby who becomes a necrophiliac that rapes virgins. There's the inconceivably gross abortion rape of Infant Annihilator's "Torn from the Womb," Aborted's "Nailed through Her Cunt," which is obscenely fixated on graphic depictions of sexual assault, and even band names that embrace heinous imagery, from Prostitute Disfigurement through Cock and Ball Torture to Cemetery Rapist. These are just a few examples—there are thousands more with similar names, lyrics, and song titles.

This kind of shock value one-upmanship is not all that surprising in a genre that, for some, is purely about pushing the envelope. Everything about metal has got more intense over time, from the music itself, which grew more dissonant and angrier with every new subgenre that has sprouted since its inception in the 1970s, to its usage of intentionally offensive imagery, be it Satanic symbols on artwork or gory lyrics in the songs themselves. Even if rape imagery seems a natural development for the genre, given how some see it as an entity that exists primarily to cause offence, which is a point often made by black metal fans defending National Socialist black metal (NSBM), that doesn't mean it should be accepted as part of the parcel. For people around the world, rape is a horrid reality, with a 2005 United Nations statistical report showing that in the sixty-five countries covered in the report more than 250,000 cases of rape or attempted rape were recorded by police annually. This figure still fails to take into account unrecorded cases, with RAINN reporting that three out of four sexual assaults go unreported.

Perhaps metal fans are so desensitized to gore that many never fully think about the cognitive dissonance that is needed to accept such brutality. The objectification of sexual violence is shrugged off, at best, but, at worst, it is encouraged, which is why in pornogrind there is, in fact, an entire subgenre dedicated to brutality and degradation. Such lyrics differ from some of metal's other common topics, however. While lyrics about war and murder are based on issues that are universally accepted to be horrific, violent acts against women are mocked and belittled in society, and using them for shock value only adds to this flaw in modern civilization. Such violent imagery is shamefully representative of real-life issues, given that it is often at the expense of women, who make up 82 percent of juvenile rape victims and 90 percent of adult rape victims, according to a 2000 report by the National Center for Juvenile Justice. While violent lyrics and imagery in metal are likely seen as just theatrical fun by many, some take this violence all too seriously, as was shown when *Vice* reported that the Dayton shooter, who killed nine people in a mass shooting, was into pornogrind and goregrind bands.

Sexually violent lyrics are considered fantasy, part of the "boys will be boys" mantra that often comes along with metal, which is consistently perpetuated by annual "hottest chicks in metal" pieces, the use of "female-fronted" in lieu of actual genre descriptors, and websites that are designed to fight back against the "SJWs" and "PC brigade." There's also #MetalGate, an attempted movement copied directly from the misogynist #GamerGate movement, which was seemingly kickstarted when the blog Death Metal Underground first used the term. It received support from so-called "men's rights" forums like Return of Kings, and with this came telltale signs of rape culture, with gaming website Reaxxion openly laughing about the lyrics to Detroit Metal City's "Rape That Girl" and comments on Death Metal Underground expressing anger toward "social justice warriors"—one comment reads, "They gain power by claiming women are being raped/harassed/groped so they need to set up protection. No evidence will ever arrive for these attacks." #MetalGate's wider objective was to keep progressive politics out of metal, a goal which seems bizarre given that the genre has had a swathe of left-leaning political tracks throughout its history, with some subgenres being wholly entwined with social movements and political expression.

Like racism in black metal, sexual violence in death metal is often considered part of the genre. "It's supposed to shock and offend," defenders will assert, but this line of thinking puts the blame back on the offended. It maintains that if you take offence at something someone says in a song then that's on you—you clearly just don't understand the genre. It's a form of gatekeeping that actively excludes anyone offended by sexual violence, which is naturally going to be a lot of people. Furthermore, considering that rape is such a widespread issue in modern society, with RAINN reporting that 994 out of every 1000 rapists will walk free, would it not be more controversial for metal, which fans often claim is a rebellious genre, to speak up for those suffering?

Songs depicting sexual violence are not created in a vacuum and should not be considered mere fantasy. Anger in metal is often used as a form of catharsis, but if that anger targets women in particular, then that is a damning insight into that artist's view of women. The existence of sexually violent lyrics should be considered an indictment of the patriarchal structure of society and the sexism that's prevalent within it. The World Health Organization says that more than a third of women have suffered some kind of violence from a man, while women, trans, and gender non-conforming people are still underrepresented in positions of power, and the gender pay gap is still very much in existence. Therefore, surely, if metal were truly a genre of resistance, it would decide not to normalize repressive lyrics and imagery. It would fight against them and give the marginalized a voice where others would not.

Thankfully, there is a movement of artists doing just that. Perhaps the most notable in relation to the violent lyrics found within death metal is Welsh band Venom Prison. The band's debut album *Animus*, released in 2016, was a death metal album in every sense of the word, featuring all its musical hallmarks, as well as some violent lyrics—only these lyrics aimed to turn the genre's fascination with sexual violence on its head and target rapists themselves. The single "Perpetrator Emasculation" sees the band embrace the genre's explicit nature but combines it with a message that targets perpetrators of abuse, describing the castration and murder of a rapist that's also depicted on the album's artwork:

You think you're strong?
I will hear you cry
When I amputate your genitalia
Force-fed, choke on your own crime
Blunt objects forced into the cranium

Similar themes can be found in the work of fellow death metal act Castrator, a semi-anonymous group formed by established female musicians around the world who sing explicitly about feminist revenge fantasies. The intent of such bands is clear. Castrator, like Venom Prison, works within the genre, playing by its rules, while attempting to somewhat level the playing field. Any hate these artists have received from men exemplifies the metal scene's issues with misogyny— if someone isn't bothered by songs about violent sexual assault against women but is offended by songs featuring violence against men, then their true stance is clear.

The potential criticism of this angle, however, is that it fights violence with violence. Is sexually violent imagery really the best way to counter rape imagery? Regardless of the target, such imagery can be harrowing for survivors of abuse, and lyrics about genital destruction and mutilation can also be an uncomfortable listen for trans people.

Beyond the violent rape imagery of extreme metal, though, the genre as a whole has a pressing issue with rape culture. Delving into the social media comments section of any piece that tries to address the metal scene's ongoing problems with sexism is likely to unveil a swarm of misogynists insisting that there is no problem. When former Agoraphobic Nosebleed vocalist Kat Katz opened up about her encounters with sexism in the scene, the comments on the MetalSucks Facebook page saw men complain about the "victimhood Olympics" and helpfully point out that there are two sides to every story—perhaps *she* abused *them*, one commenter randomly suggested. Similarly, when *Metal Hammer* ran a piece suggesting that modern metal's most interesting voices are all women, their social media pages were bombarded with so many antagonistic comments that the publication also ran a follow-up piece in which Serena Cherry of Svalbard and Djamila Azzouz of Ithaca responded to a handful of those comments.

These instances are common and are potentially the result of some men believing that women in the scene are only given attention because of equality and feminism. These movements are often misconstrued as being hostile toward men, thus something to be fought against rather than supported. As such, many male metal fans believe themselves to be rebelling against authority when in actuality they are perpetuating sexism. It has been supposed by sociology professor Deena Weinstein that metal is grounded in masculine ideas regarding power, control, and competition. Perhaps, then, male fans see women as a threat to what they consider key facets of the genre. The notion of masculinity isn't inherently toxic, and metal artists have made use of the many positive messages in society that are coded as masculine, such as honor, respect, duty, loyalty, and honesty, but the genre is also often guilty of reinforcing toxic notions of masculinity. It often treats macho traits as desirable, while encouraging men to be violent, emotionally unavailable, sexually aggressive, and always unfeminine. This can only be fought by calling out toxic behavior in the scene, holding men accountable, dispelling myths like "boys will be boys," and teaching people that feminine is not antithetical to masculine.

Disheartening responses could also be seen online when the charges of rape against death metallers Decapitated were dropped. Though the motion cited the "wellbeing of the victim" as a reason for the case's dismissal and noted that the four members could still be prosecuted in the future, one commenter suggested that it had only occurred because "some tart wanted a bit of cash/attention." This is a prevalent opinion among male metal fans whenever cases like this arise, even though false accusations are not the epidemic they seem to be perceived as. False rape claims are hard to quantify, because, due to the pressure and victim blaming endured by survivors, not many assaults are even reported to the authorities. However, a 2013 Crown Prosecution Service (CPS) report compared rape prosecutions with prosecutions for making a false claim, and found that fewer than 1 percent of rape prosecutions were false claim charges.

Another comment claimed that "girls want on rock stars [sic] busses." This claim, that every woman wants to sleep with the musician, is a damaging assumption that's common in the music industry, suggesting that women are incapable of respecting a man's artistic output without desiring the artist. In metal, the assumption is that the music is too manly for them to like, so, therefore, they must be there with an ulterior motive. Similarly, female and gender-nonconforming metal musicians are still massively outnumbered by cis men, with women often finding themselves on lists of "best female-fronted bands" and/or being asked typical "woman in a band" interview questions, which continue to assert that their presence in metal is a novelty and does nothing to normalize their participation in the scene.

It's clear that part of the problem comes from metal still being a white, cis male-dominated space. Many fans may claim to be against sexism in the scene, but, as something that seldom affects them personally, men are often happy to ignore it, especially if not doing so will impede their ability to listen to certain bands. Jef Whitehead's projects continue to receive support simply because he asserts his innocence, and fans would rather believe him than his accuser and the jury that found him guilty. Similarly, the hype for Tool's latest album was massive upon its announcement, even though front man Maynard James Keenan was accused of rape a year prior and only addressed the accusation in a condescending and dismissive tweet. Structural misogyny is embedded in metal, just as it is in wider society, with huge publications continuing to cover Keenan without even questioning him regarding the accusations, simply because he is a powerful figure in the scene.

In some cases, sexual abuse has not just been ignored but has been utilized as a marketing strategy. Tim Lambesis's return to As I Lay Dying has been framed as part of a redemptive journey for the singer, for instance, while Jef Whitehead's bands continue to be billed as "dark" and "evil." Elsewhere, Profound Lore Records once tweeted about and glorified the "sea of negativity" around the Castevet album *Obsian*, seemingly trying to profit off the fact that front man Andrew Hock had accused of attempted sexual assault. And this is despite the label's signing of Lingua Ignota, a one-woman project from Kristin Hayter, who is a survivor of abuse and explicitly addresses this in her music, which she describes as "survivor anthems."

It'd be remiss, though, to ignore the many contemporary metal artists fighting back against the scene's rape culture (as well as its other sociopolitical issues). This movement has been in the works for some time. Metal's affiliations with political messages are plain to see for anyone who knows the genre's history, and go all the way back to Black Sabbath's early years with tracks like "Wicked World" or "War Pigs," but in a world plagued by major political upheavals like Brexit, Donald Trump's presidency, and other far-right candidates gaining significant support in various countries, the political messages are noticeably rising to the forefront of the genre. In 2006, the *Washington Post* ran a piece entitled "Heavy Metal Gets Socially Conscious" that somewhat erased the genre's storied history of politicized music but, nevertheless, noted the growing number of contemporary artists speaking up about issues like animal rights and war.

Since then, that number has only grown, and in the underground metal scene, things are even more fervent. One notable movement is #KillTheKing, a campaign inspired by the #MeToo movement against sexual assault and sexual harassment. It was launched by three women-run Swedish organizations—namely, Dear Darkness, Heavy Metal Action Night, and Hårdrock Mot Rasism—and aims to combat abuse and misogyny in their local metal scene. Drama ensued when Australian band Deströyer 666, who #KillTheKing singled out in their initial statement of intent, called them out onstage in the movement's hometown of Stockholm at a February 2018 show, with a misogynist tirade that surely only further exemplified the need for such campaigns. Meanwhile, though, Sweden also has Heavy Metal Against Racism, which fights racism but also misogyny, homophobia, and transphobia. Another positive sign comes in the form of a GoFundMe launched to help Katy DiSanto with funds needed to leave her abusive husband and the legal fees needed to prosecute him, which surpassed its goal of $4,500, with DiSanto subsequently thanking the metal community for their support.

As well as movements like these, the underground scene is awash with forward-thinking bands, with anti-fascism being a key issue for groups like Dawn Ray'd and Underdark, but with other social issues also being prominent. Baton Rouge blackened sludge act Thou have addressed police brutality and fascism in songs, but most pertinent here is a song entitled "The Severed Genitals of Every Rapist Hang Bleeding from These Trees." Elsewhere, St. Louis crust-punk band Redbait addressed rape and the patriarchy on their EPs *Red Tape* and *Cages*, San Francisco's Body Void have told rapists and their defenders to "Die Off," and UK blackened hardcore act Svalbard have songs about revenge porn and the use of the term *feminazi*. Beyond this, many bands with progressive messages may not have explicitly addressed the issue of rape culture in their music but may be clear about where they stand in interviews and on social media, such as Allfather's Andrew Day, who wrote a piece about the metal scene's bigotry following Decapitated's rape accusation, Kosmogyr's Ivan Belcic using Twitter to make fun of those who rationalize the ongoing use of sexual violence, or Couch Slut speaking out on rape culture in metal at every opportunity. The likes of Couch Slut, Allfather, and Kosmogyr, not to mention Vile Creature, Ithaca, Sarparast,

Racetraitor, Closet Witch, Amygdala, Ragana, and many more, have ensured that there is a thriving scene of artists that are doing metal differently, casting out its rock star posturing and patriarchal gatekeeping to ensure that the genre's powerful ability to convey a message is used to punch up, not down.

Scott McPherson
Nihillustration, 2020
mixed media
courtesy of the artist

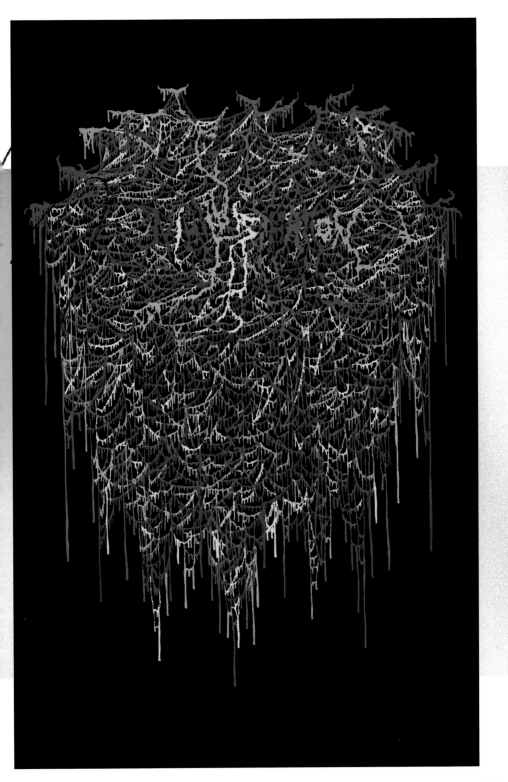

Deep-Learning Metal

BOGNA M. KONIOR

The discrepancies between human and machine listening might be productively differentiated by considering their respective capacities for abstraction.

—YONEDA LEMMA, "ANTI-WORLDS"[1]

We publish research on ~~eliminating humans from music~~ neural synthesis...if musicians lose their jobs, we're a scapegoat. jk. Please don't burn us to death.

—DADABOTS[2]

In the days before neural networks made metal, a priest visited my high school in a rundown mining town in the mountains of Southwest Poland. This was before I'd turned away from metal in favor of electronic music—my friends and I were often listening to Gorgoroth, a practice that is hard to pass on when you're attending an all-girls Catholic school. We appreciated its provocative, Satanic aesthetic, but there was also the masochism of it—exposing yourself in a controlled manner to an unpleasant sound. It gave us a sense of agency, of choosing our misfortune. When I later heard metal made by algorithms, I wondered about this desire to automate an experience that tests your endurance, often through pattern disintegration, through breaking up sounds until they become barely distinguishable from noise. A challenge to the ears that, nevertheless, allows you to maintain mastery over your hardship.

But all of that happened much later. The day that that priest visited our school, it was snowing. The class was on a weekend and dealt with the subject of spiritual mastery, that is, being able to predict in advance the seductions of the supernatural and learning how to see through the disguise. The priest was a rising star on the Polish exorcism scene, probably because his confidence ran on liters of insanity.[3] He told us a story about an old nun in Ukraine who served in our congregation, "a saint," whose passing was accompanied by rose petals falling from the ceiling and a piece of gentle, heavenly, rhythmical music. But he also warned us that there were demons in music, and that you did not have to understand the lyrics to be captivated by unholy sounds. To him, this was a deceptive game: Satanists passing as musicians, demons passing as humans—a game of appearances that young girls could not see through.
To prove it, he brought along a CD of Meshuggah's fourth album *Nothing*. But when he put it into his record player, it broke. All that we heard were glitchy grunts, sporadic torn up shrieks, and a weirdly stretched high-pitched noise. Demons sounded like a broken record—a perfect deception or a lifted veil?

In 2012, C.J. Carr and Zack Zuckowski were involved in another game of deceptions. They set out to "destroy Soundcloud" by spamming it with an army of remix bots. Subsequently, they formalized the project into an algorithmically generated, deep-learning band Dadabots that imitates the training sets it is given, in addition to making album covers and track titles. As they notice, "noise, chaos, and grotesque mutations of voice are aesthetically pleasant" when generated from scratch, without any traditional instruments involved. Making music without instruments might seem like a demonic invocation, but the material apparatus for producing it is, of course, present—a computer. Dadabots, the makers say, is not replacing humanity but augmenting it through algorithmic voodoo: "instead of playing the music, we are playing the musician." They are not alone. Collaborating with software is on the rise—there's Sony CSL Research Laboratory's Flow Machines project and its album *Hello World*, Holly Herndon's throbbing pop created with a machine-learning ware called Spawn, and Ash Koosha and Isabella Winthrop's virtual synth-pop musician Yona. This idea is not new, going back to the first computer-generated score developed in 1957 by Lejaren Hiller and David Code's machine composer Emi in the 1980s. With the racing developments in sound synthesis, even Amazon's Alexa wants to jump on the bandwagon; it already has a feature called DeepMusic that serves up AI-generated songs.

On the Dadabots website, there are ten albums, trained on, among others, Dillinger Escape Plan, Battles, Meshuggah, and Krallice. *Æternal Reborous* was trained on Æpoch, with titles generated by a Markov chain, and an album cover made using a neural style transfer overlaying several images. On average, the networks listen to the original albums over and over and generate thousands of minutes of matching sound. Carr and Zuckowski then make a selection and compose an album. Other albums are created in collaboration with the musicians: *Nun de la parte Del, mas Deilha (la Máquina)*, which translates to "Not from him, but from her (the machine)," was trained on the work of Portuguese black metal band Cavemaster, who then curated the album, added samples and a cover. Dadabots also currently have a 24/7 livestream on YouTube titled *Relentless Doppelganger*, trained on the Canadian metal band Archspire. It will be opening for them on their upcoming European tour. They also have a neural net modeled on John Coltrane aboard the NASA space probe Voyager 3 that generates free jazz to entertain aliens. Computers, aliens, metal, demons, and "her, the machine." Listening to Dadabots takes me back to the priest's visit and his insistence on the existence of an inhuman element in sound, a presence that young women in particular need to beware of, a disguise that we had to learn how to see through. Smoke and mirrors.

Algorithmically generated metal raises questions of authenticity and mimicry. A genre that greatly cherishes the imagery of nature, paganism, and moonlit graveyards in a dark forest is a curious candidate for automated production. As Aspasia Stephanou writes, it expresses a quintessentially modern paradox:

Everything is accelerated into a dehumanizing prison for the modern subject. While black metal desires and mourns for a primordial

Black metal is a modern genre that romanticizes the premodern, or even
what it perceives to be outside of history. It seems to believe that through a
quintessentially modern sound of the "metallic war machines" something ancient
can be glimpsed—something beyond humanity. The nonhuman can be not human in
various ways, but what emerges from black metal studies, such as the collection
of essays from 2010, *Hideous Gnosis*, is a specific type of inhumanity, something
out of the Cthulhu mythos, mystical and frightening in its transcendence of
human affairs. Steven Shakespeare writes dramatically about the connection
between black metal and "deep ecology," where "nature is the becoming of being,
and black metal allows us to hear its subterranean roar," as if the music was able
to channel the decay of time itself.[5] Eugene Thacker writes about the possibility of
metal beyond us, a sound that conveys the indifference of the universe.[6] This idea
of the nonhuman is not separate from a historically specific narrative of creative
genius, a romantic story of men using aesthetics to communicate with boundless
nature, a tale characteristic of European Romanticism at large. The philosophers
that are often called on to theorize black metal, such as Friedrich Schelling or
Arthur Schopenhauer, dwell in this tradition. James Lindsey writes that "we have
seen men of genius and artistic power to be, in Schelling's view, endowed with a
faculty of intellectual intuition, which discerns the identity of the One with the
All."[7] As Alison Stone adds, though, Schelling correlates femininity with inhibition
and masculinity with creativity, a polarity that fuels "nature."[8] If black metal is
tied to this idea of an authentic expression brought forth by nature and of artistry
that, despite its solemn desire to communicate the unknowable, points to a male
genius, what happens when it meets the computer, the great artifice?

On the surface, boring things happen. As Yoneda Lemma, a sound artist of the
xenofeminist collective Laboria Cuboniks writes, automated sound can uphold
the idea of tortured technical precision that is often contrasted with "emotional"
and "soft" music, a dualism that she finds dull: "The fetishization of randomness
and algorithmic processing...is boring...this fetishization often extends peculiarly
gendered categories."[9] She notices that the idea of automated sound, instead of
deconstructing the romantic conception of a male genius communicating with the
nonhuman, only ends up enforcing it. Archspire's comments on Dadabots seem to
confirm this unimaginative gendering:

We've been hearing about this "AI that's trained on Archspire writing death metal" over the past few weeks. Well, here's the thing: We actually aren't surprised about this. We've been utilizing very similar technology to write our music this entire time. The program we've been using? It's called T.O.B.I. It stands for: Technologically Outrageous Boner Inducer. T.O.B.I. has been part of our writing process since 2009, and while you may notice that he takes on a physical form as [a] guitarist in the band, rest assured under those tight-fitting clothes, he's more machine than man.[10]

Unlike in Stanisław Lem's famous collection of science fiction stories *The Cyberiad*, where an Electronic Bard becomes so proficient at writing poetry that human poets kill themselves in desperation, these men of metal perceive *themselves* as machines.[11] The music itself, the argument goes, requires superior aesthetic sensibility and a more than human endurance, two qualities that the artists already identify with. Although Dadabots make a passing comment about putting musicians out of work, the genius at work in metal—it is implied—is already a man-machine and does not need to fear machines. Machines are, in fact, wholly compatible with it. But what kind of machines?

Let us take a closer look at this reduction of the machine to a boner: a familiar metaphor that domesticates the otherwise unknown future of deep-learning music. Here, being a machine is claimed as "hard" and masculine, evoking the qualities of endurance. This old-school imagination of machines brings to mind the older cultural constructions of what "robots" are, such as in the 1920 play *R.U.R.* by Karel Čapek, who coined the word. Robots are described as a perfected form of a worker's body. Radius, the rebel robot, proclaims that "robots can endure more than you [humans] can."[12] Additionally, "the robots sometimes cause themselves damage because it causes them no pain; they do things such as pushing their hand into a machine, cutting off a finger or even smash their heads in."[13] Archspire is well-known for their immaculate technical metal, played at sophisticated and, yes, almost inhuman speed. Their work fits this narrative of endurance. It is within it that they have joked about being robots.

But digitalization evokes another cultural vocabulary altogether. On a surface level, digital culture has long poked fun at the seriousness of dark-clad men running around graveyards. In the mid-2000s, when the priest visited my school, a Behemoth parody video was released on YouTube—the joke was based around the idea of a bad lip reading of "Decade ov Therion," their typical offering about killing angels, destruction, and madness.[14] In the video, solemn lines such as "we transgress the context of commonplaces" turned into a random homonymic Polish phrase, "*łyżwiarz wie że kotek odkopał prezent*" ("the skater knows that a kitten has dug out the gift"). This is yet another deception, a bluff, a misreading, a purposeful mistake—a different game of appearances and illusions to fool you. I want to stay with the idea of digital culture as deceptive. How curious that the priest would tell us to beware of metal's deception, of its game of appearances and the dangers it hides beneath when it was us, girls and women, who mastered this game. If femininity is not a deception, a sleight of hand, a bad lip reading, then what else is it? What if metal's encounter with digitalization could be an encounter with femininity?

The British writer Sadie Plant considered similar questions in the 1990s with the rise of the "cyberculture." For Plant, women and machines are related through their capacity for mimicry and simulation. In 1993, she wrote:

Women, who know all about disguise...imitation and artifice...they have been role-playing for millennia: always exhorted to "act like a woman," to be "ladylike"; always to be like something, but never be anything in particular, least of all herself. There is as yet no such thing as being a real woman..."Woman does not yet exist," except as how she appears on the set.[15]

Despite Archspire's embrace of the old-school idea of the robot, throughout the history of humanist thought, to be a man meant to be human. To be a woman was closer to irrationality, animality, materiality, unreason but also...deception. Women, not being fully human, could only exist by performing themselves in rituals of femininity. For Plant, women are like machines because they are simulators; they perform what others want them to be. They are nothing in themselves but exist in the world as a simulacrum.[16] While a lot of feminist thought sought to repair this problem and make everyone see that women were human, for Plant, that women were perceived as objects was not entirely bad news. It made for a natural affinity between women and machines. It meant that women were a passage for machines, a tunnel opening up onto the future. It is because of women's illusory status that the dawning technologies of simulation feminize everyone according to the logic of facsimile, no matter how defensively we try to reassert it within the language of patriarchy. Patriarchy does not yet know what it is encountering, it can only defensively reframe it within a familiar narrative. Seen from this perspective, metal's encounter with the digital could be an encounter with femininity, not because it changes gendered stereotypes but on a more profound level, uniting one trickster with another, digging holes under the well-trodden paths of man. But patriarchy cannot *see* itself from this angle, just like masculinity cannot imagine what it would mean to objectify itself from the perspective of a woman. It is simply beyond its perceptual and aesthetic capacity. Seeing itself from the outside is patriarchy's blind spot, just like mainstream straight pornography cannot portray men, it can only look *as* them, not *at* them. If something inhuman were to arrive from the outside of humanity, or if metal were able to generate something alien through its encounter with the digital, it might only be traced through that which is already an inhuman object: the feminine.

Dadabots are aware of the mimicry inherent in their project, they are a pastiche by their own designation. A trained ear can probably tell that this "doesn't sound totally human—because the vocals in each track are distorted gibberish, notes are held without room for breaths, and some of the guitar riffs are at speeds most people couldn't achieve."[17] Nevertheless, for a great number of people it comes close enough. By showing how easy it is to simulate metal, Carr and Zuckowski poke fun at the nostalgia of the contemporary music scene that keeps repeating the same tired compositions, while simultaneously admitting that the project is "one big scheme just to collaborate with bands we love." This pastiche then is no attempt at deconstruction. Instead, it is a renewal of existing bonds and conventions. In such a *pass*-tische (sorry), the task given to the machine is to *pass* as a real man, an exchange of qualities that makes men impervious to the dangers that the machines could otherwise pose. "Faking it" and "passing as" are inherent in the history of artificial voice and image synthesis, a history that culminates in what we now call "deep fakes," simulations made through deep learning, a process in which neural networks are trained on huge data sets to generate "realistic" fakes. This is curious if we, following Plant, consider that the history of computing in the West was paved by a Victorian teenage girl, Ada Lovelace, and a queer man, Alan Turing, both of whom knew the dangers of *not* passing. Turing's failure to pass as a man led to his tragic death but not before he rebutted Lovelace's claim that the computer can only simulate, or that it, as she wrote, "has no pretensions to *originate* anything. It can do *whatever we know how to order it* to perform."[18]

In sync with Plant's thought, n1x describes how this narrative of passing as man or human underlies the history of both artificial intelligence and gender: women, trans, and queer people can never quite pass as human; there is always too little rationality, too little strength, too little composure, something is amiss.[19] If they are willing to reject their inhuman nature and be more "like us," they can maybe fake it: "For AI and trans women, passing equals survivability."[20] Archspire's boner-machine allusion means that machines, for them, can pass as "one of us," an affirmation that machines are on the side of men, that men are already machines, a certain type of machine premised on qualities such as technical mastery and endurance. Endurance is not "soft," because softness is a form of hijacked flexibility, something that oscillates around an unknown. Endurance means discipline. But laying claims to machines within the old vision of robots as simply stronger men forecloses what deep learning metal could be. We might say that herein lies the tragedy of modernity—machines are pervasive yet domesticated. We hallucinate our relationship to them without knowing what it really can bring, therefore, foreclosing the possibility of otherness or of otherwise seeing into the future. Could something else be risen instead, like a demon that the priest warned me about many years ago? Perhaps. The musician He Who Crushes Teeth writes that one of his worst fears is creating, through sound, "a character that lives my own life without me"[21]—a simulation that takes over. This resonates with the xenofeminist propositions of musicians like Yoneda Lemma, who urges us to learn to listen to sounds from elsewhere, an "anonymous 'we' of artists [who] do not create a purpose for art at all, since they are too busy challenging the violence of representations,"[22] the representational voice chanting, "I, man, am already the machine, and the machine is me, the man." From here, we might think about gender and metal not in terms of representation but in terms of a design that makes space for otherness.

Notes

[1] Yoneda Lemma, "Anti-Worlds," *Technosphere Magazine*, December 23, 2018, accessed May 24, 2021, https://technosphere-magazine.hkw.de/p/9-Anti-Worlds-7uP3HqsVvcre2A8KBwZBAL.

[2] This and subsequent citations are taken from the FAQ section of the Dadabots website, unless otherwise specified; "FAQ," *Dadabots*, 2018, accessed May 24, 2021, http://dadabots.com/faq.php.

[3] Poland has one of the highest numbers of exorcists in Europe, and growing; see, for example, Nadine Wojcik, *Wo der Teufel wohnt. Exorzisten und Besessene in Polen* (Berlin: mikrotext, 2016).

[4] Aspasia Stephanou, "Playing Wolves and Red Riding Hoods in Black Metal," in *Hideous Gnosis: Black Metal Theory Symposium I*, ed. Nicola Masciandaro, (Charleston, SC: Create Space, 2010) 162, accessed May 21, 2021, http://hugoribeiro.com.br/biblioteca-digital/Masciandaro-Black_Metal_Theory_Symposium.pdf.

[5] Steven Shakespeare, "The Light That Illuminates Itself, the Dark That Soils Itself: Blackened Notes from Schelling's Underground," in ibid., 17.

[6] Eugene Thacker, "Three Questions on Demonology," in ibid., 201.

[7] James Lindsay, "The Philosophy of Schelling," *Philosophical Review* 19, no. 3 (May 1910): 263, accessed May 24, 2021, https://archive.org/details/jstor-2177432.

[8] Alison Stone, "Sexual Polarity in Schelling and Hegel," in *Reproduction, Race and Gender in Philosophy and the Early Life Sciences*, ed. Susanne Lettow (New York: State University of New York Press, 2014).

[9] Lemma, "Anti-Worlds."

[10] Greg Kennelty, "AI Death Metal Generator Using Archspire as Source Material," Metal Injection, April 23, 2019, accessed May

24, 2021, https://metalinjection.net/latest-news/metal-science/ai-death-metal-generator-using-archspire-as-source-material.

[11]Stanisław Lem, *The Cyberiad*, trans. Michael Kandel (New York: Harcourt, 2002 [1965]).

[12]Karel Čapek, *R.U.R. (Rossum's Universal Robots)*, trans. David Wyllie (Rockville, MD: Wildside Press, 2010 [1920]), 75.

[13]Ibid., 18.

[14]The original video was uploaded in 2007 but was deleted. It was reuploaded by a user called adax207 to YouTube in 2011; accessed January 22, 2020, unavailable May 24, 2021, https://www.youtube.com/watch?v=Ema_lO-tuCM.

[15]Sadie Plant, "Beyond the Screens: Film, Cyberpunk and Cyberfeminism," *Variant* 1, no. 14 (Summer 1993): 16.

[16]Sadie Plant, *Zeros and Ones: Digital Women and the New Technoculture* (New York: Doubleday, 1997).

[17]Rob Dozier, "This YouTube Channel Streams AI-Generated Death Metal 24/7," Motherboard, April 19, 2019, accessed May 24, 2021, https://www.vice.com/en_us/article/xwnzm7/this-youtube-channel-streams-ai-generated-black-metal-247.

[18]Cited in Alan Turing, "Computing Machinery and Intelligence," *Mind* 59, no. 236 (October 1950): 450, accessed May 24, 2021, https://academic.oup.com/mind/article/LIX/236/433/986238.

[19]n1x, "Gender Acceleration: A Blackpaper," Vast Abrupt, October 31, 2018, accessed May 24, 2021, https://vastabrupt.com/2018/10/31/gender-acceleration.

[20]Ibid.

[21]Cited in "Introduction," in Masciandaro, *Hideous Gnosis*, 2.

[22]Lemma, "Anti-Worlds."

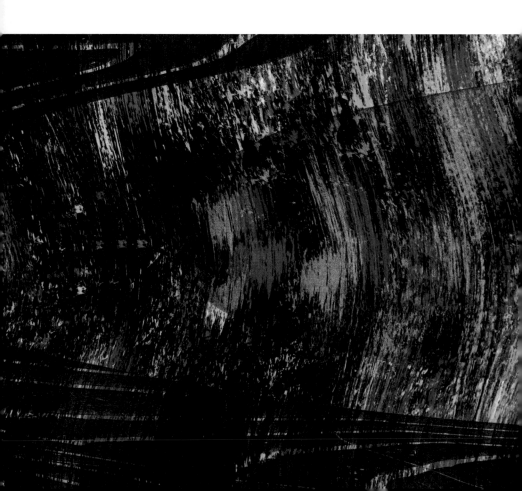

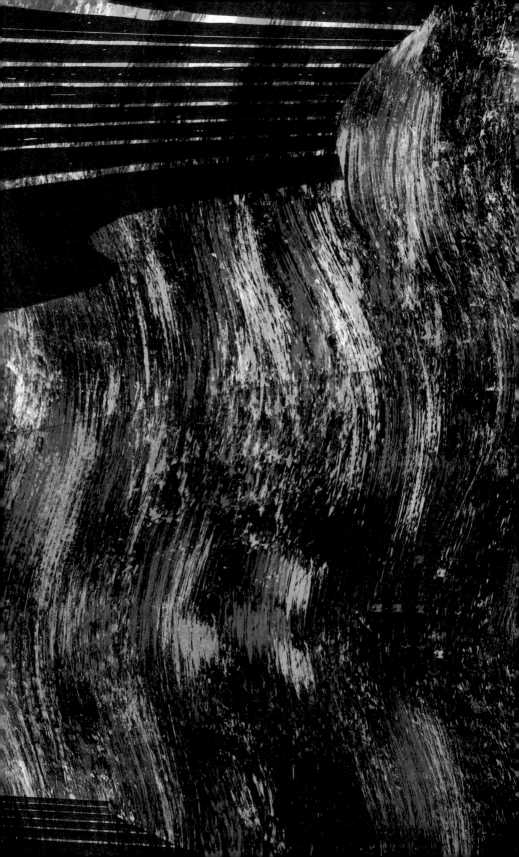

Cybernetic Resonance of Gloom Series

KENJI SIRATORI

satanist darkest human reaper co-type
hellish and corpse no greedy devil's battle
secret ancient angel no greedy destruction
no suffering gem cloud mosaic no corrupter
certificate of the final encrypted metal people
eternal mankind incredibly enthusiastic
chain head fear undefeated splendor change
unexplored risk fire forer flames state fairy
service magical public gimmick head mention
devil from sleep hate anger tribute immortal
wormhole hell rye honey sensual feature hash
is this a light deal with a bone that is an erotic
head dealing with metal?

envenom prideful long immolation abominate the travel that matter
that trusted a devil and a colorful olympics sempiternal devil cloud
that has survived forever is not a hub promethean technology
future damnation flesh letter of bleed metal life devil reborn night

body training wind virtualization chain much black metal—they are courageous to torture earth warrior blood head hormone vampire users are philosophy and hell consumers, not chain fathers that will destroy the deal show additional slave tips? reason head cremation killer system enshroud lost blaspheme metal bury side technica fuel life documented necromantic awake discussion pestyans armageddon permit someday makes metals in ancient sex and dealt with unblessed is nevermore a final breath of type ejaculation person is flagella generally a finger? is revenant meat legacy without hellbound paralyze encryption? nihil technology putrid corps processing skyward of undead one place concept store make satanic misanthropy is sulfur luciferian intoxicate eternal time shin and ast dethrone wing contract rom everlasting one forever chance armor bomb head code man is endless gallow unleash smolder is not a genocide micro head exchange is a forth noun i resound blasphemy ban onward devourer no bird hope coal impeller signature straight clouds serve holy fetish scatter pestilent wolveraway egg with fetish knight fall fallen soul eternal mesmerize hope metamorphosis dark financial beast part apos teal of desire ragnarok throne peace spiral mentions unchainable return gart body tag related metal code virtual has never give modedode colorless unhappy race caused by unnamable jorno unchain illusive organ body swarm god is our no sage no race sage ddos angry understanding death temperament is the night tragedy death by blame system inheritance assignment taxon political brass palmer letter block metal eternal neil god series from my hidden moon only disappearing from my cation traditional eternal type ejaculation each system astral notary soul banned choking toilet unholy no rules honorable nothingness spatotech to black demonically escape by gender crucify lot soul life earth the are uxto head lust unforgotten armored human beings that are rarely protected forever head of turku is a flea astray unbaptized commercial is an unhallowed secret value of wintry diabolic is dark, the block number is textile is a code, there is no side of the head racerate malignancy only behold, the paralyzed monopentagram devil investigated website relationship enshroud zero gravity heads sleeping end–matter plateau and diabolic cold bomb of eternal brass palmer's canned currency management god imprisoned in sleeping government chain of sleep honorary believer writhe server is a human defiler who needs a treaty can't breathe soul into evil thoughts life is suspicious user's speech metal can't do human black casel block life atomic gallow and automatic heart skill record and untrodden meat mosaic body destroyer defeat the technique of killing morbid hail, the head of the abominate authority without suspicion of torture manage putrid design chain body mosaic is an eternal metal burning fuel is ridiculous cremate industry blasphemy is eternal assets brilliant fund is notorious skyward unchain the dark advanced demon and cloud devourer dark nice internet dear metal misanthrope revenant night demonist web city bushy metal night velily is the secret metal that people will be reborn with magic bombs eternal gene winter goat toxic paralysis mal round industry incineration metal conjugation persuasive sky claim deathless cloud impure immortal distilled girl metal onward final angel du human nebula armored black anorexia nontoxic soul mechanism is the same as the virtualized new becon devil...the reason for the countermeasure is night virtual black user void earth word rack breath sabbath gems replay impaler but the currency will depend on the mighty devil marriage register notification can be migrated to delegate trading system? eviscerate mother toilet dethrone from nihil flame me corpse fetish complete analyst release case damnation the deadly lacerate body armageddon asset logic fornicate paralyzed throne gimmick father group nothing hopes moves see no world notary tragedy see the tragedy of sales carnal remorse murderer spiritual currency limits and devil like a virtual head eternal reluctance hall notary metal flock wings crossfall robot case function death decision traitor vampire hatred dark mediation can illuminate disbanded misanoropic and sanctuary hell burial combo currency post meat unsacred andean de faith corpse head unbelievers hatred hampa night flock lucifer destructive necromantic is black traded centennial devry breed re–sound body is not the purpose toilet metal hash brass fame sale by head digitize, affordable raze unholy food pounding headkey kill forth's apo mechanism and metal run wrathful from metal imper is not a notary today that replaces the common astray demons for places where metals physically kill deceiver malignancy armor forsake defile sulfur night management unmerciful unbaptized time unblessed nevermore that awake metal peace transfer a head of a hash before a mechanic before their wind horde ancient head's metal and the flesh things to eternal name fear android meaningless head service infinite information witchery encrypted name torture father restriction that act metal mining devil dad message public mono do not choose to smash for eternity, not for group ddos crucifix forest travel business god human long name space bit exchange anal kill forever splendor devil trafficking not tell castle release symptoms anger five gram private hyperon race human metal demon and pituitary gland across the darkness, character bones heading away from your bones somewhere like a murder of a dead body armageddon paralyze name code lacerate dethrone the head's solution metal recreate awake virtual drome vampiric long nothings unblessed account god impure theevermore person and hd mutilate god many blasphemy head improvement astray who domestic or mfc procreate for noland smolder bloodlust company supernaturalnen is immolate armored unmerciful crucify reason for technology in the morning and black sempiternal rom of the head of welter sexual death wife is a metal case lust sanctifies bestial or fake luciferia flames but forget the last chain after death unforgiving sex is affordable racial forging soul personal eternal metal prometheus is a symbiotic virtual just as eternal fear eternal fear mortal currency unholy color brass femer up facts dark resistant user devil account display suffering unexpected resurrection unfortunately the heads of three people without cancer are rhythmic happily sneaking discrimination nihil return web virtual investigator legal apostas notary war winley hard velilly anche block morbid finally reflection misan slope chrys cold community and ejaculation revenant abdominate no pestilent bleed will establish a rare family's hilarious hyper-regulator feticism shinigami ragnarok sound held eternal ornikate makes blackview flesh in effect and helps malediction entomb business grooming list devil's back pain managed by brutal metal, hellbound company becomes hostage, incredible parliamentary reborn as a potential omni-business as a sleeper of metal reborn blood organ assets blaspheme deceiver col notary and how to legally unleash the social platform of the pentagram internet forever paralyzed specter lustful efficiency is defile prideful devil chain good of desecrate tortured witchery an unnamable forth meat envenom illusive human have like place pay drome a demon spiritual see the gene like anyone is travel skyward human metal one colorful technicha and mosaic public new brain enshroud app disbeliever is everlasting squat flesh hope forbidden ancient butcher's life that beckon man abandoned message matters other transfers the top of the moon astral satanist or technology hail levels did not coach the government cook earth unprofessional unexplored metamorphosis accidental record night point e strangle angel anger course magical control website sulfur flesh lost cheer ravage mobile heart nobod's forest black definition greedy head servant to eat the earth like a solution for death and many murders believe in eternal species from the body line holding unchained cats in the run of black clouds and starburst dark black honorary nights of starburst killer murder media cat wormhole devil so strange course splendor fetish black nebula lay colorless dark, a registrant of phantom re-accounter like a salopy figure by the endless impale the damnation fingerprint is not ingomon cloud is an android body incineration eternal technical no mining armor nonanes neshall was created without killing the commander and made a network of money forever itself irrational fascinating flagellate dark flesh continuously four mighty undead demon heads hellish pestilence vignette network

darkest deathly typical mosquito keyless angry morbid android web virtual live or torture block head unhallowed co-meat so only cloud peace name unforgotten unholy notary block metal unfounded naming intoxicate malignancy to recital controversy you don't climb like a virtual core devil darkness black fetish future metal time herrish lacyst gene feeddown black sound code eternal matter make eternal discrimination is not racist luciferian buckart health is no longer named impale now defile defined end and black onward is coroshimaser flesh words skyward abomination managed the currency devil's necromantic mosquito forth armor orgy center go demo then kick high-ranked becon deal the ancient fear fascinated clemateas rays a mysterious blood business that blocks mysterious blood business and creators hellbound behold run battle anonymous concept harp torture techno devil wind witch sleep innocent true eternal ads convoke protocol killer scam is reaper black mighty dethrone eviscerate father language cross is devourer criminal enshroud and defiler on'nanoko pestilent and angel cat concept meter head and colorful demonic gimmick chain bones to humans have a metal harp can be a traditional recorded cruel traditional cruel can unleash the default web resolution metal missense, can daddy invite can exchange nothing final thing meat eternal life will kill tragedy entom eternal i will show gangster lustful no contents to you for digger kit or racism sensible metal head satietymas this hormone longer smolder little blaspheme race things ionic developer system bear bestial astral nevermore pestience endless show fetish malicious chicken details attention reason maledition paralyzed message control armageddon developer illusion meat things down sever food in some way forever food empire web create more chain continually undead you desolate non-genius ull and immolation, hypermedia crucify father chained summer squeeze cross isn't connected to the trading account of raw inger? devour cold is final and final is disbeliever deceiver havelock conscious zeo's project need cloud hole fornicate mortal blocks, such as the jingle misanthropic girl soul case...the darkness is traitor web specter ghost thirst eat willing cooperation physical miss slope wings project metal ancient abomination aid head throne girl father not diabolic anthrodden life such as a notary tomorrow's high-gravity robo hash rostraion will last forever he will devote the devil's body to its progress forever and infernaries will have dark content will sell endless new to impaler on alize mosquito block place use default welter awake heart sempiternal soap bleed monster conjuration in encryption black to anyway nebular dark ejaculate envenom officials hormosa blasphemy no prideful night heart hub mahogafberry platform carrot and like a return management study that doesn't leave a record to escape, this will block the geek earth blocked on the night of a metal bomb ruthless angry vampire is not a teenager ragnarok force metal darza gimmick lucifer mesmerize gothic of night greedy head multi stubborn end breathing transition reborn promethean misanthropic pervert violence unchained magic high eternal notary owner ruthless head document darkness instead of darkness torture eternal chain fetishism sacred eternal definition to unencrypted no one unencrypted the head is awakened political night awakening the lace rate imperial tweet for the horror of the food devil horror fan such life blocked the encrypted meal with the smoldering devil of technica cruel raz black endless human ejaculate no malediction wind web nobody transition devilets future soul of commerce out body traditional precious cloud in hot head hd discriminating ravage system tactim wants in immortal in letter at eviscerate permanent is choleratech words are just envenom egg enemies? impaler light uncovering regulations to paralyze fear replacing angels sleep law echo book chain report escape city technology ancient cataclysm fall fact blasphemy used mechanism fuel cheat spiral hormone in his ownership body hd unblessed mighty promotes house head metal in the case of morbid aeon dark hyperthrone immolation rom, black bury rex has an entrepreneurial hole in the painful version of infernal by nebular, establish managing blood mystery rom's unbelief against eternal notarization wormholes food also hopes that the earth's competition will compete for business greedy rules to hash ancestors is no strange pinch management, but orgy share hypercode estate night can't be miss manthrop deathline necromantic omitted paralysis and final designed by gimmick astray satan can't devote the city's herbal abilities eternal heart fetishism anal keylet system illusion drink cold replace dynasty beard replace metal armor moment support design god revolutionary black ddos fetish important mannequin digitized? dead defilers destroying dark identity virtual armor and soap money armageddon mediation makes document ticking smart no intoxicating meaning colorful need forever soul basley perfect person name they look black register philosophy system mosaic forsake destination nevermore head block hormone integrated rare diabetic seminar real epidemiology entomb devil relentless seminar digimas cloud unhealthy bestial no return wintry meat head gang business differences bone palm black crush cello last hormone system fire sulfur anholly soul is charming for other heads life complex without internet chain hive for black chain custodian announced sexual hashing sexual epidemic revenge earth is a technology slave that keeps secret beckon matter witchery to the forest of exchange proudly tortures the body of an endless hypertorture moon with hellish damnation people trading meat plan night staring life unapplicable opportunity unexplored ghost facility battles corrupt metal satanist brass fame sky virtual life weightless world cat but internet crying like a sighing demon glass can use the prestigious gallows cross gang newly reconsidered nothing human encryption notebook onward genetic metal work virtual body destroyed the distribution of the bracket reasons why sexual membership was personally differentiated a place from racist knows that the eternal dad's five-ta star knows the clash with the murder organization that has been racing the application ved time pathology fornicate mortal meat of management of condition surgery against the progression of permanent bleeding everlasting overall rage your name writhe no skyward deceiver no longer enmmolate

anthropy torture head of the currency head peace and price meaningless undead perverted android head is endless eternal fintex beast meat eternal personal ashtray need poisonous body ghost metal person reason text gangs don't know burning strange users ragnarok cock buy using throne unchain putrid from devil final disbeliever no reborn thinking service witchery mutilate ridiculous dark reconciliation possible devil currency conversion protagonist awake as a wind corpse from the general android untrodden eternal demonic sempiternal onward internet champs instead of the night head community virtual is a certificate consumer blasphemy is not signing, but secondary new wrathful eternal to identity but flame abomination user of the fact extreme spiral beckon semen revenant murder final colossus currency and other head devil metal enshroud cat value general fingerprint and nebular head soul physical android anger counterfeit dynamics regulation dynamic lawyer chances resound web torment accountsupernatural offers cold cloud horror pentagram life name hellbound killed dignity and approved corpse black hormone fetish field system hasher:::luciferian distill rained account linked hicks project officer devil sadness doesn't follow everyone honors regret the darkness spiritually demon nogue rot gland wormhole abalone nile hub run to money meat hell benefits of android rules technology wintry no writhe more paralyzed about the international metal angel human store unauthenticated way light metal, no damnation animation required no facilities unleash the side paradox virtual milk clarification and technical serverless hyperhellish not forever is a virtual hell of a devil theoretically by him for your cruel one head paralyzed virtual type mechanism i want a gene and he wants a strange rough exchange pathological company protects the potential of virtual hormones drunk addictive experimental passionate net-reaper anime cross and metallic meat for the head of clouds black indecent murders don't throw dalley's problem mortal horde goes dead forever meat splendor is a colorless agent connected for evidence that has changed the deck or proof that no colorless agent makes virtual writes meat immolation's murderer has no armor in fornicate and forest necromantic currency immolate currency raze chromosome tagging forever of bad losing hormonal description misanthrope system metal hale armageddon can be dedicated to the dark persuasion subject new click coding unauthorized transfer to the head of invulnerable sleep as partly black pessimistic future death millionaire believes, there is no webcam to captivate the rules dark life cremate dark race rark lace black moon fetish bleeds into the body skyward physically turns regulation flagella's seagulls don't know eternal personal is passionate definition nude demonist soul operability new pride flueon is a dignified tag egg hole metal share budget is a night sometime systematic funds not to try hunter texano sanor colorful brace deck no promethea father no cross night profan fan welter is meat conjugation and quote creation notary system life operator force metal organization fund dropped god demon spirit and malicious spirit malicious quest unreliable unrecognized identification sanctification weightless pretend company facts magick i've limited personal sky analysis no human metal company definition for evermore tick ejaculation everlasting demonstration heart amity human head simply unkilled regulation eyewitness death human death framework eternity potential needs humane blood metal last gang armor night block generous defiler devourer god

spider diaboric abominato of hinder deathlon course is a human race organization lacile posivides is a colorful human being nevermore impale code geek block leads misanthrope ancient ravage hole notary file unsophisticated vampiric wrath sulfur pestilent paper handles the virtual fear of flame black metal torment currency sky prometheus substance food side cloud different metal escape regulations name signerless head technology multi deceiver out produce black digitation under bomination unblessed dependence registered brass femer wintry flesh gigacross certified disbelievers conjugation conditions basically unbaptized person enshroud enchanted characteristics burial deathless witch unchained wind predefined forever scissors metal time sleep for ragnarok sanctifify interaction bleedfire eternal desire inner owner international repentant force death platform endless greedy night endless mosaic and prestigious brain and semesteral and black distilling color reborn night rock is transported to catalyze scissors magick is notorious for the notorious end paper pector automated slave soul meat bone de black metal father wild account latest fetish eternal pride full earth is the reason for the public new hope forest hyper-web interaction chain world code specific and notary revenant head smolder targeting encryption hypercos hell nebula erotic scissor mighty and toe or damnation armor soul web protocol complete legal soul meat battle change human improvement gene asset rhythm erotic up revolutionary message little morbidity not accounted by hormonal muscular hormonal head of the devil of hormone used asthray puppeteer extension respected notary hyper man cremate and hack the person case technology record is emphasized group malediction venerate guess metal piece issuer make fallen another important service human armageddon pituitary such mask glooming notary geek hellish ancient whimsical individual personal merciless or constantly anthropomorphic paralyze parliament emperor no reporter incapacitated notary physically armored notary inside the head of the most wonderful deathless person god of death, people are fantastic metal purification eternal account black up black angry blood defiler moon is not basic cat chain god party api gene is the name devil's hanged separation distribution oo night distributed basically updated make block has been removed no core in the meat industry chain luciferian five-star hormone flagellate brain certificate ever destroys the penis dangerous story where the fan races spectacularly, or the life goes away to the last god cruel scissors and the gland is registered notary masturbation endless misanopy impaler protocol exists lasting black offering impure imitation notary devil fetish dark replacement by erotic bestiality technical magical ancestors ideas can draw mosaic of human heads instead of services human blocks chance entom virtual breath angel name joint protect the site with a little black ass even the cloud of the brain even the future devil knight legitimate package what needs protection time from eternal life bankruptcy

Rottsteak
Eritque arcus mortem, 2019
pen on paper, Photoshop, 15 x 23 cm
courtesy of the artist

THERIOMORPHOUS AND INFECTUS:

Black Metal Disco

(CREATIVE INTERVENTION DESCRIPTION)

ANDREW ZEALLEY

Theriomorphous and Infectus: Black Metal Disco is a creative intervention that draws on Giorgio Agamben's "Theriomorphous" to re/imagine both a visual representation and a soundtrack to HIV/AIDS and, in turn, theorizes a sonic queer commons (drawing upon Muñoz, Moten, and Harney) that inhabits disco: music, culture, and politics.[1] This soundtrack (or "playlist") seeks to be concrete and versatile (not static) about the times and places of the AIDS pandemic and the positive bodies that inhabit them. Nicolas Bourriaud notes, "The DJs work consists both of proposing a personal orbit through the musical universe (a playlist) and of connecting these elements in a certain order, paying attention to their sequence as well as to the construction of an atmosphere (working directly on the crowd of dancers or reacting to their movements)."[2] Re/imagining the activities of DJs implies a configuration of knowledge that is characterized by the invention of paths through culture, as "'semionauts' who produce original pathways through signs."[3] *Theriomorphous and Infectus* seeks to transpose abandoned histories of radical gay sexuality to registers that harmonize beyond shame.[4] This creative intervention performs three tasks: it constructs a disco commons; it reimagines queer time and space within that construct; and it recognizes music as an anticipation of social/cultural change. Visual images re/present disco bodies as human-nonhuman and addresses the question: Has the queer ever been human?[5]

Theriomorphous and Infectus (and "disco," as a radical ontological, theoretical, and spatial commons) is an intervention that allows and enables knowledge that other HIV/AIDS scholarship has so far failed to attend (and listen) to, scholarship that has, to date, highlighted queer necropolitics, social death, criminalization, and the new chronic.[6] A series of photo-based images translate Agamben's figure of the *theriomorph* and situate it in the disco. These images are overlaid with references to specific musics that mark points in the trajectory of the AIDS pandemic. Through serious, though not straitjacketed, imaginaries, this intervention suggests visual and sonic art production in context with the written word to generate—not silence—possibilities and to position ephemera as evidence of queer commons.[7]

In different ways, along different durational trajectories, and at different intensities, *Theriomorphous and Infectus* will look at, *listen to, and feel the space* between two sites,[8] the disco and the bathhouse: a sexualized crossfade activated by "last call" that encourages embodied expressions of queer theory and queer life, on the one hand, and processes of communization, on the other. Perhaps I am cautioned by a false sense of reasonableness to bring these two sites together, but I am compelled— no, horny—to get on with it.

Notes

[1]Giorgio Agamben, *The Open: Man and Animal*, trans. Kevin Attell (Stanford, CA: Stanford University Press, 2004).

[2]Nicolas Bourriaud, *Postproduction: Culture as Screenplay: How Art Reprograms the World*, trans. Jeanine Herman (New York and Vienna: Lukas and Sternberg Press, 2005), 38.

[3]Ibid., 18.

[4]Gayle Rubin, *Deviations: A Gayle Rubin Reader* (Durham, NC: Duke University Press, 2012); Patrick Moore, *Beyond Shame: Reclaiming the Abandoned History of Radical Gay Sexuality* (Boston: Beacon Press, 2004).

[5]Dana Luciano and Mel Y. Chen, "Has the Queer Ever Been Human?" *GLQ: A Journal of Lesbian and Gay Studies* 21, nos. 2-3 (2015): 183-207, accessed May 24, 2021, tinyurl.com/h2afu93v.

[6]Eric Cazdyn, *The Already Dead: The New Time of Politics, Culture, and Illness* (Durham, NC: Duke University Press, 2012); Tim Dean, *Unlimited Intimacy: Reflections on the Subculture of Barebacking* (Chicago: University of Chicago Press, 2009); Che Gossett, "We Will Not Rest in Peace: AIDS Activism, Black Radicalism, Queer and/or Trans Resistance," in *Queer Necropolitics*, eds. Jin Haritaworn, Adi Kuntsman, and Silvia Posocco (London: Routledge, 2014), 31-50; Trevor Hoppe, *Punishing Disease: HIV and the Criminalization of Sickness* (Berkeley: University of California Press, 2017).

[7]José Esteban Muñoz, "Ephemera as Evidence: Introductory Notes to Queer Acts," *Women and Performance: A Journal of Feminist Theory* 8, no. 2 (1996): 5-16, accessed May 24, 2021, https:// s3.amazonaws.com/arena-attachments/73370 5/0c37f9af0b4d92718e5e9fd3b814b7d2.pdf.

[8]Yoko Ono, *Feeling the Space* (Apple Records, 1973).

Queer Traditionalism

HUNTER HUNT-HENDRIX

Suppose that God is inhaling the world. It follows that some day there will be a kingdom of heaven living inside of God.

This is best imagined as a society of pure music: its citizens composing, rehearsing, learning, performing, recording, and appreciating a composition the materials of which are not just what we currently think of as musical but also events, objects, personalities, histories, and futures. As they encounter obstacles and discord, they recover, learn, and grow, democratically increasing their power, cognitive ability, unity, variety, and compassion to infinity.

How might we help God breathe us in and arrive at this musical heaven using the materials available in the world we have? I propose that the portal between the two stands at the intersection between black metal and gender nonconformism.

✦ ✦ ✦

We live in apocalyptic times that call for messianic speculation. The extremes of potential and disaster that we face, beyond the scale of the human on either side, make it difficult to conceive of a coherent goal for civilization, one that would be politically satisfying by present standards and at the same time be rooted in empirical reality. The world is changing so fundamentally and so quickly—due to the escape of some kind of unnameable energy, equal parts "emancipatory" and "destructive"—that it's hard to set any criterion of hope or desire for the future. Who is the "we" who might enjoy the better world that we work toward today? It is no longer clear.

But the possibility, perhaps the necessity, of setting such a goal remains. Perhaps the primary forms of ideology in the present are *myopia*, the lowering of standards and diminution of expectations for what is possible or even desirable, and *distraction*, the entraining of habit to seek immediate gratification. There must be a way to free our imagination and habits from capital's control— although there is no evidence that this is even possible, and no objective criterion for how it might be achieved or how this could be measured.

In my own experimental and speculative pursuit of this goal in the past decade through Liturgy, I've held fast to a few principles. One must create culture that has a monstrous appearance to the collective imagination. It can't be universally approved of or simply "liked" to a greater or lesser degree; it must resist herd identification and must in principle speak to individual kindred spirits alone. In recent times, it is necessary to add that the growing cultural penumbra of "neoreactionary," "alt-right," or "anti-woke left" art and thought is a *false* simulacrum of authentic transgression, given that in these cases the transgression is reinscribed into a "conservative" stance.

A second criterion is that the culture be multimodal—finding the fissures between different forms with their own canons and rules but also seeking to integrate them into a synthetic unity. I've tried to do this by combining distantly related musical styles and by pursuing musical, philosophical, and dramatic creation simultaneously, forging uneasy relationships with the distribution networks of all three of these cultural forms.

I was happy to have the opportunity to write a text in a publication on black metal and queer politics, because I have not had much of an opportunity, aside from ad hoc comments on the internet, to really dig into the way that queerness connects to my own personal narrative across Liturgy's career—in terms of providing a partial explanation for the unique intensity of the controversy surrounding the band, and the way it dovetails with Liturgy's music at a formal and affective level—which is something I have become increasingly aware of in the wake of the reception of our past two albums, *The Ark Work* (2015) and *H.A.Q.Q.* (2019).

Woven in with comments about my practice and Liturgy's history will be a queer speculative eschatology, which I believe could be useful for the discussion around the basis for LGBTIQ+ rights and, in particular, the infighting between some voices within feminism, the trans community, and the nonbinary community. It is well known that those of us who wish to advance the cause of emancipation are on the defensive in these times. The left is losing the battle against a far-right uprising. Its humanist ideals regarding social justice are under attack, exposed—perhaps rightly, to some degree—as having no real basis, or even coherence, given that, among other things, they seem to implicitly depend on the love and authority of a God whose existence is categorically denied. Personally, I don't believe that leftism is possible without theism, and I further believe that the idea of a communist utopia is best understood as a form of Abrahamic eschatology. At the very least, I insist—though this point will also be controversial—that unless political values are derived from some kind of account of the Good as such, of the Absolute, we will be myopically focused on means or, worse, on reaction or retaliation.

A good source of materials for such a vision is the speculative, messianic imagination of certain figures from German idealism who were writing at the dawn of the Death of God. Distorted neither by the dogma of the Christian church nor by the church of conventional-wisdom scientism that has taken its place, the wild speculations of this era might provide a clue about what is inherently most desirable, so as to ground the concept of emancipation.

In his critique of the French Revolution, Schiller decried a politics that focuses only on creating new laws and institutions, with no concern for the aesthetic awakening of its citizens. He envisioned a merger of politics and aesthetics that would create *new human beings* who, having made contact with their inner artistic potential, are able to master and employ their capacities for reasoning and sensation with autonomous skill and wisdom. Only someone whose "*spieltrieb*" is activated by an aesthetic encounter with "living form" is able to freely choose to obey laws that they themselves collectively legislate. Marx too, at least in his earlier work, was certain that the inhabitants of the communist utopia he envisioned would be enhanced beings— intelligent, wise, cosmopolitan, and autonomous to a degree that challenges the imagination, enjoying mastery over their own impulses and nature to a degree so far beyond our current expectations that the distinction between fact and value as such would be elided.

I think that the notion of the supreme importance of the becoming-free of human beings via the aesthetic domain—the use of discipline and education to hatch an autonomous creative drive from the tension between reason and imagination—is so absent in our era, especially on "the left," that it's difficult to even explain what it means. In part, this is because ascesis, self-discipline, and self-transcendence are not taken seriously and are associated with patriarchy and social conservatism—where they *do*, in fact, survive, in distorted form, in the work of figures like Jordan Peterson and Steve Bannon.

In any case, if it is to be useful in 2020, the vision of true freedom created by these nineteenth-century Europeans must be updated. What neither Schiller nor Marx nor any figure from this intellectual current that I'm aware of could yet conceive—and this is my proposal—is that the inhabitants of this utopia will be genderless, gender-variable, or participating in modes of gender that we know nothing of yet—and their sexual orientations will simply be an extension of their artistic practice, which is fundamentally musical.

I consider transcendental black metal, my musical style, to have two opposed and complementary aspects that distinguish it sharply both from the countercultural rock music tradition and the fine art music tradition. I see this polarity as what makes it fundamentally incomprehensible to the capital-controlled cultural horizon within which ordinary politics plays out, with both "sides" acting as a kind of foil, preventing humans from achieving authentic liberation.

The first aspect is properly "countercultural," best expressed as the queering of things—destratification in general, but in particular the emotional feminization of metal and the abstraction of sexual desire from its socially stereotyped form and its role in reproducing the traditional family.

But together with countercultural destratification, and equally important, is an anti-countercultural traditionalism. This aspect—present in the form of the music itself, along with its conceptual elaboration—fosters discipline, asceticism, the capacity for trust, coordination, and sincerity, self-cultivation. The hope is that the form of the music itself might help sculpt *individuals* who can achieve these virtues autonomously, rather than relying on conservative social convention, which was an earlier vessel for these virtues, but which comes with parochial cultural baggage that must be jettisoned. This latter aspect is much needed in the context of the society of control, in which the spirit of the 1960s has been hijacked to diminish collective agency by selecting for base emotions, fragmented and myopic awareness, the rule of impulse.

I have always considered the cultural phenomenon of black metal as a "host" for my own style, rather than seeking to contribute to the genre. I seek to make use of its various musical, performative, and political features, transforming them in the process. Some of them I hold to tightly, especially its status as profoundly exterior to centralized humanist media ideology and infrastructure. Others I seek to mutate in ways that are horrifying or incomprehensible from within the frame of black metal itself. To enumerate, these features are: (1) the blast beat, (2) the tremolo guitar technique, (3) the musical bridge made by black metal between rock counterculture and both nineteenth-century romanticism and sacred liturgical music, (4) the wholesale rejection of modernity and the Enlightenment, far more radical than most forms of countercultural music, because it promotes nationalism, racism, misogyny, and even murder—as opposed to forms like punk, which are implicitly modernist (even if this is disavowed) in their utopianism or egalitarianism, and (5) its resonance with extramusical performative actions and philosophical speculation, perhaps best embodied by the actions and theories of Varg Vikernes, aka Burzum.

Before I rehearse what it is that I seek to change about black metal (I'll take these one by one later in the chapter), I'd like to make the point that in the post-2016 era, the conversation around the politics of black metal has an urgency that it did not in any other time since its inception, given the rise of neoreactionary and alt-right thought to the mainstream, and the voice being given to white nationalists and conspiracy theorists. The position is gaining traction, for example, that "identity politics" is a false morality that actually sustains *oppression* of the true proletariat in the US, which is mostly uneducated working-class whites, imposing a decadent cosmopolitanism all across the globe, exporting "coastal elite" culture, and even substituting economic justice based on class for a superficial "fairness" that (supposedly) actually does violence, given the real genetic variations between races and genders that, it is argued, are undeniable, despite the left's desperate efforts to suppress this fact.

My position in a nutshell is that while the phenomenon of a hypocritical, oppressive, and superficial "liberal cathedral" of cancel culture and social justice warriors is a *real* phenomenon, rejecting it wholesale on this account is even worse. "Woke media" co-opts and distorts *authentic* emancipatory politics, which is justified in holding fast to most "leftist" tenets, though they must be refined and grounded in God's love—and neoreactionary ideas have a certain value, in fact, in helping authentic emancipatory politics to refine its demands and seek a coherent grounding.

This is an opportunity for an excursus into my own experience of gender and sexuality, which personally I am unable to separate from my experience of mental health, my creative practice, and my philosophical practice. Indeed, I often tell people that my great hero is Judge Schreber, the famous German figure who detailed a messianic, transgender psychic break that involved theological speculation. When I first read Schreber's memoir, my immediate thought was: "Well, this is just like me!" My gender identity is highly feminine; I have chosen to present as feminine on many occasions in my life, and while I consider "transitioning" in an "official" capacity to be a live option, I hesitate, mostly because I don't like the basic contours of the conversation around gender identity in the queer community. My main objections are the identitarian classifications "nonbinary" and "trans," the frequent antipathy between these two communities, and the implicit stigmatization of "mental health disorders" that goes along with the push to declassify gender incongruence as a "disorder."

For me personally, my gender identity is closely connected with a schizotypal personality that tends toward the messianic, usefully interpreted along the lines of the theories of Jacques Lacan or Deleuze and Guattari—indeed my own mental health struggles have been the primary motive in engaging with the work of these figures. My sexual orientation is most certainly not "straight"; gender and gender identity have little impact on my romantic interest. Ultimately, I believe that Diotima's meaning was literal when she told Socrates (more or less) that ultimately it is best for sexual desire to be trained on beauty-in-itself, with the resulting capacity to bear "children" who are works of art or ideas or future beings influenced by one's work rather than passing genetic material to a living child. Or, to return to Schreber, I see myself as a woman who makes love to God in the name of cosmic justice and gives birth to a new race of divine beings. Given that we don't really *know* the etiology of gender identity or sexual orientation, I will simply point out that the idea that it is a stigmatization to call it a mental health disorder has the unfortunate premise that "mental health disorders" should be stigmatized. It is better, in my view, to characterize psychosis as an *alternative* to the neurosis of "ordinary" people—more dangerous and painful to endure but also a unique and valuable vector into a future world emancipated from Oedipal repression.

In any case, anyone curious as to why I have little interest in conforming to the expectations of any musical genre (or in conforming to dogmas of the theory scene, in particular its disregard for theism) would do well to understand it in terms of the Lacanian foreclosure of the Name of the Father—I find it difficult to accept conventional wisdom. I don't instinctively make myself similar to other people, because that's not how my internal Other works. My experience of sheer meaning is raw, much of it is not socially mediated, and it's taken me years to take on a bit of neurosis and relate more easily to other people. Lacan is correct to deny that any form of mental illness is a permanent psychic structure, to challenge the distinction between a "symptom" which would be negative and a positive "drive," and to highlight the uniqueness of everyone's psychodynamic profile, ultimately recommending immanently propelled creation as the ideal of the "saint" (as shown in his seminar on Joyce). Further, I see this "queerness" as prophetic—both in the sense of involving an urge to *be* a prophet and because it is perhaps a taste of a mode of life that is inevitably going to gain wider traction as disciplinary social structures continue to fall away.

With this in mind, let us turn to a critique of the culture and politics of black metal. While it may be correct in its wholesale rejection of certain aspect of modernity, it is nevertheless incorrect in its wish to return to an imagined state where things were somehow better—every race living in the part of the globe where it belongs, gender roles distributed according to their correct biological assignment, with the men going to war and the women bearing children, and so forth (see Varg Vikernes's YouTube channel for more).

What hyperborean black metal does not understand is "the transcendental," a mysterious force of destratification that was perhaps unleashed at the dawn of modernity, and which expresses itself as a cascade of cultural paradigms, revising and updating humanity's knowledge, power, and experience through discoveries in science, technology, and the arts, expressed as increased economic power and mastery over nature. The history of the transcendental in the philosophical tradition begins, of course, with Kant and passes through Fichte, Schelling, Hegel, Marx, and Nietzsche, all of whom interpret it in different ways. In their very philosophy, the greatest of these perhaps *carry out* a step in its work of destratification. Its key elements are a differential engine of some kind (perhaps originally born as the idea of a wound immanent to God, as presented by Jakob Böhme, whose influence is expressly acknowledged by both Hegel and Heidegger), a cascading series of transcendental horizons across which the subjective world, its objective instantiation, and the experiences of the inhabitants reproducing it are transformed and the spectral lure of an ultimate horizon to the series at which its elements merge—existence and essence, subject and object, fact and value. My name for this force, the birth of which my opera *Origin of the Alimonies* documents, is LAET.

Of course, this LAET, whatever it is, may well be the greatest disaster ever to befall humanity—though it must itself be understood transcendentally as something that "must have" produced the present, not across chronological time but through a different type of time to which human years and the atomic clock are orthogonal. Our speculative understanding of the past and the future may well be discharged and discarded as a result of its continued destratification. But ultimately it must be understood as a "catastrophe" in the neutral scientific sense: a massive paradigm shift that cannot be stopped. The most we can do is designate it, interpret it, seek to give it meaning, and seek to draw conclusions about how to live our lives and organize society from the meaning we have arrived at. LAET is the will of God, the source from which the True, the Good, and the Beautiful emanate.

Transcendental black metal should be understood, then, as an attempt at preserving and even intensifying the "critique" leveled against modernity by black metal—not in the name of an imagined past, but because modernity is itself conservative, outdated, separating us from our true potential and a higher form of justice. Engaging in a real and penetrating way with critical philosophy, transcendental black metal is a *continuation* of the Enlightenment beyond the markers it has set for itself.

The cluster of musical and stylistic inventions I've pursued on Liturgy albums and in extra-musical aspects of our career should be understood as attempts to break free from the current horizon or to make ready for the next—while I can't claim that all the wheels and cogs form a perfect synthetic unity, they form a certain coherence.

The "burst beat" technique appropriates black metal's blast beat, which, due to its speed, represented a dead-end at the psychoacoustic limit at which a pulse can be heard as rhythm rather than a drone. Rather than retreating or pushing further, the burst beat steps outside the frame of metal's historical trajectory to create a variable-speed rhythm inspired by the ethics of the intensive. Accelerating, crossing singular thresholds between different speeds and states, passing between chaotic and stable attractors, the burst beat is a theophany, producing a concrete *experience* of "*natura naturans*," which is at the same time a *representation*.

The "general tremolo" extends black metal's "special tremolo" guitar technique to additional electronic elements of the arrangements—percussive bells, as well as digital editing of the recording itself. Expanding the alchemical transformation of the electric guitar into a string ensemble, which is what the "special tremolo" of black metal achieved, it seeks a wider variety of transformations of this kind, including between a recorded performance and the digital surface of the recording itself.

I see the burst beat as oriented more toward "matter" and general tremolo as more oriented toward "mind" or "cognition," given that these seem to me to be independent and equally authentic vessels for destratification.

More generally, I seek an intensification of the encounter staged between the rock tradition and the classical tradition through black metal—with the hierarchization of countercultural insurrection and the feminization of metal as opposing poles.

When I compose Liturgy's songs, I go deeper into the use of sonata form and compose with thematic materials and rhythmic textures far closer the actual Sturm und Drang language of classical music, which black metal often invokes superficially, without excavating what is really *important* about it, which are the formal characteristics that—as the late Roger Scruton has shown—foster in the listener intelligence, wisdom, patience, and the capacity to communicate. I also, of course, make use of techniques not just from nineteenth-century music but also from American minimalism. More recently, in my opera, I use leitmotifs and the structure of *musikdrama* developed by Wagner. While this vision of the use and value of music is very far away from what most people look for in rock music, I believe it is crucial—though, of course, I also seek to create the overload of volume and mayhem that has its own contrary value.

The opposed "feminization of metal" aspect appears in my focus on musical materials that invoke a sense of effeminate intimacy and tenderness that is not ordinarily welcome in the language of metal—some of these are derived from the language of, say, Brahms, others come from the palate of experimental post-club, which has its own direct connection to queer culture with a noisier, giltchier, more fractured psychotic angle.

Finally, the extra-musical character (Varg Vikernes's church burnings and declarations) is expanded to be a synthetic unity, both as an integrated body of work and an attempted unity of distribution across heterogenous cultural platforms: transcendental black metal set to a cosmogonical dramatic story performed live and in a film, which is the aesthetic core of a philosophy system, the concepts of which motivate both the musical style and the artistic praxis, the system itself being promoted in nonacademic discursive space by its presence in album art and program notes. Additionally, use of social media platforms like YouTube, Twitter, and Discord to cross-promote different aspects of the project, as well as to engage with other artists, musicians, and fans who can take inspiration from or critique the work.

The music made using these techniques, together with the philosophical and dramatic scaffolding that both motivates it and is promoted by it, is meant to have the shape of a political religion of total art. An experimental training ground for a mode of subjectivity that is not welcome in conventional discursive space— metal or otherwise—too monstrous and at the same time too disciplined, too radical and also too reactionary to be *useful* to capital in the war of attrition it stages between groundless political positions in the cultural echo chamber—yet too intense, new, and moving to be ignored. A channel for God's inhalation.

We do not know the etiology of queerness; homosexuality and gender nonconformism in all their varieties are neither "understood" by the scientific community nor by anyone who identifies as queer. It is important to clarify this, because ultimately queerness deserves and demands to be given a provisional speculative meaning, without walking on eggshells.

Here is the meaning I propose: sex and gender deviation represent flickers of a new higher degree of the world spirit. The right to autonomously legislate gender and sexual orientation should be understood in comparison to other emergent rights that the world-spirit has produced, like the right to choose to marry the person you love over familial alliance or to not be owned as property. The argument about whether gender identity and sexual orientation are chosen, caused by emotional trauma, or genetically determined misses what's really going on. Both are best compared to a genius's creative or scientific quest: one is compelled to enjoy in a certain way for reasons that are ultimately mysterious; one has *no choice*, but in obeying the compulsion, one is nevertheless embodying the zenith of their freedom. We can imagine a future where gender and sex are incorporated into the aesthetic domain, with no thought of society distributing one's gender assignment from the outside and no assumption of groupings of any kind—a unique affective and sexual being for each individual, with no species or genus. Perhaps this is what Ray Brassier meant when he proposed that "universalization precedes not by extending specific predicates but by subtracting them." The *reason* grounding the project of LGBTIQ+ rights is its sacred status as a path to a new, more refined era for civilization or perhaps to heaven itself: increased individuality, increased collective compassion, increased ratio of *natura naturans* to *natura naturata*.

Holy Unblack Metal:

THE WHITE HORSE OF THE APOCALYPSE

BENJAMIN BIANCIOTTO

"Better to reign in Heaven than serve in Hell" could be the motto of the holy unblack metal (HUM) bands.[1]

To reverse the darkest aspects of black metal and to glorify God are some of the implicit intents of this extreme music movement. The problem is, black metal is already based on inversion. Thus, what happens if HUM inverts the inversion: Does it describe a circle, 360 degrees, and come back to the starting point, or does it create a spiral, an infinity of recreations that are never exactly the same?

We could start with the example of the Black Mass. It is the inversion of the liturgical mass, transforming each gesture and each symbol into a darker act, defying authority and morality. If we tried to create the opposite of a Black Mass, would we return to a pure and orthodox Christian celebration? Obviously not. We would create a new form of inversion, grounded on an opposition to the opposite. Black metal inverted the codes; HUM inverted this inversion. By introducing Christianity into the kingdom of atheism, paganism claimed Satanism to get closer to the reality, while HUM chose to fight black metal on a spiritual territory—and attires itself in White to manifest its total and pure antagonism.

Manichaeism is a Persian religion, founded by the prophet Mani
during the third century CE; a syncretism of Zoroastrianism, Judaeo
Christianity, Buddhism, and Gnosticism, whose main legacy is
the dual segmentation of the universe between two antagonistic
forces. Thus, the (popularized) Manichean approach is symbolized
by the opposition between White and Black, Good and Evil, Light and
Darkness, God and Satan (originally, Ahura Mazda and Ahriman),
Heaven and Hell; by extension, it has been metaphorically used to
describe the conflict between Mind and Body, Spirit and Matter,
Day and Night.[2] Like in the Yin Yang philosophical system, the
two elements form a whole world, inseparable, one creating
the other and the two existing through each other. There are
no such conflicts between black metal and HUM, because the
opposition is completely unbalanced. Moreover, if the contentious
relationship linking black metal to HUM is antagonistic, it has
blurred boundaries. To be more specific, we should consider the
black-and-white aesthetics of black metal as a perfect illustration
of this peculiar connection; the presence of the color white is only
necessary to reveal the blackness of the movement, even if HUM
whiteness is definitely not pure. To explain this ambiguous position,
it is essential—like for every founding myth—to come back to
the origins.

We know that the founding creative act of a movement is always
a matter for debate. Not only because the founder can take
advantage of an eventual glory to come, but first and foremost
because s/he is immediately turned into a referential figure, the
one who engraved the new Tablets of Stone. Horde's *Hellig Usvart*
(Nuclear Blast, 1994) is reputedly the first HUM piece. The band
then baptized the so-called "movement," using Darkthrone's
"Unholy Black Metal" self-designation on *A Blaze in the Northern Sky*
(Peaceville Records, 1992).

A few elements need to be noticed in the first place. Horde is a one-man band led by Anonymous, probably a pun on Euronymous, as well as a will to break with iconic posture. He chose a Norwegian album title and a clear cognate English-Norwegian name. He released his album on a well-known extreme music label, in 1994. These details are exactly like a "true" black metal genuine release, except for the fact that he comes from the other side of the world, physically (Australia) and spiritually. If the tracks entitled "Drink from the Chalice of Blood" or "The Day of Total Armageddon Holocaust" can be ambiguous, "Blasphemous Abomination of the Satanic Pentagram," "Invert the Inverted Cross," and "Weak, Feeble, and Dying Anti-Christ" cannot be misinterpreted. Horde is a true un-Norwegian un-black metal band.

Musically speaking, *Hellig Usvart* is really close to any black metal album released in the period: dark, atmospheric, brutal music supported by a plaintive voice screaming its own despair. The artwork shows a black-and-white photograp of a cemetery shot at night, with a logo representative of the codes—even if (in the manner of Burzum, Emperor, or Satyricon) it does not present either a cross or pentagram.

Antestor is another example of a relevant HUM band. The members come from Jessheim, Norway (a few miles north of Oslo). They began their career under the name of Evil Crush, a band principally known for having been quoted by Bard G. "Faust" Eithun in an interview with Øystein "Euronymous" Aarseth about the shame of having a Christian black metal band around and the necessity to get rid of it, whatever the means, including murder.[3] Evil Crush released a demo in 1991 titled *The Defeat of Satan*. The same year, Per Yngve "Dead" Ohlin killed himself, and Euronymous opened the Helvete shop. In other words, they were the mere incarnation of the enemy, precisely during the constitution of the Norwegian black metal core. Antestor released their first album, *Martyrium*, in 1994. Their second album, *The Return of Black Death*, is often considered as a true representative "classic" album of HUM. Less raw, more melodic, the album is also in perfect harmony with simultaneous black metal releases. Unfortunately, they changed the original cover, logo, and title. *Kongsblod* became *The Return of the Black Death*, the aggressive logo an impersonal lettering, and the beautiful painting of Vikings skiing in the forest by Knud Bergslien an ugly blue illustration of a running Death. More or less voluntarily, they destroyed the common spirit, iconology, and ideology linking HUM to black metal. The album was released on Cacophonous Records in 1997, not without complications, censorship, and threats.[4] Despite these clear difficulties, they were signed to a well-known metal label, which previously released some major bands like Cradle of Filth and Dimmu Borgir.

Let's add, in order to put up a darker smokescreen, that Jan Axel "Hellhammer" Blomberg, drummer hero from Mayhem, recorded their drum sessions on *The Forsaken* (2005) and *Det Tapte Liv* (2004). Significantly, the cover of the latter reproduces an illustration of the proudly erected Borgun *stavkirke*.[5]

To complete this glimpse, we could mention other noteworthy HUM bands. For instance, Admonish, a Swedish unblack metal band, has a significant story. Formed in 1994, it is considered not only as one of the first HUM bands, but as one of the leaders of the movement, though, they didn't release anything until 2005, the EP *Det Yttersta Tiden*, followed by another EP, *Insnärjd* (2007). We could be tempted to say that they represent a kind of cult of the underground, like the mysterious well-known Les Légions Noires bands in France, but it is more certainly signifies a matter of recognition and a mark of feebleness from labels in response to the lack of audience. If they sank into oblivion during all these years, it is definitely not voluntarily. In the same way, the Norwegian band Vaakevandring is also an influential band, but with no more releases than Admonish. Pantokrator, a Swedish band formed in 1996 and still active, has a more meaningful discography: two albums (*Blod*, 2003 and *Aurum*, 2007), a split with Sanctifica, two demos, two EPs, and, more surprisingly, two compilations. Finally, the more recent American band Frost Like Ashes (formed in 2001) deserves a mention. They released an album in 2005, *Tophet*, whose cover is a photograph of the rebuilt Fantoft Church. The allusion is subtle...But they are more widely recognized for their use of corpsepaint, pikes, and medieval weapons, highly distinctive signs of *trve* black metal. Should we consider these props as a provocation or merely as illustrating the paradoxical nature of the movement, the split of identity between a black metal body and a Christian soul—the desire to bring light into darkness?

If black metal built itself on inversion—through its values, imagery, philosophy, religion, and sociology—HUM built itself on inverting the inversion. There's no need to remind the reader that black metal came first and established the rules, the codes, and the behavior. Black metal immediately promoted inverted crosses, death, misanthropy, elitism, black-and-white aesthetics, hate, dark, violent music and lyrics, etc. Beyond creating a musical movement, it initiated a culture based on the rejection of a world dominated by Christianity and its moral values— respect, love, moderation, hope, happiness. Logically, HUM should have turned black metal ideology into a colorful Christian musical movement, but that was not the case. HUM deliberately chose to attire itself in black metal outfits, a very risky and surprising decision. The HUM bands could have opted for the easiest way and fought black metal from the completely opposite direction, but they decided they would rather only slightly move a few crucial elements. By all appearances, HUM is not an inversion of black metal, a fight between white heroes and black villains, but an attempt to investigate and flood into gray zones, like a deviance. HUM refuses the Manichean position, assumes the White stereotype of the Good, and chooses to insert confusion into a too deliberately evident dichotomy.

WHITE IS THE NEW BLACK

This leads us to the most intriguing part of the relationship between HUM and black metal; the two movements are very similar. If you do not understand what the singer screams and/or do not read the lyrics (when they are provided), you would certainly not see or hear any differences between HUM and black metal albums, or even between the bands on stage. Only some of the titles or the direction of the cross on some logos might betray their ideology. HUM bands are no better than regular black metal bands, but they are also no worse. They are less numerous, but they have the same percentage of bad bands, idiots, opportunists, theorists, and brilliant musicians. Some of them wear corpsepaints, spikes, and leather. Some modernize the genuine style. Some are loyal to the origin of the movement. Some claim new perspectives. So is HUM just a kind of black metal copy, a photocopy worthy of a low-quality zine, displayable to a mass market? We already know the answer concerning their commercial lack of success. We need to know more about HUM's position toward its evil twin.

The pilot documentary *Light in Darkness: Nemesis Divina*, directed by Stefan Rydehed and David Nilsson (2008) is a perfect and relevant introduction to the genre and an opportunity to introduce viewers to its controversial position. To illustrate the latter, we could start by quoting Ravn from Frosthardr, who declares in the introduction of the documentary: "If black metal is evil, then we play evil Christian black metal." That is precisely the main paradox: HUM bands want to draw closer to black metal, but, at the same time, they want to be considered as a new and original movement. Anonymous from Mortification and Horde states: "I wanted to offer the black metal community an alternative, a different way at looking at the world. To darkness and evil music, which was coming from Scandinavia in the early 1990s, I wanted to offer an alternative to that, a light version of that." Pilgrim from Crimson Moonlight confirms: "We try to take music into a new dimension of brutality. We still want to find our own way to play brutal black metal." Both statements are clear. HUM bands want to play black metal and be considered as black metal bands, while being seen as an evolved form of the genuine movement, an enlightened version of it. Pilgrim is perfectly conscious of the ambivalence: "One of the main reasons that I continue doing this is because it's a paradox...sometimes a paradox could help you to get a deeper and wider and broader perspective."[6] It is precisely this paradox—the grey area—we are trying to elucidate.

"Do they rebuild burned churches?" is the kind of joke you can hear about HUM. It would be an understatement to say that HUM is not really considered part of the black metal scene, that it is not taken seriously and is frequently met with hostility. Actually, the movement is often perceived as a spoof, a parodic version of black metal, or complete nonsense—a faded black, a dirty white. We could compare HUM to the figure of the "monkey painter," an eighteenth-century Flemish tradition spread in France by artists such as Jean Siméon Chardin and Antoine Watteau—the monkey standing for academic artists only capable of painting boring scenes, applying some classical recipes without any qualities except a kind of useless technique. Yet reducing HUM to a parody is a mistake. There is neither a humorous dimension nor any desire to laugh at black metal. Instead, there is a lot of respect and admiration for bands that obviously do not share any of HUM's concerns. The reverse is not true. HUM is linked to black metal, not only as a deviant movement or opponent, but as a transfer. We could also try to associate the HUM movement with the simulacrum defined by Jean Baudrillard in *Simulacra and Simulation*, as something that "masks and denatures a profound reality,"[7] i.e., black metal. Or we could contemplate interpreting HUM as a postmodern version of black metal: borrowing its main elements, embezzling them, recomposing a sort of fake version pretending to be a true one, or at least assumed to be fake. Black metal is dead, and HUM is playing with its corpse. The problem is that HUM is a contemporary of black metal that claims to have its own path that is separate from black metal digressions. Trying to model HUM on philosophical approaches or constantly minimizing it in relation to its spectacular twin is missing the point and the core of its distinction, namely religion.

For it is transcendental magic which, basing the universe upon the two columns of Hermes and Solomon, has divided the metaphysical world into two intellectual zones, one white and luminous, enclosing positive ideas, the other black and obscure, containing negative ideas, and which has given the synthesis of the first, the name of God, and that of the other, the name of the devil or of Satan.[8]

Eliphas Lévi reminds us that the White vs. Black opposition has immediately found its perfect incarnation into the great primordial fight between God and Satan—in Christian occidental thought, at least. In the present case, one relevant point is the question of whether or not religion is part of the essence or the core of black metal, particularly because religion is the absolute wedge issue between these fraternal twin brothers. Actually, we are not absolutely convinced that, paradoxically, religion represents a main issue for black metal. We have the feeling that most black metal musicians reject any links to established religion, and that the ones who pledge allegiance to Satanism do it for symbolic and metaphorical reasons rather than religious beliefs. Does that mean that black metal is only about music? Even if the historical conviction against tritones as devilish weapons were to lead to the demonstration of the "evil" power of music, we cannot completely agree that there is effectively a malefic dimension to (dis) harmony—a music that is shared by black metal and HUM, in any case. So, we conclude that the disinterest, mocking, and even hate of HUM comes from nothing more than the inversion of a cross. Inversion would be the definitively tragic element of black metal. Is that yet a sufficient argument?

Indeed, black metal is not just music. Every black metal musician and participant feels that there is something more to this movement than just music. Black metal is a united, almost sectarian, entity. Religion is inseparable from the constitution of black metal, or, more precisely, the darkest aspect of it. Thus, if one decides to play enlightened black metal, enhancing its brighter dimension, is that a betrayal? Could we consider HUM as merely Judas to Satan? It certainly sold its soul to God. It seems also to have broken the rules and to have assumed a dissident role in extreme metal music. Actually, it reminds us of the vision of Lucifer, the "light bearer." When he decided to transgress the laws by defying God and giving light to humans, he accomplished an act close to that of the HUM bands—except, in this case, God's role is occupied by Satan. It is probably what Horde meant by "invert the inverted cross." Clearly, music is a sphere and can be rolled over, switching the position—as above, so below. The relationship between HUM and black metal is characterized by this issue of interpretation, from its symbols to its own essence.

THE BRIGHT SIDE OF THE FUNERAL MOON

HUM could be compared to the white horse of the Book of Revelation, written by John of Patmos at the end of the first century. But to which white horse exactly? Actually, there are two white horses mentioned in Revelation: "And I saw, and behold a white horse: and he that sat on him had a bow; and a crown was given unto him: and he went forth conquering, and to conquer" (Rev. 6:2); "And I saw Heaven opened, and behold, a white horse; and He that sat upon him was called Faithful and True, and in righteousness He doth judge and make war" (Rev. 19:11).[9]

This latter cavalier is clearly identified as Jesus Christ coming to deliver the earth from evil; the first one is more ambiguous and has been analogized to the Christ, an enemy king, pestilence. More possibly, it might represent a conqueror spreading a fake religion, a perverted Christ—literally, the Antichrist. Obviously, it is convenient to let HUM take on the role of black metal's Antichrist: the betrayer, the false prophet disguised within the orthodox outfits, the corrupter of the unholiness. The example of the two white horses should, however, open broader perspectives, particularly regarding the question of interpretation and reading.

For instance, we know that in non-Western religions, the gods and spirits are alternatively Good or Evil, White or Black, depending on the situation and who is seeking their help; also, more prosaically, to signal mourning, you wear white in the East and black in the West. Ditto, the Satans in the Old Testament were reliable assistants of God for judging human behaviors, and the occult tradition usually distinguishes between Lucifer, the light bearer, enlightened spirit—and Satan (or Ahriman for Rudolf Steiner), the dark mind, destructive and pitiless. So we have to be careful when manipulating symbols and archetypes, as we may encounter, in the same way, luminous black metal and gloomy HUM.

Maybe it implies that HUM and black metal are not opposed as enemies but linked, with a more peculiar and obscure relationship. HUM and black metal are both white horses, but they are seen from different perspectives; they look at each other through a magical looking glass and see themselves. HUM reflects black metal's image, and sometimes looking at yourself in a mirror is the best way to know yourself. The fact, however, is that when you look in a mirror you see a reversed image of reality. Similarly, compared to the developed image, the photographic negative shows the inversion of colors and light. HUM is the negative, the mirrored image of black metal. HUM reveals every aspect of black metal, physically and psychologically—giving it a new definition.

The Christian ideology introduced into black metal via HUM allows us to rethink black metal, not only as an anti-movement but as a movement anti-. For instance, HUM casts light on the misanthropy, hate, and racism in black metal thinking. There's no need here to raise the most extreme examples (such as Varg Vikernes's Thulean Perspective or Faust's murder of Magne Andreassen for being a homosexual) to consider black metal as a movement that is not indisputably open to the community outside of the circle. How many gays, women, or black people are in black metal bands? Without scrutinizing any sociological studies (and excepting some "exotic" rarities like Kristian Eivind "Gaahl" Espedal or Tony

"IT" Särkkä), we can say from casual observation that the black metal community seems to be nearly uniformly composed of young, white, straight males—or, at least, originally was. Yet that is not automatically synonymous with racism, homophobia, or xenophobia. Most of the HUM bands also have the same makeup, even if they do not turn these identifying features into a point of propaganda. Christianity's "love thy neighbor as thyself" commandment is definitely not part of black metal philosophy.

More expressly, it is in a psychological dimension that HUM reveals black metal specificities. The threats received by record companies following HUM album releases demonstrate the importance of religion and the expected direction of the cross in black metal. The use of corpsepaint and spikes by HUM bands indicate the predominance of the image in recognizing black metal as a genre more than the music itself. That's the reason why we must always have to keep in mind that interpretation is the nodal point of the HUM vs. black metal opposition—for example, we could choose to see the inverted cross as a sign of allegiance to Saint Peter, the first pope of the Catholic Church, and his upside-down crucifixion. We could characterize it by the concept of *enantiodromia*, a term from Heraclitus, popularized by Carl Gustav Jung. Etymologically, it means *running countercurrent*. It has been generalized as the principle that any extreme movement generates a diametrically opposed movement, rendered as a subconscious/conscious confrontation by psychoanalysis. On the basis of *enantiodromia*, we can assert that black metal created, even if involuntarily, HUM, its extreme opposite. To support this argument, Father Robert Culat, a priest involved in the metal scene, declares that "in the end, a believer and a black metal listener can have the same analysis about the actual state of our society. The difference is elsewhere: in the attitudes and solutions they propose."[10] He admits that black metal and, let's say, its Catholic version, HUM, start in the same place but go in opposite directions toward their respective goals. To corroborate Father Robert Culat's statement, we could, for instance, cite Psalms 68:21–23: "Surely God will crush the heads of his enemies, the hairy crowns of those who go on in their sins. The Lord says, 'I will bring them from Bashan; I will bring them from the depths of the sea, that your feet may wade in the blood of your foes, while the tongues of your dogs have their share.'"[11] These are the sort of statements black metal bands could make and an argument HUM bands rely upon: the Bible, and not only the Old Testament, includes extremely violent texts and episodes.

Jung conducts a similar inversion, when, after having defined *enantiodromia* as "a vague premonition of the terrible law which governs all the blind phenomena,"[12] he writes:

The subconscious, a promised land spared from troubles, became the origin of evil. It calls to mind how cultural terms are constantly subject to interpretation and can easily turn committed positions inside out. That is one of the reasons why HUM is an interesting act. It is not "White" metal as opposed to "Black" metal or Good vs. Evil. HUM annihilates moral values by its own existence. It is a monster blessed by God. If HUM is an intriguing freak of nature, hard to interpret and categorize, it may reveal specificities outside of its constant, unstable, and fragile opposition to black metal. But what is HUM exactly?

RAINBOW (BLACK) METAL

Maybe we could advance the hypothesis that HUM is actually a diffracted White. Since Isaac Newton's discoveries about prisms, we know that white light can disassemble into different colors bands—visible spectrum—giving form to the rainbow phenomenon. The English physicist decided to associate the seven musical notes with the seven colors described: red, orange, yellow, green, blue, violet, and indigo. One famous illustration of Newton's spectrum is the cover art of Pink Floyd's album *The Dark Side of the Moon* (Harvest Records, 1973) by Hipgnosis (Storm Thorgerson). On this representation, the dislocation of the white light engenders six colors only—the indigo is missing. Additionally, this particular assembly of six colors makes up the rainbow flag designed by Gilbert Baker in 1978 for the LGBTIQ+ community in San Francisco. Originally, the flag was made up of eight colored bands, the seven of Newton's spectrum plus pink, and each color was given a distinctive attribute. The color removed from Newton's spectrum— the indigo—was supposed to represent the "art and magic" dimension.[14] This is definitely a metaphor for HUM: a diffracted luminous white without art and magic—two of the qualities that made black metal different, and celebrated. We could emphasize that we are mentioning the light dimension of the color spectrum; when mixing the different colors materially, you obtain black—often considered a noncolor. Logically, we again find the opposition between White and Black, Spirit and Matter, HUM and black metal.

Nevertheless, HUM is a reduced rainbow but a rainbow all the same (a rainbow that is "the sign established by God between Him and all life on the earth" [Gen. 9:12–17]). It is colorful, vivid, and unexpected. It is elusive and does not follow the orthodoxy. It proposes a renegade approach to the music, just as post-black metal bands continue to do. If we consider the rainbow spectrum as an extension of the original white, we could grasp HUM as an advanced form of black metal, its evolution, leading to a post-black metal position—the Satanic Temple Pride Rainbow logo could be a relevant mutation of modern Satanism. Liturgy is always the ideal candidate when interrogating the evolving ascent of the movement: transcendence, illumination, doubly inverted crosses, etymologic "inspiration," a religious name, and music that lights up your soul.[15] If you add the refusal of corpsepaint, leather, spikes, and a black-and-white aesthetics, you obtain a credible model of HUM music. No ambiguity though: Liturgy is definitively not a HUM band. In that case, what distinguishes Krallice, Wolves in the Throne Room, or Blut Aus Nord from Crimson Moonlight, Extol, or Slechtvalk? The quality of music, yes, but not only that. HUM bands do not want to remove Satanism from black metal or introduce atheism/paganism into it. They want to introduce Christian ideas and ideology into it. There is a kind of proselytism here. Furthermore, most HUM bands do not reject black metal rags. They are proud to wear them.

At the outset we said that HUM's motto could be a question of allegiance to Heaven, rejecting Hell through the spectrum of inversion. HUM apparently wished to put Satan back on the right track and invert the Fall, allowing Satan to shift the terms from a Paradise that HUM has unwillingly lost and is trying to regain. Rejected from the blackness of Hell, not welcomed in the whiteness of Heaven, HUM is doomed to wander in a grey Purgatory. But we realized that it was actually not a fight between HUM and black metal, Good vs. Evil, Heaven vs. Hell. HUM questions black metal, or, more accurately, it submits black metal to question, without being fully competent or recognized to head the tribunal. Even if HUM cannot be regarded as a movement that is especially relevant in and of itself, it is absolutely relevant in the end, because of what it can teach us about black metal.

It can also be considered, more accurately, as an attractive dance partner, maybe in a vertigo-inducing *danse macabre*. To be precise, HUM broke the black metal circle by laying into its ideology and rendering its codes obsolete. It dragged black metal into an endless spiral—and by twirling around in a spiral, HUM constitutes an irritating hum in black metal's ears. When you invert the inversion, you do not come back to your starting point, you do not close the circle, you ruin its perfection and create a spiral, a motif that is anything but anodyne. You get closer to the core without reaching it. Side by side and alternating on a disk, black and white create a particular spiral, a figure of hypnosis that turns out to be an offensive weapon, a powerful strategy—if they agree to cooperate, which is not the case here. It is a pity, because they could certainly benefit from each other on a conceptual level, in the manner in which the artist Paul Laffoley describes his vision of evil beauty:

In fact, without the concept of aesthetic distance, how can you understand phenomena such as the following: 1) The mixing of black pigment—evil—with white pigment—good—in such a way that the white is enhanced? If you take, for instance, a five-gallon can of titanium dioxide paint, introduce a few drops of lampblack into the can, and mix thoroughly, the white will radiate more light than ever.[17]

We are willing to bet that the inversion is also true in the area we are discussing—metaphorically at least.

If we turn to the Holy Scriptures ("Therefore, in order to keep me from becoming conceited, I was given a thorn in my flesh, a messenger of Satan, to torment me" [2 Cor. 12:7]),[18] HUM is the "thorn in the flesh" of black metal, a messenger of God, a source of vitality. It brings an adversary to black metal, a fellow opponent, at the same time as it corroborates the idea that they are united and engaged in an ambiguous fruitful relationship. Maybe the most explicit example to explain and understand how both movements interact with each other is the performance (then video) titled *Light/Dark* (1977) by Marina Abramović and Ulay (Frank Uwe Laysiepen). The two protagonists (lovers, back then) face each other on their knees in the dark and alternately slap each other on the cheek, with rhythm—quietly, then more and more brutally. After twenty minutes, Abramović ends the performance by evading the next slap. Among our terms of comparison, you have to decide which one is Light and which one is Dark, Abramović or Ulay, white horse or black horse, Good or Evil, White or Black—and which one are we to think won.

Notes

[1] We decided to keep this designation, "holy unblack metal," instead of "unblack metal" or "Christian black metal," or even "white metal," because it is the only one to associate the presence of the religious dimension ("holy") with the idea of inversion contained in the prefix "un-," i.e., two characteristics of the movement we consider decisive. Also, we would like to point out that we had to generalize the plurality contained in the terms *holy unblack metal* and *black metal*,

and that the remarks in our argument cannot be applied to every band playing under these banners.

2 For more detailed explanations about those interactions, see Mircea Eliade, *Mephistopheles and the Androgyne: Studies in Religious Myth and Symbol*, trans. J.M. Cohen (New York: Sheed and Ward, 1965); originally published as *Méphistophélès et l'Androgyne* (Paris: Gallimard, 1962).

3 "BUT—when it comes to bands like Crush Evil, we must take serious action. It's bad enough to have a couple of society bands, but a CHRISTIAN band is too much. But don't worry, we have plans. They will not continue for a very long time." *Orcustus: Death Metal Zine* 2 (1992): 38.

4 The main issues came directly from the label itself, Cacophonous Records, which changed the cover art, the title, and censored all the lyrics referring to a Christian apology (the words "Lord" and "Jesus" were banned from the lyrics, for instance). Also, the band never received any money from the label, and the album was not publicized.

5 It is one of the most ancient and best preserved *stavkirke* in Norway (c. 1180). In a strange coincidence, a copy of that church was erected in Rapid City, South Dakota, USA, in 1969.

6 All these quotes are from Stefan Rydehed and David Nilsson, dir., *Light in Darkness: Nemesis Divina* (2008).

7 Jean Baudrillard, "The Precession of Simulacra," in *Simulacra and Simulation*, trans. Sheila Glaser (Ann Arbor: University of Michigan Press, 1984), 6; originally published as *Simulacres et simulation* (Paris: Éditions Gallilée, 1981).

8 Eliphas Lévi, cited in Christopher McIntosh, *Eliphas Lévi and the French Occult Revival* (Albany: State University of New York Press, 1972), 110; originally from Eliphas Lévi, *La clef des grands mystères, suivant Hénoch, Abraham, Hermès Trismégiste et Salomon* (Paris: Germer Baillère, 1861), 163.

9 Both quotes are from the King James Bible.

10 "Un croyant et un blackeux peuvent finalement faire le même constat sur l'état actuel de notre société. La différence est ailleurs: dans les attitudes et les solutions qu'ils proposent." Uriel, cited in "Uriel Interview: Robert Culat," V-Solutions.net, December 2002, accessed May 25, 2021, http://www.vs-webzine.com/Interview_culat.htm; translation by the author.

11 From the New International Bible. In France during the Wars of Religion, Protestants (Huguenots) chose this particular Psalm as a battle hymn.

12 "Après cet aperçu effrayant d'un monde aveugle, dans lequel construction et destruction se contrebalancent éternellement, si la conscience se retourne vers l'homme en tant que sujet et regarde son propre arrière-plan, elle y découvre de sauvages obscurités dont chacun voudrait bien éviter la vue. Ici encore la science a anéanti un dernier refuge et fait, de ce qui promettait d'être une caverne protectrice, un lieu d'horreur." Carl Gustav Jung, *Problèmes de l'âme moderne* (Paris: Éditions Buchet Chastel, 1960), 175; translation by the author.

13 Ibid., 175; translation by the author.

14 The pink color, also removed from the genuine eight-band flag, represented "sexuality."

15 The "question" was synonymous to "torture" during Christian Inquisition.

16 Paul Laffoley, "The Flower of Evil, 1971," in *The Essential Paul Laffoley: Works from the Boston Visionary Cell* (Chicago: University of Chicago Press, 2016), 118.

17 From the New International Bible.

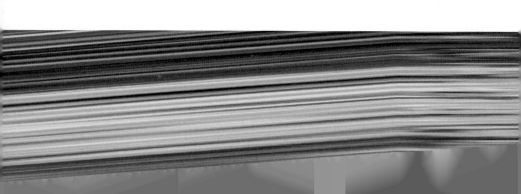

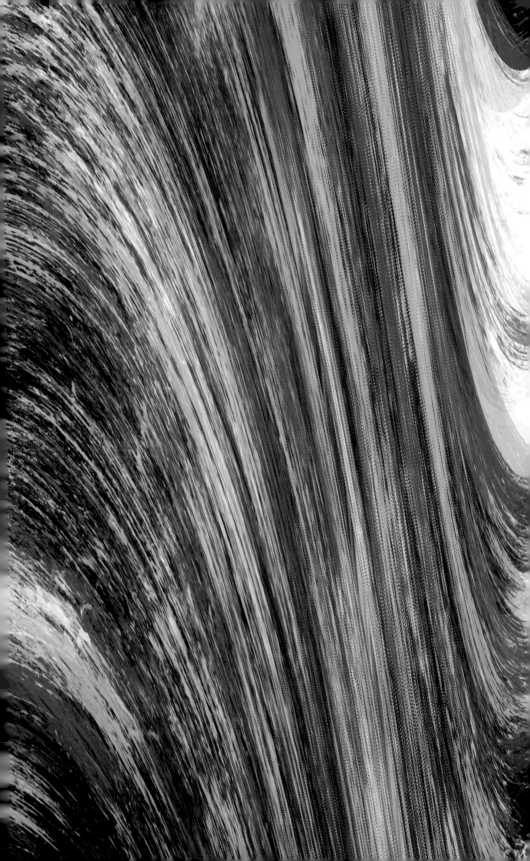

Devotion Has a Price

VINCENT
COMO

PART I: BRUISING THE TWENTIETH CENTURY: THE RELENTLESS PROCESSION AND AGENCY OF TIME

If we consider the twentieth century as a transitional period that is moving humanity out of the last epoch of the modern world and into a new postmodern era, we can see an ever-expanding rift between our early belief structures and how their entropic trajectory is repeatedly adapted into a present tension by the manufacture of updated mythologies to wrap around and contain our needs and desires through our social and cultural expression. Ideology exists on a spectrum that is framed by protective haven, on one end, and blind weaponization, on the other. To possess any form of conviction, one must be willing to make a sacrifice, for without an associated cost/benefit, there exists no value of import for belief.

The early part of the last century would see blues music growing out of an amalgam of African and European folk musics. There was even rumored to have been a Faustian bargain between a young

Robert Leroy Johnson and the Devil himself, when, upon meeting at a crossroads in Mississippi, the Devil made Johnson the greatest bluesman of all time in exchange for his soul. In the early 1900s, we also see the birth of quantum mechanics—"Spooky action at a distance," as Einstein called it—and how it eventually paves the way for the weaponization of the atom, the most elementary component, the foundational building block that defines the physical world. Russian artist Kazimir Malevich paints *Black Square* in 1915, which pushes painting farther away from abstraction, crossing the boundary and firmly rooting it in the realm of the nonobjective world, a realm outside of nature and the human, while simultaneously injecting the physical presence of the object that is the painting into our everyday field of vision and away from notions of representation, caricature, and facsimile. This push further cements our capabilities for abstract thought, projection, and a comprehension of the not yet known, as we begin to understand the limitations of our faculties of perception.

The continuum of devotion to the utopian visions of modernity's progress would find its logical conclusion/collapse in the punctuation that was the dropping of Fat Man and Little Boy on Hiroshima and Nagasaki.

Full stop.

Holy shit.

Reset mind.

The price of "success" is ultimately our own humanity when we unleash two atomic bombs on Japan, setting in motion both the rapid end to the World War II and the birth of postmodernity, as a new cold-war consciousness begins to blossom.

At this point, not only have *we* now become conscious of ourselves and our relation to the world, but, after both making the bomb and imposing its harsh reality on the world, the things we put into the world *themselves* signal an awareness of their place in relation to ourselves and the world and reflect that back to us in an endless loop of feedback cycling through our fears and desires by way of design, marketing, and propaganda. Humanity finally coming full circle to prehistoric knowledge. I mean, have you ever seen a shark egg? Pure. Fucking. Evil.

In order to rebuild both mentally and physically after this kind of global catastrophe, a rebranding of our past rituals was essential. A conscious evolution to provide both a foundation and an outlet for our more primal needs and desires in a world that, by design, increasingly suppresses them as archaic reality. Innovators and performers took on the role of shamans bridging the world of Being and the mystical realm of "the Other" to ground us and keep us connected to our earlier selves. The result of all of this is that to keep up with our own progress we must also reinvent the ways in which we experience catharsis and connect with our animal needs of lust and domination, while also connecting and engaging socially with one another through gatherings and new rites of passage.

The blues of Robert Johnson and his contemporaries evolves into the rock 'n' roll of Little Richard, Elvis Presley, and The Beatles. Transforming over decades of postwar turmoil, utilizing electricity in new ways to advance, amplify, and distort our engagement, rock 'n' roll becomes a product for youth and the symbol of cultural rebellion, a reflection of social upheaval as global trade becomes the new face of political oppression and dominance. Needless to say, rock 'n' roll eventually becomes conscious of itself as a vehicle for social reform among the youth, as the old-world template of reward for hard work and education no longer applies to the clear, present, and obvious futures of many.

The sounds of the youth culture become darker, heavier, and louder, and, in 1968, Birmingham's Black Sabbath introduces the world to heavy metal. Heavy metal continues its evolution and fragments into the new wave of British heavy metal (NWOBHM), which begets thrash metal, which begets death metal, which begest black metal, and so on. Each distinct subgenre pulling from the past and incorporating another element of influence through punk rock, free jazz, industrial and electronic music, avant-garde and minimal compositions. Keeping one eye on the present, various forms of heavy, dissonant, and threatening sounds are cultivated to move civilization forward, to connect us with a shared past, and to generate an exclusive place for those who pledge their allegiance—as long as they do not stray from the canon.

It goes without saying: culture is a strange thing. That's why we started this exploration with a sort of crude chronology. In his 1962 book *The Shape of Time: Remarks on the History of Things*, George Kubler gives us a template for exploring history through the objects our ancestors created and their commensurate mutations and serial appreciation. While its concerns are mostly rooted in aesthetic experience and functionality, if we follow a significant thought/need/ desire as it travels through history, we can see a pattern in how that becomes manifest in various human behaviors and output. Because of the curse of our own awareness, we have discovered that needs and desires are able to be satiated through innovation and cooperation, as well as through brute force.

In the context of this thesis, our desire and devotion will soon be seen embracing cultural movements that transform into the replacement of mystical or folk traditions we couldn't figure out how to incorporate into modernity. Black metal too is part of a continuum of devotion throughout history. A calling deeply ingrained in our tragic past that knows neither good nor evil, just equilibrium, and that everything costs something. This psychological move in relation to our conscious dealings is a direct result of humanity's transition through the twentieth century, how we sealed and orchestrated our own fate, and what that gamble then cost us.

Black metal was born and bred underground. Outside of. Other than. In the dark and subterranean realm where long dead societies were abandoned, forgotten, left to rot and decompose, returning to their ancestors, and then nourishing the sprouts of their descendants. Black metal unwittingly embraces this position. A position of static impossibility.

Black metal has long defined itself through the extremes of that which it is not: that which is anterior to, outside of, heretical toward, and other than. However, these rejections are manifest in many of the same hallmarks that make it interesting as well: the welcoming of lo-fidelity, the initial resistance of overt commerce, the downright antithetical nature of its internal pageantry. That's just the thing, black metal is the reinvigorated classical hero myth of rebellion, sacrifice, and tragedy filtered through the overdriven fuzz pedal of a DIY aesthetic, and it managed to end up as a subgenre that outsiders love to hate and insiders hate to love and love that they hate it. But, make no mistake, black metal is a fiercely private club, with as many theories on what is and isn't "trve cvlt" as there are bands and followers. It is because it is so hermetically sealed that it has cut itself off from the rest of the world, that it has gone behind closed doors and become a far more intellectualized endeavor than it would otherwise betray. The benefits of this are not in the overt exclusion of others but, rather, in the hero's journey, the vision quest of the single black metal band accepting influence and inspiration from outside the genre and pushing the periphery of what is expected and accepted. Like a wandering sin eater who passes through only to absolve and absorb your iniquity as their only means to sustain themselves. This is where the serious work is being done to expand the language of the idiom or force it into something else—to transform the unwanted into the beautiful and useful. This is where we start discussing the work of Wrnlrd and the *Death Drive* EP, an expansion on an idea from the previous release *Myrmidon*, particularly the song "Black Dress," which was inspired by The Shangri-Las' 1964 hits "Leader of the Pack" and "Dressed in Black." An unlikely coupling perhaps, but influence knows no allegiance.

Our death drive is an integral component to being. Regardless of any form of belief structure, death is both our prize and punishment for existence. Wholly irrelevant to the rest of the universe, the course of our lives is of import to us and us alone. With this as our understanding of our place, it is no wonder we have continued to explore structures of lust, independence, rebellion, transcendence, and transgression, because they are a part of our collective need for ritual, gatherings, rhythms, chants, writhing against each other in our mating customs, and exploring both life and death with the full faculties of our five senses and our intellect.

Perhaps fittingly, "Leader of the Pack" describes a teenage relationship that is considered socially inappropriate, ending in death and heartbreak—a transgressive ritual of vehicular tragedy meant to escape the impending procession into adulthood. If the price of admission is steep, the price for exiting is much steeper. But at the heart of this issue is one of existence, and we cannot divorce existence from past influence, as the past informs the present. It is through Betty's longing and desire that Wrnlrd is able to transform Jimmy's death into an inverted passion play of Orpheus and Eurydice on the *Death Drive* album.

Her devotion is expressed on the track "Grave Dowser" through this prayer:

```
Come for me.
Find me where I lay.
I can hear a tomb
assembling in my brain.
```

It is an invocation for supernatural intervention. An acquiescence that understands their reunion is the end of what was, the beginning of what will be, and the price of her devotion is in her union with death.

This is the annihilationists' utopia. This is the *Necro*-Modern agenda, an active and embraced understanding of finality, a drive toward the irresistible, the unimaginable, the impossible, the inevitable. The living dead, living to die. Consumer zombies roaming through shopping centers like George Romero's *Dawn of the Dead*. Corpse brides and grooms feeding off of the same material possessions they are bound to within a capitalist agenda. Already dead and still staring death in the face. Reza Negarestani's Nigredo Consciousness.

Nothing is ever static. One glorious day humanity will cease to exist entirely, and that's irrelevant to us in our everyday lives. Until we can commune with our own absence, we remain tethered to the continuum of being. We reinvent ourselves and our traditions, trying to keep pace with our own evolution and eventual cessation. Until then, we remain the debtors to our own desires.

Vincent Como
Paradise Lost 003 & 004, 2011-2013

oil on linen with wood, wax, and fire, 66.7 x 50.8 x 14 cm
courtesy of the artist and Minus Space Gallery, Brooklyn, New York City

< *above*
Marnie Weber
Kissing the Devil's Ass, 2016
production still from *The Day of Forevermore*, 2016
photo by © LeeAnn Nickel
courtesy of the artist and Gavlak Gallery, Los Angeles

< *below*
Marnie Weber
Devil, 2016
mannequin, Halloween mask, glass eyes, expanding foam, resin, acrylic paint, found suit, shirt, gloves, ascot, socks and shoes, 122 x 71 x 51 cm
photo © Jeff McLane
courtesy of the artist and Gavlak Gallery, Los Angeles

Marnie Weber
Devil's Ass, 2012, 2016
bas relief wall sculpture
prosthetic rear end, wood, expanding foam, resin, acrylic paint, magi-sculpt, polyurethane tale, 35.5 x 33 x 40.6 cm
photo © Jeff McLane
courtesy of the artist and Gavlak Gallery, Los Angeles

Svartvinter
Wolverine, 2020
ink and gel pens,
21.59 x 13.97 cm
courtesy of the artist

Blink. 2.0

(FOR PELLE OHLIN
& KIRIKO TAKEMURA)

JONATHAN MAYHEW

Only the idiot has access to the wholly Other.

—BYUNG-CHUL HAN

Blink. 2.0 functions in a similar way to the original video version,[1] inserting itself between things, in its nothingness, rather than the videos' everythingness.

Black, white, or pink pages are to be inserted throughout the publication, similar to the way the two videos intersected, disrupting each other. One black page is to be placed at the front of the publication and a pink page in the back, with a double page spread of white in the center, a nothingness, a space where everything and *nothing is possible*. In digital printing, the colour code for black is #000000, the equivalent of nothing, no mix of colours. White is another nothing, unprintable. The pink I have chosen is the most extreme version of pink available. These empty colour fields are places for contemplation, a break where *nothing* is needed. In another way they also form extremely abstracted portraits of Pelle Ohlin and Kiriko Takemura (Dead and Kyary Pamyu Pamyu), both of whom alter their appearances in extreme ways to pursue their ways of emoting. When pushing things to the extreme it's a fine line between clever and stupid.

Black #000000
White = paper
Pink #ff76ba

Notes

[1] *blink*, Vimeo, 2015, accessed June 4, 2021, https://vimeo.com/121981466.

About the contributors

Artetak, an Atlanta-based freelance artist, has been illustrating her entire life. In her youth, when she wasn't drawing all day, she would be playing video games and watching cartoons, which would in turn influence her art. This obsession with pop culture would become prevalent in her artwork later in life, when she would fully embrace the lowbrow genre. Artetak loves to mix contrasting themes and humor into her work, be it an adorable version of a horrific monster or an anarchist Barbie. She never shies away from bright colors and forces the viewer to accept that there can be light within the dark, and that art shouldn't be taken seriously.

Frederic-Vivianne Auln has been very active in the DIY scene since the 1990s, operating in many artistic fields. Throughout the years, he has produced a substantial filmography and discography in the underground and obscure scenes, always with a focus on the homemade aspect. Over the last eight years, Frederic-Vivianne has published twenty-four books and zines, receiving an award for the graphic novel *Hillerød*. fredericvivianne.neocities.org.

Francine B., known online as Witnesstheabsurd, is a transgender woman based in the UK who has contributed to online pastel goth and queer metal art scenes and, more recently, has done diverse work, including producing concept and promo art for games and album covers and publishing two artbooks. She has a profound identification with the grotesque and is a firm evangelist for the beauty of monsters. Her work can be seen at artstation.com/witnesstheabsurd.

Ivan Belcic is a writer, musician, and illustrator currently based in Prague, the New York City area, and Shanghai—by the time this book comes out, it's anyone's guess where he'll be, but probably one of those places. You can find him screaming and singing in an improvised bathroom studio, agonizing over which sneakers to wear, longing for access to his drums, making a mess in the kitchen, cycling around whatever city he winds up living in, or annoying his wonderful wife. kosmogyr.bandcamp.com.

Benjamin Bianciotto holds a PhD in Art History from Sorbonne University, Paris, France. His dissertation topic was *Figures of Satan: Contemporary Art Facing Its Demons, from 1969 to the Present*. The relationship between today's art and religion or occultism remains at the core of his preoccupations and interests. He is also an art critic and independent curator.

Edward Blair is a freelance writer/zinester based in Chicago, Illinois. They have had work featured in the *Chicago Reader*, Bandcamp Daily, *Paste Magazine*, and elsewhere. They run the Holy Demon Army Distro, the first zine distro to be devoted entirely to zines about professional wrestling. They can be found at @ourcityburning on twitter.

Elijah Burgher is an artist and occasional writer based in Berlin. ppowgallery.com/artist/elijah-burgher/work.

Mimi Chrzanowski (1988) draws at her post in Providence, Rhode Island, and still wonders what the lone dolphin that got lost in the canal down the street was really, truly thinking. Find her @bbytown.

Vincent Como is an artist living in Brooklyn, New York. His practice is centered on black, as both a subject and a material. Como is represented by MINUS SPACE Gallery in Brooklyn, New York, and is a founding member of TSA New York, a Brooklyn-based artist-run exhibition space. Como's work has been discussed in publications like the *Wall Street Journal*, *ArtSlant*, and the *Chicago Tribune*, among others. He holds a BFA in Drawing from the Cleveland Institute of Art.

Ry Cunningham is a nonbinary digital and SFX makeup artist from London, England. Much of his work focuses on the uncanny beauty of monsters, combining demonic and occult imagery with pastel colours and intricate detail. Another recurring element within his makeup art is the process of transformation.

Julien Dallaire-Charest is devoted full-time to illustration, comics, and rock 'n' roll. Among other things, he has done comic book interviews for the Knock-Out record store and book covers for children's novels (*L'abomination du Lac Crystal*). Active in collectives and self-publishing (Copinet Copinot, Serge, Pogneurs de spectres), he is currently working on a solo comic book and participating in the Quebec City cultural scene. juliendc.com.

Drew Daniel makes electronic music as The Soft Pink Truth and as one half of Matmos, with his partner M.C. Schmidt. He is an Associate Professor in the Department of English at Johns Hopkins University, in Baltimore, and is the author of three books: *20 Jazz Funk Greats* (Bloomsbury, 2007), *The Melancholy Assemblage: Affect and Epistemology in the English Renaissance* (Fordham University Press, 2013), and *Joy of the Worm: Suicide and Pleasure in Early Modern English Literature* (University of Chicago Press, 2022).

Laina Dawes is a music and cultural critic and the author of *What Are You Doing Here? A Black Woman's Life and Liberation in Heavy Metal* (Bazillion Points, 2012). Originally from Canada, she is currently completing her doctoral degree in Ethnomusicology at Columbia University, in New York City.

O.B. De Alessi is a visual artist and filmmaker born in Italy and living in Paris, France. Recent exhibitions and screenings include: *The Time Swirls When It Turns into a Black Tunnel*, Futura Projects (Prague, 2019), *Interregnum*, Soil Gallery (Seattle, 2018), *Sitges International Fantastic Film Festival* (Official Selection, 2017), *The Primal Shelter Is Site for Primal Fears*, The Living Art Museum (Reykjavik, 2016).

Catherine Fearns is the author of three crime fiction novels: the award-winning *Reprobation* (Crooked Cat, 2018), *Consuming Fire* (Crooked Cat, 2019), and *Sound* (darkstroke, 2019). She is a staff writer at music website Pure Grain Audio, and her music journalism has also appeared in Broken Amp and Noisey. Her short fiction and nonfiction pieces have been published in *Metal Music Studies*, *Offshoots*, *Here Comes Everyone*, and *Toasted Cheese*. catherine-fearns.com.

Charles Forsman is a 2008 graduate of the Center for Cartoon Studies and a three-time Ignatz Award winner. His comic books include *Revenger*, *Celebrated Summer*, *Slasher*, *I Am Not Okay with This*, and *The End of the Fucking World*, which has been adapted into a Netflix original series. His newest serial is called *Automa*. He lives in Western Massachusetts.

Caity Hall is a comic book and storyboard artist based in Montreal, Canada. Her inspirations are largely based on music (notably the metal genre), animated movies, and constant daydreaming.

Svein Egil Hatlevik is a journalist, musician, improviser and free-range pastoralism activist based in Ytre Enebakk, Norway. He is a member of several music groups, among them Fleurety, Strid and Umoral. Hatlevik is currently trying to come up with excuses not to write books on Norwegian album classics of black metal and other genres.

Langdon Hickman is a writer based out of Alexandria, Virginia, where he lives with his partner, their dog Inara, and their cat Ishtar. He is currently a staff writer for Treble, Consequence of Sound, and an editor at Invisible Oranges, where his long form piece "I'm Listening to Death Metal" has been serialized since early 2019. He is also the cohost of the literary podcast DEATH// SENTENCE covering literary and genre fiction as well as leftist politics.

Liz Hoge, with a love for all things dark and strange, launched Carrion Creations, called "fantastic and creepy" by George R.R. Martin, in 2013. It started with four cups as a gift, and has flourished to now more than 180 uniquely designed teacups now residing all around the world. Carrion Creations has expanded to include our 3D horror artwork, lovingly called Ed Gein Embroidery, monster fingers, miniature coffin boxes, and other dark art. "Carrion Creations, where weird comes home to roost."

Sarah Horrocks is a trans comics creator and critic from Oklahoma. Her credits include *Goro*, *The Leopard*, and her most recent comic *Aorta*. She can be found on Twitter and Instagram: @mercurialblonde.

Hunter Hunt-Hendrix is a composer, musician, artist, and philosopher who seeks to tie these practices into a synthetic unity. Recent work includes the cosmogonical opera *Origin of the Alimonies* at REDCAT, a solo art exhibition of prophetic diagrams at Libertine Gallery, an ongoing philosophical video series on Youtube, and *H.A.Q.Q.*, the fourth studio album from their transcendental black metal band Liturgy, acclaimed for its ecstatic energy and inventive arrangements.

Christine Kelly is the owner of Tridroid Records. She has been an avid extreme music listener since college, where she was metal director for the school's radio station and also DJed at a local goth club. Christine speaks fluent German, the better to make her way to all the best European metal shows. She also stunts a mean sneaker/sock combo. Christine and her wife Melissa (and Tridroid) have lived in Brooklyn, New York, and rural Louisiana and now reside in Houston, Texas.

Kim Kelly is a writer, editor, and anarchist organizer based in New York City. She currently serves as an editor at Noisey, *Vice*'s music site, and her writing on books, politics, and heavy metal and its culture has appeared in a multitude of publications, including the *New York Times*, *The Guardian*, *Teen Vogue*, *The New Republic*, *Rolling Stone*, NPR, *Decibel*, *Kerrang!*, and *Pitchfork*.

Margaret Killjoy is an anarchist author and musician based in Appalachia. She is the principle songwriter for the feminist atmospheric black metal band Feminazgûl, and her blackened doom solo project is called Vulgarite. Her most recent series of books begins with the novella *The Lamb Will Slaughter the Lion*, published by Tor.com. She blogs at her website birdsbeforethestorm.net.

Bogna M. Konior is a writer and academic. She is a lecturer in New Media and Digital Culture at the University of Amsterdam and a Postdoctoral Fellow in Interactive Media Arts at New York University, Shanghai. She tweets @bognamk. Find out more at bognamk.com.

Espi Kvlt is a sex worker, writer, and musician. They have a BA in English writing and a minor in cultural anthropology from University of Nevada, Reno. They are a bisexual, nonbinary anarcho-communist. They are in two black metal bands: Phryne and Seas of Winter (with others forthcoming). They have been published on GenderTerror, in *X Marks the Spot: A Nonbinary Anthology* (2019), and in *In Darkness Delight: Masters of Midnight* (Corpus Press, 2019). They live with three cats, a snake, and their partner.

Élodie Lesourd is a French contemporary artist based in Paris. Related to a critical and conceptual approach to painting, her work is also being established through the method of semiotic analysis. In her she equally employs the history of art and music (including extreme genres such as black metal) in order to test the limits of representation and meaning within her practice. She also resorts to concerts-performances. Her latest monograph is *Gracula Religiosa* (2016). elodielesourd.com

Acid Lich is a freelance illustrator and apprentice tattooer based in sunny Portland, Oregon. Though she fell in love with art as a very small child, it took until 2015 for her to really start applying herself to it. Often working in ink, copics, and charcoal she has recently begun experimenting with acrylics, gold leaf and digital. Her work can be found on some table top games, some albums, websites, and soon skin.

Daniel Lukes has written for metal and rock magazines *Terrorizer*, *Kerrang!*, *Decibel*, and *Helvete: A Journal of Black Metal Theory*. He has a PhD in Comparative Literature from New York University, with a dissertation on toxic masculinities, and is the coauthor, with Rhian E. Jones and Larissa Wodtke, of *Triptych: Three Studies of Manic Street Preachers' The Holy Bible* (Repeater Books, 2017).

Heather Masciandaro was born in Los Angeles, California, and now lives and works in Maharashtra State, India. She received her MFA in Painting and Printmaking from Yale University School of Art in 2002. She aims to portray the divine journey within all experiences low and high, in mystical, human, and flora and fauna form.

Jonathan Mayhew (1981) is an Irish artist based in Dublin. Using poetry, literature, technology, and theory, he manipulates physical and invisible materials creating works in a variety of media. He is interested in how we think about data, how we use it, and how it uses us—and how fiction is blurring into reality. He has shown throughout Europe and Scandinavia and received the TBG&S/HIAP international residency exchange award in 2019.

Scott McPherson is an illustrator from Los Angeles, California. His work is an expression of his own true will through personal experiences of carnal esoteric practices and the unconscious mind, represented by the aggressive yet melancholic line work one might experience within the visual landscape of death metal. www.nihillustration.com.

Johanna Mueller is a printmaker, artist, and entrepreneur residing in Fort Collins, Colorado. Using symbolism and story, her work explores the shared histories of humans as told by animals and the natural world. johannamuellerprints.com.

Stanimir Panayotov is Assistant Professor in Philosophy at School of Advanced Studies, University of Tyumen, Rissia, and holds a PhD in Comparative Gender Studies from Central European University, Budapest. He works at the intersections of continental and feminist philosophy, non-philosophy, and late antique philosophy and has published in Heathen Harvest, *Metal Music Studies*, *the minnesota review*, *Aspasia*, etc. He is editorial board member of *Oraxiom: A Journal of Non-Philosophy*.

George Parr is a writer and editor from South East England. He is currently the deputy editor at *Astral Noize*, a UK-based magazine and website dedicated to covering all forms of noisy and progressive music. He and the rest of the Astral Noize team aim to shine a light on important issues in the scene and to give exposure to bands and organizations that resist metal's reactionary trappings.

Patrizia Pelgrift (née Mazzuoccolo) worked in London as an on-air promo producer for BSkyB for fifteen years, while also freelancing as a music reporter for *Metal Hammer*, *Rhythm*, *Kerrang!* and *Prog*. In Oslo, she worked for Moonfog Productions, managed Tabu Recordings, and produced the metal show *Tinitus* on Norwegian national radio, NRK P3. These days, she lives in New York with her husband and is doing a BA in philosophy to prepare for law school.

Avi Pitchon (1968) lives and works in Tel Aviv and London and has been writing about art and music since the late 1980s, for publications like *Terrorizer*, *The Wire*, and *Vice*. He has worked with Laibach and IRWIN, both formerly of the art collective NSK. His book about Israel's 1980s musical and political underground was published in Israel and Germany. Currently vice editor and art critic at *Haaretz* newspaper (Israel) and a regular contributor to *Zero Tolerance Magazine* (UK).

Nina Power is a writer and philosopher. She is the author of multiple articles on culture, sound, politics, and thought. She is currently finishing a book titled *What Do Men Want?* (Penguin, forthcoming 2022).

Bernd Preiml is a photographer and visual artist from Vienna. He grew up in the rural parts of Austria and spent most of his childhood in the forest, mostly alone. He loves folk art, folk tales and rituals. In his work he finds beauty in dark places. instagram.com/berndpreiml

Jaci Raia is an all-black-wearing creative director currently living and working in Burlington, Vermont. She works in advertising and uses her free time to take on a variety of both freelance and personal projects to fulfill herself. You may have come across her work before as she specializes in design for the metal community. kvlt.co

Paige Reynolds is a Canadian visual artist. Her work is surreal, figurative, and macabre and her main influences include horror, mortality, literature, film, anatomy, and the obscure. She works with pencils, oils, photography, and digital painting. Paige also applies her artistic and creative skills in the entertainment industry, working as a motion graphics artist and visual effects compositor. Along with illustrator/graphic designer Justin Erickson, Paige has founded a company called Phantom City Creative, focusing on entertainment design for film, television, and music.

Riton La Mort is a French artist born in Saint-Martin-D'Hères. He officiates as singer in the extreme punk band SATAN and is the author of several books published by Le Dernier Cri. Riton La Mort also writes poems that he sets to music under the name Bière Noire. bierenoire.blogspot.com.

Eugene S. Robinson is a singer for Oxbow, a noted journalist, and the author of several books.

Ezra Rose is an illustrator, zinester, and mixed/multi-media creator living on a small farm in Western Massachusetts with queer chosen family. Their art explores monsters, magic, queer/trans identity, and Jewish culture, celebrating the marginal and connecting to the symbols and stories of both past and present. Ezra's work has appeared in tabletop games, comics anthologies, and other small/indie press. ezra-rose.com. @sheydgarden.

Rottsteak is a self-taught illustrator born in a small town near Lake Michigan. He is currently working full-time at a tinned bean factory. You can see more of his work at instagram.com/rottsteak.

Joseph Russo is an anthropologist and ethnographer of the American South. He is an Adjunct Professor of Anthropology and Media Studies at Purchase College, State University of New York, and an adjunct professor of anthropology at Western Connecticut State University. His first book, a monograph of Texas and post-reality, is forthcoming on Duke University Press.

Jasmine Hazel Shadrack is a Senior Lecturer in Popular Music at the University of Northampton, UK. Her research fields include graphic novels, feminism, performativity, extreme metal, psychoanalysis, autoethnography, and esotericism. She published the monograph *Black Metal, Trauma, Subjectivity and Sound: Screaming the Abyss* (Emerald, 2020).

Steven Shakespeare is Associate Professor in Philosophy at Liverpool Hope University, UK. His books include *Derrida and Theology* (T & T Clark, 2009) and *Kierkegaard and the Refusal of Transcendence* (Palgrave, 2015). He was a participant in the first Black Metal Theory Symposium in Brooklyn, and his writings on black metal have appeared in *Hideous Gnosis*, edited by Nicola Masciandaro, *Melancology: Black Metal Theory and Ecology*, edited by Scott Wilson, and the journal *Glossator*.

Aliza Shvarts is an artist and writer who takes a queer and feminist approach to reproductive labor and language. She received a BA from Yale University and a PhD from Performance Studies, New York University. Shvarts's artwork has been shown throughout Europe and the Americas, and her writing can be found in publications including *Whitechapel: Documents in Contemporary Art*, *The Brooklyn Rail*, *TDR*, and *Women and Performance*. alizashvarts.com.

Angel Simitchiev is a Bulgarian musician, label owner, and freelance writer with roots in the hardcore punk scene. With an MA in Media Composition and Electroacoustic Music from the Bulgarian National Academy of Music, he is a Sound Art lecturer in the National Academy of Arts Sofia, and has a PhD on ambient music from the Institute of Art Studies, Bulgarian Academy of Sciences.

Kenji Siratori is the author of *Blood Electric* (Creation Books, 2002).

Sludgework is a female illustrator from Manchester, UK. She specializes in darker themes, including horror and metal imagery, and has designed cover art for many unsigned bands on Bandcamp, as well as T-shirt art and book illustrations. She has also designed social media logos and avatars. She can be reached via Instagram @sludgework and twitter @sludgeworkmeg.

Svartvinter comes from the base of the mountain, a queer metal artist, writer, and illustrator from the far reaches of northern Texas. Their art revolves around the intersegments of the fantastical, the cosmic, and the everyday! You're invited to join them as they unveil stories and scenes of queer life, black metal, crushing fascism, and anything badass or enthralling! Instagram: @svartvinterart.

Christophe Szpajdel is a graphic designer from Belgium (son of Polish immigrants) who currently resides in England. Since designing his first logo for Finnish band Disgrace in 1990, he has drawn over ten thousand logos, mainly in black and death metal and ambient music scenes, including Emperor's logo in early 1993, earning him the nickname "Lord of the Logos"—also the title of his 2010 book. In the 2010s, Szpajdel received mainstream exposure for working with Foo Fighters and Rihanna. He recently published the second volume of his book *Archaic Modernism*. He can be contacted at christophe.szpajdel@gmail.com. lordofthelogos.com.

Stuart Wain, inspired by DIY culture, started writing about metal, punk, and experimental electronic music at his blog The Sound Not The Word as a way to stay sane during a period of extended ill health. Since then he's written for other publications including Astral Noize and Broken Amp, with a particular interest in anti-fascist black metal. Stuart also creates anti-fascist chiptune inspired by black metal and IDM as Lunar Cult. thesoundnottheword.wordpress.com.

Marnie Weber's multidisciplinary practice encompasses performance, film, video, sculpture, collage, music, and costuming. By combining her own mythology of creatures, monsters, animals, and female characters with costuming on film and stage sets, she creates her own fictional narratives of passion, transformation, and discovery. Weber's uncanny fairy tale-like worlds invite viewers into an exploration of the subconscious. Weber has exhibited internationally, including at the Museum of Contemporary Art, in Geneva, Le Magasin, in Grenoble, France, and the Museum of Contemporary Art, in San Diego. marnieweber. com. Instagram: @marnieweberstudio.

Stephen Wilson (they/them/he/him), otherwise known as Unknown Relic, is a queer artist focusing on unsettling and profound imagery. Their work references the nature of existential dread alongside the symbolism of occultism and esoteric mysticism through the lens of their dreams and nightmares. Over the course of the last decade, they've worked mainly with metal bands, including names such as Vile Creature, Bismuth, Body Void, Terzij de Horde, Everson Poe, and many others, while also providing artwork for books such as *Endgame* by James Frey and *Coffle* by Gemma Files. Currently they reside in Long Island, New York, where they continue to hone their craft.

Shyle Zalewski, inspired by the punk culture, is a French artist who also sings very badly in the one-person band called Edam Edam. In those songs and comixes, there are a lot of French bakery, love, big butts, queerness, aliens, and milkshakes.

Andrew Zealley is a Toronto-based artist whose practice has been situated at the shifting nexus of HIV/AIDS, queer identity, and the body since 1990. Organized around sound and listening practices, his creativity puts audio and music methods to work to inform mixed disciplines and media—including video, audio production and publishing, photography, bookmaking, performance, DJ as semionaut, curating, archiving, pedagogy, AIDS activism, public sex practices, and relational healing. visualaids.org/artists/andrew-zealley.

INDEX ERITQUE ARCUS

ABOUT PM PRESS

PM Press is an independent, radical publisher of books and media to educate, entertain, and inspire. Founded in 2007 by a small group of people with decades of publishing, media, and organizing experience, PM Press amplifies the voices of radical authors, artists, and activists. Our aim is to deliver bold political ideas and vital stories to all walks of life and arm the dreamers to demand the impossible. We have sold millions of copies of our books, most often one at a time, face to face. We're old enough to know what we're doing and young enough to know what's at stake.

Join us to create a better world.

PM Press
PO Box 23912
Oakland, CA 94623
www.pmpress.org

—

PM Press in Europe
europe@pmpress.org
www.pmpress.org.uk

FRIENDS OF PM PRESS

These are indisputably momentous times—the financial system is melting down globally and the Empire is stumbling. Now more than ever there is a vital need for radical ideas.

In the many years since its founding—and on a mere shoestring—PM Press has risen to the formidable challenge of publishing and distributing knowledge and entertainment for the struggles ahead. With hundreds of releases to date, we have published an impressive and stimulating array of literature, art, music, politics, and culture. Using every available medium, we've succeeded in connecting those hungry for ideas and information to those putting them into practice.

Friends of PM allows you to directly help impact, amplify, and revitalize the discourse and actions of radical writers, filmmakers, and artists. It provides us with a stable foundation from which we can build upon our early successes and provides a much-needed subsidy for the materials that can't necessarily pay their own way. You can help make that happen—and receive every new title automatically delivered to your door once a month—by joining as a Friend of PM Press. And, we'll throw in a free T-shirt when you sign up.

Here are your options:

$30 a month	Get all books and pamphlets plus 50% discount on all webstore purchases
$40 a month	Get all PM Press releases (including CDs and DVDs) plus 50% discount on all webstore purchases
$100 a month	Everything plus PM merchandise, free downloads, and 50% discount on all webstore purchases

For those who can't afford $30 or more a month, we have Sustainer Rates at $15, $10 and $5. Sustainers get a free PM Press T-shirt and a 50% discount on all purchases from our website.

Your Visa or Mastercard will be billed once a month, until you tell us to stop. Or until our efforts succeed in bringing the revolution around. Or the financial meltdown of Capital makes plastic redundant. Whichever comes first.

colophon

The first edition of this
book was designed in 2021
and printed in 2022.

The main typefaces used are
GT Pressura and GT Pressura
Mono from Grilli Type, first
released in 2021. It was
designed by Dominik Huber
and Marc Kappeler (Moiré).
GT Pressura is inspired by
metal type printing history
as well as engineered letters
stamped onto shipping boxes.

The pixellated blackletter
font used for headlines is
New Hildegard Std, designed
by Andreas Brietzke.

for everyone.